The Best American Sports Writing 2010

The Best AMERICAN SPORTS WRITING™ 2010

Edited and with an Introduction
by Peter Gammons

Glenn Stout, *Series Editor*

A Mariner Original
HOUGHTON MIFFLIN HARCOURT
BOSTON • NEW YORK   2010

www.hmhbooks.com

ISSN 1056-8034
ISBN 978-0-547-15248-6

Printed in the United States of America

DOC 10 9 8 7 6 5 4 3 2

Contents

Foreword

TWENTY YEARS AGO, in the foreword to the inaugural edition of this book, I repeated an anecdote I heard Tim Horgan, longtime sports columnist for the *Boston Herald,* tell at his retirement dinner. He said that when he was approached by aspiring students of sports writing he always asked why they wanted to write about sports for a living. Invariably the students would respond to Horgan by saying, "Because I love sports."

"Wrong," Horgan would admonish. "You have to love the writing."

I have never forgotten those words. They are the reason, as I explained in that first edition, why this book is called *The Best American Sports Writing,* two words, and not *The Best American Sportswriting,* the compound word, which would be a different collection entirely. First and foremost, this is and has always been a book for those who love writing. That the writing is about sports is, of course, not insignificant, but my goal has always been to seek out stories that are so well written that the subject matter hardly matters, to find stories that readers will enjoy, not simply because of the topic, but, just as a non-athlete can enjoy the artistry of an athlete, because of the artistry displayed by the writer.

A great deal has changed since I began the work of this book twenty years ago, both for me personally and in the field of sports writing. When I began serving this book as series editor, I had just turned thirty years old and lived in an apartment in Boston's South End and freelanced while working as a librarian at the Boston Public Library. Over the ensuing twenty years *BASW* world headquarters have moved, first to a house in the suburbs and now to Vermont, hidden in the fields and woods alongside Lake Champlain near the Canadian border. I have married, buried both my parents, and watched my daughter grow up amid the clutter of this book for each of her fourteen years. Eighteen years ago I quit my job, and I have been a full-time writer ever since. I rehabbed an old rotator cuff tear, started playing baseball again, pitched in over-thirty baseball leagues for ten years, and retired once more. I have coached girls' softball and Little League; learned to ski, snorkel, kayak, and skate and to make my own beer, maple syrup, and applesauce; given dozens of talks; visited scores of schools; written hundreds of columns and features, over forty juvenile books, and a full dozen adult titles; and edited several other anthologies. I've made some friends I'll have for the rest of my life and lost track of some others because, quite frankly, the curse that every writer lives is that every hour or minute we spend doing what we love is an hour or minute we spend away from those we care about. I easily spend six or eight hours almost every day writing (I usually have to ask my daughter, to her amusement, what day of the week it is), and hours more each day reading, usually for this book, sometimes while sitting on an exercise bike, or on the porch, or at the kitchen table eating, or in my chair watching a ball game. Though the work of this book never ends, it has surrounded me for so long I sometimes barely notice.

In an earlier edition of the book I told the story about how I came to be selected to serve as series editor, something for which I am forever grateful and still a bit mystified, because, to be honest, I did not know how to do this when I started. I cannot imagine that anyone would know how to do this, really. Like the act of writing, this is a "learn by doing" experience.

My first editor, undoubtedly trying to impress me with the magnitude of my task, told me that the series editor for another *Best American* title kept file cards of publications, meticulously checked them off each time they arrived, and notated the cards in regard to their contents, and that I should do the same. I bought a big box of file cards and dutifully began creating a similar card file system.

Then I looked at the pile of material waiting to be read. Deciding that anything that got in the way of reading should probably be ignored, I tossed the cards. I have kept things simple and never used any kind of grading or ranking system for the stories I read beyond this: Stories I want to read again go in one pile. Stories I don't want to read again go into another, and when that much larger pile topples over, those stories either get recycled or go into my woodstove. As the deadline approaches I keep going over the "read again" pile until it gets small enough to send to the guest editor.

Of course, any changes in my life pale when compared with the changes that have taken place in writing and journalism. Twenty years ago—before anyone had ever called me "sir"—I had just made the transition from writing features and other freelance assignments in longhand and then going into work early to type them out on an electric typewriter. I was beginning to work on a Magnavox Videowriter, a first-generation word processor that, to a nontypist like myself (I use my thumb and two fingers on each hand and type at the speed of my mind, which is not very fast), seemed absolutely magical. When I was selected to edit this annual collection, the job came with the caveat that I had to buy a computer. It cost most of my advance, and now my wristwatch probably contains more computing power.

Writers for newspapers and magazines were making—or had just made—a similar transition to computers, and there was, of course, no such thing as the online world, which has changed almost everything everywhere, but few places more so than the commercial worlds of newspaper, magazine, and book publishing. There is no point in hashing over the obvious here, but anyone involved in any of these businesses knows that everything has changed, and in the last few years of economic recession, not for the better. There are, unquestionably, fewer print outlets for writing than there were twenty years ago, and space in those that remain has become more precious. The online universe, which did not even exist, now offers outlets to everyone, ranging from purely commercial platforms to the virtually noncommercial world of the blog. This is both a bad thing, because the best writing is generally done by professionals, and a good thing, because the best writing is not *always* done by professionals. Quality, not byline, matters.

It has never been easy to earn a living as a writer, and it is particularly difficult now, but it probably has never been easier *to* write. Resources are instantly accessible. In an hour I can research what used to take me weeks to do. But those same resources are now also at the fingertips of readers, not all of whom appreciate the care and talent it takes to turn raw facts into fine writing.

In these pages we argue otherwise, because the only thing that has not changed over the last twenty years is the most important thing of all—the quality of the writing. I am amused that every three or four years some magazine (or, now, website) sees fit to run a story that bemoans the "death of sports writing" or some similar "get off of my lawn" nonsense, and then sends it to me for consideration in the next year's edition.

Although I agree that a great deal has died over the last two decades, and perhaps a small portion of the output described by that compound word "sportswriting" has reached an end, I am something of a historian of both genres and believe that rumors of the demise of either are highly exaggerated. While I have yet to meet the writer who became better at his or her craft by going on television or the radio, there always have been and continue to be great writers who value the written word above all others. But the notion of some kind of "golden age" of either sportswriting or sports writing is simply the kind of selective nostalgia that still prefers Mom's meatloaf to any other.

From my chair, sports writing seems to be doing quite well. The reason, of course, is the writer. Despite the conveyor belt of change, in both technology and the marketplace, that seems to speed up even more from year to year, the writers who have appeared in this book and who I read each year have neither cowered in fear before the word nor been frozen into silence.

Quite the opposite. Many of us who retain faith in the page probably write more and better than before. It's in the blood, and despite all the logical arguments that can be made against pursuing writing of any kind as an avocation, at the end of each year I end up with a box of about two hundred stories that I want to read again, stories that I worry over as the pile gets smaller and the decisions become more difficult, just as I did twenty years ago. At the end of the process I still seem to find seventy stories or so that I feel are worthy of being sent to the guest editor. Unless the guest editors have collectively chosen to lie, each has had a difficult time selecting the twenty to twenty-five stories that eventually appear in this book, not because they can't find enough stories, but because they have a hard time paring the number of stories down to a manageable size.

Now I am the one who regularly gets phone calls or letters or e-mails from aspiring writers who call me "sir" and approach me in much the same way they approached Tim Horgan. I tell them the same thing he did: you have to love the writing. That, above all else, has not changed, and I do not think it ever will.

This is a book for people who love writing, and putting it together has been a pleasure. It now takes up a bit more than two feet of shelf space on my wall, and I recently took a look at the entire collection. Join me as I flip the pages once more.

1991

If I were to pick one story that is emblematic of my hopes and dreams for this collection, it might just be Florence Shinkle's quiet, gentle tale "Fly Away Home," about an older couple who raced pigeons, a story that proved, I think, the wisdom of creating a book of sports writing—writing about sports—rather than sportswriting. It is an understated story whose pace matches the emotional tone of its subjects, a perfect game story for a competition that takes place over hours and sometimes days, a story that requires patience. When I sent this one off to guest editor David Halberstam, I was rooting for it, and—big surprise—he did not let me down.

1992

Every once in a while I encounter a story that hits me like verbal satori. Paul Solotaroff's visceral and unvarnished profile of steroid-abusing body builder Steve Michalik, "The Power and the Gory," still gives me chills and remains as vital today as it was then. Yet, for all its power, the story is not overwritten—Solotaroff's work needed no artificial enhancement, and Michalik's experience needed no embellishment. A brutal recitation of the facts was powerful enough.

1993

One of the joys of editing this book in the early years was that nearly every writer was a discovery. While I had previously read their work, I had passed over bylines like the signs along the freeway. Now, having to pay attention, I suddenly began to realize that around almost every curve was greatness—Charlie Pierce and Bill Nack and Pat Jordan and Mark Kram and a host of others. When I look back at some of these early editions, I am sometimes astounded by the roster of writers we managed to assemble, and in this edition Peter Richman's nuanced, sensitive portrait of Tommy Lasorda's relationship with his dying son, a gay man afflicted with AIDS, stands out among a lineup with absolutely no weaknesses. It was also one of the first stories to introduce the reality of AIDS to a sports audience, something Richman did with great heart and sympathy. Guest editor Frank Deford just kept picking stories, and at 464 pages, this edition is the longest in the history of the series.

1994

Sometimes a story looks into the future, and the best of those stories does so without even knowing it. Bruce Buschel's portrait of former major league outfielder Lenny Dykstra gambling at a casino was a masterful takedown, and one that, given Dykstra's more recent financial and legal problems, seems written as if Buschel had supernatural access to the inner workings of Dykstra's psyche. He did, paying attention to what Dykstra said and did and how he acted, rather than allowing who he thought Dykstra was get in the way—it's called reporting. The resulting roller coaster of words matched Dykstra's mania with absolute precision.

1995

The guest editor makes the final call on the contents each year. Unless asked, I stay out of the selection process. That keeps the book from getting stale, but sometimes one gets away. I cited a story called "Blind Alley," by the late Jeffrey Felshman of the *Chicago Reader,* in "Notable Sports Writing of 1994." It was an empathetic slice-of-life account about a group of people who bowled despite not being able to see. Felshman, whom I knew from our days at Bard College, passed away last fall. After his death, I sought his story out and read it again and wondered why the hell it didn't make the book. *The Best American Sports Writing 1995* was the short-

est edition of *BASW* ever published, something over a hundred
readers let me know as soon as it hit the stores, and I wish it had
included one more story.

1996

Before I began editing this series, I assumed that to get into this
book or another similar collection the writer had to know someone and have a line of publishing credits as long as your arm. But
when I started doing this, as someone who wasn't connected,
hardly knew anyone, and didn't have a particularly long line of
publishing credits, I realized that might not be the case. Then I
read Joel Reese's "Down and Out" in *Texas Monthly* about his encounter with former Cowboy wide receiver Golden Richards, and it
made it into the book. Although Reese has gone on to have a fine
career as a writer and editor, his story on Richards was the first of
his career.

So there.

1997

Each time I pull one of these volumes off the shelf and flip open to
the contents and pick a story to write about, it seems as if I could
write about Gary Smith. Not only has he been in the book more
than anyone else, but he has probably written more memorable
stories than anyone else. This edition includes his portrait of Tiger
Woods, "The Chosen One." If the people who have shared the
pages of this book were to select a best sportswriter of the last
twenty years, I have no doubt that Gary Smith would be included
on every ballot.

1998

The guest editor and I do not necessarily have all that much to do
with one another. Some, like David Halberstam, have chosen to involve me in the process and discuss their selections, but most have
chosen to make their selections in camera, which is certainly their
right and privilege.

Only one ever asked me to come over to his house and sort
things out over the kitchen table. That was Bill Littlefield, who is

the only guest editor I can also claim as a friend and who has been, I can state without equivocation, the best and most generous friend that, along with David Halberstam, this series could ever have asked for. Each year Bill has been kind enough to ask me and either a contributor or the guest editor to appear on his fine and original program on National Public Radio, *Only a Game*. We all usually end up sounding like a bunch of Cub Scouts during a campout and spend more time laughing than actually talking, but that's fine too. And in the You Can't Make This Stuff Up Department, I first met Bill before, I think, either of us had published a word. I was standing outside the Green Monster at Fenway Park on opening day in an old baseball uniform drinking Bloody Marys and reading poetry about baseball through a Pignose amplifier while being heckled by drunks waiting in line to buy a ticket in the bleachers. Bill had a tape recorder and was looking for a story for the radio.

It was destiny . . . or something.

1999

When this series started, I was still working at the Boston Public Library. Apart from my annual request for submissions that I send out each year to hundreds of newspapers and magazines, I would build this book from occasional weekend forays into the deep and dark recesses of the BPL, where I would flip through mounds of newspapers and magazines. Although I lost my access to the library's collection when I left the library in 1993, by the time I put the 1999 edition together for guest editor Richard Ford, I had access to the Internet. My editor was particularly thrilled that I was able to begin to supply copy for the book in electronic form, which meant it did not have to be retyped during production.

Yes, it has changed everything—everything except the most important thing of all. So far, somehow, this book still starts with a human being somewhere whose fingertips tease the words out on the page one letter at a time.

2000

One of the benefits of being the series editor, and not the guest editor, is that I get to cast a wide net and let the guest editor sort things out and decide whether a particular activity is a sport or not.

I am half-Canadian, and my late uncle Bern curled, which in parts of Canada and the upper Midwest sort of fills the same role that bowling does in other places. For the uninitiated, crudely speaking, curling consists of pushing large stones over the ice while racing alongside the stone wearing special ice-proof shoes and brushing the ice with a broom.

I used to joke that one day *The Best American Sports Writing* would include a story about curling, without ever thinking it would, but damned if it didn't happen. In this edition Guy Lawson, author of "Merl Curls Lead," and guest editor Dick Schaap both proved me wrong.

2001

You know how it is when sometimes you meet someone you admire and you're disappointed because the person's public persona and private persona not only have nothing to do with each other but don't even like each other?

That's not Bud Collins. After we finished this edition, we had dinner in Boston with our wives, and Bud, who always seemed nice on television and interesting and funny in print, was even nicer, more interesting, and funnier in person.

2002

There are a few stories that have been reprinted in this series that I absolutely *love*, stories that I have probably read ten or fifteen times over the years and never ever, ever get tired of. If I could, I would make them required reading in every school in America and put them together in a collection called *The Very Best of the Best American Sports Writing.*

And if I were making it *The Best of the Very Best of the Best,* it would include only three stories, but I know I could never choose just one of them as the absolute best. One is J. R. Moehringer's "Resurrecting the Champ," which appeared in the 1998 edition and includes one of the best, and certainly the longest, ledes I have ever read. Another is Bill Nack's "Pure Heart," about the death of the racehorse Secretariat, from the 1991 book, and the third is Bill

Plaschke's story "Her Blue Haven," from the 2002 edition. Even now I sometimes tear up just thinking about it.

If you have never read any of these stories, well, you should. Like *right now.*

2003

With the permission of Mark Kram Jr., a terrific writer who has made several appearances in this book, including the fine memoir about his father that appeared in the 2008 edition, the 2003 edition was dedicated to the memory of Mark Kram Sr., who himself had appeared in these pages a number of times.

I did not know much of Mark's personal story, but I did know him to be a writer always worth reading. He first appeared in this collection in the 1994 edition, and when I contacted him we chatted for a while in almost Aristotelian fashion: he asked me questions about this book and about writing and what I like and why, and I did my best to answer him and not sound stupid.

It was like a test. I think I passed, because every year or two after that I would get a call late some morning from Mark. He would start by asking if I had read a certain story, or a certain writer, and ask me what I thought of it. Then it was off to the races, and for the next two hours or more I would mostly listen while he told me about Muhammad Ali or talked about a story I had never read or a writer I did not know much about. Although he had every opportunity to do so, he never advocated for his own work. I never knew why he called me, and I never asked, but looking back, it seems to me now that, in one way or another, he was trying to alert me to the authentic. I think he thought that this book was important and that there were certain things he just wanted to make sure, perhaps sensing that his time was ending, that I knew or had thought about. Of the many things I treasure about working on this book, those conversations are among the most precious, and whenever I am contacted by a younger writer, I try to recall Mark Kram's generosity.

2004

I am not a hunter or a fisherman, but I don't begrudge those who are, as long as they follow the rules, do it the right way, and keep

xx   Foreword

the hell off my land. But competitive taxidermy? Even though I don't get it, I still loved Susan Orleans's story *Lifelike*, which told me everything I didn't want to know about taxidermy, and then some.

2005

There are a lot of clichés in writing, and one of them is that often the best stories are right in your own backyard. I was perusing the *New York Times* one day and saw a story entitled "How to Catch Fish in Vermont" by Pam Belluck. Since there are almost always fishermen in my backyard, even in the winter, on the ice, I had to read it. I found out that here in Vermont you can shoot fish with a gun. Really. Like, in my backyard.

I'd have never known.

2006

I get letters and e-mails about this book, which lets me know that readers care, and even those that are critical are almost always nice. The only one I remember that was not was one I received after the publication of this edition from a doctor who berated me for being a secularist and pushing a liberal agenda and warned me to get right with God, presumably because this edition included one story that touched on the social inequities that followed the New Orleans hurricane and a few others that were nonjudgmental about their gay subjects. Then I Googled the writer of the letter and discovered he had given up his license to practice in a plea bargain after being charged with rape.

True story.

2007

Derek Zumsteg's story "Bugs Bunny, Greatest Banned Player Ever" analyzes Bugs as if the cartoon is archival evidence that Bugs was a real ballplayer; the story is written like Bill James channeling Albert Einstein channeling Margaret Mead. After nearly twenty years of doing this book, it takes a lot to surprise me, but that one did, and I still think it is one of the most original stories we've ever reprinted. Editor David Maraniss agreed, and it is without question one of the most unforgettable stories we have ever published — and also the first from a blog.

2008

A lot of things are easy to make fun of, and cheerleading is one of them. But Jeanne Marie Laskas's profile of the NFL Cincinnati "Ben-Gals" did not take that easy route. "G-L-O-R-Y" is more celebratory and sympathetic than snarky and demonstrates, I think, the value of that approach. Young writers take note: do not mock your subject.

2009

The lede to the first story in this edition, "Life and Limb" by Bruce Barcott, from *Runner's World,* begins: "On the day he decided to pay a man to cut off his leg with a power saw, Tom White woke with a powerful yearning to run." I'm not having my leg or any other body part amputated, but readers may wonder whether, after twenty years of editing this series, there aren't days when I would rather poke out my eyes than do this for one more second.

Well, not very often. Even after twenty years, I usually awake with a powerful yearning to read.

And that is what unites us all who find each other under the banner of this series.

Every season I read every issue of hundreds of general interest and sports magazines in search of writing that might merit inclusion in *The Best American Sports Writing.* I also actively survey the Internet and contact the editors of some three hundred newspapers and hundreds of magazine editors and request their submissions. But I still implore and encourage everyone reading this to send me stories they would like to see reprinted in this volume. Writers, readers, and all other interested parties should feel free to alert me to either their own work or that of someone else for consideration in *The Best American Sports Writing 2011,* according to the following criteria. Each story

- must be column-length or longer;
- must have been published in 2010;
- must not be a reprint or book excerpt;
- must have been published in the United States or Canada; and
- must be received by February 1, 2011.

All submissions must include the name of the author, the date of publication, and the publication name and address. Photocopies, tear sheets, or clean copies are fine. Readable reductions to 8½-by-11 are preferred. Submissions from online publications must be made in hard copy, and those who submit stories from newspapers should submit the story in hard copy as published. Since newsprint generally suffers in transit, newspaper stories are best copied and then mounted on 8½-by-11 paper; if the story also appeared online, the appropriate URL should be attached. While there is no limit to the number of submissions either an individual or a publication may make, please use common sense. Owing to the volume of material I receive, no submission can be returned or acknowledged, and it is inappropriate for me to comment on or critique any individual submission. Publications that want to be absolutely certain their contributions are considered are advised to provide a complimentary subscription to the address listed below. Those that already do so should make sure to extend the subscription.

No electronic submissions will be accepted, although stories that only appeared online are eligible. Please send all submissions by U.S. mail—weather conditions in midwinter here at *BASW* headquarters mean I often cannot receive UPS or FedEx submissions —and the deadline, February 1, is real.

Please submit either an original or clear paper copy of each story, including publication name, author, and date the story appeared, to

Glenn Stout
PO Box 549
Alburgh, VT 05440

Those with questions or comments may contact me at basw editor@yahoo.com. Copies of previous editions of this book can be ordered through most bookstores or online book dealers. An index of stories that have appeared in this series can be found at my website, glennstout.net. For updated information, readers and writers are also encouraged to join *The Best American Sports Writing* group on Facebook.

Thanks again go out to all at Houghton Mifflin Harcourt, particularly my editor, Susan Canavan, and Meagan Stacey. Thanks also to Peter Gammons for his diligence in making the final selections. I again thank the website sportsjournalists.com for posting submission guidelines, and my family, Siobhan and Saorla. Since its inception, the work of this book has been a constant in our lives, and to their credit, I have somehow avoided ending up in the discard pile. My greatest gratitude, however, is extended to the writers who have kept me company every day of the last two decades. I hope to feel the same way in another twenty years.

GLENN STOUT
Alburgh, Vermont

Introduction

THE MAGIC OF SPORTS is not only the moment but the memory of that moment, voiced over, etched forever, taking on a life of its own with each replay, on the screen or in the mind's eye. It was Mazeroski's shot heard round the world. The Catch. Jordan's final shot, as a college freshman or an aging Bulls superstar. Andre Agassi dropping to his knees. Landon Donovan's live-or-let-die goal in the World Cup. Joe Carter's walk-off in the World Series.

Arguably the most famous sports moment of all time is Bobby Thomson's 1951 series-ending home run, but I have often wondered how many people actually saw Thomson swing the bat that day, or heard Russ Hodges holler, "The Giants win the pennant!" We all went into collective shock when we saw Kirk Gibson's homer off Dennis Eckersley disappear into the Chávez Ravine bleachers in the 1988 World Series. Both of these moments were historic, but they live on because of the way they were captured, recorded, immortalized in photographs and, more importantly, in words, spoken and written. The late Jack Buck's radio call — "I don't believe what I just saw" — accompanies the videos of Gibson's home run. Before the final game of the 2004 World Series, both Jack Buck of Fox and Joe Castiglione of the Red Sox Radio Network knew that if Boston won, their calls of "The Boston Red Sox are world champions" would be the first ever, since there was no broadcast of the World Series in 1918, when the Red Sox had last won.

Hodges's call screamed of the passion of a crosstown team that had come from thirteen and a half games back, a team to whom the word "miracle" had been applied, while Jack Buck's call described the improbability that a seemingly mediocre Dodgers team would defeat the powerful Athletics. Both were unimaginable, so when they happened, fact superseding fiction made the moment greater than any anticipated victory.

Fewer than 12,000 people actually saw Ted Williams's last home run. But we have John Updike to thank for preserving it in our memories as vividly as we will always have David Tyree's Super Bowl catch. Updike did it with his words—words that changed the way baseball was written.

The writer's job is to record these moments, to be where we can't be, to see what we can't see, to turn an event into a tablet. Or to record with a particular flair or point of view a moment we did see or did live through in a way that makes us consider it anew, that makes us consider it again and again. To capture competitive genius is a competitive art of another kind, one involving deadlines. Depending on the time zone, the writer who chronicles a game usually has an hour to get downstairs to the clubhouse, ask questions, run back upstairs, and write. And great story lines write themselves. Game 6 of the 1975 World Series ended when Carlton Fisk homered off the left-field foul pole, which gave me twenty-two minutes to write 1,500 words, which was easy, because the narrative of the game's plays had culminated in Fisk's home run. I remember little. I remember the typewriter and jamming paper in and handing the typescript to a runner, who fed it through a machine to the *Boston Globe*.

Even now, when we can touch a screen and get any game, find any box score, track down any fact or tidbit about an athlete we love or love to hate, the way the moments are preserved is important. Television does do it well, whether it is NBC's coverage of the Olympics or the days leading up to the Super Bowl or those lyrical and personal "Outside the Lines" pieces on ESPN by brilliant reporter/writers like Tom Rinaldi. But storied history has traditionally appeared in the written word, whether by Grantland Rice, Roger Angell, or Leigh Montville journeying out in the snows of Sarajevo to find Yugoslavian skiers who fought the Nazis during World War II. These writers tell us the who and the why and sometimes give us the context of the time and the place in history. What sports writers bring to these moments is as much a part of the fabric of sports as home runs or touchdowns or finish lines.

*

Sports writing is about crafting under the pressure of deadlines; it is about tireless, dogged reporting; it is about understanding the games that so fill lives; but most of all it is about people. Some of us children of the sixties were fortunate enough to come along at a time when print was king—in my case, to go to the *Boston Globe* under one of the greatest writers' and journalists' editors who ever lived, Tom Winship. That meant learning from colleagues like Bud Collins, Ray Fitzgerald, Will McDonough, Leigh Montville (the best columnist I have ever read), Bob Ryan . . . Collins convinced me that specialization was the future of sports writers, which focused me on my passion, baseball. Therefore I could be in George Brett's house three weeks before the end of his career, a week before he got his three thousandth hit, and ask him how he wanted his last at-bat to go. "I want to hit a routine ground ball to the second baseman and bust my ass down the line," Brett answered. "If I'm out, I'm out. If I'm safe, fine. I'm not Ted Williams. I just want to go out busting my ass on a routine ground ball."

As we replay such moments in the years that pass, or as we relive them by reading a book or watching an old highlight reel, we sometimes lose sight of the fact that the men and women who perform these feats are really like us. They are human. How many millions of copies of the picture of Bobby Orr flying through the air have been sold? That is the seen performing genius of an artist. Yet when I was transferred from Brigham and Women's Hospital to a room in the Rehabilitation Hospital of the Cape and Islands as I recovered from a severe aneurysm, I found Bobby Orr, being who he is, lying on my bed. Sometimes these humans are like Larry Bird and John Smoltz, who never wanted anyone else to drive. Sometimes they are flawed; sometimes they are victims of circumstance or misfortune. When the Arizona Diamondbacks rallied to win Game 7 of the 2001 World Series, Mariano Rivera was so self-assured that months later he looked back and said, "Hey, I broke three bats. That's going to happen." Sometimes the drive to greatness ends up, as it did for Pete Rose, in the runaway truck lane. But all these folks provided us with moments. They are people—they all have stories.

In 1986 I was doing a story on Dennis "Oil Can" Boyd and his personal problems. His father, Willie James Boyd, owned the Meridien, Mississippi, Eagles, a Negro League team that hosted Willie

Mays and Henry Aaron before they played in the major leagues. The elder Boyd sat in a small restaurant and talked about his culture. He had earned his living as a landscaper, but his family's passion was baseball.

"I worked for the man who was the grand dragon of the Ku Klux Klan in this area," said Willie Boyd. "I had no choice. I had mouths to feed. That was the way it was. I was working on his grounds that day in June 1964 when cars rolled up to his house. I didn't know what was happening. You didn't ask. I found out later they drove up the road to Philadelphia and murdered the civil rights boys from up north [James Chaney, Andrew Goodman, and Michael Schwerner]. That man who was the grand dragon today is destitute and shriveled with arthritis. My boy is pitching for the Boston Red Sox, in the big leagues."

Nearly fifteen years later, a Northeastern University junior named Carlos Pena sat on the couch at his family's home in Haverhill, Massachusetts. Pena was ten days away from being the tenth pick in the baseball draft, and that day he told of his journey to the United States. Just six years before, when he was fifteen, Pena had moved with his parents, brother, and sister from Santo Domingo, Dominican Republic, to Haverhill. It was January; there was more than a foot of snow on the ground. The family and an uncle moved into a two-room apartment in a triple-decker without heat. Both parents worked two jobs to raise their family, and none of the children were allowed to take English as a second language. "My dad made us sit down with a dictionary and work until we got it," Carlos said. As he awaited the upcoming draft, Carlos Pena had a 3.7 grade point average in engineering at Northeastern, his sister was dancing with the Boston Ballet, and his younger brother was on his way to getting a PhD in engineering.

"We came here in pursuit of the American Dream," Pena said as he sat on the couch.

"But wasn't it a lot more difficult to achieve that dream than you imagined?" I asked.

"Where is it written in stone that the American Dream is supposed to be easy?" Pena replied. "Toughness makes us great."

Carlos Pena was drafted by the Texas Rangers and traded to the Oakland Athletics, who traded him to the Detroit Tigers, who released him. He signed with the New York Yankees, who released him. He signed with the Boston Red Sox, who didn't pick up his contract. He signed with the Tampa Bay Rays and led the American League in home runs. "Nothing is easy," Pena told a group of inner-city Boston kids. "This country was built by people that weren't given a chance and never gave up."

Most of us never experience what athletes experience. One day, as Gary Sheffield was walking out of the Yankee spring training field, a man yelled, "You've forgotten where you came from. You never come home to the neighborhood. You're too big." Sheff grew up in a ghetto neighborhood in the Hillsborough section of Tampa. He had friends who were killed, others who spent time in jail. His uncle, Doc Gooden, had lived through a nightmarish life. A cousin was in jail. Sheffield never looked up, but when he had walked another fifty feet, he said to the person next to him, "I never forget where I came from. That's why I don't go back." That's why he sponsored the Little League and other youth programs in that neighborhood.

Sheffield often talked about his past. "I never forget. It's part of what drives me. It keeps me from going in the wrong direction. I know a lot of people thought I would end up doing the wrong things and never make it, let alone hit five hundred home runs. I never stop thinking about that. Some people think I have a chip on my shoulder. I say every day I have something to prove, to someone I can prove was wrong about me."

Dustin Pedroia is five-five and a half. Really. When he was in college, scouts said he was too small and too slow ever to be an everyday major league player. Four years after being drafted, he was the American League MVP. "I keep a list," he said. "Not really, but seriously, I remember all the people who wondered why I was even allowed to start one game. I was hitting .160-something the first month of my rookie year, and a lot of people wanted me out of here. I remember. It's motivation. It's edge. Edge is good. Baseball is such an everyday grind, you need everything you can find, every day."

Bill Parcells was discussing the importance of that edge outside a batting cage in Jupiter, Florida, during spring training in 2010, when Albert Pujols stepped out of the cage, came around, and said, "I remember everyone from my junior year in high school to my second year in the big leagues who said I wouldn't make it. It *is* edge. I hope I never lose it. Never lose that drivin' wheel."

Sports are essentially selfish. "You can't perform well enough to help your team if you don't have some selfish drive," Dennis Eckersley says. Yet when he lost to Ron Guidry and the Yankees 7–0 in the four-day September weekend known as the Boston Massacre —a loss that brought the Boston lead over New York to one game after leading by fourteen—Eckersley walked out into the clubhouse to see nearly one hundred reporters surrounding teammate Frank Duffy.

Eckersley had the bases loaded in the fourth inning with no score. Duffy was playing second base because Jerry Remy was hurt. Jim Rice was playing right field because Dwight Evans, the best defensive right fielder in the league, was hurt. Lou Piniella lofted a pop fly into the wind and the high sky in shallow right center field; five players chased it. Rice called for it, and Duffy was ducking when the ball blew back and hit him in the back. Two runs scored, Bucky Dent doubled, and when the inning was over, Eckersley was in the clubhouse, the Yankees were up 7–0, and all that stood between them and first place was a nervous Red Sox rookie pitcher named Bobby Sprowl.

Eckersley came into the clubhouse and started pulling reporters out from around Duffy. "It wasn't his fault! Leave him alone!" he shouted. "Come to my locker. I loaded the bases. I hung the g——n slider to Bucky Dent. I have the *L* next to my name. Talk to me." A perfectly unselfish act of being a teammate from a man who understood the necessity of selfishness.

"Anyone who isn't a little vain or selfish probably isn't going to drive to win," Jason Giambi used to say. "Guys who say, 'Oh, I don't care what they say or think' either don't care about anything or they're lying. That's the cliché BS."

It reminds me of the inanity of rating athletes based on their championship rings. If the number of rings is what really matters, then Luis Sojo, with four, was a better player than Ted Williams, Don Mattingly, or Carl Yastrzemski. The line between winning and losing is blurred. In 1978, Rich Gossage got Yastrzemski to pop up with two out and runners at second and third to finish the Yankees' 5–4 victory in the most famous regular-season playoff game ever played. Two years later Gossage was pitching in the American League Championship Series when Brett hit a three-run homer into the third deck of Yankee Stadium to give the Royals the pennant.

"You guys want me to talk about what it feels like to lose," Gossage said to reporters. "When two good players compete, one has to win, one has to lose. Yastrzemski is no loser—he's going to the Hall of Fame. So is George Brett. He beat me. I don't feel as if I lost to him. There's a difference." (Incidentally, Gossage is in the Hall of Fame with Yastrzemski and Brett.)

In sports, we are sprayed with clichés like graffiti on New York subways, told that one player "would really like to win," or offered racial profiles about African Americans' "talent" and white players' "intelligence." We are regaled with tales of how tough pitchers and hitters were in the good ole days, how batters were knocked down and hit in the neck or head by pitches. Toughness is one of the great clichés in sports. But a good sports writer doesn't bow to the cliché. He writes instead about what toughness costs. Take, for example, Tony Conigliaro, the youngest player ever to win a home run championship and the youngest to reach one hundred career homers, whose career was essentially ended by a pitch that fractured his cheekbone when he was only twenty-two. He was a hitter from those "good ole days," a star player and personality whose trajectory was deflected by a glorified bean ball. After the beaning, Tony C played a couple of years with the Angels, then had to retire. He tried a comeback with the Red Sox in 1975 and actually hit their first home run that season—a season in which they got all the way to the seventh game of the World Series against the Big Red Machine of Cincinnati.

Tony and I would often sit together on bus and plane rides, and he never lost the belief that he would once again be a star. He had full vision in only one eye, and pitchers were throwing balls at 90 miles an hour, and he bristled at the notion of fear. "I already know what it's like to have my career taken away from me," he said. "What else do I have to lose?" Like other great athletes, he didn't think like you or me.

Conigliaro was traded to the California Angels after the 1971 season for a relief pitcher named Ken Tatum. From the start of the 1970 season until midway through 1971, Tatum was the best reliever in the American League. Midway through that '71 season, Tatum threw a pitch that shattered the jaw of Baltimore outfielder Paul Blair. It turned out to be the turning point in two lives. Blair was never the same hitter; Tatum was never the same pitcher. "I never again could throw a pitch on the inner half of the plate," Tatum admitted long after his career was over. "I was afraid of killing someone."

Athletes are people, remember. People not unlike us. They are human. And that's what makes them more interesting, really, than any play on the field or flying leap on the court. Steve Blass threw a shutout in the seventh game of the 1971 World Series and three years later could not accurately throw a pitch to his catcher. I saw a pitch he threw in spring training land halfway between third base and home plate. I saw a pitch Bobby Sprowl threw in Daytona Beach land in the press box. Chuck Knoblauch went through the same kind of thing. Rick Ankiel, whose brain wires short-circuited in his first postseason game when he was twenty years old, battled all the way back through dark ages to be a successful major league center fielder.

"Personal or professional trauma does strange things to human beings," says a psychologist who has worked with hundreds of players. One was a very talented minor league pitcher who came down with "the thing," or "Steve Blass Disease." The young pitcher went to the psychologist's house, which was on a hill with a driveway that ran nearly a quarter of a mile to the street. They began playing catch, with the psychologist in the driveway and the pitcher by the house. The pitcher didn't want his doctor to have to go down the hill, and every pitch was perfect. When they reversed positions and the psychologist was by the house, the pitches went up off the house, and one broke a window. "When he was focused on me and my well-being, he was fine," said the psychologist. "When he was focused on himself and his delivery, he couldn't throw a strike." That pitcher never made the major leagues.

They are people. And they have flaws. Imagine if William Shakespeare were here to capture the flaws that have become so public for some of our athletes today. If the book *Game of Shadows* is accurate, when Barry Bonds turned to performance-enhancing help, it was 1999 and he was already in the argument for the ten best position players who ever lived. If the charges against Roger Clemens turn out to be valid, when (and if) he turned to help, he was already a first-ballot Hall of Famer. "Insecurity," says a psychiatrist, echoing the thoughts of one Hall of Fame player that "the bigger the star, the greater the insecurity." Watching one player angrily denying to Congress that he had ever used performance enhancers, a general manager said, "The first law of psychology is that if someone is self-absorbed [true in many of these cases], he will usually become self-delusional."

I sat in a chair in front of Alex Rodriguez when he had to admit to PED use in Texas, and I watched him sweat through his sweater, hyperventilate, and shrink. I couldn't help but be struck by the sense of human fragility. He said to me weeks later, "You know me. That's not bad. You know what? I'm not perfect."

It can be A-Rod, or the delusional Jose Canseco, whom Pat Jordan (whose autobiography, *A False Spring*, remains a literary sports classic) profiles in these pages in "Chasing Jose." It can be Sara Tucholsky, whose powerful story is told in Thomas Lake's "The Way It Should Be," the first selection in this book. It can be Jonathan Boyer's undeniable will, captured here in Steve Friedman's "The Impossible Redemption of Jonathan Boyer." It can be Jenny Crain, the runner whose tragic story is told deftly by John Brant in "Close to Home," or the tragic Bernie Kosar, whom Dan Le Batard captures in his brilliant essay, "Life Throws Bernie Kosar for a Loss." There is the heroism and greatness of Kenny Washington and Shane Battie, as well as the near-mythological figure that was Dick Fosbury. The National Football League, along with almost every sport besides football, is trying to come to grips with what the history of Kyle Turley and Ted Johnson should have taught us, and here that history is masterfully examined in Malcolm Gladwell's "Offensive Play" and Robert Sanchez's "This Is Ted Johnson's Brain."

Everyone will find glimmers of recognition in these pages, because at the end of the day, sports, or the experience of sports, are deeply personal for us. And we connect to these moments in very particular ways. I cannot watch the end to the Miracle on Ice enough, because David Silk was a friend who, when he played hockey, always knew how to play in the defensive zone. A New England kid who grew up playing on a pond in Groton, Massachusetts, Silk had something Handelian in his back-checking, intercepting the Russian pass, dumping it out across the blue line to Al Michaels's "Do you believe in miracles?"

I have known Harvey Dorfman for more than thirty years, and I know what he has done to help athletes like Kevin Brown and Al Leiter and Mark Wohlers, so it's no surprise that Karl Taro Greenfeld's "Stay in the Moment (with Doctor Baseball)" flashed through me, because of Dorfman's ability to find the vein that reduces the complicated to the simple, the anxiety to the childish love of competing in a childish game. Recently one of my closest friends, Jerry Stephenson, for thirty-five years a scout, the son of a legendary scout, and the father of a rising star in the scouting business, died, and so I have gone back and read Bill Plaschke's tribute to Phil Pote more than two dozen times. In "The Ever Elusive, Always Inscrutable and Still Incomparable Bobby Orr," S. L. Price gets Bobby Orr right: the greatest player who ever put on skates; the man who was sitting on a sick man's hospital bed, ready to greet him and help jump-start his rehab with his smile; the man who sits in the stands at Cape Cod League baseball games and thanks every kid who asks him for his autograph. Every one.

Bob Ryan and I started as summer interns the day Robert Kennedy was assassinated in 1968, in the heat of the civil rights movement. Barack Obama was inaugurated president nearly four decades later, the day after I had been reunited with Thurston Clarke and celebrated his brilliant study of that earlier tumultuous year in *The Last Campaign*. Meanwhile Ryan wrote in "NBA Leads This Race," "Where the NBA laps and relaps the field is in the area of authority." In those words, my old friend and colleague defines what we who have spent our lives in sports wish we had articulated.

This collection is about sports, which means it is about the human race, its drive and passion, strengths and weaknesses, rises and falls, and the damages caused by the need for greatness. It is the magic of sports: George Brett walking away from baseball after hitting a ground ball to second base and running as hard as he could to first base, safe or out; Rich Gossage understanding that he didn't *beat* Yaz or that Brett didn't *beat* him; Carlos Pena understanding that the cold and the embarrassment he endured as a teenager in Haverhill, Massachusetts, were what drove his family in their pursuit of the American Dream.

Better yet, as this volume of wonderful sports stories shows, it is Mallory and Liz carrying Sara around the bases. Mallory Holtman weeps. She, like A-Rod and Steve Blass, Ted Johnson and Greg LeMond, is just like us. Sports writers have devoted their lives to turning athletics back into the human condition—and in these pages they have done just that. It should have ended differently for Mallory. Don Mattingly should have won a World Series ring.

PETER GAMMONS

The Best American
Sports Writing
2010

THOMAS LAKE

The Way It Should Be

FROM SPORTS ILLUSTRATED

THE GIFT MOVED BY WIRE and satellite, leaving a saltwater trail. It came from a field on the edge of the Cascade Mountains and traveled around the world. The gift was a story. It began with a hanging curveball and ended with a strange, slow procession. It gave gooseflesh to a phys-ed teacher in Pennsylvania, made a market researcher in Texas weak in the knees, put a lump in the throat of a crusty old man in Minnesota. It convinced a cynic in Connecticut that all was not lost.

At an office in the South, one woman tried to tell another woman the story but cried so much that the second woman had to find the details on the Internet, and then she cried too. At an office in the North, a 250-pound man was wiping his eyes when a colleague walked in, so he lied and said his contacts were bothering him. At a trucking company in the Midwest, a jaded executive cried the first time he read the story and then went back and read it again, because it made him feel so wonderful.

Yes, men cried. As much as women, maybe more: a retired cop in upstate New York, his body confused by conflicting orders from his nervous system; a fire-protection engineer in Washington State, his heart rate and blood pressure soaring and plunging; a biology professor in Montana, his breath coming in long sighs; a self-described redneck logger in Oregon, warm water running in rivulets down his cheeks.

The economy was faltering then, in the spring of 2008. Gasoline was $3.56 a gallon. We were five years and four thousand dead soldiers into Iraq. The story jolted us back to sanity, people said, and restored our faith, and reminded us that goodness and decency and honor still exist.

All it took was an improbable swing by a .153 hitter.

A broken strand of connective tissue.

A situation with no clear precedent.

And an astonishing proposal from a young woman named Mallory.

> *Dear Mallory,*
> *What a fantastic person you are!*
>   *Clare King, West Allis, Wisconsin*

Mallory Holtman sleeps in a king-sized bed with seven pillows. Mounted in a plastic display case above her head is a Louisville Slugger engraved with her name, and under the bed are two forty-one-quart storage bins full of fan mail. Pictures surround her bed. There she is with Rudy Giuliani at the 2008 All-Star Game at Yankee Stadium. There she is with Justin Timberlake at the ESPYs. There's the proclamation from the day she was honored by Congress. There's the baby in Surprise, Arizona, whose mother made her Mallory's namesake.

To millions of people who know the story, Mallory Holtman is defined by forty seconds of her life. But what about the rest of it? Who is she, and what gave her that wild idea?

Her first name says nothing about her. Mallory comes from the Old French *maloré*, which means "unfortunate." The name was her brother's idea. He got it from a character on the 1980s sitcom *Family Ties*.

Her nickname is not much help either. One softball teammate used to call her Heifer, which, despite her ability to eat a cheeseburger for lunch and a top sirloin for dinner, does not accurately describe her appearance. To at least one male fan, she looks like Ashley Judd. ("You really could be her little sister," he wrote.)

It would be convenient if Mallory's tattoos had rowdy stories behind them. They do not. The dragonfly on her left ankle was applied when she turned eighteen because she wanted something girly that was not a flower. She had a flame put on her lower back to match her older sister Amanda's flame. And then, on a trip to Fort Myers, Florida, with her best friend, Kelli Spaulding, she walked into a tattoo parlor, looked through the available images, and chose a flower after all, for her left wrist.

The diamond-studded silver cross has promise. She has worn one around her neck for five years, including the four she played first base for the Wildcats of NCAA Division II Central Washington University. Was it a gift from a special young man? No. Mallory is fixated on James Dean, judging from the posters hanging in her bedroom, but she has never had time for a serious relationship. She just loves diamonds, and she figured it would be a long time before anyone gave her any, so she bought the cross for herself and wore it as she methodically chopped down Central Washington's career records for home runs, RBIs, hits, runs, and doubles. After a while she *had* to keep wearing it, if only out of superstition.

Mallory lives in Ellensburg, Washington, population 17,000, an old rodeo town 110 miles southeast of Seattle. She shares a house near the Central Washington campus with two other assistant softball coaches. They keep an arsenal of plastic yellow Nerf guns in the top of a closet, next to a string of Christmas lights, and they mix pale-green margaritas in a deluxe Cuisinart blender. Their head coach is Gary Frederick.

To explain why Mallory works for Gary Frederick, you could talk about the time he brought in a barbershop chorus to serenade his players on Valentine's Day, or you could talk about the priorities he lays out at the beginning of each season (family first, academics second, sports third), or you could tell a story, from many years ago during his days as a baseball coach, when his team was in the district playoffs. They had won the first game of a best-of-three series. Then rain came and turned the field to mush, and the rules said if another game couldn't be played, the Game 1 winner would automatically advance. But Frederick got on the phone and found a playable field, and his team played two more games and lost them both. "I'm sorry you feel that way," he said to his players when they grumbled, "but I don't want to back into a championship."

On April 26, 2008, the brilliant Saturday of Mallory's last regular-season home games with the Wildcats, Central Washington faced the Western Oregon Wolves in a doubleheader. The Wildcats lost the opener 8–1, putting themselves one loss from elimination in the race for the NCAA playoffs. Mallory was hitting above .360

for her career, and she held the Great Northwest Athletic Conference's career record for home runs. But her failing knees were already scheduled for surgery after the season, and she would not be going pro. None of her college teams had made the playoffs. This was her last chance.

> *I am a 45 yr old male who has played little league baseball and adult softball for many years. I too have never hit a homerun in my life. I had tears in my eyes while watching the story. I could totally relate to her goal.*
> *Bobby Ashworth, King, North Carolina*

Game 2, top of the second, no score, Western Oregon runners on first and second. The catcher flashes two fingers and then two more, calling for a curveball outside.

The Wolves' Sara Tucholsky stands in the batter's box. Her teammates call her the Ocho, because she wears number 8. She is a backup right fielder in a hitting slump, starting this game only because the first-string right fielder misread a line drive by Mallory in the first game and the coach made Sara a defensive replacement.

The curveball comes in at about 50 miles per hour, as yellow as a grapefruit and just as large. In a dramatization of this moment produced for Japanese television, the American actress playing Sara imagines herself in a ray of white light, hitting her first career home run. In reality she is just trying to make contact. The pitcher has missed her target. The ball is over the plate.

In the Japanese drama, Sara swings with her eyes closed. In reality she stares at the ball, picturing it as even larger than a grapefruit. She connects. There is a sound of vibrating aluminum as the ball sails toward the horizon, toward Lion Rock and Flag Mountain, over the left fielder, over the fence.

Sara runs along the white stripe of powdered limestone that Frederick poured on the field that morning. Behind the backstop, Central Washington parent Sue Wallin captures the moment on her ancient Sony eight-millimeter video camera.

Mallory sees the ball disappear. *Dang it,* she thinks, walking from first base toward the pitcher's circle to huddle with her teammates. She sees the first runner score, then the second. She looks for Sara.

But Sara is behind her, out of sight, and Mallory hears an awful noise.

Wallin turns off her camcorder.

I simply cannot express how much your team has lifted me this day.
   Al Wazlak, Virginia Beach

Mallory grew up in White Salmon, a no-stoplight town on the Columbia River Gorge in Oregon. The Holtmans lived in a neighborhood called Pucker Huddle, across the river from Mount Hood. Mallory was the baby of the family, five years younger than Amanda; twelve years younger than her brother, Gabriel; much too young to be anyone's rival. For Gabriel and his friends, she was something of a mascot. It helped that she was, in his words, "freakishly coordinated." She could ride a bike by age three.

When Mallory was six, Gabriel took her snowboarding on Mount Hood, down slopes with names like Daisy and Buttercup, but those didn't sound tough enough for Mallory. For her benefit he renamed them Deathblow and Frontside Intimidator.

When she was eight, he took her windsurfing on the Columbia River, through white spray and fifteen-foot swells, and sometimes he stole her out of school so they could go cliff-jumping into the deep green lakes along the Columbia. Gabriel was a muscular six foot four, with a black belt in tae kwon do. When she was with him, nothing could touch her.

One day on the school bus, a teenage boy said something despicable to Mallory, something no one should ever say to an eight-year-old girl, and she mentioned it that night at the dinner table. Unfortunately for the boy, Mallory knew his name. "I know where he lives," Amanda said.

Gabriel went and took care of it. Nobody bothered Mallory again.

Dear Mallory,
Will you marry me?
   Just kidding; I'm 74, happily married, and a grandfather. But I am one of countless people across the country, and probably across the world, who truly love you for what you and Liz Wallace did for Sara Tucholsky on April 26. How could we not?
   Rev. John M. Salmon, Portland

On the first home-run trot of her life, Sara Tucholsky is heading for second base when she hears a coach yelling behind her. "Get back! Get back!"

The American dramatization of this game is a six-minute film directed by Ron Shelton, who also wrote and directed *Bull Durham* and *White Men Can't Jump*. In that simplified version of the story, part of a series from Liberty Mutual that celebrates everyday virtue, Sara is injured when she trips over first base. In reality she misses first altogether, and ten feet toward second she turns to go back. But her metal cleats catch in the dirt, and she looks down to see her right knee rippling like a wave.

Sometimes there is a popping sound when a person tears an anterior cruciate ligament, one of four major threads of tissue that hold the upper and lower leg together. Sara hears no sound. What she feels is an immediate and concentrated pain unlike any she has had before. She falls to the dust, moaning, and the crowd goes silent.

Mallory turns to see Sara on her back, holding her knee. The first-base coach is still yelling, "Get back to first!"

Sara crawls back to the base, perhaps eight feet, and holds it like a pillow. Breathing deeply, she asks the first-base coach, "What do I do?"

"Don't touch her," says the base umpire, Bill Wagner. By rule, if anyone from her team tries to help her, Wagner will have to call her out.

A voice comes from the audience, near the home dugout: "She needs the wheelchair. Use my wheelchair. Get her around those bases." It's Bobbi Frederick, wife of Coach Frederick, mother to the Wildcats. She is fighting Lou Gehrig's disease. Her entreaties are lost in the chaos. She will hang on for eight more months, and Gary will sprinkle her ashes in the Yakima River, and Mallory will use her newfound political clout to have this field named Gary and Bobbi Frederick Field.

What happens next will be the subject of some dispute. Remember: Sue Wallin has turned off her camcorder. The coach of Western Oregon, Pam Knox, will recall an exchange with the home plate umpire, Jake McChesney, that goes like this.

KNOX: If she can't run, what's going to happen?
McCHESNEY: It'll be a two-RBI single.
KNOX: *What?*

Mallory will remember the same words. At least two others will say they saw Knox conferring with McChesney. But McChesney will say he never spoke to Knox.

The other umpire, Bill Wagner, who makes his living as a black-jack dealer, never had the talent to play sports at a high level, but he loves facilitating the game. Rules are his obsession. A few times a week, when he's eating lunch alone, he opens the NCAA softball rule book at random and studies one of its 271 pages.

In eight years as an umpire, Wagner had never seen a player injured on a home-run trot. Now, standing a few feet from Sara's prostrate form, he scans his internal database. *There's got to be a rule for this,* he tells himself. Later he will look it up and realize there are *two* rules for this, and he could have applied either one. Contrary to what Knox was led to believe, neither would result in a two-run single.

Rule 8.5.3.2: If an injury to a batter-runner or runner prevents her from proceeding to an awarded base, the ball is dead and substitution may be made. The substitute must legally touch all awarded or missed bases not previously touched. This would give Western Oregon all three runs, but Sara's only career home run would be wiped from the record books because she did not personally cross the plate.

The other rule, 15.10.2.3, was designed for extraordinary circumstances, such as when a fielder or runner is badly hurt and the ball is still in play: *When necessary to protect an injured player, the umpire may suspend play immediately and before resumption, award a base or bases that offensive players would have reached, in the umpire's judgment, had play not been suspended.* This would be an easy call. Sara would have made it all the way home. She would get her four bases and be credited with a home run.

There is no telling how long she lies there. To Sara, it seems like at least four minutes. To Wagner, it seems like only ninety seconds. The answer is on the tip of his brain. Subsequent evidence will show that, at least for a moment, he too believes the mistaken two-run-single theory. The confusion drags on. Finally, Mallory has had enough.

"Excuse me," she says.

And would you please thank their parents for raising such compassionate young ladies? I know that we as parents often wonder if we

have made any difference in the world. These parents need to know
that they have.
    Jamie and Becky Cripps, Kalamazoo, Michigan

Mallory is afraid of snakes, and failure, and lightning, and the high
wind that used to slice through the gorge and rattle her bedroom
window while she was sleeping in the dead of night.

"Dad," she would say, wandering into her parents' room, "I think
someone's outside my window. You have to go look."

And Greg Holtman (volunteer fireman, home builder, former
timber cutter) always got up, stumbled to the door, did a token
search of the perimeter, and came back, telling his daughter, "No
one's out there. Go to bed." This made Mallory feel better, but
sometimes, for additional security, when she was as old as sixteen,
she crawled into the queen-sized bed between her mother and father and flopped around till morning.

For Mallory's sixteenth birthday, Greg installed a batting cage
with a pitching machine in the backyard. Her mother, Christy, a
first-grade teacher for thirty years, sat in a lawn chair and provided
running commentary while Mallory worked on her swing. She
even announced what the imaginary fielders might have done:
"Oh, good catch. Robbed ya."

Mallory had a softball scholarship offer from Canisius, a Division I college in upstate New York, but she chose Central Washington so she could play for Gary Frederick and so her parents
could see her play. In her four full seasons they missed fewer than
five games. One day Greg drove 350 miles to Nampa, Idaho,
through two snowstorms, over two mountain passes, and drove
home that night. Mallory's sister knows nothing about sports,
but she attended the games too and cried for joy at every home
run.

Even when Mallory struck out, Christy found a way to make her
feel good. "Your hair looks nice," she would say, or, "Honey, you
look really great in your pants today," or, when the Wildcats lost,
"There's worse things than losing," and then they all went out for
some red meat.

Now that Mallory is famous, people walk up to Christy and say,
"You must be so proud of her."

This is how Christy replies: "We've always been proud of her."

I coach a team of 11–12 year old boys here in Pampa, Texas and we recently had an 11 year old young man hit his first homerun in the bottom of the last inning to draw our team within 2 runs. However, in his exuberance, he evidently missed 1st base or barely touched it. After he touched home and while our other kids were congratulating him, the other coach protested that he missed 1st base and the home plate umpire agreed and he was called out.

That showed extremely poor sportsmanship and I have printed this article out and mailed it to the opposing coach so that he can hope-fully learn what true sportsmanship really is. By the way, we ended up losing the game by 2 runs.

Kevin Hunt, Pampa, Texas

As it turns out, the rules have no bearing on this story. What matters is the *perception* of the rules. One way or another Mallory has been given to understand that Sara is about to lose her home run. That would mean her injury is to Central Washington's advantage. In the Wildcats' fight to avoid elimination and Mallory's quest to prolong her career, they would have one less run to make up.

But Mallory just wants Sara off the field, getting ice on her knee, and she wants to get on with the game. She does not confer with her teammates or her coach. She knows what to do. She has a brother and father who will let nothing harm her. She has a mother and sister who affirm her without condition. She has spent more than four years learning from a coach who would rather lose in the mud than win by a rainout. She has spent nearly twenty-three years getting permission for what she does next. "Hey," she says to the umpires, "can I help her out?"

"What?" Wagner says.

"Can I help her around the bases?"

"Why would you want to do that?"

Wagner scans his database for rules against this proposal. *No*, he decides, *it's not obstruction, because the fielder isn't getting in the run-ner's way. It's not interference, because the runner isn't getting in the fielder's way. Well, if she wants to let the other team score an extra run, then I'm going to let her.*

He consults with McChesney, who says, "It's Senior Day. It's their field. If they want to do it, who am I to stop it?"

Wagner turns back to Mallory.

"All right," he says. "Do it."

I would like to treat you and your team to a small something, an ice cream, a soft drink, or maybe a slice of pizza. Please accept the enclosed check with that in mind, or if you wish to donate it for another cause, feel free to do that. It is little enough.

I have three daughters, and thank God, I know they would have acted in the same manner as you and your team did, given the opportunity.

Paul Newman, Derby, Connecticut

P.S. I'm sorry to disappoint you, but though the name is the same, and we live in the same state, I am not the actor, nor am I any relation to him.

Money poured in after the game, along with candy from strangers. Gary Frederick's team got nearly $25,000 in donations, including at least one check from a soldier in Iraq. The university matched every dollar. The Wildcats got new uniforms for 2009 and new protective screens for pitching practice. Instead of riding to away games in three vans driven by the coaches, they were chauffeured around the Pacific Northwest in a luxury charter bus.

Mallory wants to be Central Washington's next head softball coach, whenever Frederick, who turns seventy-two in July, decides to retire. In the meantime she and Sara have formed a nonprofit organization, the Mallory Holtman and Sara Tucholsky Sportsmanship Defined Foundation, with the aim of doling out scholarships and teaching kids the right way to play. They have a publicist and a booking agent. Corporations pay them to deliver motivational speeches, including a recent appearance in Florida to educate five or six thousand mortgage brokers on character and responsibility.

Her mother says fame has not changed Mallory, not in the least, but Mallory does admit to one prima donna moment. Last summer, when they were on vacation at a cabin in Idaho, Christy asked Mallory to take out the trash. Mallory had just returned from several plane rides—from a televised awards show to the All-Star Game and back—and she complained about being tired.

"Mallory," her mother said, "you're with family now. You need to check yourself." And Mallory took out the trash.

*

*I am 100% disabled with Multiple Sclerosis and anytime someone
helps me I do not know whether to be embarrassed or thankful. This
was very, very kind of them and very, very wonderful.*
  Chris A. Rock, Navarre, Florida

Mallory scans the field for potential accomplices. "Liz," she says,
locking eyes with the shortstop, Liz Wallace, a Navy wife from
Montana who can turn a double play with unusual speed and grace.

Liz puts down her glove. *Yes, that's the right thing to do,* she thinks,
walking with Mallory toward Sara. She can see tears on Sara's
cheeks, powdered limestone on her right hand.

"We're going to pick you up," Mallory says, "and carry you
around the bases."

Sara nods. "Thank you," she says, overwhelmed with relief. Mallory bends down and puts her left hand under Sara's left thigh and
her right hand under Sara's left armpit. Liz does likewise on Sara's
other side. They lift her off the ground.

Behind the chain-link backstop, Sue Wallin presses Record on
her Handycam. Four days later she will hustle to her hometown
post office just before it closes and drop the eight-millimeter tape
in the mail to her daughter in Ellensburg, and it will arrive just in
time to be shown to visiting reporters, and it will be seen on national TV and played nearly 200,000 times on YouTube.

Mallory and Liz haul Sara toward second base, moving with awkward sideways steps. They must travel 180 feet. *Don't trip,* Mallory
tells herself.

"Thank you, guys," Sara says again. At 125 pounds, she does not
feel heavy.

"You hit it over the fence," Mallory says. "You deserve it."

Mallory lowers Sara's left foot to touch second base. "This has to
look hilarious to everybody who's watching," Liz says.

"I wonder if they're laughing at us," Mallory says.

The spectators do not laugh. They stand, feeling a certain eu-
phoria, their applause a mild hailstorm. Mallory lowers Sara's foot
to third base. An umpire hovers nearby, just to make sure.

As the women turn toward home, a wheat farmer named Blake
Wolf takes aim with his Pentax ten-megapixel and snares a crisp
vertical snapshot, the only known still photograph of the event.
The picture will be licensed by a nonprofit group called the Foundation for a Better Life and printed on nearly 1,400 billboards.

Sara looks up to see her teammates standing at home plate, clapping for her. Beyond her gratitude she feels a twinge of pride, because she has just hit the first home run of her career in what will prove to be her last at-bat.

Mallory and Liz do not linger. As Sara is carried to her dugout to have her knee iced, the two Wildcats walk back to the pitcher's circle for a team huddle. They are still one loss from elimination.

"All right," Liz says. "Down three-zero. Let's get these outs and go in and hit."

> *I have seen many of the greatest moments in sports: Willie Mays'*
> *catch in center field, Bill Mazeroski's World Series winning homer,*
> *Kirk Gibson's homer in the World Series. I was present to watch*
> *Hank Aaron hit his record breaking homer, saw Yastrzemski win the*
> *triple crown . . . and on and on and on.*
>
> *Nothing will live in my memory longer or with greater impact than*
> *the sportsmanship of Mallory and Liz.*
>
> *Gary Johnson, Vancouver, Washington*

There was a green metal box in the bushes outside the bank. There was a threatening phone call. The police chief showed up, along with a captain and a bomb technician. The bomb technician scanned the box with an X-ray machine and decided it was part of a hoax. He carried the box into the bank. The chief and the captain went with him. The bomb technician tried to open the green metal box, and the chief and the captain tried to help him. The green metal box was not part of a hoax. The bomb exploded, and it killed the bomb technician and the captain, and it tore off the police chief's leg.

This all happened on Friday, December 12, 2008, in a small Oregon town called Woodburn. The whole story is tragic and complicated, but the relevant portion concerns insurance. Woodburn belongs to a self-insurance cooperative called City County Insurance Services, and when the bomb exploded, the men and women of CCIS found themselves handling a crisis.

They had to spend hours on the phone in search of a grief counselor with four-wheel drive and snow tires who could be at Woodburn City Hall by 8:45 A.M. Monday. They had to fill out a bundle of paperwork for the city recorder, who would normally handle such things except she happened to be the dead captain's wife. The police chief's medical bills would total more than $500,000, which meant CCIS needed another insurance company to help pay. One claims supervisor, Susan Lavier, drove down an icy road with one hand on the wheel of her Dodge Durango and the other hand holding a cell phone on which she negotiated with the excess-coverage provider to make sure the chief got the care he would need: a plastic surgeon for his face, a vascular surgeon for his amputated leg, an orthopedist for his broken bones, an ear specialist for his perforated eardrum, a wheelchair, a wheelchair van, hallways at home wide enough for his wheelchair, a driveway level enough for the van. Lavier would have to justify every cent.

Earlier this year, CCIS recognized Lavier, Valerie Saiki, John Dalen, and Janie McCollister for their exemplary service on the Woodburn case. The company has a phrase for what they did. They call it Doing a Mallory.

I know I will never forget their good deed; whereas, had they even won the entire NCAA softball tournament, I'm sure I would have forgotten their name as soon as the next team won.
Denise and Gary Iams, Marion, Ohio

Central Washington scores twice in the bottom of the second, closing the gap to one run. Western Oregon scores again in the fourth to go ahead 4–2. Central leaves the bases loaded in the sixth. Mallory has two hits but no runs batted in. The score is still 4–2 when the game ends. Even if Sara's home run had been called a single, Central would have been one run short.

Some will say that only a woman would have done what Mallory did, that a baseball player in the same situation would have left his opponent in the dust. Some will say that only an amateur would have done what Mallory did, and only a player from a Division II college or lower, because in Division I and professional sports the purity of competition is tainted by money. There will be plenty of debate, except on one point. Almost all of us who hear Mallory's story will search the high meadows of our souls for hope that we would have done the same thing, or that we will, if we are ever given the chance.

Mallory walks off the field into the arms of her mother and father. "We're so proud of you, honey," they tell her, as always, and the evening holds the promise of a trip to Outback Steakhouse. But right now the game is over, and her softball career will expire in seven days, and the playoffs are forever out of reach. And Mallory Holtman weeps.

Shadow Boxing

FROM ESPN.COM

MIAMI — THE OLD MAN opens the door and shuffles into a familiar room. The air smells of stale beer and discount brand cigarette smoke. The tables are taken by men with no names. They are all friends. They are all strangers. A different journey brought each of them here, to the pool hall on NW Second Avenue, but that doesn't matter anymore. Their journeys are over. Most don't share the details, not even their last names. Some don't remember the year, or how long they've been coming here. They have no past.

The old man walks clumsily to a table. He has a story. The act of telling it, of having people hear it, keeps him from disappearing forever. One night, he says, he fought Muhammad Ali. Almost won, he brags. Some believe him. Some don't. Most don't care. He's just another wacko wandering the streets with some tale about how his life could have been different.

They ignore him, pretending he's not even there. He's got to show them.

The old man gets up and throws punches into the air.

The people around him laugh.

He sits back down, invisible again.

Part One: Lost

In the Beginning

The search started off six years ago with a phone call.

The man on the other end is Stephen Singer, a New Hampshire car salesman who collects things in his spare time. Most of all, he collects all things Muhammad Ali. It's a fetish. He prizes the light box he keeps on the wall of his office. With the flick of a switch, you can see an X-ray with a thin crack: Ali's broken jaw.

He tells me the story of the boxer who disappeared, starting by explaining his latest mission: collecting the signatures of all fifty men who fought Ali. The first thirty-five or so came easy. Singer got a professional autograph collector to help with those. Then, the pro came to a dead end; Singer decided to continue on his own.

He peered into another world, in which a brush with fame didn't grant immortality. One by one, he found them. Some took months. He searched dank boxing gyms and dusty public records. He found a man who'd given up the ring for a European carnival. He located a notarized letter from a fighter turned Mafia hit man. A rabbi acted as a middle man in a small Argentine town for the passport of a fighter who'd been dead since 1964. He was number forty-nine.

One fighter remained. What had happened to Jim Robinson, who'd fought Muhammad Ali in Miami Beach on February 7, 1961?

Singer tried everything. He contacted boxing historians and even enlisted Ali's old trainer, Angelo Dundee. He found a boxer in Philly named Jim Robinson . . . who never fought Ali. Private detectives and former FBI agents helped. Robinson was a ghost. He had no known date of birth, no known full name. No known family. No ties. No public records linking him to a place or a time. In the exhaustively well-chronicled life of Muhammad Ali, Singer has stumbled into the one hole, a man who'd shared a moment in time and space with one of the most famous humans ever, only to vanish. An old Associated Press story said Robinson was from Kansas City, which is why Singer is on the phone with the local paper's feature writer, who happens to be me. He tells me there isn't much more information to build on; nobody has ever really thought to search for the fighter before.

In a way, Jim Robinson didn't begin to exist until someone realized he was missing.

Hooked

Singer asks me to help, so I collect everything already known about Robinson. Turns out, although sports people throw around the phrase "go down in history" a lot, in real life, history doesn't amount to much. Jim Robinson's name appears maybe a dozen times in print.

The night of the fight, he ran into the Miami Beach Convention Hall, carrying an old Army bag full of his gear. The reason he seemed harried? He was a last-minute replacement, used to fighting for pocket change. The guy who was supposed to box that night, Willie Gullatt, didn't show.

Ali biographers figure Gullatt got scared. With good reason. Until that point, the old stories say, few considered Ali a great fighter. That all changed the day before he fought Robinson, when heavyweight contender Ingemar Johansson, in town training for a title fight with Floyd Patterson, invited the young Ali, still known as Cassius Clay, to spar.

They stepped into the ring, and by the time the men climbed out after two rounds, the history of boxing was forever changed. Ali threw a blur of punches, a jab, then two more, his feet dancing, a combination, right, left, right. Each punch landed—hard. Johansson lumbered forward, throwing a roundhouse right, which didn't come close, and the big heavyweight stumbled and almost fell.

Ali danced and talked in rhyme.

The next night, Gullatt, who also seems lost to time, didn't show up. Jim Robinson got the call, even though Ali outweighed him by sixteen and a half pounds. Robinson came out fast, throwing wild punches, which Ali dodged, waiting for an opening. About a minute into the fight, he saw his chance. Bam! Bam! Pow! Pow! The shots to the head put Robinson down. He struggled to stand, but the referee counted to nine, then stopped the fight.

It had lasted ninety-four seconds.

Afterward, the *New York Daily News* wrote, "It was all a mistake." The *Miami News* wrote, "If promoter Chris Dundee had canvassed the women in the audience, he couldn't have found an easier opponent for Clay."

Three years later, Ali beat Sonny Liston in Miami to become champion, and the next night, a few miles up the road in a tiny auditorium, Robinson lost to a journeyman named Jack Gilbert. Robinson was already fading away. Boxing records show he kept fighting, losing much more often than he won, finally stopping in 1968.

There's been only one sighting since then. In 1979, a photographer shooting pictures for *Sports Illustrated* went to find Ali's earliest opponents. Michael Brennan located Jim Robinson, whom people down in Miami called "Sweet Jimmy." Most of what's known about his life comes from the brief blurb that ran with the photos. He lived off veterans' benefits. He claimed he was born around 1925. He claimed he was wrongfully convicted of armed robbery. Most days, he just hung out in the seedy Overtown neighborhood, at the pool hall owned by Miami concert promoter Clyde Killens.

The photos show a haunted man. His jaw juts out, like he's lost teeth. His eyebrows are bushy; once, they probably seemed delicate. A visor throws a shadow across his eyes. A deep scar runs along his left cheekbone. In one, he leans up against the wall of a Winn-Dixie. In another, he walks down railroad tracks, the skyline of Miami rising behind him. He never smiles.

Brennan shot the photos on a Friday night and Saturday morning. Sweet Jimmy smelled of booze and Camel cigarettes. Brennan remembers the last time he saw him. It was in the morning, on the railroad tracks, and he slipped the old fighter twenty bucks. Sweet Jimmy turned and walked off, negotiating the crossties. He never looked back.

"Tell Clay I ain't doing too good," he said.

The Paperless Trail

We all live parallel lives on paper.

Long after we're gone, the details of our existence will remain part of the public record; in time, they will be all that's known about us, a skeleton of facts, the human whys long decayed. That's what made Sweet Jimmy's disappearance strange. It's hard to disappear. Search engines record everything: our arrests, the amount we paid for our house, the times we've defaulted on a credit card or paid our taxes late. No piece of our past is truly private. The love of a wedding day is public record, as is the hatred of divorce. Public records allow me, in less than two minutes, to learn that Muhammad Ali has a home or office at 8105 Kephart Lane and that his wife has owned a Lexus, license plate LA1, with an AM/FM cassette player and a standard tilt steering wheel. The invasiveness can be scary, but also strangely reassuring. Someday, through these strings of ones and zeroes, people will know we were here. It's impossible not to leave a trail. Finding Jimmy, I was sure, would take a day. Two, tops.

That was six years ago.

I stuck with the search, first while with the *Kansas City Star*, then at ESPN. Everywhere I turned, I found pain and loss, a procession of wasted lives, people who never fought Ali and, thus, won't ever have someone come looking for them. Did any of these men hang in the pool hall too, never knowing someone a few feet away shared the same name? A James Robinson born in 1929 was shot a few blocks from the pool hall in 1984, his murderer yelling, "I told you I was gonna kill me a black son of a bitch." A James Robinson died of a gunshot to the head in Overtown in 2007, likely a suicide, but he turned out to be just fifty-four. A Jimmie Robinson was beaten to death under an overpass near the pool hall in 1991. He had an old arrest for being in a park after hours, and his only address was the Camillus House, a local homeless shelter. His date of birth made him too young to have fought Ali in 1961. The Miami medical examiner's office said 227 people have died in Miami since 1980 and never been identified. Any of them could be Sweet Jimmy.

I ran hundreds of searches, through every imaginable database, called every Miami boxing authority still alive. Dundee helped by going through his wealth of boxing sources. The VA struck out, as did the military records center and the Social Security office. Current and former law enforcement officers tried to help. The police union sent Sweet Jimmy's picture to old beat cops. The county and city cold-case detectives searched. They found no J. Robinsons who were African American and the right age. The Florida Department of Corrections said it had never had custody of a Jimmy, Jim, or James Robinson who fit the description.

Finally, I began to realize that I was looking for Jimmy all wrong. I was looking for him the way I'd look for myself. He'd lived off the grid, managing to go through life and, according to society just out of reach around him, never exist.

It was pointless to look for Sweet Jimmy in my world.

I had to go search in his.

Starting Over

The first stop is in Miami Beach at the Fontainebleau Hotel. Elvis and Sinatra stayed here. Bond spied on Goldfinger's card game here. The man I've come to see stands ready to grab my luggage — an old bellhop, name tag reads *Levi*. Yes, that's my guy, Levi Forte, an old boxer who fought with Sweet Jimmy. He's been here forty-four years, and the tourists whose bags he carries have no idea that he once stood in the ring with champions, just like most folks didn't know that Beau Jack, the old man who shined shoes downstairs, had headlined Madison Square Garden twenty-one times, more than any fighter before or since.

I show Levi the photograph. He studies the drooping chin, the delicate eyelashes, the wild beard. "That's him," he says. "I haven't seen that guy in I don't know when."

The last time was about thirty years ago, and both men were passing by the famous Fifth Street Gym. Levi thought Jimmy would turn and go up the stairs. When he didn't, Levi stopped him.

"You Jimmy Robinson?" he asked.

Jimmy seemed surprised and pleased. The question made him real again, briefly.

"You know me?"

"You fought The Man," Levi said.

The tourists pile out of their cars as I step back into mine. Before I can put it in drive, I hear a knock on the glass. Levi fills my window. He's got a story. One he needs to tell me before I'm gone forever, to prove that he ever existed at all.

"Don't forget," he says. "I was the first guy to go ten rounds with George Foreman. December 16, 1969."

A Line in the Water

Next stop: Overtown.

Though it's just a few blocks from the downtown American Airlines Arena, home of the Miami Heat, you can feel the world changing as you turn off Biscayne Boulevard, each street bleaker than the one before, buildings giving way to boarded-up facades giving way to empty lots. People walk toward my car when I stop at traffic lights. Minor laws and small courtesies don't apply; a cop had advised me to run the red lights. People huddle beneath the overpasses. Drug lookouts in white T-shirts eye me warily from corners and the rooftops. Nobody enters Overtown undetected.

It didn't always feel like this. In the '60s, when Sweet Jimmy fought Ali, blacks-only hotels and nightclubs filled each block. The best musicians in the world—who could play, but not stay, on Miami Beach—saved their best and wildest sets for Overtown. Everybody came, booked by promoter Clyde Killens: Sam Cooke, Aretha Franklin, Count Basie, B. B. King, John Lee Hooker, everyone. That time and place is as lost as Sweet Jimmy. "You get off of Second Avenue," says Gaspar Gonzalez, a documentary filmmaker who made a movie about Ali's time in Miami, "and there's a hopelessness there. It's an island. There's no sense the world is bigger than that. People are desperate in a way you can't communicate. You're behind God's back."

Driving through the streets, I finger a stack of homemade posters I brought, each with Sweet Jimmy's photo and a local 305 phone number I set up. I explain on them that ESPN is looking for this man, but don't include his name. I tape them up around the neighborhood, and I drop them off at all the restaurants, shops, and liquor stores. I e-mail them to the secretaries at the local churches; nobody sees or gossips more. If Sweet Jimmy is alive, he's probably in Overtown. Finding a focal point is both satisfying and heartbreaking. All this time, Singer and I didn't know where to look for Jimmy, who never knew anyone was looking.

It's as if he was shipwrecked.

A Message in a Bottle

Three days after I return home from my first trip to Miami, my phone starts ringing.

The first caller, Melvin Eaton, claims, "I've been knowing old Sweet Jimmy for years."

He says the last time he saw Jimmy was five or six years ago, and that Jimmy never stopped reminding people that he fought Muhammad Ali. He'd shadow-box and brag. "That's all he talked about," Melvin tells me. "That's all he talked about. 'I'm the one who fought Ali. I'm the one who should have been the greatest.'"

A few days later, a woman calls. Her name is Brenda. "I see him every day," she says. "He's my friend. He be in Overtown around Twelfth Street and Second Avenue every day. He be on the street and asks for a dollar for a soda or a beer."

I ask her to go to that corner and put the phone in his hand. "They told me he just walked off," she says later, and I'm not sure whether she really knows Jimmy or just wants to feel like somebody with a mission, with a purpose, even if just for a few thin moments.

These calls point me to the door of Jimmy's world. I go back to Miami. As I'm sitting in the medical examiner's office, waiting to read the files of a few dead James Robinsons, a private investigator suggests checking Camillus House.

It sits on the edge of Overtown, a gateway. Miami has 994 people living on the street, and almost all of them end up here at one time or another. Outside, a man and woman push a stroller toward the shelter door. Another man steps inside holding a baby rattle. I walk up to the front desk, holding a flier. "I'm looking for someone," I tell the lady manning the desk.

Her name is Patricia. As she studies the photo, sadness darkens her face, as though a cloud is passing overhead. She slumps. Every day, unwanted people come through that door, and now, finally, someone has come for one of them—and it might be too late. "I never forget a face," she says. "He is homeless."

"Is he alive?" I ask.

She shakes her head. She doesn't know.

Part Two: The World Where No One Exists

Ghosts of the Pool Hall

The pool hall is boarded up, its secrets buried inside. The past is gone. It never happened. No sign of the white father and son who ran a watch repair business here until the '50s, when the son got polio. No sign of Killens, who took over the building; no sign that it once attracted the best sharks passing through Miami; and no sign of Jackie Gleason, who liked to stand atop the tables and sing.

It's the only building left on the block. Once, Ferdie Pacheco, Ali's fight doctor, had an office next door, but it burned in the 1980 riots. Crime took over the avenue. Cops often found themselves at this address. One night, they found a police motorcycle in the back that someone had stolen. As the years passed, fire and the wrecking ball cleared out the rest of the block. The promoter Killens died in 2004, but not before heroin took his son. At the end, Killens sat in his home around the corner with the shades drawn. He stopped listening to music.

The pool hall was condemned in April 2005. Killens's daughter made some poor business decisions and lost the property. It's been empty ever since. Rolling doors, like smaller versions of a garage's, are locked shut. Cinder blocks fill the upstairs windows, where a few apartments used to be, and boards cover the glass painted with the address: 920.

The current owner lets me inside. The tables are gone. The room's painted orange and turquoise, the colors of the Dolphins and nearby Booker T. Washington High. There's a toilet out in the open; the interior walls have been ripped out. The floor's been ripped up. A homeless person lives in the backroom, with a basket of clothes and cardboard boxes spread out to form a bed. There's a pile of trash in the corner with a shoe sitting on top. There's a welcome mat.

There is no sign of Jimmy.

Overtown 101

Overtown surrounds the empty pool hall, split north and south by I-95 and east and west by I-395. The concrete canopy is a daily reminder of what the neighborhood used to be, what it's become, and why.

Building the interstates in the late '60s forced thousands from their homes, destroyed a vibrant business district, and further cut them off from the rest of Miami. Population declined, from forty thousand to where it is today, just more than ten thousand. A new kind of economy rules the neighborhood now. A beer or two for a bath. Penicillin or tetracycline might buy you a place to sleep for a night. A crack rock buys just about anything.

The ZIP code, one of the poorest in the country, has more sex offenders than any other in Florida. It's a dumping ground for addicts, pedophiles, and the insane. In the shadow of a booming downtown, people live invisible lives. At the corner of NW Third Avenue and Eleventh Street, I talk to a group gathered beneath I-95. They're looking for cops.

"Police tell us to go home," one guy says, eyeing me suspiciously. "It's martial law in Overtown."

There's one woman in the group. Her arms are disfigured with scars, like she's been in a car wreck. In a way, she has. I'm told later: infections from years of heroin use. She's seen my fliers and asks if I could help her too. She wants to find out about her daddy. She gives his name. Any little bit of information will help her reconstruct the past, and a past is at the core of our humanity. A story is what makes us real.

Under the overpass, they talk about Sweet Jimmy, whom they haven't seen in a while, and about how people down here just vanish. "Give an emergency contact number," the woman tells her friends. "Let somebody know your name in case you go missing."

They go back to sitting around, their words muffled by the whine and hum of the car tires overhead. They're waiting, for the next hit, the next drink, the next meal, the next green mattress at the Camillus House, waiting for someone to come save them, for their body to end up at the morgue with a tag that says REMAINS, UNKNOWN, for the cops to tell them they can't stay here any longer. They're waiting for tomorrow, which will be just like today. The concrete shades them from the hot south Florida sun, and if you stand in just the right spot, sometimes a breeze blows nice and cool on your face.

They're waiting on the breeze.

Lessons of the Street

It takes a while, but eventually I make friends in Overtown, and their help opens the neighborhood. Smiles replace stares. The barriers fall away. One morning, local social worker Al Brown and I walk into a barbershop on NW Third Avenue.

"Gentlemen, gentlemen, how are you?" Al says. "I got a gentleman here who's looking for a guy that fought Muhammad Ali. Called him Sweet Jimmy."

A voice calls out from a backroom: "Sweet Jimmy's dead."

One of the old barbers introduces himself. "My name's Payne," he says. "I used to cut Jimmy's hair, and the guy in the back used to cut his hair. When he was walking the streets, before he went to the homeless shelter."

"Do you know what happened to him?" I ask.

"He got involved in drugs and walked the streets awhile," Payne says.

"Did he have a job?"

"No job. The street, man. He became an addict, and whoever he knew from the past he would rely on."

Payne knows a guy named Mr. Big, who was friends with Jimmy. He lives down the street in a squat, turquoise building, across from the empty lot where the old Harlem Square club, site of Sam Cooke's famous live album, used to be. Al knocks on Mr. Big's door until he steps out into the sunlight, squints a bit, then tells us he thinks Sweet Jimmy left town.

"How long ago?" Al asks.

"A good while," Big says. "Back in the '80s."

Finally, I am learning some things. I learn most people here didn't really know Jimmy, they just saw Jimmy. They didn't know his last name or his hometown. None actually saw him fight Ali. He moved silently through their lives, as two-dimensional to them as he was to those who read his name in the old boxing records and yellowed newspapers.

I learn there are two groups of old-timers who live here. There are those who held down jobs, like Big and Payne, and there are the hustlers. Both groups knew Jimmy, but as the years passed, he seemed to spend less and less time with the people who kept a foot in the real world. Irby McKnight, a local organizer who's helping me look, moved into the neighborhood the year Jimmy quit fighting.

"When I first met him," he tells me, "he used to be loud and obnoxious, but he was well-dressed. I used to say: 'Where'd this man get these old clothes from?' And people would say: 'That's Sweet Jimmy.' 'You ain't telling me nothing.' 'Oh, you don't know him. He was a boxer and he fought Muhammad Ali.'"

I learn a third thing too, more slowly than the other two. I learn about the people searching with me. In the beginning, I wondered why they were doing it. I thought about that a lot, especially when I left them in Overtown every day to go back to my fancy hotel, and finally I understood: as long as they help me look, they are a part of my world and not of his. As long as they help, they exist to me.

"He Forgets About Tomorrow"

We keep looking for people who'd remember, driving every street in Overtown, Mr. Big and Al pointing out the former sites of flop-houses and restaurants and nightclubs where Sweet Jimmy spent his days. One by one, they vanished. Wrecking balls took some; ri-ots and fires took others. Sweet Jimmy's world tightened until, fi-nally, only the pool hall was left. He outlived his neighborhood. Old-timers moved or died. Not many folks who knew him are left.

"I tell you who would know," Al says. "Shorty, who used to work at the racetrack."

"Yeah," Big says, "Shorty, he'd know about it. Shorty saw him fight."

"Whatever happened to Shorty?" Al says.

"Shorty around," Big says. "I saw him yesterday. He hangs around the corner here by Payne's. Catch him around here in the evening time. Racetrack Shorty."

The next day, we're parked next to an apartment building when Shorty Brown comes outside, a faded hospital bracelet on his arm. The skin hangs loose around his neck.

"Is Sweet Jimmy dead?" I ask.

"If he died, he didn't die here," Shorty says. "He didn't die in this town. If he'd died in this town, you'd know."

Jimmy hustled for money, Shorty explains. Worked his angle, a game with a belt and a pencil, and he was good at it. Shorty is the first of many who try to explain this quaint street hustle, and no-body can do it. Is it real? Is Jimmy real? Did Shorty ever actually see Jimmy? "He used to come to the racetrack and break every-body," he says. "Out at Gulfstream. The last time I saw him, him and Sonny Red screwed with everybody on the racetrack. They put him in jail."

"Who was Sonny Red?" I ask.

"Sonny Red was one of those little hustlers. They go around swin-dling people. Sweet Jimmy liked that life."

Guys like Shorty, and Jimmy's friend Benny Lane, who called af-ter seeing the flier, paint a picture. The kids made fun of Jimmy's heavy, heel-first walk. He always carried a deck of cards and dealt a mean three-card monte. He laughed at his own jokes when no one else did. He shadow-boxed when the fellas would yell, "Sweet

Jimmy!" A guy punched him one night at the pool hall after Jimmy kept on about the man's wife. By then, Jimmy couldn't fight back. "He was always looking to tell a joke or get a joke or say something funny," Benny says. "Get a laugh. A short laugh. Not a long laugh. That's Jimmy."

The years passed. More teeth fell out. He put up his game with the belt and pencil, shedding another thing that made him different from the faceless men and women who wander the Overtown streets. "He wasn't in the best of shape," Benny says. "He drank kinda heavy. And, uh, his mouth was kinda raggedy. Kinda like mine."

Sometimes, Benny and Jimmy would talk. About women, about whatever current events led the news, about home. Now Benny can't remember where Jimmy was from. He thinks Jimmy says he went to school in Kansas City. Sometimes, Jimmy'd pack up and leave for a month or so. He said he had a brother. "He talked about his family," Benny says. "He didn't forget about them."

This picture of Jimmy is the saddest. Not some historical footnote, but Jimmy the man, making it as best as he could. A man who thought about his family and missed his home. Benny tells me that Clyde Killens and a few others who'd made money off Jimmy's fighting watched over him. "Sometimes they cash his check," Benny says, "and give him an allowance because he liked to gamble, and he didn't care. If he gets in a game, he forgets about tomorrow."

As we are about to pull away, Shorty comes running after my car. He's remembered one last thing. "Sweet Jimmy was a disabled vet," he says. "He gets checks from the Army. He gets a check every month. We used to gamble it out of him every month. He said, 'I'm getting 740.' He always told us, 'I get 740.'"

Shorty remembers the check. Benny thinks that Jimmy might have used Killens's address. The current residents remember mail showing up every now and then for a Robinson.

The last letter arrived about a year ago.

Is Anything Real?

The stories go on as long as you care to listen, and they mirror one another mostly, though the few contradictions make it impossible to know what's fact and what's a cocktail of real memory and decades of street life. One guy who fought Jimmy twice claimed Sweet Jimmy was an impostor, that he didn't fight Ali. I'm as sure as I can be that he's wrong, but I can't be positive. In a way, that's perfect: the possibility exists that the only things people know about the man who called himself Sweet Jimmy are made up. Brenda, who claimed she still sees him, turned out to be high, crazy, or running a scam.

All the twists and turns add up to one thing: I didn't get to him in time, and he's probably lost forever.

I keep asking whether anyone actually saw him leave, or saw his dead body, or went to a funeral. Nobody did. One person thinks they remember a program from a funeral, but it's gone too. It's comforting to those here to imagine him packing up and moving away. The alternative is horrifying: that he died unnoticed, surrounded by people who used to be his friends. That he's in the potter's field down on Galloway Road.

"A lot of people remember him but they can't remember the last time they saw him," says James Hunt, who managed the pool hall from 2002 until it closed in 2005.

Sometimes, Jimmy seems close enough to touch, sitting patiently in the pool hall every day, while Singer and I and everyone else look for him in other places. I can see him hiding in the smoke and the shadows, no past, no future, wearing charity clothes they gave him down at the Camillus House. I see his beard, and I imagine the long-forgotten passions that birthed his deep scar. I am close enough to know what his mouth looks like, to see the teeth disappear, and then, he's gone too, swallowed, a figment of the fractured memory of Overtown. Watching someone be forgotten is like watching them die, and the more people forget, the more it's like he never existed at all. *He used to tell some story,* they say, *but I really wasn't listening.*

In those final years, he got quieter, an outsider even here. Regulars shooting pool wouldn't let him in on games. "If he got some money," Hunt says, "he'd play a few games of pool and claim he could have been one of the world's best. When he said things like that, a lot of people ignored him. He always said he could have beat Ali, but he got in the way of the punch."

He didn't like to be called homeless. "I pay rent," he'd say. Nobody remembers where, or if that was even true. Maybe it was a defiant act of pride in a life full of compromises. He walked in the moment the pool hall opened, earlier if Hunt came to clean. Sweet Jimmy would help for a few free games and a soda. He liked Pepsi. People gave him their leftover food. First of the month, he shot a few games of pool, fifty cents a rack, and bought tobacco. He rolled his own cigarettes. Sometimes, Hunt would ask him why. Jimmy'd smile and say, "So I can make 'em as big as I want." The folks who'd loaned him money would line up then too.

"Jimmy," Hunt would say, "when you get through paying out, you won't have any left."

"No," Jimmy'd say, "but I can make it."

"He always said, 'I can make it,'" Hunt remembers.

Then the pool hall closed.

He never saw Sweet Jimmy again.

Part Three: Where the Hell Did He Go?

The Thing with Feathers

The most important thing in a search isn't a database or contacts or cops. It's hope, and Overtown is methodical in its assault on hope, just as it is unforgiving in its ability to chip away at reality.

Sometimes, people are lost for big reasons; sometimes, they are lost because of a typo.

I am in the Miami library, reading through all the issues of the African American paper, when I see an item that mentions the name of the man originally scheduled to fight Ali February 7, 1961: Willie Gullatt. I know immediately why I've been unable to find him. The white papers, and later books and magazine articles, misspelled his name.

He's in the phone book.

The next afternoon, I am sitting under his carport as Willie, who has just lost a leg to surgery, holds court with his neighbors. He's beloved, with folks crowding around to hear stories and others honking when they drive past. They call him Big Willie. I want to believe that somewhere in America, in a similar fashion, Big Jimmy is telling neighbors about the night he fought Ali. Seeing what his life could have been makes me mourn for him, and makes him seem both closer and further away than ever before.

"I'll be seventy-five October sixth," Willie says. "And still getting me some unda-yonda."

He grins, and his audience falls out.

"I ain't did nothing since I had the operation," he says, "but she gonna get right after a while."

After some small talk, I finally get to ask the question: "What happened that night?"

Money, he says. Promoter Chris Dundee, Angelo's brother, offered Ali $800 and offered Willie only $300. He told 'em where to stick it.

"What did you do instead?"

He smiles, wistfully, remembering an Army duffel bag full of bootleg whiskey. "Got drunk," he says.

Looking back, he's got a lot of regrets. "If I coulda, woulda have left that women and that drinking alone," he says, "I believe I could have had a shot at the championship. But I didn't have the sense I have now. If I'd have had the sense, I'd let that booze alone. Left that damn liquor alone and went out there and had a shot at the championship."

But that's all in the past. Now the triumphs are more modest. The folks in the neighborhood want to throw him a barbecue for Labor Day.

"Sunday?" one asks.

"Every day is Sunday with me," he says.

CSI: Miami

Hope is good.

Hope keeps the city of Miami cold-case detectives in business. They sit in a small office with a green door. Files fill the room, each a different victim, people like Sandra Jackson who await closure inside a brown expandable folder, her entire existence reduced to the details of her death: *found at empty lot . . . 3-23-85 . . . 14:34 . . . 1255 NW 38th St.*

Inside, Andy Arostigui helps me run Robinsons through the system again. Nothing. There's an internal database of information that doesn't rise to the level of public information but might be useful to them one day. Among other things, it tracks nick-names. He gets the officer who manages that system to search Sweet Jimmy. Nothing.

Sitting with Andy and me are two cops from Daly City, California, in town to find witnesses for a murder case. I explain that I've been in Miami for a long time looking for a missing boxer. Frank Magnon and Al Cisneros dictate notes back to their home office to help me search another law enforcement database for Jimmy.

"This isn't even a state," says Frank, who's worked down here before. "It's an island of a country. It's like a vapor. They walk in and they're gone."

I fill them in on the search: the fliers and the phone calls, the people in Overtown, the pool hall and barbershops, Mr. Big and Racetrack Shorty.

"His world kept shrinking and shrinking and shrinking," Frank says, "until there was nothing left for him. Some of these guys just drop off the face of the earth."

"And don't want to be found," Al says.

"There was nothing left," Frank says. "He might have decided to just not wake up one day. Sometimes people just say, 'I've had enough.'"

A woman circles the office, pouring the little plastic thimbles of café cubano for the detectives and me. All the homicide guys in the bullpen outside the green door get a midday shot of caffeine too. Andy finishes his last possible search. Sweet Jimmy's not here. In the beginning, I wanted to sit across from Jimmy and have him tell me about his life. Now, near the end, I just want to find a body.

"I got a feeling," Andy says, "you're gonna find him at the medical examiner's office."

Naming Our Dead

It's time to meet Sandy Boyd.

We've spoken on the phone many times; she's the cold-case detective of the medical examiner's office. Naming the dead is one of our human responsibilities, she believes, and she is tireless in her work.

Her office is like Andy's, terraced in files. These are the people who died alone, who died with nothing in their pockets, who died in horrible fires or in dark waters or, improbably, both: a few they found in burned-out cars buried in silt at the bottom of the canal. These are the people who died seeking a new life, like the body who fell from the wheel well of an airplane, and those who died running from their old ones, like the young suicide victim who broke into a half-built skyscraper and jumped. Scratching out RE-MAINS, UNKNOWN and writing in a name is a triumph. "One day, I'm gonna solve all these cases," Sandy says. "Little by little, day by day, these cases are gonna get solved. They are someone's loved one."

The folks at the ME help me narrow the search. Elise Bobbitt, who runs the indigent burial program, says Sweet Jimmy isn't in one of the city's potter's fields. Sandy figures that there's been only one unidentified African American body in the right age range found since the pool hall closed. The captain of a river detox boat saw him floating in the Miami River on December 8, 2008, and fished him out. His body's still downstairs, waiting on a name.

Sandy walks me through the morgue, past the autopsy room. "You don't want to see in there," she says.

She explains the logistics of death. When a body comes in, it goes to Cooler 1, which has big stainless steel doors and looks like a restaurant walk-in. The bodies with names and family go to Cooler 2 after autopsy to await funeral home pickup. Cooler 3 is for bodies they're still trying to identify. Cooler 4 provides extra storage space.

She takes me through the doors to another building, opens the door to the Decomposed Autopsy room and the smell of death almost knocks me down—a combination of really strong blue cheese and old buttermilk. This is where Cooler 5 lives. There's a person on the table. He's got a tag on his left toe. Bleached spots dot his body and his skin is sloughing off in sheets.

Down the hall is Room M164: the bone room. She opens the door. There are rows of metal shelves with cardboard boxes. "These are all unidentified," she says.

Most contain full skeletons. One is from 1957. She opens a box; the skull inside is missing a few teeth. It's waiting on a name. In the back are the boxes from 2004 on.

Could any of them be Jimmy?

Back at her desk, she goes through the computer system. Of the fourteen unidentified skeletal remains found since 2005, all can be eliminated, for one reason or another. And we also eliminate a final loose end.

"I can show you the guy from the river," Sandy says.

She digs out the file and hands me a Polaroid. The body is shrouded in blue so only the face is visible, offering the dignity in death he never had in life. His eyes are closed and his nose looks as if it's been broken. He's got a slight overbite and his front two teeth just stick out on his bottom lip. He doesn't have a scar.

Case 2008-03065 is not Sweet Jimmy.

He's not here.

Out There . . . Somewhere

Sweet Jimmy is gone. He didn't leave a record. He doesn't exist on paper, just in the minds of those left in Overtown. He won't even exist there much longer. I walk into James Hunt's home one Saturday morning, and he tells me the news.

Three days earlier, Racetrack Shorty died.

"They're dropping like flies," James says.

Instead of getting closer to finding Jimmy, I'm getting further and further away. The old boxer grows more elusive every day. There is more talk about a brother who supposedly came looking for him. Some people say the brother took Jimmy home. Others say the brother never found him.

I ask everyone the question: where did he go?

"I think Missouri."

"He might be in Clearwater."

"St. Pete."

"His brother took him to Tampa."

"They say he took him up to Louisiana and he died in Louisiana."

"New Orleans."

"I heard he went to Belle Glade."

"He went to Texas."

"He had an accent that would be more Georgia."

"Georgia, Alabama, I don't know."

"Ohio."

He's everywhere. He's nowhere. He's out there somewhere.
He's got to be.
Doesn't he?

Everything Is Equivocal

Al Owens lives north of Liberty City, in a house on a corner. He
fought Jim Robinson twice. He looks at the photo on the flier.

"That ain't him," he says.

The first time they fought was three months before the Ali bout,
the second seven months after. When he got into the ring the second time, he says it was a different guy. He remembers the night
because a crowd of hustlers from Second Avenue screamed for Al
to kill Jimmy. "They wasn't following him to see him win," he says.
"They was following him to see him get his ass whupped."

It was a long, hard fight, and Al says he repressed the memory of
it until an autograph collector began writing him letters. Al says he
knew Jim Robinson, and he knew Sweet Jimmy, and he claims he
saw them together. Then, he says, Jim Robinson quit boxing to join
the Army and the street hustler Sweet Jimmy began fighting under
his name. "He had the same beard," he says. "He had the scar already. He wore the same visor. The visor was the thing for the guys
playing three-card monte."

But Al is a strange character too, and his memory doesn't stand
up to scrutiny. The timeline he lays out is, simply, impossible. He
too has lost pieces of himself along the way.

I send three photos—two of a young Jim Robinson in boxing
gear and one taken by Brennan—to a lab in England for scientific
comparison. The Centre for Anatomy and Human Identification
uses a six-point scale, ranging from "Lends No Support" to "Lends
Strong Support." One means they are absolutely not the same person; six means they absolutely are. Their report:

> There are numerous morphological and proportional similarities be-
> tween the man in image 1 and the man in images 2 and 3. There are no
> apparent morphological or proportional differences which cannot be
> easily explained by the effects of 20 years of aging, or the differences in
> camera angle, lighting and resolution; hence, there is nothing to indi-
> cate that the man in image 1 is not the same man shown in images 2
> and 3. However, these same factors (time, difference in angle, lighting,

expression, resolution, etc.) also make it difficult to be more conclusive.

On their scale, they give it a four: lends support.

Even science is equivocal. Nothing in the strange search for Sweet Jimmy is certain. Everything is gauzy, covered in a haze of mights and maybes, his disappearance a mirror held up to his life.

Going Home

One stop remains before I step out of Sweet Jimmy's world for the last time and return to mine. On my final Sunday morning in Miami, I show up for my shift volunteering in the Camillus House kitchen. After slicing four hams and dicing a crate of onions, I make my way to the exit. I see a familiar face coming in. Two minutes either way, I'd have missed him.

His name is Shelly. He's eighty. He's weathered smooth, like a piece of driftwood, with milky eyes. His rap sheet reaches back to the '70s, with busts from trespassing to auto larceny to drug possession. I met him yesterday, in the street, and he told me he saw Sweet Jimmy leave town. He said he and Jimmy were close, hanging out in the pool hall together. But he seemed out of it, and in a hurry, and standing in the middle of an Overtown street isn't the place for an interview. I thought I'd never see him again.

"Shelly!" I say.

He tries to place me. I remind him we'd spoken yesterday and he seems to remember.

"Do you need anything?" I ask.

"A Pepsi," he says.

I return with two sodas, and we sit in the courtyard, surrounded by other homeless men and women. They are gathered around a radio, listening to gospel and R&B, the old soul hits, staring intently, as if the music has the power to take them away. The tops of some waterfront luxury condos rise high above the shelter, and hidden behind them is the American Airlines Arena, its outdoor Jumbotron flashing messages from another dimension.

"I miss Jimmy," Shelly says.

We talk for an hour and a half. He tells me the story again, and it's the same as he told it yesterday. That's what makes me believe him, because the streets have left his mind fractured, full of images he can't order. I don't think he is capable of remembering a lie.

He says he arrived here ten years ago: March 15, 1999. He repeats the date over and over. Later, he says he's been here twenty years. I know for sure he was arrested here in 1973, so who knows.

He tells me about his parents, back in Atlanta, who left one day to go to the store and never came back. He tells me about the pool hall regulars trying to hang together after it closed but ending up scattered, about Clyde Killens making sure they all had something to eat, and about the last day he ever saw Sweet Jimmy. They were sitting in the pool hall.

"He told me a long time ago," Shelly says, "his brother was gonna come for him, you know. But I didn't know when. Jimmy said he had a brother. I didn't believe it until I saw him. His brother came and got him and took him home. I'm probably the only one who seen him get in the car. Everybody know he left town, but I was there when he got in the car and hauled ass. Shook my hand and every damn thing. Shook my hand. Said, 'I'll see you when I come back.' I never saw him no more."

He points up at the perfect blue sky. "I'll see him again."

A deformed pigeon, large tumors growing off its head, pecks around the concrete patio for crumbs. A crackhead stops throwing himself into a chain-link fence and crawls around under my chair, checking every stray cigarette butt for leftover tobacco. A man who looks too healthy to be here leans back in his chair, closes his eyes, and sings a song about taking a journey. Shelly sits quietly with the addicts and the sick, all huddled together, unwanted. I don't know if he really saw Jimmy leave, or if his mind's playing tricks, or if he knows his story makes him matter, if only for a moment, to a person who'll buy him a soda and listen to him talk. I believe that, to him, right now, looking for shade in Overtown, it's as true as the day he was born. Shelly takes a sip of his Pepsi and thinks about all the people who've come and gone.

"They disappear like the wind," he says.

Epilogue

The journey ends where it began. Six years after he first called, Stephen Singer leads me back through his office until we're standing in front of what he calls the masterpiece: two large frames six feet across containing a collage of photos, programs, ticket stubs, and, of course, forty-nine signatures. There's an engraved plaque: JIM ROBINSON'S WHEREABOUTS UNKNOWN . . . AUTOGRAPH MISSING.

He's no longer searching for Jimmy. "I moved on," he says. "I haven't really thought about it for a couple of years. I'm way past that. I've got real work to do."

I find myself wondering why I haven't moved on.

It's easy to believe the journey of Sweet Jimmy is unique. It's not. Singer's collection is a reminder of how a boxing life often goes completely off track.

Tunney Hunsaker, the first opponent, spent nine days in a coma after a bout.

Trevor Berbick, the final opponent, was beat to death with a steel pipe.

Herb Siler went to prison for shooting his girlfriend.

Tony Esperti went to prison for a Mafia hit in a Miami Beach nightclub.

Alfredo Evangelista went to prison in Spain.

Alejandro Lavorante died from injuries sustained in the ring.

Sonny Banks did too.

Jerry Quarry died broke, his mind scrambled from dementia pugilistica.

Jimmy Ellis suffered from it too.

Rudi Lubbers turned into a drunk and joined a carnival.

Buster Mathis blew up to 550 pounds and died of a heart attack at fifty-two.

George Chuvalo lost three sons to heroin overdoses; his wife killed herself after the second son's death.

Oscar Bonavena was shot through the heart with a high-powered rifle outside a Reno whorehouse.

Cleveland Williams was killed in a hit-and-run.

Zora Folley died mysteriously in a motel swimming pool.

Sonny Liston died of a drug overdose in Las Vegas. Many still believe the Mafia killed him.

"That's the saddest one," I say to Singer.

"They're all sad," he says. "They're all sad in their own way."

Even finding Sweet Jimmy isn't certain to provide any answers about his life; he might not remember he ever fought at all. Many old fighters end their lives stripped of their memories. The night Jimmy fought Ali, the main event was a light heavyweight title fight between Harold Johnson and Jesse Bowdry. Today, Johnson lives in a Philadelphia VA nursing home and has good days and bad days. His memory is going. Bowdry's wife answers the phone in their St. Louis home. "He's not gonna remember," she says. "He has dementia."

Even Ali is a prisoner in his own body, a ghost like Sweet Jimmy, lost in a different way. He paid a price for his fame, just as the men who fought him paid a price for their brush with it. Nothing is free. Confronting the wreckage reminds me of an old magazine story, written by Davis Miller. There's a haunting moment, in 1989 when things were turning bad. Ali stands at the window of his suite on the twenty-fourth floor of the Mirage Hotel in Las Vegas. His once-booming voice comes out a whisper.

"Look at this place," he says. "This big hotel, this town. It's dust, all dust. Don't none of it mean nothin'. It's all only dust."

A fighter jet lands at an Air Force base out on the desert. Ali watches it through the glass, the lights on the strip so bright it seems like they'll burn forever.

"Go up in an airplane," he says. "Go high enough, and it's like we don't even exist."

Offensive Play

FROM THE NEW YORKER

ONE EVENING IN AUGUST, Kyle Turley was at a bar in Nashville with his wife and some friends. It was one of the countless little places in the city that play live music. He'd ordered a beer, but was just sipping it, because he was driving home. He had eaten an hour and a half earlier. Suddenly, he felt a sensation of heat. He was light-headed, and began to sweat. He had been having episodes like that with increasing frequency during the past year—headaches, nausea. One month, he had vertigo every day, bouts in which he felt as if he were stuck to a wall. But this was worse. He asked his wife if he could sit on her stool for a moment. The warm-up band was still playing, and he remembers saying, "I'm just going to take a nap right here until the next band comes on." Then he was lying on the floor, and someone was standing over him. "The guy was freaking out," Turley recalled. "He was saying, 'Damn, man, I couldn't find a pulse,' and my wife said, 'No, no. You were breathing.' I'm, like, 'What? What?'"

They picked him up. "We went out in the parking lot, and I just lost it," Turley went on. "I started puking everywhere. I couldn't stop. I got in the car, still puking. My wife, she was really scared, because I had never passed out like that before, and I started becoming really paranoid. I went into a panic. We get to the emergency room. I started to lose control. My limbs were shaking, and I couldn't speak. I was conscious, but I couldn't speak the words I wanted to say."

Turley is six feet five. He is thirty-four years old, with a square jaw and blue eyes. For nine years, before he retired, in 2007, he was an offensive lineman in the National Football League. He knew all the stories about former football players. Mike Webster, the long-time Pittsburgh Steeler and one of the greatest players in NFL history, ended his life a recluse, sleeping on the floor of the Pittsburgh Amtrak station. Another former Pittsburgh Steeler, Terry Long, drifted into chaos and killed himself four years ago by drinking antifreeze. Andre Waters, a former defensive back for the Philadelphia Eagles, sank into depression and pleaded with his girlfriend — "I need help, somebody help me" — before shooting himself in the head. There were men with aching knees and backs and hands, from all those years of playing football. But their real problem was with their heads, the one part of their body that got hit over and over again.

"Lately, I've tried to break it down," Turley said. "I remember, every season, multiple occasions where I'd hit someone so hard that my eyes went cross-eyed, and they wouldn't come uncrossed for a full series of plays. You are just out there, trying to hit the guy in the middle, because there are three of them. You don't remember much. There are the cases where you hit a guy and you'd get into a collision where everything goes *off*. You're dazed. And there are the others where you are involved in a big, long drive. You start on your own five-yard line, and drive all the way down the field—fifteen, eighteen plays in a row sometimes. Every play: collision, collision, collision. By the time you get to the other end of the field, you're seeing spots. You feel like you are going to black out. Literally, these white explosions— *boom, boom, boom*—lights getting dimmer and brighter, dimmer and brighter.

"Then, there was the time when I got knocked unconscious. That was in St. Louis, in 2003. My wife said that I was out a minute or two on the field. But I was *gone* for about four hours after that. It was the last play of the third quarter. We were playing the Packers. I got hit in the back of the head. I saw it on film a little while afterward. I was running downfield, made a block on a guy. We fell to the ground. A guy was chasing the play, a little guy, a defensive back, and he jumped over me as I was coming up, and he kneed me right in the back of the head. *Boom!*

"They sat me down on the bench. I remember Marshall Faulk coming up and joking with me, because he knew that I was messed up. That's what happens in the NFL: 'Oooh. You got effed up.

Oooh.' The trainer came up to me and said, 'Kyle, let's take you to the locker room.' I remember looking up at a clock, and there was only a minute and a half left in the game—and I had no idea that much time had elapsed. I showered and took all my gear off. I was sitting at my locker. I don't remember anything. When I came back, after being hospitalized, the guys were joking with me because Georgia Frontiere"—then the team's owner—"came in the locker room, and they said I was butt-ass naked and I gave her a big hug. They were dying laughing, and I was, like, 'Are you serious? I did that?'

"They cleared me for practice that Thursday. I probably shouldn't have. I don't know what damage I did from that, because my head was really hurting. But when you're coming off an injury you're frustrated. I wanted to play the next game. I was just so mad that this happened to me that I'm overdoing it. I was just going after guys in practice. I was really trying to use my head more, because I was so frustrated, and the coaches on the sidelines are, like, 'Yeah. We're going to win this game. He's going to lead the team.' That's football. You're told either that you're hurt or that you're injured. There is no middle ground. If you are hurt, you can play. If you are injured, you can't, and the line is whether you can walk and if you can put on a helmet and pads."

Turley said that he loved playing football so much that he would do it all again. Then he began talking about what he had gone through in the past year. The thing that scared him most about that night at the bar was that it felt exactly like the time he was knocked unconscious. "It was identical," he said. "It was my worst episode ever."

In August of 2007, one of the highest-paid players in professional football, the quarterback Michael Vick, pleaded guilty to involvement in a dogfighting ring. The police raided one of his properties, a farm outside Richmond, Virginia, and found the bodies of dead dogs buried on the premises, along with evidence that some of the animals there had been tortured and electrocuted. Vick was suspended from football. He was sentenced to twenty-three months in prison. The dogs on his farm were seized by the court, and the most damaged were sent to an animal sanctuary in Utah for rehabilitation. When Vick applied for reinstatement to the National Football League, this summer, he was asked to undergo psychiatric testing. He then met with the commissioner of the league, Roger Goodell, for four and a half hours, so that Goodell could be sure that he was genuinely remorseful.

"I probably considered every alternative that I could think of," Goodell told reporters, when he finally allowed Vick back into the league. "I reached out to an awful lot of people to get their views —not only on what was right for the young man but also what was right for our society and the NFL."

Goodell's job entails dealing with players who have used drugs, driven drunk and killed people, fired handguns in nightclubs, and consorted with thugs and accused murderers. But he clearly felt what many Americans felt as well—that dogfighting was a moral offense of a different order.

Here is a description of a dogfight given by the sociologists Rhonda Evans and Craig Forsyth in "The Social Milieu of Dogmen and Dogfights," an article they published some years ago in the journal *Deviant Behavior*. The fight took place in Louisiana between a local dog, Black, owned by a man named L.G., and Snow, whose owner, Rick, had come from Arizona:

> The handlers release their dogs and Snow and Black lunge at one another. Snow rears up and overpowers Black, but Black manages to come back with a quick locking of the jaws on Snow's neck. The crowd is cheering wildly and yelling out bets. Once a dog gets a lock on the other, they will hold on with all their might. The dogs flail back and forth and all the while Black maintains her hold.

In a dogfight, whenever one of the dogs "turns"—makes a submissive gesture with its head—the two animals are separated and taken back to their corners. Each dog, in alternation, then "scratches"—is released to charge at its opponent. After that first break, it is Snow's turn to scratch. She races toward Black:

> Snow goes straight for the throat and grabs hold with her razor-sharp teeth. Almost immediately, blood flows from Black's throat. Despite a serious injury to the throat, Black manages to continue fighting back. They are relentless, each battling the other and neither willing to accept defeat. This fighting continues for an hour. [Finally, the referee] gives the third and final pit call. It is Black's turn to scratch and she is severely wounded. Black manages to crawl across the pit to meet her op-

ponent. Snow attacks Black and she is too weak to fight back. L.G. realizes that this is it for Black and calls the fight. Snow is declared the winner.

Afterward, Snow's owner collects his winnings; L.G. carries Black from the ring. "Her back legs are broken and blood is gushing from her throat," Evans and Forsyth write. "A shot rings out barely heard over the noise in the barn. Black's body is wrapped up and carried by her owner to his vehicle."

It's the shot ringing out that seals the case against dogfighting. L.G. willingly submitted his dog to a contest that culminated in her suffering and destruction. And why? For the entertainment of an audience and the chance of a payday. In the nineteenth century, dogfighting was widely accepted by the American public. But we no longer find that kind of transaction morally acceptable in a sport. "I was not aware of dogfighting and the terrible things that happen around dogfighting," Goodell said, explaining why he responded so sternly in the Vick case. One wonders whether, had he spent as much time talking to Kyle Turley as he did to Michael Vick, he'd start to have similar doubts about his own sport.

In 2003, a seventy-two-year-old patient at the Veterans Hospital in Bedford, Massachusetts, died, fifteen years after receiving a diagnosis of dementia. Patients in the hospital's dementia ward are routinely autopsied, as part of the VA's research efforts, so the man's brain was removed and "fixed" in a formaldehyde solution. A laboratory technician placed a large slab of the man's cerebral tissue on a microtome—essentially, a sophisticated meat slicer—and, working along the coronal plane, cut off dozens of fifty-micron shavings, less than a hairbreadth thick. The shavings were then immunostained—bathed in a special reagent that would mark the presence of abnormal proteins with a bright, telltale red or brown stain on the surface of the tissue. Afterward, each slice was smoothed out and placed on a slide.

The stained tissue of Alzheimer's patients typically shows the two trademarks of the disease—distinctive patterns of the proteins beta-amyloid and tau. Beta-amyloid is thought to lay the groundwork for dementia. Tau marks the critical second stage of the disease: it's the protein that steadily builds up in brain cells, shutting them down and ultimately killing them. An immunostain of an Alzheimer's patient looks, under the microscope, as if the tissue had been hit with a shotgun blast: the red and brown marks, corresponding to amyloid and tau, dot the entire surface. But this patient's brain was different. There was damage only to specific surface regions of his brain, and the stains for amyloid came back negative. "This was all tau," Ann McKee, who runs the hospital's neuropathology laboratory, said. "There was not even a whiff of amyloid. And it was the most extraordinary damage. It was one of those cases that really took you aback." The patient may have been in an Alzheimer's facility, and may have looked and acted as if he had Alzheimer's. But McKee realized that he had a different condition, called chronic traumatic encephalopathy (CTE), which is a progressive neurological disorder found in people who have suffered some kind of brain trauma. CTE has many of the same manifestations as Alzheimer's: it begins with behavioral and personality changes, followed by disinhibition and irritability, before moving on to dementia. And CTE appears later in life as well, because it takes a long time for the initial trauma to give rise to nerve-cell breakdown and death. But CTE isn't the result of an endogenous disease. It's the result of injury. The patient, it turned out, had been a boxer in his youth. He had suffered from dementia for fifteen years because, decades earlier, he'd been hit too many times in the head.

McKee's laboratory does the neuropathology work for both the giant Framingham heart study, which has been running since 1948, and Boston University's New England Centenarian Study, which analyzes the brains of people who are unusually long-lived. "I'm looking at brains constantly," McKee said. "Then I ran across another one. I saw it and said, 'Wow, it looks just like the last case.' This time, there was no known history of boxing. But then I called the family, and heard that the guy had been a boxer in his twenties." You can't see tau except in an autopsy, and you can't see it in an autopsy unless you do a very particular kind of screen. So now that McKee had seen two cases, in short order, she began to wonder: how many people who we assume have Alzheimer's—a condition of mysterious origin—are actually victims of preventable brain trauma?

McKee linked up with an activist named Chris Nowinski, a former college football player and professional wrestler who runs a group called the Sports Legacy Institute, in Boston. In his football and wrestling careers, Nowinski suffered six concussions (that he can remember), the last of which had such severe side effects that he has become a full-time crusader against brain injuries in sports. Nowinski told McKee that he would help her track down more brains of ex-athletes. Whenever he read an obituary of someone who had played in a contact sport, he'd call up the family and try to persuade them to send the player's brain to Bedford. Usually, they said no. Sometimes they said yes. The first brain McKee received was from a man in his midforties who had played as a linebacker in the NFL for ten years. He accidentally shot himself while cleaning a gun. He had at least three concussions in college, and eight in the pros. In the years before his death, he'd had memory lapses, and had become more volatile. McKee immunostained samples of his brain tissue, and saw big splotches of tau all over the frontal and temporal lobes. If he hadn't had the accident, he would almost certainly have ended up in a dementia ward.

Nowinski found her another ex-football player. McKee saw the same thing. She has now examined the brains of sixteen ex-athletes, most of them ex-football players. Some had long careers and some played only in college. Some died of dementia. Some died of unrelated causes. Some were old. Some were young. Most were linemen or linebackers, although there was one wide receiver. In one case, a man who had been a linebacker for sixteen years, you could see, without the aid of magnification, that there was trouble: there was a shiny tan layer of scar tissue, right on the surface of the frontal lobe, where the brain had repeatedly slammed into the skull. It was the kind of scar you'd get only if you used your head as a battering ram. You could also see that some of the openings in the brain were larger than you'd expect, as if the surrounding tissue had died and shrunk away. In other cases, everything seemed entirely normal until you looked under the microscope and saw the brown ribbons of tau. But all sixteen of the ex-athlete brains that McKee had examined—those of the two boxers, plus the ones that Nowinski had found for her—had something in common: every one had abnormal tau.

The other major researcher looking at athletes and CTE is the neuropathologist Bennet Omalu. He diagnosed the first known case of CTE in an ex-NFL player back in September of 2002, when he autopsied the former Pittsburgh Steelers center Mike Webster. He also found CTE in the former Philadelphia Eagles defensive back Andre Waters, and in the former Steelers linemen Terry Long and Justin Strzelczyk, the latter of whom was killed when he drove the wrong way down a freeway and crashed his car, at ninety miles per hour, into a tank truck. Omalu has only once failed to find CTE in a professional football player, and that was a twenty-four-year-old running back who had played in the NFL for only two years.

"There is something wrong with this group as a cohort," Omalu says. "They forget things. They have slurred speech. I have had an NFL player come up to me at a funeral and tell me he can't find his way home. I have wives who call me and say, 'My husband was a very good man. Now he drinks all the time. I don't know why his behavior changed.' I have wives call me and say, 'My husband was a nice guy. Now he's getting abusive.' I had someone call me and say, 'My husband went back to law school after football and became a lawyer. Now he can't do his job. People are suing him.'"

McKee and Omalu are trying to make sense of the cases they've seen so far. At least some of the players are thought to have used steroids, which has led to the suggestion that brain injury might in some way be enhanced by drug use. Many of the players also share a genetic risk factor for neurodegenerative diseases, so perhaps deposits of tau are the result of brain trauma coupled with the weakened ability of the brain to repair itself. McKee says that she will need to see at least fifty cases before she can draw any firm conclusions. In the meantime, late last month the University of Michigan's Institute for Social Research released the findings of an NFL-funded phone survey of just over a thousand randomly selected retired NFL players—all of whom had played in the league for at least three seasons. Self-reported studies are notoriously unreliable instruments, but, even so, the results were alarming. Of those players who were older than fifty, 6.1 percent reported that they had received a diagnosis of "dementia, Alzheimer's disease, or other memory-related disease." That's five times higher than the national average for that age group. For players between the ages of thirty and forty-nine, the reported rate was nineteen times the national average. (The NFL has distributed $5 million to former players with dementia.)

"A long time ago, someone suggested that the [CTE rate] in boxers was twenty percent," McKee told me. "I think it's probably higher than that among boxers, and I also suspect that it's going to end up being higher than that among football players as well. Why? Because every brain I've seen has this. To get this number in a sample this small is really unusual, and the findings are so far out of the norm. I only can say that because I have looked at thousands of brains for a long time. This isn't something that you just see. I did the same exact thing for all the individuals from the Framingham heart study. We study them until they die. I run these exact same proteins, make these same slides—and we never see this."

McKee's laboratory occupies a warren of rooms, in what looks like an old officers' quarters on the VA campus. In one of the rooms, there is an enormous refrigerator, filled with brains packed away in hundreds of plastic containers. Nearby is a tray with small piles of brain slices. They look just like the ginger shavings that come with an order of sushi. Now McKee went to the room next to her office, sat down behind a microscope, and inserted one of the immunostained slides under the lens.

"This is Tom McHale," she said. "He started out playing for Cornell. Then he went to Tampa Bay. He was the man who died of substance abuse at the age of forty-five. I only got fragments of the brain. But it's just showing huge accumulations of tau for a forty-five-year-old—ridiculously abnormal."

She placed another slide under the microscope. "This individual was forty-nine years old. A football player. Cognitively intact. He never had any rage behavior. He had the distinctive abnormalities. Look at the hypothalamus." It was dark with tau. She put another slide in. "This guy was in his midsixties," she said. "He died of an unrelated medical condition. His name is Walter Hilgenberg. Look at the hippocampus. It's wall-to-wall tangles. Even in a bad case of Alzheimer's, you don't see that." The brown pigment of the tau stain ran around the edge of the tissue sample in a thick, dark band. "It's like a big river."

McKee got up and walked across the corridor, back to her office. "There's one last thing," she said. She pulled out a large photographic blowup of a brain-tissue sample. "This is a kid. I'm not allowed to talk about how he died. He was a good student. This is his brain. He's eighteen years old. He played football. He'd been playing football for a couple of years." She pointed to a series of dark spots on the image, where the stain had marked the presence of something abnormal. "He's got all this tau. This is frontal and this is insular. Very close to insular. Those same vulnerable regions." This was a teenager, and already his brain showed the kind of decay that is usually associated with old age. "This is completely inappropriate," she said. "You don't see tau like this in an eighteen-year-old. You don't see tau like this in a *fifty*-year-old."

McKee is a longtime football fan. She is from Wisconsin. She had two statuettes of Brett Favre, the former Green Bay Packers quarterback, on her bookshelf. On the wall was a picture of a robust young man. It was McKee's son — nineteen years old, six feet three. If he had a chance to join the NFL, I asked her, what would she advise him? "I'd say, 'Don't. Not if you want to have a life after football.'"

At the core of the CTE research is a critical question: is the kind of injury being uncovered by McKee and Omalu incidental to the game of football or inherent in it? Part of what makes dogfighting so repulsive is the understanding that violence and injury cannot be removed from the sport. It's a feature of the sport that dogs almost always get hurt. Something like stock-car racing, by contrast, is dangerous, but not unavoidably so.

In 2000 and 2001, four drivers in NASCAR's elite Sprint Cup Series were killed in crashes, including the legendary Dale Earnhardt. In response, NASCAR mandated stronger seats, better seat belts and harnesses, and ignition kill switches, and completed the installation of expensive new barriers on the walls of its racetracks, which can absorb the force of a crash much better than concrete. The result is that, in the past eight years, no one has died in NASCAR's three national racing series. Stock-car fans are sometimes caricatured as bloodthirsty, eagerly awaiting the next spectacular crash. But there is little blood these days in NASCAR crashes. Last year, at Texas Motor Speedway, Michael McDowell hit an oil slick, slammed head first into the wall at 180 miles per hour, flipped over and over, leaving much of his car in pieces on the track, and, when the vehicle finally came to a stop, crawled out of the wreckage and walked away. He raced again the next day. So what is football? Is it dogfighting or is it stock-car racing?

Football faced a version of this question a hundred years ago, after a series of ugly incidents. In 1905, President Theodore Roosevelt called an emergency summit at the White House, alarmed, as the historian John Sayle Watterson writes, "that the brutality of the prize ring had invaded college football and might end up destroying it." Columbia University dropped the sport entirely. A professor at the University of Chicago called it a "boy-killing, man-mutilating, money-making, education-prostituting, gladiatorial sport." In December of 1905, the presidents of twelve prominent colleges met in New York and came within one vote of abolishing the game. But the main objection at the time was to a style of play—densely and dangerously packed offensive strategies—that, it turns out, could be largely corrected with rule changes, like the legalization of the forward pass and the doubling of the first-down distance from five yards to ten. Today, when we consider subtler and more insidious forms of injury, it's far from clear whether the problem is the style of play or the play itself.

Take the experience of a young defensive lineman for the University of North Carolina football team, who suffered two concussions during the 2004 season. His case is one of a number studied by Kevin Guskiewicz, who runs the university's Sports Concussion Research Program. For the past five seasons, Guskiewicz and his team have tracked every one of the football team's practices and games using a system called HITS, in which six sensors are placed inside the helmet of every player on the field, measuring the force and location of every blow he receives to the head. Using the HITS data, Guskiewicz was able to reconstruct precisely what happened each time the player was injured.

"The first concussion was during preseason. The team was doing two-a-days," he said, referring to the habit of practicing in both the morning and the evening in the preseason. "It was August 9, 9:55 A.M. He has an 80-g hit to the front of his head. About ten minutes later, he has a 98-g acceleration to the front of his head." To put those numbers in perspective, Guskiewicz explained, if you drove your car into a wall at twenty-five miles per hour and you weren't wearing your seat belt, the force of your head hitting the windshield would be around 100 gs: in effect, the player had two car accidents that morning. He survived both without incident. "In the evening session, he experiences this 64-g hit to the same spot, the front of the head. Still not reporting anything. And then this happens." On his laptop, Guskiewicz ran the video from the practice session. It was a simple drill: the lineman squaring off against an offensive player who wore the number 76. The other player ran toward the lineman and brushed past him, while delivering a glancing blow to the defender's helmet. "Seventy-six does a little quick elbow. It's 63 gs, the lowest of the four, but he sustains a concussion.

"The second injury was nine weeks later," Guskiewicz continued. "He's now recovered from the initial injury. It's a game out in Utah. In warm-ups, he takes a 76-g blow to the front of his head. Then, on the very first play of the game, on kickoff, he gets popped in the ear-hole. It's a 102-g impact. He's part of the wedge." He pointed to the screen, where the player was blocking on a kickoff: "Right here." The player stumbled toward the sideline. "His symptoms were significantly worse than the first injury." Two days later, during an evaluation in Guskiewicz's clinic, he had to have a towel put over his head because he couldn't stand the light. He also had difficulty staying awake. He was sidelined for sixteen days.

When we think about football, we worry about the dangers posed by the heat and the fury of competition. Yet the HITS data suggest that practice—the routine part of the sport—can be as dangerous as the games themselves. We also tend to focus on the dramatic helmet-to-helmet hits that signal an aggressive and reckless style of play. Those kinds of hits can be policed. But what sidelined the UNC player, the first time around, was an accidental and seemingly innocuous elbow, and none of the blows he suffered that day would have been flagged by a referee as illegal. Most important, though, is what Guskiewicz found when he reviewed all the data for the lineman on that first day in training camp. He didn't just suffer those four big blows. He was hit in the head *thirty-one times* that day. What seems to have caused his concussion, in other words, was his cumulative exposure. And why was the second concussion—in the game at Utah—so much more serious than the first? It's not because that hit to the side of the head was especially dramatic; it was that it came after the 76-g blow in warm-up, which, in turn, followed the concussion in August, which was itself the consequence of the thirty prior hits that day, and the hits the day before that, and the day before that, and on and on, perhaps back to his high school playing days.

This is a crucial point. Much of the attention in the football world, in the past few years, has been on concussions — on diagnosing, managing, and preventing them — and on figuring out how many concussions a player can have before he should call it quits. But a football player's real issue isn't simply with repetitive concussive trauma. It is, as the concussion specialist Robert Cantu argues, with repetitive *subconcussive* trauma. It's not just the handful of big hits that matter. It's lots of little hits too.

That's why, Cantu says, so many of the ex-players who have been given a diagnosis of CTE were linemen: line play lends itself to lots of little hits. The HITS data suggest that, in an average football season, a lineman could get struck in the head a thousand times, which means that a ten-year NFL veteran, when you bring in his college and high school playing days, could well have been hit in the head eighteen thousand times: that's thousands of jarring blows that shake the brain from front to back and side to side, stretching and weakening and tearing the connections among nerve cells, and making the brain increasingly vulnerable to long-term damage. People with CTE, Cantu says, "aren't necessarily people with a high, recognized concussion history. But they are individuals who collided heads on every play — repetitively doing this, year after year, under levels that were tolerable for them to continue to play."

But if CTE is really about lots of little hits, what can be done about it? Turley says that it's impossible for an offensive lineman to do his job without "using his head." The position calls for the player to begin in a crouch and then collide with the opposing lineman when the ball is snapped. Helmet-to-helmet contact is inevitable. Nowinski, who played football for Harvard, says that "proper" tackling technique is supposed to involve a player driving into his opponent with his shoulder. "The problem," he says, "is that, if you're a defender and you're trying to tackle someone and you decide to pick a side, you're giving the other guy a way to go — and people will start running around you." Would better helmets help? Perhaps. And there have been better models introduced that absorb more of the shock from a hit. But, Nowinski says, the better helmets have become — and the more invulnerable they have made the player seem — the more athletes have been inclined to play recklessly.

"People love technological solutions," Nowinski went on. "When I give speeches, the first question is always: 'What about these new helmets I hear about?' What most people don't realize is that we are decades, if not forever, from having a helmet that would fix the problem. I mean, you have two men running into each other at full speed and you think a little bit of plastic and padding could absorb that 150 gs of force?"

At one point, while he was discussing his research, Guskiewicz showed a videotape from a 1997 college football game between Arizona and Oregon. In one sequence, a player from Oregon viciously tackles an Arizona player, bringing his head up onto the opposing player's chin and sending his helmet flying with the force of the blow. To look at it, you'd think that the Arizona player would be knocked unconscious. Instead, he bounces back up. "This guy does not sustain a concussion," Guskiewicz said. "He has a lip laceration. Lower lip, that's it. Now, same game, twenty minutes later." He showed a clip of an Arizona defensive back making a dramatic tackle. He jumps up, and, as he does so, a teammate of his chest-bumps him in celebration. The defensive back falls and hits his head on the ground. "That's a Grade 2 concussion," Guskiewicz said. "It's the fall to the ground, combined with the bounce off the turf."

The force of the first hit was infinitely greater than the second. But the difference is that the first player saw that he was about to be hit and tensed his neck, which limited the sharp back-and-forth jolt of the head that sends the brain crashing against the sides of the skull. In essence, he was being hit not in the head but in the head, neck, and torso — an area with an effective mass three times greater. In the second case, the player didn't see the hit coming. His head took the full force of the blow all by itself. That's why he suffered a concussion. But how do you insure, in a game like football, that a player is never taken by surprise?

Guskiewicz and his colleagues have come up with what they believe is a much better method of understanding concussion. They have done a full cognitive workup of the players on the UNC team, so that they can track whatever effect might arise from the hits each player accumulates during his four years. UNC's new coach, Butch Davis, has sharply cut back on full-contact practices, reducing the toll on the players' heads. Guskiewicz says his data show that a disproportionate number of serious head impacts happen on kickoffs, so he wonders whether it might make sense, in theory, anyway, to dispense with them altogether. But, like everyone else who's worried about football, he still has no idea what the inherent risks of the game are. What if you did everything you could, and banned kickoffs and full-contact practices and used the most state-of-the-art techniques for diagnosing and treating concussion, and behaved as responsibly as NASCAR has in the past several years—and players were still getting too many dangerous little hits to the head?

After the tape session, Guskiewicz and one of his colleagues, Jason Mihalik, went outside to watch the UNC football team practice, a short walk down the hill from their office. Only when you see football at close range is it possible to understand the dimensions of the brain-injury problem. The players were huge—much larger than you imagine them being. They moved at astonishing speeds for people of that size, and, long before you saw them, you heard them: the sound of one 250-pound man colliding with another echoed around the practice facility. Mihalik and Guskiewicz walked over to a small building, just off to the side of the field. On the floor was a laptop inside a black storage crate. Next to the computer was an antenna that received the signals from the sensors inside the players' helmets. Mihalik crouched down and began paging through the data. In one column, the HITS software listed the top hits of the practice up to that point, and every few moments the screen would refresh, reflecting the plays that had just been run on the field. Forty-five minutes into practice, the top eight head blows on the field measured 82 gs, 79 gs, 75 gs, 79 gs, 67 gs, 60 gs, 57 gs, and 53 gs. One player, a running back, had received both the 79 gs and the 60 gs, as well as another hit, measuring 27.9 gs. This wasn't a full-contact practice. It was "shells." The players wore only helmets and shoulder pads, and still there were mini car crashes happening all over the field.

The most damaged, scarred, and belligerent of Michael Vick's dogs —the hardest cases—were sent to the Best Friends Animal Sanctuary, on a 3,700-acre spread in the canyons of southern Utah. They were housed in a specially modified octagon, a one-story, climate-controlled cottage, ringed by individual dog runs. The dogs were given a final walk at 11 P.M. and woken up at 7 A.M., to introduce them to a routine. They were hand-fed. In the early months, the staff took turns sleeping in the octagon—sometimes in the middle, sometimes in a cot in one of the runs—so that someone would be with the dogs twenty-four hours a day. Twenty-two of Vick's pit bulls came to Best Friends in January of 2008, and all but five of them are still there.

Ray lunged at his handlers when he first came to Best Friends. He can't be with other dogs. Ellen lies on the ground and wants her stomach scratched, and when the caregivers slept in the octagon she licked them all night long. Her face is lopsided, as if it had been damaged from fighting. She can't be with other dogs either. Georgia has a broken tail, and her legs and snout are covered with scars. She has no teeth. At some point, in her early life, they had been surgically removed. The court-ordered evaluation of the Vick dogs labeled Meryl, a medium-sized brown-and-white pitbull mix, "human aggressive," meaning that she is never allowed to be taken out of the Best Friends facility. "She had a hard time meeting people—she would preempt anyone coming by charging and snapping at them," Ann Allums, one of the Best Friends dog trainers, said, as she walked around Meryl's octagon, on a recent fall day.

She opened the gate to Meryl's dog run and crouched down on the ground next to her. She hugged the dog, and began playfully wrestling with her, as Meryl's tail thumped happily. "She really doesn't mind new people," Allums said. "She's very happy and loving. I feel totally comfortable with her. I can grab and kiss her." She gave Meryl another hug. "I am building a relationship," she said. "She needed to see that when people were around bad things would not happen."

What happens at Best Friends represents, by any measure, an extravagant gesture. These are dogs that will never live a normal life. But the kind of crime embodied by dogfighting is so morally repellent that it demands an extravagant gesture in response. In a fighting dog, the quality that is prized above all others is the willingness to persevere, even in the face of injury and pain. A dog that will not do that is labeled a "cur," and abandoned. A dog that keeps charging at its opponent is said to possess "gameness," and game dogs are revered.

In one way or another, plenty of organizations select for gameness. The Marine Corps does so, and so does medicine, when it puts young doctors through the exhausting rigors of residency. But those who select for gameness have a responsibility not to abuse that trust: if you have men in your charge who would jump off a cliff for you, you cannot march them to the edge of the cliff—and dogfighting fails this test. Gameness, Carl Semencic argues, in *The World of Fighting Dogs* (1984), is no more than a dog's "desire to please an owner at any expense to itself." The owners, Semencic goes on,

> understand this desire to please on the part of the dog and capitalize on it. At any organized pit fight in which two dogs are really going at each other wholeheartedly, one can observe the owner of each dog changing his position at pit-side in order to be in sight of his dog at all times. The owner knows that seeing his master rooting him on will make a dog work all the harder to please its master.

This is why Michael Vick's dogs weren't euthanized. The betrayal of loyalty requires an act of social reparation.

Professional football players too are selected for gameness. When Kyle Turley was knocked unconscious, in that game against the Packers, he returned to practice four days later because, he said, "I didn't want to miss a game." Once, in the years when he was still playing, he woke up and fell into a wall as he got out of bed. "I start puking all over," he recalled. "So I said to my wife, 'Take me to practice.' I didn't want to miss practice." The same season that he was knocked unconscious, he began to have pain in his hips. He received three cortisone shots, and kept playing. At the end of the season, he discovered that he had a herniated disk. He underwent surgery, and four months later was back at training camp. "They put me in full-contact practice from day one," he said. "After the first day, I knew I wasn't right. They told me, 'You've had the surgery. You're fine. You should just fight through it.' It's like you're programmed. You've got to go without question—*I'm a warrior. I can block that out of my mind.* I go out, two days later. Full contact. Two-a-days. My back locks up again. I had reherniated the same disk that got operated on four months ago, and bulged the disk above it." As one of Turley's old coaches once said, "He plays the game as it should be played, all out," which is to say that he put the game above his own well-being.

Turley says he was once in the training room after a game with a young linebacker who had suffered a vicious hit on a kickoff return. "We were in the cold tub, which is, like, forty-five degrees, and he starts passing out. In the cold tub. I don't know anyone who has ever passed out in the cold tub. That's supposed to wake you up. And I'm, like, slapping his face. 'Richie! Wake up!' He said, 'What, what? I'm cool.' I said, 'You've got a concussion. You have to go to the hospital.' He said, 'You know, man, I'm fine.'" He wasn't fine, though. That moment in the cold tub represented a betrayal of trust. He had taken the hit on behalf of his team. He was then left to pass out in the cold tub, and to deal—ten and twenty years down the road—with the consequences. No amount of money or assurances about risk freely assumed can change the fact that, in this moment, an essential bond had been broken. What football must confront, in the end, is not just the problem of injuries or scientific findings. It is the fact that there is something profoundly awry in the relationship between the players and the game.

"Let's assume that Dr. Omalu and the others are right," Ira Casson, who co-chairs an NFL committee on brain injury, said. "What should we be doing differently? We asked Dr. McKee this when she came down. And she was honest, and said, 'I don't know how to answer that.' No one has any suggestions—assuming that you aren't saying no more football, because, let's be honest, that's not going to happen." Casson began to talk about the research on the connection between CTE and boxing. It had been known for eighty years. Boxers ran a 20 percent risk of dementia. Yet boxers continue to box. Why? Because people still go to boxing matches.

"We certainly know from boxers that the incidence of CTE is related to the length of your career," he went on. "So if you want to apply that to football—and I'm not saying it does apply—then you'd have to let people play six years and then stop. If it comes to that, maybe we'll have to think about that. On the other hand, nobody's willing to do this in boxing. Why would a boxer at the height of his career, six or seven years in, stop fighting, just when he's making million-dollar paydays?" He shrugged. "It's a violent game. I suppose if you want to you could play touch football or flag football. For me, as a Jewish kid from Long Island, I'd be just as happy if we did that. But I don't know if the fans would be happy with that. So what else do you do?"

Casson is right. There is nothing else to be done, not so long as fans stand and cheer. We are in love with football players, with their courage and grit, and nothing else—neither considerations of science nor those of morality—can compete with the destructive power of that love.

In "Dogmen and Dogfights," Evans and Forsyth write:

> When one views a staged dog fight between pit bulls for the first time, the most macabre aspect of the event is that the only sounds you hear from these dogs are those of crunching bones and cartilage. The dogs rip and tear at each other; their blood, urine and saliva splatter the sides of the pit and clothes of the handlers . . . The emotions of the dogs are conspicuous, but not so striking, even to themselves, are the passions of the owners of the dogs. Whether they hug a winner or in the rare case, destroy a dying loser, whether they walk away from the carcass or lay crying over it, their fondness for these fighters is manifest.

STEVE FRIEDMAN

The Impossible Redemption
of Jonathan Boyer

FROM BICYCLING

THE CHILD MOLESTER prays before every meal. He offers thanks
for his friends, and the food he is about to eat, and the wonderful day ahead. When he wakes at 6:30 he brews himself a cup of
tea and answers e-mail and he walks his dog, a twelve-year-old rott-
weiler named Cody, three blocks to the beach next to the Pacific
Ocean, where they walk some more, and where the child molester
thinks about his purpose in life, imagines ways he might help
others.

He rides his bicycle an hour and a half a day, longer on weekends,
and, afterward, he takes a sauna beneath ceramic infrared heaters.
He drinks water that is alkalized with cathodes and cleansed of microbes by ultraviolet light. He sleeps on an electromagnetic pulsating pad. He doesn't smoke, or eat processed foods, or drink alcohol. He has been drunk twice in his life, both times when he was
fourteen years old. Once was from drinking champagne, the other,
whiskey. He doesn't eat candy. "And I don't do Halloween." He
doesn't watch television, or listen to the radio, or read the newspaper. He lives "in a media void." The books he reads are "biblical, or
historical, or nutritional." He says he avoids fiction because, "I have
so little time and I don't want to waste it." That said, he has a weakness for Jack London and has read every Sherlock Holmes novel,
as well as *Crime and Punishment*. One of his favorite movies is *Gladi-
ator*. He is slightly cold-blooded, with a temperature that runs from

95.8 to 96.5. He comes from money on his mother's side; his family owns a summer estate in Gloucester, Massachusetts, and a ranch in Wyoming. He has a pilot's license. He doesn't care for eggplant. He loves olive oil, but hates olives. He sells bicycle parts and nutritional supplements from a shop on a lightly used municipal airstrip. Many of his clients are middle-aged and they want better lives. "Being able to help them," he says, "is incredibly fulfilling." He thinks fluoridated water is bad for people, and that it was foisted upon the nation as part of a government conspiracy to cover up poisonous byproducts created by atomic weapons. Saturday mornings he attends services at a Seventh-Day Adventist church, and in the summertime he travels to Moab, Utah, where he joins other men as they sit around campfires in the high desert and talk about finding meaning in the world. He says things like "Iron sharpens iron and one man sharpens another," and "Regardless of my mistakes, [God] will take them and make them blessings." He is fifty-three and he lives in Carmel-by-the-Sea, California, with his mother, in the house in which he grew up, and on the rare occasion when he eats at a restaurant in his hometown, people look at him funny and ask how he's been, if he's okay. One of his closest friends is the chief mechanic at a local hotel. Another is a man who has been divorced five times and who lives on a hilltop nearby, behind an electronic gate, at the end of a driveway in which sits a black Porsche 911, in a house filled with centuries-old wooden carvings imported from Afghanistan, with a pet macaw named Lorenzo and the hide of a snow lion on the floor of one room and the hide of a mountain lion on the floor of another room. The mountain lion had eaten Lorenzo's cousin, Harpo, and tried to eat Lorenzo, and the child molester's friend had shot it.

The child molester and I spend four days together in late spring 2007. It's terrible and perhaps unfair to refer to him as "child molester," because he accomplished things as an athlete that few others have, and over the past few years he has, by almost any measure, lived the life of a world-class do-gooder. But "child molester" is exactly how a lot of people who know a little bit about him, especially those who have never met him, think of him even if they don't refer to him that way.

We share meals, before which we always pray, and he makes me a salad at his mother's house, and we walk on the beach and he suggests some foods I might try to lose weight and improve my health. We have dinner at the house on the hilltop, where I admire Lorenzo and the hides on the floor. We talk a lot about cycling and how the child molester came to be the first American to race in the Tour de France and why European racers seemed to accept him more than his countrymen did. We talk about amphetamine-aided descents and the transience of athletic glory and how society can corrupt a man and how we all have choices, that we all need help.

We talk about his improbable triumph, as a middle-aged man just three years out of jail, in the 2006 Race Across America (RAAM), a three-thousand-mile coast-to-coast bicycle race. We talk about his participation in Project Rwanda, a nonprofit organization working to improve the lives of the impoverished citizens of that country. We talk about religion and television, organic food and how, as a child, he dreamt of being a veterinarian in a game park in Africa. The subject he wishes didn't have to come up, but that he knows must, comes up on our third day together. We're up to 1997, when the cyclist was newly and, as it turns out, unhappily married, stagnant in his professional life. We both know what happens next. Silence. The longest silence in the time I have spent with him.

"Now," he says, "starts the whole different chapter in my life."

Of course, a lot of people don't care about the different chapters in the child molester's life. One chapter will do. That one chapter—the one titled "child molester"—is enough for them. The child molester prays? Good for him. Let him pray. He wants to help poor Africans? Keep him supervised and far from minors. He was a great athlete and he wants to be a good man? The first doesn't matter, and he gave up his rights to the second. That's what happens to child molesters. That's their fate. That's how a lot of people think. That's how I thought when I flew out to California to meet Jonathan Boyer. And then we prayed together.

He was so chubby as a toddler that people called him "Fatso." That's a fact. Here's another: his father was a dreamer and a drifter, a man who, after a bar-stool conversation in the desert with a stranger about hidden treasure, would leave his wife and three children and disappear into Mexico for weeks at a time. "A man who had a natural lobotomy for responsibility," his wife, Josephine

Swift Boyer, told her oldest son, Winston. The family lived in Moab, Utah, until 1961, when Josephine packed up her three children —eight-year-old Liza, six-year-old Winston, and the baby, five-year-old Jonathan, whom everyone called Jock (after a friend of Josephine's) —and took them to her parents, the Swifts, in Pebble Beach, California. Moab was so remote in those days that Winston Boyer, senior, had to flag down the California Zephyr at the Crescent Junction station to get it to stop. As the train pulled away, the elder Boyer drove alongside for twenty miles in his red Ford station wagon. ("The cheapest one made, with two doors," Liza remembers.) He waved at his departing family, and the family waved back, at their father and husband, and at their dog, a black, tan, and white sheepdog named Timbo. "The saddest day of all of our lives," Liza says. Jock says, "It was like yesterday. Indeed, the saddest day of my life."

Liza says that Jock "went from being the happiest, hugging-est, most generous and least shy, quickest to make friends, of all of us, to a child who was worried and sad. It took him a while to bounce back."

Two years later, the brood moved to Carmel. Their next-door neighbors in Carmel rode bicycles, so Winston and his little brother would tag along. Jock wouldn't see his father for six years. Other men in Carmel, though, took the boys under their wings. Sam Hopkins, another neighbor and a local cycling icon who had started racing competitively at age fifty, encouraged the Boyer boys to enter some events. Jock loved it from the beginning.

A local restaurateur, Remo d'Agliano, who had raced in Europe, coached the Boyers, and though there was no cycling culture to speak of—this was the early '70s—the Boyers finished at the top of almost every race they entered, along with another local boy named Tom Ritchey. Jonathan rode a black ten-speed Raleigh Competition, which was stolen from school after two weeks. Hopkins sold him a blue LeJeune for $180, which happened to be exactly the amount the insurance had paid for the Raleigh.

Winston drifted away from the sport because competition made him nervous. Ritchey liked long rides in the hills, and didn't enjoy the criteriums, with their short, narrow courses with tight corners, so he stopped road racing too. That left Jock.

Partly because of d'Agliano's urging, partly because of competitive zeal and adolescent restlessness, he decided he wanted to race in Europe. The summer before his senior year (at Monterey's York School), he enrolled in an intensive course in French at the nearby Monterey Institute of Foreign Studies, where for nine weeks, seven hours a day, he studied the language. He also rode and waited tables at d'Agliano's restaurant. When he graduated high school, he had been accepted at the University of Colorado. He had also qualified to ride in the junior world championships in Munich. He asked the university if he could delay his freshman year. Then he took the $350 he had saved from waiting tables and bought a plane ticket to Paris. From 1973 until early 1977, he raced as an amateur for little-known teams such as UVSE Saint Eloy les Mines and ACBB Paris. Like almost all new racers at that level, he traveled between hotels where, he says, "the water smelled like urine, the beds sagged, and the sheets were made of that stuff that doesn't even feel like fabric." In one of the hotels, he got fleas. In another, crabs. Always strong in the mountains, he grew stronger, fashioned himself into an elite climber. He learned, and he won, and he learned and he won some more.

In May 1977, a professional team, LeJeune BP, invited him to join. That's when he realized how little he knew. "It was incredibly hard," he says. "There were more riders, better bike handlers; people were smoother in the pack. And the fitness levels were hard to believe. As an amateur, when you thought you were tired, that was nothing compared with the pro level. What I learned was that as an amateur, you don't know what being really tired is. Think of being completely exhausted, then train and ride as much as when you're fresh. That's what it means to ride as a professional."

His first professional contract was three thousand francs, or four hundred dollars a month, which was about five hundred francs more than most newly minted professionals. That's because Boyer was an American, a novelty. His citizenship wasn't the only thing that set him apart. By 1980, Boyer was showing up to races lugging suitcases packed with twenty pounds of fruits and nuts, and a blender to mix them. He was also reading the Bible regularly. Later, reporters would say that other riders perceived him as an oddball. (If true, it would be impressive; cycling counts as its recent champions a marble-shooting, pigeon-hunting, disco-hopping Italian who died of a cocaine overdose; an ecstasy-ingesting German who most experts—and riders—believe might have beaten Lance Armstrong had he been able to stop overeating during the offseason; and an American whose lawyers said a never-born twin might have been the cause of the positive blood test that got him banned for two years from cycling.) The fruit-and-nut eater won the 1980 Coors Classic, where overexcited and underinformed television announcers referred to him as "Jacques BoyAY," instead of "Jock BOYer." The same year, he finished fifth in the world championships, then accepted an offer from another team, Renault-Gitane, that wanted him to help Bernard Hinault in the mountains of the 1981 Tour de France. (Hinault, the Badger, had already won the Tour in 1978 and 1979, would win in 1981, then go on to win the race in 1982 and 1985.) No American had ever raced in the Tour before, much less finished, much less helped a teammate win. Boyer did all three.

Like winning a Pulitzer Prize, or discovering a distant comet, the distinction of being the first American to race the Tour de France might have furnished a first sentence for future obituary writers when they considered the life of this quiet, wiry vegetarian. His thirty-second-place finish paved the way for Greg LeMond, who became the first American to win the Tour, in 1986, as well as the 7-Eleven team, which with sprinter Davis Phinney and mountain climber Andy Hampsten was the first American squad to successfully race in Europe, serving as a model and an inspiration for modern-day stars such as Lance Armstrong. Boyer was twenty-six, and though he might not have known it, his fame was already receding. Infamy was decades away.

He has long eyelashes, graying hair, hazel eyes, and the kind of looks that in another era might have been called matinee idol. He is five feet ten and a half inches tall, and his weight ranges from 145 to 150, as it has since he was a teenager. He looks about fifteen years younger than his age. He credits this to clean living, which I presume includes the electromagnetic pulsating pad and the infrared sauna and the ultraviolet-treated water, and not just exercising a lot and eating vegetables. He favors black jeans and pullover sweaters, athletic sandals with socks. On Saturdays, when he attends church and celebrates the Sabbath, he wears a button-down shirt and polished black boots. He walks slightly duck-toed.

The first time we meet, at a restaurant in Carmel, he says he likes snakes, especially pythons and boa constrictors, and loves roasted potatoes. Before we eat, he says a prayer. His voice is nasal, slightly high-pitched, absent any strong regional accent. He is something of a flirt, and when the waitress comes to take our order, he asks her how to say "poached" in Spanish and is rewarded with a big smile.

I ask how he'd like to be remembered, and he says, "I don't know. It's not something I think of. Perhaps as someone who made a positive impact on people." I ask if he has any regrets and he says, "I could have raced a little less," which he believes would have prolonged his career. He tells me that he knows himself better than he ever has. He says he realizes now that there was a lot of anger in his life, that "I have always had difficulty dealing with emotional issues."

He admits that he avoids television as much from weakness as strength. "If there's a program on, I'll get sucked into it, and then before you know it, two hours are gone. I'm a very emotional person. I get very affected by things."

He says that people are capable of great good and great evil. "I think we need to realize any one of us, given the right or wrong situation, we will do anything . . . Iraqis are no different than Americans. Muslims have the same makeup as Christians. We're all from the same stock. We can't point fingers and say 'I would never do that' and 'Those people are monsters.' We're part of the same race."

For three days, he doesn't mention his crime and I don't ask about it. We don't discuss how it has changed his life, how it has altered the way people relate to him, how it has changed how he moves through the world. He talks about God a lot and forgiveness and meaning, and I imagine it must be exhausting, not talking about something but talking about it all the time. I imagine it's what his life is like every day.

He generally shuns interviews, but he has agreed to meet because he is proud of his work for Project Rwanda, and he believes the publicity for it will be a good thing. He has been to Rwanda recently, will be piling a group of Rwandans into a 1972 Bluebird bus and driving them to race bicycles in the Utah desert the week after we meet, then will be returning to Rwanda a month after that.

He doesn't take antimalarial medications before his trips, because he says he doesn't need them. On his most recent trip to Africa, he says, "I ate enzymes, herbs, and mushrooms. I was incredibly healthy the whole time. I made it so my body was impossible for any parasite to live in." He says he is working on developing a wafer that will help mitigate the effects of giardia, "that will prevent against microbes and viruses and parasites you catch in foreign countries." I dutifully take notes and wonder which is more delusional, Boyer's efforts to develop a cracker that will save the planet, or his belief that his good works will make anyone forget—or forgive—what he did.

He finished tenth in the world championships in 1982. In 1983, he finished twelfth in the Tour. Boyer thought he would be in the top five in 1984, but he fell to thirty-first because of two crashes, dehydration during a stage he thought he could win, and the vagaries of athletic chance. In 1985, the American who started it all did something odd. Instead of racing in the Tour de France, he entered RAAM. The year before, he had been discussing, with a television producer, a feud in American cycling. A group of ultracyclists, who specialized in riding hundreds of miles at a time, were touting the cross-country race as the ultimate test of cycling prowess, and then there were racers like Boyer. "The ultracyclists wanted to be recognized as serious athletes," he says. "We just thought they were good at staying awake."

On the day after Thanksgiving in 1984, Boyer told the producer, "I could beat those guys," and the producer said, "If you really mean that and are really serious about that, you owe it to the racing cycling community to do it."

He enlisted a van and a crew. He invested in a motor home, a motorbike, a pickup truck, and a rented sedan. The first day, he rode 445 miles. The second day he made it 400 miles, then another 400 miles after that. He was going so much faster than anyone else (he averaged 14.3 miles per hour, including rest breaks) that he could sleep more than his competitors. He rode into Atlantic City more than four hours ahead of his closest competitor.

"I won five thousand dollars," he remembers. "And I spent twenty-five thousand dollars to do it."

In 1986, still recovering from the physical stress of his costly victory, he skipped the Tour. In 1987, living in Italy and racing with the 7-Eleven team alongside Eric Heiden and Bob Roll and Andy Hampsten, he finished ninety-ninth, his worst finish ever. It was his last year as a pro and his highest-paid. He made $50,000 and retired. With LeMond's victory in the world championships and the Tour de France, and Hampsten and Phinney's stage wins in the Giro d'Italia and the Tour, everyone was talking about American cycling. People were already starting to forget the man who had helped start it. "As I look back," he says, "I should have gone straight into mountain bike racing. When you stop racing, I think every athlete goes through the same thing, you go through a real serious depression . . . you're completely lost, nothing grounding you . . . I just remember it as being a really hard period."

He started a new career importing bicycle parts into the United States, in partnership with a Dutchman he knew. He traveled to twenty-six countries a year, worked with eighty customers. He lived in Holland, would drive five hundred miles to the French office, near Lyon, in the afternoon, and back the next morning. He rode a motorcycle, drove 150 miles per hour on the autobahn.

"I had a house," he says, "but no home. I was fried." In 1992, he moved back to the Carmel Valley, and after his Dutch partner severed business relations (". . . a disaster. Basically I was kicked out without any shares . . ."), he imported and sold bicycle parts and supplies on his own. In 1992, he was baptized at the Seventh-Day Adventist church in Pacific Grove, six miles from Carmel. Two years later, he met a woman at the church who lived in Seaside. They started dating, and in 1997 they married.

Seaside, California, police officers arrested Boyer on May 16, 2002, after a seventeen-year-old girl told them the cyclist had molested her from 1997 to 2000. She was barely twelve when it started. On September 12, 2002, he pled guilty to seven counts of lewd and lascivious acts upon a child, and three counts of penetration by a foreign object or genital penetration on a person younger than sixteen. He said he was remorseful. On November 19, he was sentenced to twenty years in state prison, a sentence that was immediately stayed, then he was put on probation for five years, and sent to the Monterey County jail for a year. At the sentencing, state superior court judge Gary E. Meyer noted that Boyer posed little threat to the girl or to others and that he was a good candidate for rehabilitation. Those are the facts. He slept in a dorm with sixty other men. Breakfast was served at 4:00 A.M. He read fifty books, including the complete works of Christian evangelist Philip Yancey. He was released on July 7, 2003, after serving eight months. In 2006, at age fifty-one, he won the solo enduro division of the Race Across America. His probation ended November 7, 2007. Those are facts too.

In some states, a sixteen-year-old who fondles his fourteen-year-old girlfriend is guilty of a crime, just as guilty in strict legal terms as someone who stalks playgrounds, snatching and raping children. If you can accept that when it comes to sex offenses, even child molesting, there is a moral spectrum of heinousness, then should we try to put Boyer's crime—and Boyer—in some sort of context? Boyer thinks we should. "It's too bad all those [criminal] charges get put in the same box," he says. "The fact is they're so varied, the charges . . . they go from one end to the other . . . you do have predators out there, the perverts, you do have people who are bent on molesting countless kids and who have issues with children. Then you have others who have overstepped certain boundaries and get put in the same . . . uh . . . same sort of description."

What exactly did Boyer do? According to court records, he twice "puts [his] hand inside of Jane Doe's pants and touches Jane Doe's vagina," and "digitally penetrates Jane Doe's vagina" a total of eight times. Once, during the act, he spoke French.

Boyer refuses to discuss the specifics of the crimes. His friends say his public silence is to protect the girl, now a young woman.

Lars Frazer is a photographer based in Austin, Texas. He has known Boyer for twenty years, and says the cyclist "became best friends with a thirteen-year-old girl who fell deeply in love with him. She had a high level of maturity and he showed poor judgment. When Jock said, 'This is not appropriate, it's not appropriate for us to have this level of friendship,' she lashed out," and the police were notified.

"Knowing what I know," says Frazer, "he shouldn't have spent a day in jail. He's not a predator. I have two daughters, six and three and a half, and there's no question I would let them spend time alone with Jock. They know who he is, and they love him."

David Frost, a friend of Boyer's for thirty years, who works as a

deputy district attorney in Monterey County, says, "I purposefully
didn't read the files and I don't want to. I'm sure it'll never happen
again. It's not something anyone will have to worry about. He's got
a very strong character."

Others aren't quite as sympathetic.

In a precise and careful e-mail, Monterey chief assistant district
attorney Terry Spitz said, after reviewing the file, "We are prohibited by the state bar ethics code from charging a crime based on a
hunch or suspicion. We must have probable cause to believe the
defendant actually engaged in the conduct charged. Of course,
Boyer admitted to . . . engaging in such conduct."

Facts matter. Even a man as heavily invested in intention as Boyer
knows that. He also knows that while facts might be immutable,
faith is redemptive. "We can't go through life without tragedies,"
Boyer says. "It's what we do with the tragedies that define us. It
strengthens our ability to help. One thing I've learned is that all of
us are hurting. Each day we're given opportunities to help people.
My purpose is to take those opportunities. Each day people cross
our path who need some sort of help. Not necessarily something
that's life-threatening. I think it's important, as a Christian, to help.
You get lifted up when that happens, you get encouraged, you get
hope, your trust grows. With every opportunity taken, you're given
a bigger, better opportunity later."

I ask Boyer about the girl. Does he worry about her? I don't
know how she feels, because I haven't been able to track her down.
(The fact that I tried angers some colleagues, who tell me that I
would be victimizing her all over again if I contacted her. The fact
that I fail distresses others, who argue that a story containing even
a measure of sympathy for Boyer, without his victim's perspective,
is an outrage.) Absent her thoughts, I ask Boyer how he thinks
she's doing. I ask how he thinks what happened affected her.

"It depends on which direction she chooses," he says. "If you let
something destroy you, whose fault is that? God doesn't want you
to be destroyed. We all have an opportunity to choose a path that
will make us stronger. I just hope she's making the right choices in
her life despite the past. We all are responsible for our choices. I
was responsible for my choices and I take full responsibility."

Then he tells me the story of Corrie ten Boom, the Dutch Christian woman who hid and saved Jews during World War II, and was imprisoned in a concentration camp for her efforts. He recounts the story of how, after the war, a concentration camp guard from Ravensbrück, where she had been imprisoned, approached her.

"He said to her," Boyer tells me, "'I know that God forgives me, but my question is, do you?'"

("For a long moment we grasped each other's hands," ten Boom wrote in her book, *Tramp for the Lord,* which I looked through after I left Boyer. "The former guard and the former prisoner. I had never known God's love so intensely as I did then.")

"We can't look at the pain we've caused," Boyer says. "We have to look at the good we can do, and though it can't erase the past, it certainly can eclipse some of the damage. Our choices are today."

Does Boyer see that the tale's power comes because it's the victim who is the narrator, the *victim* who is extolling the virtues of forgiveness? Does he understand that he's not the best person in the world to be suggesting that the child he molested would be better off if she would simply forgive and move on? Then again, what's the difference what he says? Or what anyone says? Don't a man's actions matter more than his words?

In January 2008 I receive a telephone call from Dan Cooper, a stock trader in Chicago. Cooper, one of the central supporters of Project Rwanda, is devoted to financing it and getting others to finance it. He has heard about the time Boyer and I spent together, and he is worried. "This is going to have a direct impact on my ability to keep the team sustainable," he tells me. "Project Rwanda has become the good-news story of cycling. *Bicycling* magazine comes out with a story about Jonathan Boyer being a child molester, that good-news story could very easily evaporate."

The next day, Cooper would fly in a private jet with the president of Rwanda to meet the president of Starbucks, who was hosting a dinner at the behest of the president of Costco. Cooper was hoping to raise a lot of money. "We got to know Jonathan before we invited him to be part of the Rwanda team," Cooper says. "We know the background and the drama that unfolded there . . . Externally, it's a little bit of a wild card when it comes to public perception."

Cooper and I talk for almost thirty minutes. He says Boyer would resign from the program "in a heartbeat" if he thought his presence would hurt the project. He says that only two people know exactly what happened between Boyer and the child. He says Boyer "is as close to a walking angel as I've met. I've never seen a guy who's been more self-sacrificing of himself than Jonathan . . . being around Jonathan makes me better. There are very few people I can say that about."

Cooper is more reflective than insistent, as interested in talking about pain and redemption as he is about corporate sponsorship. It's easy to understand his success at fundraising.

"This guy is wearing this huge, horrible scarlet letter," he says. "And at the end of the day, a guy can't keep paying for his crimes over and over and over again, especially someone doing so much good and spreading so much love as Jonathan."

Getting arrested and serving time for child molesting—no matter the circumstances or mitigating factors—tends to winnow the number of a man's friends. Tonight, Boyer is having dinner with three who stuck by him. There is Ricky Gonzalez, chief mechanic for the past twenty-six years at the nearby Bay Park Hotel, a regular customer at Boyer's shop, and the crew chief on the latest RAAM victory, who Boyer says "is like an older brother to me." Winston Boyer, Jock's real older brother, who is as impish and bawdy as Jock is pious and tightly wound, is there too. The host for the evening is Peterson Conway, owner of Peterson Conway Imports in Carmel, speaker of six languages, ex-husband of five wives, world traveler since he joined the Peace Corps thirty-eight years ago at age seventeen and landed in Afghanistan, where James Michener hired him as his translator; he is also the owner of the Porsche and the mountain lion rug and Lorenzo the macaw, as well as the 8,500-square-foot house on the seventeen acres sprawled near the top of Jack's Peak, the highest spot on the Monterey Peninsula, where we are all gathered. "What Sean Connery is to cinema, he is in my life," Boyer had told me earlier. Maybe it's because I had already been overloaded with sentiments about men sharpening men, and Nazi criminals seeking forgiveness, and the dangers of fluoride, but at the time, the statement didn't seem as weird to me as it does now.

We sit at a counter made of Italian marble, beneath ceilings that once covered a maharaja's harem quarters, behind a door built in the eighteenth century, shipped here from India. Winston Boyer and Conway drink wine and Jock and I and Garcia have water as we talk about cycling and love and Lorenzo's dead cousin, Harpo, whose sad fate had led Conway to climb the tree outside his house with a shotgun and spend a night waiting for the animal that is now a rug. We swap stories. Conway remembers a moonlit night in Katmandu, and bowls of hash, and the strange sensation of cold cobblestones and hot liquid on his bare feet, and the stoned realization that it was the blood of oxen whose throats had just been slit, in an adolescent rite of passage, by teenaged Ghurka soldiers. Winston Boyer recounts the time he was scheduled to show a collection of masks he had photographed at a famous New York City art gallery, until, he says, the gallery owner ran into some financial and legal difficulty and got caught up in a murder investigation that involved sadomasochism. The man with the most notorious stories of all doesn't mention them. Conway flambés a flan with a miniature blowtorch and we all sample the best cheese I have ever tasted and then Winston's phone rings and he looks at it while we all look at him.

He smiles a tight smile. "Mom," he says, and he and Jock look at each other and we all chuckle.

Jock leads us in prayer before dinner, thanking God for the food, and his wonderful friends and the blessed day. I hear Conway mutter something I think is Farsi before he serves chicken in herbs that taste better than any herbs I have ever tasted, and the best tea I have ever tasted. "Don't bother asking him for the recipe," Jock says.

Over dinner we discuss Boyer's latest RAAM victory. There was a bad crash in Kansas, a potentially lethal hot-rodder in Arkansas, and dead-of-the-night searches for fresh fruit in East St. Louis, Illinois. There were terrible digestive problems and a racing heart rate and chafing so severe it required massive applications of lidocaine, which made it necessary for Boyer to drop to all fours in order to urinate. There were sleep-deprivation-induced hallucinations from coast to coast.

"I relate to pain," Boyer says. "Even now, for some odd reason, I'm at home in pain. It seems to be some old friend of mine.

"One of the things that draws me are natural disasters . . . adverse atmospheric conditions really draw me and I have no idea why. I'm attracted to natural upheavals . . . if there's this huge thundershower, lightning, huge windows, blizzards, I just want to be part of it."

"I attribute all this," Winston Boyer says, "to Jock not taking drugs."

Boyer and his wife separated in 2000, divorced in 2003. He hasn't dated since he was released from prison, he says, but now he's ready. He would like to meet someone, fall in love, settle down and start a family. His friends talk about fixing him up, joke that he wants a younger woman, and I make sure I don't obviously cringe. (A few minutes later, one says that thirty-two would be the ideal age.) Does Boyer know how what under most circumstances is merely manly joshing takes on a sinister, sickly cast, because of his history? If so, he doesn't show it. There is something reserved about him, guarded, which makes sense, because he's a smart man, he learned French in a summer, taught himself about nutrition and fitness, trained himself to be one of the best cyclists in the world. He forged a magnificent athletic career from—among other things—being cagey and hiding weakness.

Dinner is over, and the flan is delicious, and there is some more talk of past races, adventures, and misadventures. Soon, Boyer will drive down the mountain and to his mother's house, where he will sleep on his electromagnetic pulsing pad, then wake in the morning, to his tea, and his walk on the beach with Cody, and his professions of gratitude to God, and to his best efforts to get on with his life.

Thirty-five years ago, when Boyer was first winning cycling races and dominating the sport in California, one of his chief competitors was Tom Ritchey. When Boyer went to France and opened the era that would lead to American dominance in the Tour de France, Ritchey turned his hand to building bikes and, with a handful of other men, created and rode the first mountain bikes. He launched Ritchey Design and was elected into the Mountain Bike Hall of Fame in 1988, and today heads up his eponymous company that is one of the sport's leading manufacturers of high-quality bicycle components.

I meet Ritchey after four days with Boyer, on my way from Carmel to the San Francisco airport. Ritchey has ridden his bicycle from his home in the lush and green Woodside hills, where it sits among those of Internet millionaires and venture capitalists. We meet at Bucks of Woodside, a breakfast joint famous for flapjacks and Internet start-up deals. People are dressed in jeans and casual-looking, high-performance, expensive athletic gear. Ritchey is tall and lean and fit, wearing cycling shorts and a bicycling jersey. He orders oatmeal.

He tells me that a few years earlier, he realized his life was empty: money and status and a home among venture capitalists and Internet millionaires hadn't brought him real happiness; his business had gotten away from him; he was in his midforties, and while he had most everything he had ever wanted, he wanted more, and he didn't know how to get it.

When an acquaintance invited him to Rwanda, to take part in a project designed to help the citizens of that country, he was skeptical. "I'm not a giving person," he says. "I had never done anything like it. And I went there with prejudices, strong opinions." In Africa, everything changed. That's where Ritchey became involved with Project Rwanda. He designed a bicycle to help coffee farmers more efficiently transport their crop, and asked Boyer to be project director and coach of the Team Rwanda racing team, to help with publicity and awareness for Project Rwanda. "To me," he says, "Rwanda represents new beginnings. Goodness, mercy, hope. Rwanda is me . . . It's anyone having to work through serious disappointments in life."

It takes Ritchey about fifteen minutes to get from his adolescent race victories, through his middle-aged despair, to rebirth in Africa, and his oatmeal sits, cooling. He weeps while he talks, unapologetically and sloppily. He weeps when he speaks of his midlife crisis, and of the joy he discovered in Rwanda, and of the men's retreats he attends in Moab once a year, where, "We have a campfire every night, talk about our lives, share each other's burdens. We're honest about what's going on. We've got to take out the sword and put each other at point all the time . . . It's a deeper way of relating, of connecting." Ritchey tells me I should think about attending one year. He gives me a Project Rwanda T-shirt and some Project Rwanda coffee.

Everything about the breakfast meeting—Ritchey's existential crisis, the men's groups in the desert, the sloppy tears, certainly the

T-shirt and coffee—is slightly but not entirely surprising. Boyer and I had talked a lot about despair and new beginnings. When I had asked him for names of people who knew him, who might be able to share their perceptions of him, maybe he picked someone he thought might be in tune with the theme of his life as he had discussed it with me. Maybe he thought I was sympathetic. Or maybe he wanted someone who he thought knew him well. Certainly he wanted someone who could talk about his good works in Africa. In any case, while Ritchey is eloquent on the subject of men and meaning, and the economic calculus of African coffee production (Rwanda grows an enormous amount of coffee; the problem is inadequate systems to transport the product, which is where the bicycle comes in), his knowledge of Boyer is incomplete. Though they raced together when they were young ("We were more competitors than friends," Ritchey says), and they ride together now ("Very few people ride at the pace I do . . . He's someone I enjoy spending hours and hours and hours with in the saddle"), there loom three decades between adolescence and middle age. So, granted, Boyer has been wonderful at spotting talent in Rwanda and conscientious about training young Rwandans to be elite cyclists. And yes, Boyer has been giving and honest and warm during their time in Africa and in the Utah desert. And sure, pain can help heal, and the point of the sword and all that stuff.

But what about the girl? What would the young woman she's become say? How much weight would she give Boyer's good works?

Ritchey had told me earlier during our breakfast that even during his greatest financial success, "I didn't know who I was." Now, he says, through pain and self-reflection, he has found the answer. "I am who my friends are," Ritchey says. "The people who are in my life are who I am. I had a realization: the people in my life right now are the reasons I am here. People like Jock."

I ask about what he says to people who want to know about Jock's crime. I ask what I can say to people who, when I'm telling them about Boyer's good works, and his athletic accomplishments, berate me when I get to the words "child molester." The people who tell me I'm doing harm by writing with anything other than indignation when I write about this particular crime. This particular criminal.

"You either believe people can change or you don't," Ritchey says. "It's that simple. You either experience that grace, that forgiveness, that ability to be merciful, or you don't."

Here are the facts of Jonathan Boyer's life: He won eighty-seven races as an amateur, forty-four as a professional. He was a member of the United States national team fifteen times. He competed in nine world championships.

Here are the facts: He lives with twenty-four-hour guards, behind walls, in a four-bedroom house in Musanzi, Rwanda. He has been here since autumn 2007. He travels the country looking for promising cyclists, testing them, training them, encouraging them to join Team Rwanda. He has tested fifty riders, and from them formed a team of eleven. The team has raced in Algeria and Namibia and South Africa and Morocco and Cameroon and the United States. At the 2008 Continental Championships, in Morocco, Team Rwanda placed tenth out of fourteen. Next year, Boyer hopes to test about three hundred to four hundred more riders. Virtually every one of the Rwandan cyclists comes from a place with no electricity or running water, and not enough food. "They're definitely used to hard times," Boyer says. "They have an emotional stability beyond my comprehension." Boyer and I talk in November 2008. He has just returned from a race with his team in Morocco, and the next day will be departing for Lethoso. He wants to make sure I write about his recent work; that people learn about the impact the cyclists are making in their communities, in the country, in all of Africa. "People see Team Rwanda, and their first thought is, 'genocide.' They see these guys riding, and they witness miracles happening. It blows people away." He tells me that in four to six years, he plans for Team Rwanda to be racing in the Tour de France.

Here are the facts: Jonathan Boyer closed his business, moved out of his mother's house, left the United States to make a new life in a country where hundreds of thousands of people were murdered fifteen years ago. Here are the facts: He is fifty-three years old, divorced, single, a convicted child molester living in Africa, helping people. He returns to Carmel, California, every October, for his birthday, so he can register as a sex offender, then goes back to Africa. Since he's been in Musanzi, two Rwandans he knows—

a cyclist and a cook—have become fathers. The proud parents
named their boys Jonathan.

You pray before every meal. You give thanks for the food you are
about to eat, and for the friends who believe in you, and for the
wonderful day ahead. You wake at 6:30, and you drink two cups
of coffee before you walk your dog. You ride your bike, and that
helps. You keep busy, and you eat right, and that helps too. But
there are quiet, still moments that must feel like lifetimes when
you wonder if you will ever be forgiven.

You cheated your business partner. You lied on your income
taxes. You betrayed a confidence. You gossiped about your best
friend. You neglected your child. You hit your wife. You cheated on
your husband. Maybe you did worse. Maybe you did much worse.
You were cowardly. You acted out of lust, or wounded pride, or anger. You hurt people.

You're not a world-class athlete, and you were never convicted
of a crime. You don't have to endure reporters' questions or public censure. You have to confront only yourself. You only have to
make it through your own still, quiet moments. Do you apologize
to those you hurt? Would it change anything? Do you give your
clothes to the Salvation Army? Do you volunteer at a soup kitchen?
Do you move and start your life over? Do you do good works to forget your sins or to atone for them? Does it matter? Does it change
anything? Does it change what you did? Does it change who you
are? And who are you? Who *are* you?

MIKE MAGNUSON

Whatever Happened to Greg LeMond?

FROM BICYCLING

So BEFORE I GOT DIVORCED, I loaded a bike and a suitcase and a laptop into my pickup, said goodbye to my wife and children, and drove away from my home in southern Illinois to meet Greg LeMond.

I was going down to the Tour de Georgia to find him, and the date I ended up arriving there, April 20, 2006, was exactly nineteen years after LeMond's brother-in-law accidentally shot him while they were turkey hunting in California. LeMond had won his first Tour de France the previous summer but in 1987 had been having a bad spring; after breaking his wrist in a minor race in Belgium, he'd come back to the States to heal and decided that as long as he had some free time, he might as well have some fun — then he lost 70 percent of his blood volume and nearly died.

He recovered, of course, and two years later pulled off the first great comeback in American cycling history, the one not much of anyone seems to care about these days: he won the 1989 Tour de France on the last stage, improbably erasing a fifty-second deficit to the great French racer Laurent Fignon in just a twenty-five-kilometer time trial, taking the yellow jersey by eight seconds, which was the narrowest Tour victory ever and, meantime, setting a record for fastest time trial in Tour history. And as if this weren't enough, LeMond won the 1989 world champion road title a few weeks after that.

For anyone much under the age of forty, or people older than that who didn't get into the sport until Lance Armstrong's own miraculous comeback in 1999, it can be difficult to understand —and believe—how popular LeMond was, how significant his victories felt, how deeply he touched lives.

His early career promised greatness: in 1979, he became the first American to win the junior world road race championship, then four years later, he won pro worlds—again the first time for an American—by attacking and holding off the pack through the last eleven kilometers. The next year, 1984, he rode his first Tour de France and won the white jersey, for best young rider.

It was the 1985 Tour that began to establish him as a legend: his teammate Bernard Hinault had already won four Tours and, nearing the end of his career, wanted a fifth to equal the record that at the time was shared only by Jacques Anquetil and Eddy Merckx. LeMond was obviously stronger but, under pressure from his team, agreed to support Hinault rather than take his first victory; in return, Hinault promised to help LeMond take the yellow jersey the next year. But the Badger repeatedly attacked LeMond in 1986 so that his win—another first for an American—was achieved not only with little support from his team but in the face of what many fans believe was outright hostility. It was a cowboy win, reckless and individualistic and raging against the establishment, and because the race had also appeared at length on U.S. television, American cyclists responded: when LeMond had turned pro, in 1981, there were about 10,000 licensed road racers in the United States; at the peak of his popularity, no more than ten years later, there were around 40,000.

After his comeback in 1989, LeMond's celebrity reached heights no one thought possible for a cyclist: he made the cover of *Sports Illustrated*, was named the magazine's Sportsman of the Year (first time for a cyclist), visited the White House, did a guest spot on Johnny Carson, appeared on the Wheaties box as well as on a promotional giveaway stuffed inside Chex cereal boxes, and was the star of a $12 million Taco Bell ad campaign that featured TV commercials and the giveaway of 300,000 water bottles carrying his signature. He was not merely a star. He was an icon.

As much as we Americans loved him, the French loved him maybe even more, even though he'd taken a Tour away from a French rider. For a time after his comeback he was the most popular athlete in all of France, according to a couple polls. I think they loved LeMond so much because he was a calamity, the kind of person for whom everything seemed to be going wrong at all times. Yet somehow, with a sort of cheerfully honest determination, he could still succeed—for instance, on the final, ceremonial stage into Paris for his first Tour win in '86, LeMond crashed three times. He had panache, in the classic French Cyrano de Bergerac sense: noble, reckless, faulted in an endearing and particularly human way. Get knocked down, get up, keep going, and somehow find exuberance and joy throughout the experience.

Maybe panache is one thing in a great champion like Greg LeMond and quite another thing in an ordinary person like me, but I have always wanted to exhibit that quality in my bearing, in my endeavors, my way of life, to be someone you can laugh with and laugh at, who knows life is serious but regards it with humor, who always has something going wrong but finds a way to make it right.

The trouble with things forever going wrong, of course, is that eventually something will go wrong that can't be made right. Eventually, there will be no cheerful rallying back.

Greg LeMond was at the Tour de Georgia, and a bunch of us journalists were getting to meet him because he was supposed to be in another process of cheerfully rallying back.

The Trek Bicycle Corporation, which produced LeMond's eponymous brand of bicycles, was unveiling his new line of carbon-fiber race bikes. Trek should have had a great business partnership on its hands: it also made the bikes Armstrong had ridden to all seven of his Tour victories, and the combined star power of the two greatest American champions was the kind of thing marketing and PR teams dream about.

But LeMond had been publicly feuding with Armstrong and generally speaking out about doping. The American public, the bicycle-buying public, had not been amused by his remarks. Trek would later say, as part of a lawsuit between the company and LeMond, that it had received complaints and that the controversy was hurting sales.

LeMond's most notorious remark: "If Lance is clean, it is the greatest comeback in the history of sports. If he isn't, it would be the greatest fraud." His funniest: with the drugs they have these days, "one could convert a mule into a stallion." Or I thought it was funny at the time he said it. Not many people seemed to have agreed with me. A lot of cyclists I'd meet thought LeMond was jealous of Armstrong.

This was just the latest calamity that, sure, in a way may have been central to LeMond's appeal but had also kept him from achieving the kind of superstardom that Armstrong had forged out of his comeback. From the 1990 marketing fiasco, when Taco Bell had to recall all those promotional water bottles after one of the mouthpieces came off and a child nearly swallowed it, to the decade-long floundering of his bike brand before Trek got involved, to his partial ownership of Bruegger's Bagels, LeMond had always seemed to be chipping away at his own legacy: we don't want our heroes to sell us breakfast; we want them to sell us hope. Lately, his brand had been rumored by industry and media sources to be in trouble. I guess the idea in April 2006 was that if the media met LeMond and found out he was an okay guy we would be more inclined to write good things about his bikes and people would be more inclined to buy them.

We met LeMond in the German-themed town of Helen: a place where all the buildings look like they're in Berchtesgaden and the locals talk with that pleasant twang folks have in the mountains of the Southeast. In a couple of days, the Tour de Georgia would pass through Helen on its way to Brasstown Bald, where on the murderous 20 percent pitch to the summit Tom Danielson would do his best to put time into Floyd Landis but it couldn't be done, not this year. Floyd was unbeatable this year. A mule was going to win the Tour de France.

We stayed in a very nice, very quaint hotel called the Helendorf, behind which flowed the lazy waters of the Chattahoochee, and on the morning of April 21 we were assembled near the river in the early morning, sipping coffee and making journalistic small talk. A shaft of light poked through the trees. And Greg LeMond appeared in it.

He announced himself as if nobody knew who he was. "Hello, I'm Greg LeMond."

It was him all right. But not the 5 percent body-fat, boyish-blond Greg LeMond in all those classic bike-racing photographs guys like

me once had taped on our walls. He had the smile, the joyful demeanor, the classically piercing blue eyes, but this was a gray-haired,
burly fellow who looked more like a retired NFL running back
than a Tour de France champion. He was also the happiest, most
folksy person you'd ever met in your life. He looked at the journalists one by one, at the Helendorf and the river and the shaft of
sunlight, and he said the obvious: "Isn't this a great place?"

He said, "I'm so happy we're here."

The Trek people ushered us inside the building, into a conference room where we listened to a presentation about the new
bikes, which looked magnificent to me — but then, most bikes do.
LeMond stood near a new bike that was nicely displayed on a little
riser, and he began his remarks by saying, "I used to be a bike
racer."

None of the journalists laughed or looked surprised. To me, this
would be like meeting Bill Clinton and having him say, "I used to
be president of the United States."

LeMond had intended the irony, and had hoped for a laugh and
seemed momentarily shaken by the lack of response. He said a few
more inconsequential words, giving off an uncharacteristic nervous impression, as if he wanted to do the right thing for Trek and
not say anything that could lead anywhere dangerous, but for him
to rein in some small part of himself by necessity he had to rein in
all of himself. He handed over the floor to one of the Trek people
who began explaining the intricacies of the new bikes.

I didn't listen. I couldn't. Greg LeMond was in the room, sitting
not twenty feet from me, and I could tell he wasn't listening to the
presentation either. He was peering into his hands and picking at
his fingernails and poring over in his mind things I couldn't even
guess what they were. He is twenty-two months older than me, and
even though I didn't know him then, I always felt like I had, and
had always admired him, and his presence in my life had been as
significant as anybody I'd ever known. I had never been a great cyclist but had always considered cycling to be one of the centers of
my life, and there is no doubt that when I bought my first fancy
road bike in early August 1986, when I changed from that person who tooled around on a bike for no reason to a person who
dreamed of riding too far and too hard, I did so because Greg
LeMond had won the Tour de France the month before. I remem-

ber at the time seeing the pictures of Greg in the newspaper and in *Sports Illustrated,* that grinning, almost astonished look he had on his face. When he was pictured off the bike, he seemed always to have one of his hands to the top of his head, as if saying, without words, "My God, can you believe this is happening to me?" I remember thinking, what a humble guy, an ordinary person achieving extraordinary things.

Whenever I had ridden a bicycle, I had said to myself, "My God, can you believe this is happening to me?"

It would come to pass, in the process of trying to write a story about LeMond, that I would interview him for a couple of hours during the days in Georgia and, a few months later, for another couple of hours at his house in the suburbs of Minneapolis. I recorded all this with an old microcassette recorder, on a number of little tapes that I carry with me in my briefcase to this day. On those tapes LeMond is exactly like the person I imagined I had known my whole life: funny, smart, completely without ego, totally self-deprecating, and honest to a fault. When I was in the presence of Greg LeMond, I couldn't help thinking, yes, this man is my friend.

I also read every document I could find on the subject of Greg LeMond and watched every LeMond clip on YouTube, both in English and French, and in the process I transformed myself into a walking encyclopedia on all things Greg LeMond.

In my career as a writer and in my life as a cycling enthusiast, meeting and hanging out with Greg LeMond topped the list of things I had been able to do, and because, like Greg LeMond, I am not the type of person to keep my mouth shut, I told everybody I knew the great story of how I met Greg LeMond and what a fantastic person the guy is, how funny, how genuine, what a regular guy. I told people how I had come to learn, through meeting Greg LeMond, that truly great people have nothing to prove and can therefore be some of the friendliest, most humble people in the world.

When all my friends and colleagues and fellow cyclists who loved Armstrong would defend their own hero, I would say, "I don't know Lance Armstrong and what he's all about, but I've met Greg LeMond, and all that talk about Greg being crazy or angry or jealous of Lance, that's a bunch of crap. Greg is totally cool."

I never wrote the story.

In fact, after I drove away from LeMond's house in 2006, I hardly wrote a word for the next two years and lost interest in cycling and essentially fell apart in almost every way a grown man can fall apart. I would say it's a miracle that I am alive and even more a miracle that I once again sling my leg over the top tube of my bicycle and take it out for a ride nearly every day of the week.

Once in a while, during those two years, friends of mine would ask, "You still writing?"

I would lie. "I've got six projects going," I'd say. "I love writing."

Or people would look at me, at a certain puffiness you don't see in cyclists who ride twenty-five hours a week the way I once had. "You still riding your bike?" they'd say.

"Here and there," I'd lie, "but not like I used to."

Sometimes people would say to me, "Whatever happened to Greg LeMond?"

I would stare at my shoes and say, with complete honesty, "I don't know."

I still don't know. The last time I saw him was at his house, on July 26, 2006, several hours before the story broke that Floyd Landis had tested positive for testosterone doping after his miraculous comeback in Stage 17 of the Tour de France. LeMond was happy about the Tour and thought it had been raced cleanly, something that mattered a great deal to him. We talked for a couple of hours, then he walked me to my truck, which was parked at the end of his driveway. The skies were as clear blue as LeMond's eyes. We shook hands, and I drove away. Within an hour, I was in downtown Minneapolis having coffee with my mistress. She was smoking a cigarette and was not happy with me for having taken so long talking with Greg LeMond, whose name she didn't recognize. The next day, while I was driving from Minneapolis back to southern Illinois, a twelve-hour drive over not-very-scenic interstate, I heard on the radio that Floyd had been caught, and I said to my mistress, "This is going to be a calamity. Greg will definitely speak up about this."

She didn't care. She changed the radio to a station that played pop music and said, "Is that all you think about is bikes?"

It was—though right about then that was starting to not be true anymore. For years I had more or less done nothing with my life but ride my bicycles or work on my bicycles or read books about riding or books about working on bicycles, and I certainly had gotten much out of the lifestyle, the kind of benefits any cyclist knows so well. Then for reasons that I can only begin to approach by saying I had lost my mind, I had betrayed my wife and taken up with a mistress who was overweight, smoked heavily, was in her midtwenties, considerably younger than me, and had been a student in a class I'd taught the previous spring. I liked her, I guess, but I could never pinpoint why. She seemed like the person I was before I took up cycling but wasn't uptight about her weight or how much she smoked. Maybe I admired that about her.

I can't remember. Anyway, it wouldn't matter. A week from the day I drove away from Greg LeMond's home, I would meet another mistress, this one a person my age who didn't smoke and who loved bicycles as much as I did, and I fell in love with her as with no other woman I'd ever met. The smoker found out that I had taken up with the cyclist—I told her, actually—and we got into a huge argument and she went to my wife and told her what had been going on, then went to the university and told them what had been going on, and as you might imagine, I got kicked out of my house and came within a couple of millimeters of losing my job and ended up living with nothing, sleeping on the floor in a rented room and only seeing my children every other weekend. I lost the cyclist, the one I loved, as well. She lived halfway across the country from me and didn't know the extent of the collapse I had been going through. I didn't have the guts to tell her, so I just let it go and stepped away from my bike and checked out of the world.

The day I sat in the conference room at the Helendorf Hotel with the journalists and Greg LeMond and the Trek representatives, I wish I could have known what was going to happen to me and done something to stop it. Or maybe I knew somehow what was on the road ahead and just hoped, when it was all over, that I would land miraculously back on my feet.

On July 26, 2006, the day I was sitting in Greg LeMond's house in the suburbs of Minneapolis, in his study, a warm room with books on the shelves, some nice leather furniture, a couple of trophies, which I didn't bother to ask about because they didn't seem to be a big deal to Greg, he was asking me about my life, my career, not

because he was kissing my ass to come off like a swell guy in a magazine but because he is a swell guy, a regular guy. Outside the window to the study, the spacious green manicured lawn of his estate
looked perfectly elegant in the July-afternoon sunshine. He seemed
a little edgy, though. His son Geoffrey was scheduled to come home
from France later in the day, and the thought of the flight, the
travel, the connections, and so forth, concerned LeMond. Apparently, Geoffrey had ridden L'Étape du Tour, the event that lets am-
ateurs ride a stage of that year's Tour de France, and had a great
time, and after that, he'd gone to stay with some friends of the family. Greg himself was thinking about going along with him the next
year and riding L'Étape. It struck me that Greg wouldn't really be
going there because he wanted to ride; he wanted to be near his
son. He paused somewhere in there, when he had been talking
about his son—maybe he was thinking about what it would mean
to return to France at the time of the Tour; maybe he was thinking
about things a writer like me had no right to know—and became
more serious than I'd seen him.

He remained oddly quiet.

For a second, I wanted to tell him how fucked up my life had become. I wanted to say, "Man, I'm cheating on my wife, and I
brought my mistress with me on the trip here to the Twin Cities.
She's in downtown Minneapolis right now, smoking cigarettes,
hoping I keep it snappy during my interview with you." I felt like
crying and asking him for advice. Surely Greg LeMond would know
what to do?

But I kept my business a secret. He had secrets too, I suppose.

Neither of us could have known right then that Landis had tested
positive for testosterone, and that this would eventually lead to
LeMond appearing in a California courtroom and admitting he
had been sexually abused when he was a child. We had no way of
knowing that on this very hour we were talking, somewhere in
France professional cycling was teetering on knife edge over the
very issue that had made this great champion, this terrific man,
into a controversial, unpopular figure in his own country, not because of what he had done but because of what he had said.

Instead, Greg was running his hand through his hair and saying
how Landis had raced clean, and the proof was, look, he got tired
and had a bad day in the mountains then came back and had a

good day. "That," LeMond said, "is what happens when riders race clean." He also said what a great person Landis was and how well the French would receive him and how, just a couple of months ago, he had met Floyd's father and really thought Floyd's father was a fine person.

He fell silent again. I got the feeling I shouldn't be looking at him. Somebody was moving around outside the window: a gardener fiddling with an extension cord. People were talking in other parts of the house. Maybe LeMond was listening to see if his son had come home.

I could remember the day LeMond met Floyd's father, because I was there. Geoffrey LeMond was there too.

On the day of the Brasstown Bald finish, the Tour de Georgia held a VIP party at the summit of the climb, in a park-service interpretive center. LeMond was one of the VIPs. Earlier in the day, in a driving rainstorm, he had stepped up to the bandstand at the start of the stage and fired the starter's pistol. This took place in a parking lot of a school, and the rain was falling so hard that no crowd had assembled; nobody seemed to be there but journalists and bike racers. When the emcee announced LeMond's name, the racers at the line hardly looked up. Rain pelted their helmets; they stared at their handlebars; this was going to be a miserable day in the saddle. LeMond fired the gun, the riders rode off, and within two minutes, the rain quit. Just as suddenly, when LeMond stepped down off the starter's stage, he was surrounded by cycling fans. Where they came from, I couldn't guess, and he shook their hands and signed autographs, all the time looking around nervously for Geoffrey's whereabouts. Geoffrey was in the Waffle House hospitality tent drinking coffee. Geoffrey was twenty-one years old at the time, a bit taller than his dad, and very skinny, and considerably more shy, or at least in this context he seemed to be. Geoffrey looked like he might be a quiet aspiring poet in a coffee shop; Greg looked the wisecracking guy in charge of the paint department at Ace TrueValue.

An hour later, I was in the back seat of a car with LeMond, on the way to Brasstown Bald. Geoffrey was in the front seat with one of the guys from Trek. We were laughing and joking and talking about what great cycling roads we were driving on. As we got closer to the mountain, we could see that crowds had gathered; cars were parked everywhere on the roadside, and people riding bicycles were everywhere. This was a huge crowd, though overall apparently the race was drawing about half as many fans as the previous year. Armstrong wasn't racing in the Tour de Georgia this year.

When we reached Brasstown itself, we could drive only so far up the mountain: no cars were allowed all the way to the top. So we parked in a VIP lot and started walking the last two kilometers up the steep road. Our group was LeMond and his son, several other journalists, and several Trek folks, and we walked right along the road's centerline. Maybe 1,500, maybe 2,000 people were lining the road behind barriers, and this slow, uphill parade to the top was simply astonishing to witness. However much LeMond may have irritated or bored the American public, however much he had supposedly offended and angered Lance Armstrong and throngs of yellow-braceleted fans, amid the crowd here on this steep pitch of a Georgia mountain, LeMond walked to resounding cheers. No one said a harsh word. People took pictures. He shook hands. The grin on his face was the winning grin we loved so long ago; it was as if he were walking slowly up the last two kilometers to a Grand Tour victory of the American mind.

At the top, while the race approached, the idea was that Greg would autograph posters for the various VIPs who were in attendance, and there were many in attendance, though I didn't recognize any of them. People milled around and drank wine and munched snacks and watched the race on big-screen TVs. It would be ninety minutes or so before the leaders would reach the base of Brasstown. The VIPs seemed to be comfortable with the situation, and folks were drinking and talking and acting as if they had all known each other for years and years, which they may well have. The only people who looked out of place were several women and several girls wearing the modest dresses and prayer caps of the Mennonite faith. The Landis family, of course. The young girls played, and the women supervised. It warmed the heart to see it.

On the far side of the gathering, a long line of people had formed, people waiting to meet Greg LeMond and have their poster signed. The poster was a picture of LeMond victoriously crossing the finish line in the 1989 World Championships, ahead of Dimitri Konyshev and Sean Kelly. In the picture, LeMond is soaking wet after a brutal day in the rain at Chambéry, France, and he's not making a victory salute: his mouth is wide open as if to express a lifetime of joy and pain and ecstasy all in one marvelous, inexpressible yell. When he was signing these posters, LeMond was sitting down at a chair, in front of a table, with Geoffrey not too far from his side, but when Landis's dad appeared in front of him, LeMond stood and shook the man's hand.

"I really admire your son," LeMond said. "This is mine."

Eventually, three months later, in late July, it was time for me to take my leave of Greg LeMond. We left his study and walked past his kitchen, which was modern and behind which was a room that I couldn't see well but appeared to have some magnificent French-looking paintings on the wall. We wandered outside through his three-car garage that contained the usual stuff people have in garages—weed trimmer, lawn mower, garbage cans, some bikes—and walked onto his large asphalt driveway that overlooked a few terraced drops leading to a grassy area with some woods beyond. I was sad to go and wanted to come out with something profound to mark the occasion, but all I could think to say was, "This property would make an excellent cyclocross course."

He laughed and said that it certainly would. One of these years, maybe he'd get around to building one.

My pickup truck—a beat-up, scratched-up old Ford—was parked at the end of the drive, and he approached it with me. In a rack in the pickup's bed was my trusty steel 'cross bike, very dirty, and I had been mountain biking with it, a lot, and had cracked the frame at the top of the seat tube but was still riding it daily. The bike was a disgrace. The truck was a disgrace. And here I was with one of the most famous people in the sport of cycling.

He said, "You're still riding that?"

"Yes, sir," I said. "Every day."

"Aren't you afraid it might crumble underneath you? You could get hurt if that happened, you know?"

"I know," I said. "But right now, it's the only functioning bike I have."

This was true. Money was tight for me, and when money is tight, it's hard to keep a fleet of top-end bicycles in the stable. Greg looked at the bike, at the truck, at me, and he could see I was just being honest with him, talking to him man to man.

He said, "Why don't you take one of my bikes out of the garage?"

He had one of the brand-new LeMond carbon-fiber bikes in there, with the Bontrager carbon clincher wheelset and everything. Those wheels alone were probably worth twice as much as my 'cross bike when it was brand-new.

He said, "You should take that carbon bike. Looks like you could use one."

I have replayed this moment in my mind at least a thousand times. I leveled my eyes into his, the famous blue champion eyes, the eyes that had seen victory on the most magnificent platforms in the cycling world, and I said, "No thanks, man. I'll get by."

He didn't press the issue. He knew I was just too proud to accept a handout, and that was the end of it. We shook hands, and I drove off into the distance and into a downward spiral it would take me two years to halt.

I don't know whatever happened to Greg LeMond. Since I saw him last, he's been in the news a few times: once for appearing at the Landis hearing and admitting that he had been molested as a child, another time for suing a land developer in Montana, another time for suing the Trek Corporation, which finally severed all ties with him and discontinued the manufacture of LeMond bicycles, and another time for appearing at one of Lance Armstrong's press conferences and grilling him on his drug-testing program. It was enough to make me wonder if maybe Greg, finally, had used up his chances, had lost his panache. But maybe that's where the guys who have it need to get before they can surprise us by unveiling it once more — maybe what the rest of us think of as its disappearance is part of its existence.

The other day my twelve-year-old daughter called me on the phone, freaking out about a ghost program she had watched on TV.

"Dad, I'm losing it," she said. "That ghost was so intense!"

"If the ghost shows are too much for you," I said, "watch something else."

"But ghost shows are my favorite!"

I live halfway across the country from her these days and haven't seen her in months. Money's still awfully tight for me. I can't pay my bills, let alone buy a plane ticket. The only lifeline I have to my daughter is a cell phone and conversations about what she's watching on TV.

She said, "How soon do I get to visit you, Dad?"

I still see Greg LeMond on a regular basis, not the real Greg but the Greg of my imagination, which is the American imagination, the one where people from anywhere, from any circumstances, have the opportunity to make their dreams come true. The Greg I see is a thirteen-year-old kid who lives in the country at the top of a large hill that might not even have a name. It is not a col; it is a change in elevation on the surface of the earth. The kid will have Greg's youthful blond hair and that youthful wild-eyed grin, and this kid will get on a bicycle and bomb down that steep hill and charge back up it again, and do this over and over till he thinks, oh, maybe I'll do something else. When he gets off his bike, maybe he'll take his fishing pole to the river and try to catch the world-record smallmouth bass; maybe he'll dream of driving racecars or flying airplanes or growing up someday to become the champion of the world in sport. He is a kid who is hopeful and strong, interested in everything and everybody, and he will know the world is wide open for him to explore. He will be the best America has to offer, humble, joyful in victory and, in losing, honored to have competed with the winner. No harm will come to this kid. Nothing bad will ever happen to him. At the end of his day, when he goes home to his family and reports what he experienced in the world, he will say, "Wow, isn't that something? I can't wait to go see it all again."

CYNTHIA GORNEY

Ripped. (Or Torn Up?)

FROM THE NEW YORK TIMES MAGAZINE

THERE WAS NO MOON over the tennis stadium, but it was after midnight, the risers still crowded, and Rafael Nadal was playing the Argentine David Nalbandian. This was in Indian Wells, California, three months ago, at a tournament in the desert called the BNP Paribas Open. People had taken off their visors and straw hats, and the night now was windless and warm, and although Nadal is number one in the world and Nalbandian was that week number eleven, Nadal was having a terrible first set. He'd try one of his scary forehand drives, the whole arm whipping around so fast and the wrist snap so fluid that it's like watching a thick rope flicked and hissing, and he'd *uuunhh* the way he does as his racket meets the ball, the sharp grunt that for an instant would be the only sound in the stadium, and then the ball would splat straight into the net. Or the ball would go long, meant to drop spinning just inside the baseline but instead sailing a whole foot out, and thousands of people would wince all at once. "It's okay, Rafa, come on." Sometimes the stadium fans love to roll the R in the Spanish manner, especially when they're singing to him, *"RRRAfa, RRRAfa,"* but these were sober, unaccented voices calling from the risers to Nadal, who didn't look up.

He'd been playing this way for an hour. It was a best-of-three-sets tournament, and finally he lost the first, 3–6. If he lost the second, he was done.

He sat and drank some water. He took off his shirt, which made spectators start wolf-whistling, and put on a fresh one. Nalbandian changed his shirt too, but nobody wolf-whistled at him. The umpire called for the start of the second set.

I said to some people near me, Rafa's not going to win this match, is he.

The look they gave me was amused, knowing, and kind. A woman said, "Watch him." She was smiling.

Nadal set down his water bottle beside a second water bottle. He lifted the second one, took a sip, and replaced it in the exact spot where it stood before. As he readied himself to serve, he tucked his sweaty hair behind his ears with one hand, left ear first, then right ear. He reached around to his backside to pull loose his shorts. The Spaniards who travel with him call these his *manías*, his on-court tics; Nadal is messy at home, and when he was a teenager in Majorca, his mother used to complain about his room. But in competition, his rituals are precise, like those of many sports champions. Nike, which pays Nadal more than $3 million a year to wear its clothes, has never designed a pair of shorts that kept Nadal from loosening the seat just before he serves the ball.

Now he started to play. At tournaments, teenage girls scream when they see Nadal walk onto a tennis court, literally shriek and leap to their feet and clutch each other; women older than his mother shiver and elbow their friends; men raise their cameras aloft; there's flash-popping and Spanish flag–unfurling and a rising swell of noise and applause, and at some point Nadal lifts one arm and smiles at spectators, which sets off momentary pandemonium among the women. (Once, pressed between two middle-aged ladies who had worked their way to the front of a crowd staring through a wire fence at Nadal on a practice court, I asked the one on my left to speak specifically of the appeal. "Um, his tenacity," she said. "His energy. His . . ." And the lady on my right snapped, without taking her eyes off Nadal: "His hotness. Just get to it.") He is barely twenty-three, and I've heard people describe him as an evolutionary leap, the kind of new life form that materializes every few generations in tennis and makes everybody ecstatic and argumentative and eloquent. There is debate among serious tennis watchers, for example, as to whether Nadal's victory over Roger Federer in the Wimbledon final last year was the greatest tennis match ever played or whether it has only been *called* the greatest tennis match ever played when, in fact, Nadal's victory over his Spanish countryman Fernando Verdasco in the semifinals of the Australian Open in January was greater.

Each match went on for more than four and a half hours. Each was desperate, operatic, repeatedly to-the-brink-and-back; each ended with Nadal collapsing to the court in triumph and the spectators exhausted and perspiring, and if you are not a tennis person, I suspect this may be somewhat hard to fathom—the idea that watching two men spend that many hours hitting a ball could actually make your heart pound so hard that you have to keep jumping up and yelling and grabbing your own head. But let me just suggest that if there were ever a time to understand why people invoke Shakespearean tragedy and ancient gladiators and so on when they carry on about competitive tennis, now is that time.

Wimbledon, which starts this week, will feature Nadal as a looming presence whether he plays the tournament or not. Two weeks ago, he received a diagnosis of tendinitis in both knees and announced that he would immediately start anti-inflammatories and recuperative therapy to try to make himself, in his words, "100 percent ready to play." This served only to crank up the plotline: Federer, the Swiss champion who many people believe is the most brilliant tennis player in history, is locked into unpredictable, week-by-week, multi-episodic combat with the Spaniard whom Andre Agassi recently called a "freak of nature" and who has taken Federer's place as the top-ranked player in the world.

Nadal lost the French Open three weeks ago, yes. He lost shockingly, unexpectedly, before even reaching the quarterfinals. The knees might or might not have been a factor; Nadal refused to make any injury excuses for his defeat, but in any case, it was the first match he ever lost at the French Open, which he had won four times in a row. Because he left early, before he and Federer could face each other, there will always be an unanswered question attached to Federer's championship: the French was the only one of the four Grand Slam tournaments, the majors, that Federer had never been able to win. He was beaten there by Nadal four years in a row. In last year's final, in fact, Nadal obliterated him so completely that people either stared in fascination or averted their eyes, as though witnessing a dreadful car wreck. For a few days, when I was at the French Open, Nadal's defeat made for richer drama than anybody else's victory, and I would not really have understood why that was had I not also been at Indian Wells in the middle of the night in March and watched Nadal's face during that

second set against Nalbandian, especially when Nadal began moving faster and faster, coiling, springing, powering the ball into back
corners, missing, driving again. After a time, I realized a new sound
was coming from Nadal in between the hitting grunts, an even
more guttural sound that was low, feral, and drawn out between
intakes of breath. He was growling.

Nadal's postmatch press conferences always begin the same way:
the door beside the lectern opens, he walks in loose-limbed and
with his hair disheveled and he sits down and says politely into the
microphone, "Hello." He still grapples with English, being in his
daily life a speaker of Spanish and Mallorquín, which is a variant of
Catalan and even harder to understand, unless you grew up on the
island of Majorca. So it comes out "HHAllo," and he takes the English questions first. I've seen him do this with a half-eaten chocolate chip cookie in his hand, grinning and wiping crumbs from his
mouth; but after he finished beating Nalbandian, he looked dark
and irritated.

"I am not happy," he said. "I am not happy about myself in the
first two sets." It was almost 3 A.M. Nadal won the second set 7–6 in
a tiebreaker and the third 6–0, and by the time everything was over,
Nalbandian looked as if somebody had been hitting him with a
broom all night. "I was scared about his backhand," Nadal said. "I
think I didn't go to the match with a clear idea of how to play."

He needed a shave, though in truth he usually looks as if he
needs a shave; it's part of the allure. When he's pleased, he has a
way of smiling with half his mouth too, as though he's shyly just
starting to realize how good he feels; the effect is of a young Harri-
son Ford, but with unbelievable biceps, and the combination of
on-court savagery and off-court humility has disarmed people who
have followed tennis closely for decades. "I don't think I've ever
seen a guy acting as natural, as a champion, as Rafael Nadal," the
French writer Philippe Bouin told me recently. Bouin has been
covering tennis for thirty years for the sports paper L'Équipe. He is
regarded as a sage in the tournament newsrooms, and when I first
met him, at a tournament in Miami, he mused aloud about the
extraordinary relationship between Nadal and Federer, each of
whom regards the other as the most admirable and dangerous
competitor he has ever faced.

"You must remember," Bouin said gently, in his lovely accented English, "that in tennis you have to *kill* the other." Not just play better. Sometimes the one who plays better can lose. It's a sport of splendid cruelty, for all its decorum and finicky trappings; every winning point comes when the other guy, in front of a whole stadium of people staring directly at him, is forced by his opponent into inadequacy. He lunges for the ball but whiffs, he whacks it long, he hits it into the net, he screws up. From the stands, you sometimes see players surrender not because they don't know how to return the shots coming at them but because the specter of this impending inadequacy has suddenly just taken over their brains. It transpires right in front of your eyes: something sags, and they go sort of limp; you can see their faces and their posture start registering *get me out of here.*

When he's on — which is most of the time but not always, thereby heightening the suspense — Nadal is better than anybody at making this happen to opponents. If he does play Wimbledon these next two weeks and wins, or if he holds off and recuperates and perhaps goes on to win the U.S. Open in September, he will have earned legitimate entry into the ranks of the all-time greats — not just the world number ones, in other words, but the players whose names make up those best-ever lists that are constantly being debated and rearranged by fans. Federer floats around at the top of those lists, along with a dozen or so others (Agassi, Pete Sampras, John McEnroe, Sweden's Bjorn Borg, Australia's Rod Laver, and so on). Two of the three reasons for preparing to consider Nadal for these ranks, contentious as such propositions tend to be, are straightforward:

1. He wins on all three court surfaces on which the world's four most important tennis tournaments are now played: the grass of Wimbledon, which Nadal won for the first time last summer; the hard acrylic composition used at the Australian Open, which Nadal won in January, and the U.S. Open, which has so far eluded him; and the soft red clay of the French Open, on which Nadal and Borg share the record of four straight titles. (On clay, in fact, Nadal is the best player who has ever lived. Until losing to Federer two years ago in Hamburg, Nadal had a streak of eighty-one victories on clay, a record that took on such a life of its own that people around Nadal felt a certain relief when the streak ended.) Being a

three-surface champion at this level of competition is almost impossibly difficult, requiring three kinds of pacing, strategy, and ball attack; it's as if an international track star won gold in the 100 meters, the mile, and the steeplechase. There are undisputed great players—Sampras, McEnroe, and Jimmy Connors, for example—who never in their careers mastered the French Open's clay.

2. He spent three whole years second in the world only to Federer, who during those years could not only outplay everybody but, in many people's opinions, could probably have outplayed anybody who ever lived and nonetheless could not get past Nadal in Paris. Nadal was a phenomenal number two. His number-two-ness was heroic and inspirational, and he was known to mention it quite cheerfully in press conferences: "I'm not the best, but I am a *very* good number two in the world."

3. He thrills people. Federer thrills people too, but the Nadal thrill is so different from the Federer thrill that studying the two of them is like a gorgeous immersion course in the varieties of athletic possibility. Federer is elegant and fluid and cerebral, so that his best tennis looks effortless even when he is making shots that ought to be physically impossible. Nadal is muscled-up and explosive and relentless, so that his best tennis looks not like a gift from heaven but instead like the product of ferocious will. His victories and his taped-up knees and his years as a *very* good number two in the world all resonate together, as though the rewards and the wages of individual effort had been animated in a single human being: if you hurl yourself at a particular goal furiously enough and long enough you may tear your body up in the process, but maybe you can get there after all. People have loved watching Nadal create trouble inside Federer's head. This is how they characterize it in tennis, that Nadal makes Federer crazy, that Nadal's refusal over and over to be beaten by Federer in Paris was the one problem that Federer—who usually has uncanny on-court telepathy about what his opponent plans for three shots hence and exactly how to wreck it—was unable to figure out.

Then Nadal finally beat Federer at Wimbledon too, and then at the Australian, where Federer famously picked up his runner-up trophy and looked at the assembled reporters and burst into tears, causing Nadal to put an arm around him, the young Spaniard at once respectful and consoling, and murmur something private into his ear. That Nadal now has the capacity to outplay Federer on multiple surfaces—that the signature game of the world's highest-ranked tennis player is not a beautiful ballet unto victory but an imperfect, bruising, savage refusal to yield—this is why Nadal thrills people. This and the biceps. "Every tennis lover would like, someday, to play like Federer," Philippe Bouin told me. "But every man wants to be Rafael Nadal. Which is different."

Nadal has played tennis left-handed since he was eleven, but he uses his right hand to sign autographs, wave, play golf, turn on video games, and react fast to most things that require a hand. "Watch," he said to me in Spanish one afternoon this spring, nodding toward his publicity man, Benito Perez-Barbadillo, who was lounging around nearby. "Benito! Throw something at me." Perez-Barbadillo tossed his cell phone. Nadal's right arm jerked up and grabbed the phone out of the air, and he smiled and shrugged. "Whatever involves feeling, I do with the right."

The word he used was *sensibilidad,* which means many kinds of feeling, literal and perceptual and emotional, and the assertion that Nadal does everything of *sensibilidad* right-handed seemed sort of preposterous, given what tennis requires of the hand that is holding the racket. Hitting a tennis ball in elite competition is like a cross between boxing and pitching a baseball, situationally complicated like either but executed at much faster speed and requiring split-second calculations about many more variables: how hard; how high; angle of racket head; wind speed; court surface; how much ball spin; what kind of ball spin (top, side, or back?); where exactly to aim within an area thirty-nine feet long by twenty-seven feet wide; opponent's weaknesses, state of mind, footing stance, and location not at this exact instant but in the time it will take for the ball to cross the net, etc. *Sensibilidad* of the left hand, I wondered—surely Nadal possesses that when he holds a tennis racket?

"That's the only thing with the left," he said. "Well, I'm ambidextrous when I eat. But playing tennis right-handed—I can't do it. I'm clueless. Benito could beat me."

Perez-Barbadillo made a face at him, and Nadal scrunched amiably into his armchair, his long legs crossed at the ankle on the low table in front of him. We were in the players' lounge at the Indian Wells tournament, which is not one of the four Grand Slam events but is the inaugural U.S. stop of the year and draws nearly every top player in the world. Massive posters of Nadal were plastered all over the tennis complex, like Times Square billboards, so that from on high he was smiling or making killer faces over the carnival array of standard tennis tournament commerce: frozen-lemonade stands, food courts, oversize yellow balls for collecting autographs. Nadal sometimes has burly guys in sunglasses with him when he walks on the pathways between courts, and although it's plain why they accompany him — parents shove their autograph-ball-brandishing children through adult crowds toward Nadal, and once I heard a young woman repeat in a low, ominous voice, "You *don't* ignore me, you *don't ignore me*," as she was trying to catch his eye — the fans adore him partly because he moves so sweetly in their midst.

He signs the balls and the bare arms and the T-shirts. He rumples small boys' hair. He waits while people press up alongside him to pose for snapshots. The Nadal personality stories that circulate among tournament fans are all variations on a single theme: the young man is *educado,* as they say in Spanish, not so much educated in the formal sense (Nadal left conventional schooling after he turned pro at fifteen), but courteous, respectful, raised by a family with its priorities in order. Nadal may have the on-court demeanor of a hit man, as far as the party across the net is concerned, but you will never see this champion hurl his racket during a match.

The only lead coach Nadal has ever had — highly unusual in tennis, where frequently players discard coaches one after another in their effort to ascend the competitive ranks — is one of his paternal uncles, Toni Nadal. Toni is the impassive man, usually in sunglasses and a cap and with his arms crossed placidly over his chest, that the television cameras turn to periodically during Nadal's matches. Among the numerous Rafa-and-Toni stories I heard in the stands: that Toni declared years ago that if he ever saw Rafa lose his temper on the court (racket-hurling is the standard tantrum, but there's also cursing the line judges, sulking, and yelling at spectators), their coaching relationship would end on the spot. Or that Toni refuses on principle to carry Rafa's rackets for him. Or that they always fly commercial because Toni scoffs at the idea of a tennis star, even one worth scores of millions, believing that he merits a private jet.

These accounts turn out to be exaggerated, but not by much. "No, no, I've never delivered ultimatums to him," Toni said dismissively in Spanish when I met him in Miami in March. "He knows he can't throw a racket. He just knows. As far as I'm concerned, it's shameful when he orders a *meal* and doesn't finish it. Understand? Same thing with rackets. These rackets cost money."

It is true, Toni says, that he taught Rafael years ago to put his tennis shoes on carefully, not mashing his feet over the backs and slopping around as though in slippers. It is also true that Toni expects Rafael to carry his own rackets; that Rafael plays left-handed because of something Toni figured out long ago; and that at a tournament a few years back, when Rafael's manager, Carlos Costa, asked Toni to make Rafael stop eating the chocolate croissants he was wolfing down before a match, Toni raised his eyebrows at Costa and said no. "*Que tenga dolor de estómago,*" Toni said. Let him get a stomachache. Tomorrow he'll know not to do it again.

"It's about respect," Toni told me. "It's really easy for these guys to start thinking the world revolves around them. I never could have tolerated it if Rafael had become a good player and a bad example of a human being. I was at a symposium recently and a trainer said to me, 'Look, if you ask a young player's father which he'd rather get at the end of this process—a courteous person or the French Open champion—you *know* what that father is going to say.' And I said: 'No, that's all wrong. Because if that player is brought up courteous, brought up as a respectful person, he's got a better chance to reach the championship of the French Open —because it's going to be easier for him to accomplish the hard work.'"

Both Toni and Rafael still live in Majorca, along with multiple Nadal relatives, in a nontouristy little city called Manacor, about fifteen miles from the beach. A four-story building has served for many years as an informal family compound, housing Rafael's parents, his younger sister, his grandparents, and various other relations. Rafael has his own apartment there, with workout machines and the PlayStation he likes to take with him on the road, and in the Majorcan tradition, there are also Nadal weekend houses at the beach. It is not an athletics-obsessed family—one of Rafael's grandfathers is a retired orchestra conductor, and his father, the oldest of five brothers, owns real estate and a window-and-glass business in Manacor. But Toni, the second oldest, learned tennis as a child, on what was then one of the few courts in Majorca; he was nationally ranked in Spain before becoming a tennis teacher and then opening his own club on the island. Miguel Ángel, the youngest of the brothers, was a professional soccer player when Rafa was born.

There was a lot more soccer than tennis during Rafa's early childhood, in fact. Miguel Ángel was picked up by one of the best teams in the country; he played for the Spanish national team in three World Cups, and some of his own first instincts about Rafael came from watching the boy play against his adult relatives during a keep-away game in which people in a circle try to pass a ball back and forth to one another past someone at the center of the circle. The only way for the middle person to get out and become a passer is to intercept a pass. "He *liked* being the middle," Miguel Ángel told me. "We'd all do our tricky maneuvers to try to get the ball past him. Any one of a hundred little kids, you do those kinds of moves on him, he'll start crying. But Rafa, no. He'd keep fighting to get the ball."

The family apartment hallways and local streets served for ball-handling practice too, and before long, Rafael was the leading scorer even on teams of boys older than he was. "I was passionate about soccer," Rafael told me. "I still am. Odd, though — playing soccer always made me much more anxious than playing tennis. On soccer days, I'd be out of bed by six in the morning, all nervous. But I was always calm when it was time for a tennis match. I still don't know why."

In tennis circles, Nadal is occasionally mentioned in the same sentence with Tiger Woods, as in: some matters appear explainable by upbringing and training, and some by a felicitous accident of natural design. (When Agassi used the term "freak of nature," he hastened to add that he meant it as a compliment — Agassi was at the French Open issuing public praise of Federer and observing that only the freak of nature from Majorca had kept Federer from multiple French Open victories already.) Like Woods, Nadal started what would become his career sport when he was a toddler; Toni remembers his nephew having been no older than three. "He was at the club one day, and I handed him a racket, we had some little ones, and then tossed a ball at him," Toni said before practice one morning in Miami. "When he hit it back — two-handed, he wouldn't have been strong enough otherwise—I said to myself, 'Okay, this is not normal.' His feet, especially, the way he'd move himself into good hitting position when I tossed balls at him. This is a rare thing in a child."

Rafael's parents have a standard policy of declining interview requests; their support for him is by all accounts unwavering but uniformly private, and when I asked Toni how the family managed the destined-to-do-this challenge, how you help a gifted child flourish without oppressing or souring him, he shot me a look that was at once mocking and stern. "I don't believe anybody's destined to do anything in this life," he said. He is firmly *antireligioso,* his term, and he also seems to take pleasure in placing the game of tennis—"being able to pass a ball back and forth over a net," as I've heard him describe it—into its proper perspective in the universe. (Once when I used the word "drama" in a question about Rafa and Federer, Toni interrupted me midsentence. "This is not drama," he said. "Drama is people in Africa who don't have enough to eat. Drama is people no one ever smiles at. There is no drama here.") The primary athletic goal when Rafa was little was ensuring that he had fun, Toni said, and because the boy was the first grandchild, that wasn't hard to do.

"He was the family toy," Toni said. "We're all close. Everything was really a form of athletic training. He didn't come back to the club much when he was three, he'd get bored; but then when he was four, he'd come once or twice a week, and I started throwing balls at him a little harder. He still liked soccer more than tennis, and he was very good. Left-footed shooter. I started paying him when he scored—one euro for a left-footed goal, two euros for a right-footed goal."

The payment offers were partly Uncle Toni humor, he said; as Rafa grew, the two of them developed a series of running jokes in which Toni simultaneously teased, prodded, and made himself comically huge. He invented a mythical backstory in which he too was a famous *futbolista,* now retired, having played soccer brilliantly for a professional team in Italy. Toni had been known as El Gran Natali, he assured Rafa, and when *futbolista* friends of Miguel Ángel came to visit one day, Toni persuaded them to use this name in hearty greetings and to come up with tales for Rafa about the Great Natali's exploits on the field. But there was also a practical motive for the euros-for-goals deal: Toni was assessing Rafael's reactions, testing to see how instinctively and with what kind of power the boy used one side versus the other. "It's been said I was very clever for having changed him into a left-hander," Toni told me. "But it's not true. Because Rafael was left-footed, I thought he might turn out to be left-handed in tennis. When he started, he was playing with both hands—and he hit harder from the left." This is Rafael's recollection as well; whatever else he did every day with his right hand and foot, his physical strength seemed more concentrated on the other side. By the time he was eleven, he was playing competitive tennis regularly—so well, indeed, that Toni had already remarked to Rafa's father, "This boy will be the Spanish national champion someday"—but he was still grasping the racket two-handed, for forehand and backhand alike.

"So I asked him, 'How many top ten players play with two hands?'" Toni said. "He told me, 'None.' And I said, 'You're not going to be the first.'"

Nadal's arms, both of them, have inspired over the years a fervent subgroup of admirers, especially once he began appearing at international matches in what became his trademark outfit: sleeveless shirt, wide headband knotted around the unruly hair, and his celebrated *piratas,* rakish knee-length shorts that made him look like a surfer who lifted weights in his spare time. When Nike altered the ensemble early this year, in what everybody involved insists was a mutual decision by the company and Nadal's entourage (the idea was to move him into something more grown-up), there was a brief but spirited insurrection among the fans. The Vamos Brigade, an international Nadal-watching website frequented mostly by enamored and effusive women, set up a special discussion devoted to Nadal's new short-sleeved shirts and more conventional shorts; the title was "Official Mourning Thread." "I found that if I just stared at his face long enough, I could make the sleeves disappear and see him sleeveless in my brain," one correspondent wrote. Lamented another: "I miss the arms!!! The big, muscled, tanned arms." Perhaps the young man was ready for a change, someone suggested. The response was quick and curt: "Please leave us alone to grieve."

The arms have also been considered with more seriousness of

purpose, as have the legs, by observers trying to dissect the mechanics of Nadal's power and to guess at the cumulative toll his style of play may be taking on his body. The coach Robert Lansdorp, who has worked with Pete Sampras and Maria Sharapova, among others, uses the informal label "reverse forehand" for Nadal's most characteristic stroke, his searing, spinning, miserable-to-return forehand drive. The crowds around Nadal's practice courts love to watch him up close as he repeats this stroke over and over; his racket appears to rip across the top of the tennis ball, shooting it toward the net like a twirling missile, not only brutally fast but also heavy-feeling and unpredictable on the bounce. The "reverse" part comes at the finish, which is sometimes not the traditional across-the-chest follow-through, but rather a defiant full-arm snap upward, as though Nadal were whipping a lariat over his head or delivering an Italian obscene gesture—almost the opposite, Lansdorp observes, of what coaches generally teach tennis students to do.

"It's not that he's the only one who hits this," Lansdorp says. "Nadal just does it to an extreme, and he's really mastered that reverse forehand to a great extent. He can do it from anyplace, almost to any ball, and make winners. He can hit it cross court, down the line, wherever he wants to go. And he's probably done it since he was ten. Thank God nobody changed it and told him, 'Hey, that is not the way to hit a forehand.'"

The ferocity of Nadal's spinning forehand was quantified three years ago, in fact, when a San Francisco tennis researcher named John Yandell used a high-speed video camera and special software to count the average number of revolutions of a tennis ball hit full force by Nadal. "We've measured the spin rates on the forehands of quite a few of the top players, including Nadal, Federer, Sampras, and Andre Agassi," Yandell told me when I visited the apartment from which he runs his online teaching site, www.tennisplayer.net, where videos and explanations of many famous players' strokes are posted. (A brief Yandell video analysis of Nadal's stroke can be found on nytimes.com.) "The first guys we did were Sampras and Agassi. They were hitting forehands that in general were spinning about 1,800 to 1,900 revolutions per minute." Sampras's serve, the deadliest in tennis during his five years as the world number one, was so hard to return partly because it combined so much speed with so much spin, Yandell said. "One guy who played against him said to me once: 'John, I can return to guys who serve faster than Pete. But the problem with Pete's serve is you're trying to return a bowling ball with a badminton racket.'"

Yandell chuckled. "Federer is hitting with an amazing amount of spin too, right? Twenty-seven hundred revolutions per minute. Well, we measured one forehand Nadal hit at 4,900. His average was 3,200. Think about that for a second. It's a little frightening to contemplate. It takes a ball about a second to travel between the players' rackets, okay?" He grabbed a calculator and punched in numbers. "So a Nadal forehand would have turned over eighty times in the second it took to get to Federer's racket. I don't know about you, but that's almost impossible for me to visualize."

Left-handedness has its own strategic advantages, in tennis as in baseball; Nadal has a strong two-handed backhand, but the geometry of tennis courts means the evil whirling forehand, his toughest shot, is easily aimed at the weaker backhand of righty opponents like Federer. It's not unreturnable, the way Sampras's serve often seemed to be; every competitor Nadal plays gets that shot back to him sometimes. But it tends to pin players at the back of the court, where they use all they have just trying to stay alive defensively. And it never, ever eases up. The coach Jose Higueras, who was also born in Spain but now directs elite player development for the U.S. Tennis Association, says he first saw Nadal play in Majorca, when the boy was fourteen. Rafael had reluctantly given up soccer by that time, after his soccer coach insisted that he devote himself to one sport or the other. He was fulfilling his uncle's predictions on the court: he won several junior national championships and was the first three-time consecutive winner of the international Nike Junior Tour. The Spanish national team was scouting him—Nadal would be brought on at sixteen and two years later help Spain win the 2004 Davis Cup—and Higueras says that as he watched the teenager, he was struck at once by the very quality that so reliably beats down Nadal's opponents now.

"The intensity, in every single shot he hit at that age, was unbelievable," Higueras says. "When you see him practice, it's pretty spectacular. Every ball he hits with the same intensity and power. Every day, it's like it's going to be the last practice of his life."

Juega cada punto como si fuera el último. They say at the tournaments that this is what Toni Nadal still hammers at his nephew: play every point as though it were the last—of the game, of the match, of the day, of your life. "It's out of respect for the sport," Toni told me when I asked him about it. "If you're going to do a thing, do it absolutely the best you can. Did I ever say it to him directly? No. In my family, there were lots of things my father never said to me. You just see them, in the attitude. From the time Rafael was little, he'd win that first point of the match, which nobody ever pays much attention to, and he'd yell, '*Vamos!*' All pumped up. Let's *go!* And you play like you train. As he grew up, he got used to training as though each point were the last one."

Nadal didn't shoot toward the top of the player rankings once he joined the pro tour at fifteen, in 2001. His first ranking was at number 1,002; it was 2003 when he cracked the top 100. He had a lot to learn. He couldn't "read" the court the way players like Federer did, intuiting where both ball and opponent would go next. He played hard from the back of the court, where his endurance and insistent groundstrokes gradually wore out his opponents, but he wasn't yet nimble or tricky at the net. His serve was oddly flabby for a player of such power—it still can be, in fact, though recently it has improved in both speed and precision. Once when I was talking to Toni, I wondered aloud whether in retrospect the two of them had sacrificed a certain *sensibilidad* when they settled on Nadal as a left-handed player, whether he's stronger with the left but might have been more exacting and coordinated with the right. I used the word *problemas* in my question, recalling Rafa's occasional critiques of his own serve, and then backtracked: wait, the guy's the best in the world, probably not right to call them problems, exactly. Toni watched me flounder and then started laughing.

"See what getting to be number one does!" he teased. "Here you are, thinking, 'Whoa, must watch my words carefully here.' Yes. It's possible he'd be serving better if he played right-handed. Throwing the ball perfectly is hard for him, and he doesn't always hit it at the correct height. The whole thing is just not something he does very well. We're working on it."

The relationship between Nadal's technique and his injuries has pursued him for years now, less because there's specific research to back it up (if you haven't suffered from hurting knees yourself at some point, you surely know someone who is not an elite athlete and has) than because it almost hurts to watch him play. The man just works so hard, and all the time, and at such tremendous velocity. And he has been doing this at tournament level, before spectators, since the age some children start T-ball. "More speed, bigger problems," Nadal's doctor, Angel Ruiz-Cotorro, told me when I visited him in Barcelona after Nadal lost at the French Open. "Tennis has changed a great deal in recent years. We used to talk about injuries: the elbow, the shoulder, the wrist. But in recent years, with the change in equipment materials—the rackets, mostly, but also the strings—we have whole new pathologies. Everything's faster. You're hitting the ball faster and harder, and in new positions, which creates problems with the spine, the knees, even the hips."

The tally of Nadal's ailments over the years is honestly not as impressive as that of many professional athletes: a stress fracture in his left foot, a banged-up elbow from a fall outside a tennis court, random knee and joint pains, the tendinitis. People imagine the whipping forehand must wreak havoc on his shoulders, but so far, at least, it has not. "We've been doing prevention stuff for years— some with weights, some with rubber resistance bands, always before starting play and after finishing," Ruiz-Cotorro said. "But Rafa's never put huge work into those shoulders, despite what people think. They came with the genes. If you look at his family, you'll see the same powerful constitution." (This is true; in their forties now, Toni and Miguel Ángel are both built like American football players.)

There is no question, though, that hardcourt surfaces are tougher on the body—the joints, the tendons, the back—than grass or clay. The harder Nadal works to hold his number-one ranking and try for tennis's career Grand Slam (titles in all four majors), the more he needs to dominate not only clay but also the harder-pounding material that covers the courts of the U.S. Open. The image of Nadal in poetic self-immolation, the glorious athlete pushing himself resolutely toward his own undoing, is so mesmerizing and distressing that I've heard it raised by spectators and coaches and by former competitors who now run the tournaments Rafa enters. Ruiz-Cotorro said he feels twinges of it himself, not just with Nadal but with many of the elites he's charged with trying to keep both healthy and in play. "It's brutally demanding, this obligation to win," he said. "But in order to do it, you use the best weapons you've got."

His remedies? Ruiz-Cotorro sighed. "Tendinitis is hard to treat," he said. "The first thing you have to do is decrease the inflammation and rest. He's resting now. But for an athlete like this, the word 'rest' does not exist."

Ruiz-Cotorro observed that since way back in the early *piratas* days, a kind of magnifying glass has been applied to everything that happens to Nadal on the tennis court. When I told Nadal about all the people who worried aloud to me about the level at which he is using up his body—this was back in March, it must be remembered, while he was winning everything in sight—he laughed and threw up his hands and looked for an instant less like an international tennis champion than a righteously ripped twenty-two-year-old being told he was going to hurt himself if he kept snowboarding so fast.

"They were saying this three years ago, that I couldn't last," Nadal said. "And after four years, I'm better than I ever was. This irritates me, no? I'm tired of people telling me I can't go on playing like this. In the end this is what makes me win, lose, everything. I can't control how I play. I want to keep getting better. And the most important part is the head."

After the Swedish player Robin Soderling beat him in the fourth round of the French Open, Nadal held one unsmiling press conference and then quickly went home with his support team, pleading to be left alone. He celebrated his birthday with his girlfriend and his family, the first time he had done so in five years, since the day falls during the tournament he had more or less come to own. Around the tournament site, the postmatch dissections traversed a wide range of physical and psychological territory, all of it speculative: Nadal's knees were bothering him. Or Nadal was depleted by the nonstop competition schedule. Or Nadal was rattled by just having lost a tournament in Madrid, in the finals and on clay and to Federer. Or Nadal was psyched out by Soderling, whose world ranking was only number twenty-three but who nonetheless hits powerful, flat balls—minimal spin, that is—that Nadal, even though he'd always beaten him before, finds a challenge to return.

At the press conference, the reporters kept after Nadal, in English and in Spanish, poking about for some revelatory quote. He had moments of looking like himself in the match, but not many. Soderling, who has a reputation for mental surrender under pressure, seemed to have been possessed by some sort of cosmic visitation. (Martina Navratilova, calling the match on television, cried out in admiration, "Soderling is playing out of his mind!") Nadal appeared heavy-footed and off-kilter from the first set on, and people who know his game grew increasingly perplexed as they awaited the familiar surge that smashed Nalbandian at Indian Wells and dozens of other opponents over the years. "Up until the end, everybody was saying, 'Something will happen, something will,'" Philippe Bouin told me when I found him at the French Open press center. "We've seen this movie many times. John Wayne never dies at the end of the movie. But this time, the cavalry was not there."

Nadal himself kept declining, with mounting frustration, to buy into any sort of Superhero Collapses Mysteriously narrative. "You know, guys, I lost," he said at one point, sounding uncharacteristically tetchy. "I *lost*. That's what I can say. I didn't play my best tennis today." People close to him say they could see it right away, both in the stadium and on television; Miguel Ángel Nadal, who was watching in Manacor, told me he watched the beginning of play and simply knew, one athlete to another, that this time the champion was going to struggle. It happens, Miguel Ángel said, and shrugged. "Same as when you go out in the street and you look up at the clouds and you know," he told me. "It's not going to be a good day."

In every Rafael Nadal press conference I've attended since March, somebody inevitably asks him about the pressures of being number one. He always has the same reaction: a certain expression flickers across his face, like *would you guys please just get over this,* and then he says something along the lines of: "I promise you, I don't get up in the morning thinking about being number one. I get up in the morning thinking that I've got a match, and I need to try to play as well as I possibly can." That rendition of the I Don't Think About It response was delivered in Spanish, to some reporters at Indian Wells, but I've heard it in Nadal's less-fluid English too, over and over: I'm fine, I don't dwell on it, I just want to play my best tennis.

One of Nadal's most endearing traits, since he assumed a starring role in international tennis, has been his public admiration for Federer. Nadal makes a practice of complimenting his opponents' abilities, even when he has just come from stomping all over them, but when he talks about Federer, he still sounds like the adulatory apprentice. "You are a great champion," Nadal said in English to Federer, in front of the whole tennis-watching world, at the Australian Open awards ceremony. "You are one of the best of history." Nadal had beaten him, of course, and some months earlier pushed Federer from the world number-one spot, and even after one has heard him deny it a dozen times, it's hard not to think it must be unsettling for the very good number two to adjust to the burden of finally having made it—of having achieved what he wanted, so that now the fight is no longer to get there but to stave off the hungry competitors behind him, one of whom is the master himself.

"Inside him, I don't think anything has changed—he still thinks Federer is the best," his manager, Carlos Costa, told me when I was in Barcelona the day before the French Open final. Like the rest of Nadal's support team, Costa was philosophical and undefensive about the loss to Soderling; the champion played a lousy match, they said, and it happened to be against a very good player playing the match of his life. "I haven't talked to Rafa about this," Costa said. "But I think there may have been some tension. 'I *never* lose here, so many years, I've never lost at center court, *record record record.*' This is just my thought. I'm not going to touch it now. Maybe later."

I went back to Paris to watch Federer in the final against Soderling, whose run of playing out of his mind held right through quarterfinal and semifinal matches against players of much higher rank. During the Nadal-Soderling match, the French spectators were snarky to Nadal, cheering lustily as it became clearer that the trophy-hogging Spaniard was going to lose. But they love Federer, and shouted him on now as he glided about the court, appearing not to break a sweat as he did law-of-physics-defying things with the tennis ball, like causing it to arc gently over the net and land on the forecourt clay and just stop, right there, while Soderling would scramble from the back court in a futile attempt at a return. "Ooh la la," said the man sitting beside me, who turned out to be Jean-Paul Loth, a retired French competitor who for ten years was captain of the national team. The cosmic intervention had come to an end; there was some intense second-set action, but Federer would take the match in straight sets, and as Soderling's game unspooled, Loth watched and shook his head. On a regular day, he said—Nadal playing like Nadal, Soderling playing like this—the Spaniard would have made swift work of the upstart from Sweden. "And if Nadal had had a chance to be in this final," Loth said, "Federer would never win."

The most important part is the head, Nadal had told me. Tennis improvement manuals are full of this instruction, as are all manner of other guides for trying to live the life you want, and as Federer sank to his knees in joy when the last point was over, I wondered whether Nadal was in front of his television in Manacor, or whether he spent the finals afternoon the way Costa guessed he would, on a family friend's fishing boat in the Mediterranean. Nadal loves fishing. He competes when he's on fishing boats too—he can't help himself, he likes to see who will get the biggest catch. I asked him once how he envisioned his adult life when professional tennis was over, and the first thing he said was, "A boat."

He'll still live in Majorca, he said. He and his mother have started a foundation, aimed at improving the lives of children in developing countries; he'll have some role in the foundation, and in sports. "If my career lasts for three more years, it lasts three more years," he said. "I still want to improve at tennis. If it's two years, then it's two. If it's five more years, perfect." Then he'll buy the boat, he said, but not a huge one. "A normal-sized boat," Nadal said. "To go fishing in the sea."

DAVID OWEN

The Ghost Course

FROM THE NEW YORKER

IN 2005, A SCOTTISH GOLF-COURSE CONSULTANT named Gordon Irvine took a fishing trip to South Uist, a sparsely populated island in the Outer Hebrides, fifty miles off Scotland's west coast. South Uist (pronounced YEW-ist) is about the size of Martha's Vineyard and Nantucket combined. It is virtually treeless, and much of its eastern third is mountainous and uninhabited. Gales from the Atlantic strike it with such force that schoolchildren hope for "wind days." Irvine had approached the island's golf club, called Askernish, and offered to barter greenkeeping advice for the right to fish for trout and salmon in the lochs nearby, and the club had welcomed the free consultation. It had just nine holes and a few dozen members, and the golfers themselves mowed the greens, with a rusting gang mower pulled by a tractor. Irvine walked the course, in driving rain, with the club's chairman, Ralph Thompson, and several regulars, and then the group went to lunch at the Borrodale Hotel, a mile and a half down the road.

At lunch, one of the members surprised Irvine by saying that Askernish was more than a century old and had been designed by Old Tom Morris, a towering figure in the history and folklore of the game. Morris, who was born in 1821 and looked a little like Charles Darwin in an ivy cap, was the founding father of modern golf. In the 1860s, he won four of the first eight British Opens and became the head professional of the Royal and Ancient Golf Club of St. Andrews, serving there for four decades as the chief greenkeeper of the Old Course, golf's holiest ground. He also designed or redesigned several of the world's greatest courses, among them Muirfield, Prestwick, and Carnoustie, in Scotland, and Royal County Down, in Northern Ireland.

Irvine was polite but dismissive: the course he'd walked that morning was a cow pasture with flagsticks stuck in the ground, and he doubted that Morris, whose courses he knew well, had ever come near it. But another club member said that this was not the original Askernish, and that Old Tom's layout had had eighteen holes and was situated closer to the sea. Most of the original holes, apparently, had been abandoned, probably beginning around the time of the Second World War. Ralph Thompson said that the club possessed a news clipping from 1891 which described Morris's creation of the course that year, and which quoted Morris calling the layout "second to none." Irvine was curious enough to take another look, and after lunch Thompson drove him back.

This time, Thompson led him to a grassy dune at the western end of the seventh hole, and when Irvine climbed to the top and looked toward the Atlantic he saw a stretch of undulating linksland running along the ocean, between the beach and the existing holes. For Irvine, the experience was like lifting the corner of a yard-sale velvet painting and discovering a Rembrandt. There were no surviving signs of golf holes in the waving marram grass, but the terrain, which had been shaped by the wind into valleys, hollows, and meandering ridges, looked so spectacularly suited to the game that he no longer doubted the Morris connection. Despite the rain, Irvine could easily imagine greens and fairways among the dunes, and he told Thompson that, if the club's members would agree to work with him, he would donate his time and expertise, and help them restore their lost masterpiece. A resurrected Askernish, he said, would provide a unique window on the birth of the modern game.

Not everyone on South Uist was pleased with this idea. The land in question had long been used as a common grazing area by local tenant farmers, called crofters, and a group of them protested that the construction of golf holes would violate their legal rights. One of the crofters described the golf project as a "land grab," and said that old property documents relating to the area made no mention of Old Tom Morris. For the aggrieved crofters, the plans brought to mind one of the most notorious periods of Scottish history, the Highland Clearances. Beginning in the eighteenth century, wealthy landlords gained possession of large sections of northern Scotland, which until then had been controlled by Gaelic-speaking clans. The new landlords attempted to impose what they viewed as economic rationality on their holdings, most of which were still farmed and grazed as they had been during the Dark Ages, by subsistence farmers working tiny plots. This transformation, which has been described as the wholesale substitution of sheep for people, involved waves of eviction, consolidation, and forced expatriation. By the late nineteenth century, the chieftains of the northern clans had either sold out to others or become landlords themselves, and the old Gaelic culture had been weakened or obliterated in many places, and sentimentalized elsewhere. A fad for kilts, tartans, and bagpipes took hold in the rest of the country, even as genuine Highlanders were being shipped off to Canada or put to work in the factories of Birmingham.

The Askernish project seemed, to the protesting crofters, like the clearances all over again. Ralph Thompson soon began to speak of making the restored Askernish—which the sportswriter John Garrity has described as a "ghost course"—the anchor of a much larger development, including additional golf courses and a hotel. He created a website and solicited nonresident life memberships, at £2,500 apiece, in the hope that fees from abroad would help to finance the construction. The crofters complained that the club's members were courting golf-playing "dandies" from the mainland and the United States, and were doing so at their expense. "What a cheek," one crofter said this past December. "They have gone on top of our *grazing* land and done with it what they want." The crofters began legal action to stop them.

Getting to South Uist today isn't as hard as it was in 1891, when the sole option was a slow, unreliable steamer, but it still requires determination. When I visited the first time, in 2007, I flew from Inverness to Benbecula, one island to the north; South Uist doesn't have its own airport but is connected to Benbecula by a half-mile-long causeway. In the air, I looked down, through breaks in the clouds, on the fjord-like creases that rumple Scotland's west coast and on the waters of the Minch, the stormy channel that separates the Outer Hebrides from mainland Scotland. This past December, I visited again, taking a ferry from Oban, which is a two-and-a-half-hour drive from Glasgow, by way of Loch Lomond. The ferry sails three or four times a week and sometimes makes a brief stop at Barra, which has a tiny airport whose schedule depends on the tides, since the runway is a beach. The South Uist ferry passes Mull, Coll, Muck, Eigg, Rum, Sanday, Sandray, Vatersay, Hellisay, Gighay, and other small islands, and in good weather the trip takes about six and a half hours. Until 1974, cars had to be loaded and unloaded with a crane, like freight; nowadays, you drive on and drive off.

The first time I visited South Uist, Ralph Thompson, the Askernish chairman, came to meet me. He manages the island's main agricultural-supply store, which stocks sheep feed, onion sets, shotguns, and other local necessities. He was born on the mainland in 1955, but, as a child, he spent summers on South Uist, where his grandparents lived. One reason he liked those visits, he told me, was that he was allowed to go for weeks without bathing, because his grandparents' house, like almost all houses on the island at that time, had no running water.

Even today, South Uist is short on modern conveniences. The lights went out one afternoon as Thompson and I were having a beer in the bar at the Borrodale, and he began counting. When he got to "five," the lights came back on, and he said, "If you count to five and the power comes back, it means a swan hit the line." Later, we drove south on the island's main road—a single lane for most of its length, with frequent bump-outs for yielding to oncoming traffic and for overtaking sheep—and crossed a causeway to Eriskay, a smaller island. Thompson spotted, in the distance, a ferryboat approaching from Barra, and he pulled over to watch it. He wasn't expecting anyone, but there are so few activities on South Uist that residents have evolved an unusually low threshold of amusement. We watched the ferry for fifteen or twenty minutes, and didn't pull away until the last of a handful of departing passengers had boarded.

Sometimes, entertainment arrives on the island unexpectedly. Early in 1941, a freighter, the SS *Politician*, ran aground in the sandy shallows between South Uist and Eriskay. Its cargo included more than twenty thousand cases of whiskey, and, over several weeks, groups of islanders rowed to the wreck and made off with thousands of bottles. They hid the whiskey in cowsheds, rabbit holes, and lobster traps—and significant portions of the adult population of several Hebridean islands stayed drunk for weeks. In 1947, the Scottish novelist Compton Mackenzie wrote a fictionalized account of the wreck and its aftermath, called *Whisky Galore.* Two years later, the book was made into a movie, filmed mostly on Barra. For its release in the United States, it was retitled *Tight Little Island;* too late, James Thurber suggested *Scotch on the Rocks.*

Most people think of the word "links" as a synonym for golf course, but it's actually a geological term. Linksland is a specific type of sandy, wind-sculpted coastal terrain—the word comes from the Old English *hlinc,* "rising ground"—and in its authentic form it exists in only a few places on earth, the most famous of which are in Great Britain and Ireland. Linksland arose at the end of the most recent ice age, when the retreat of the northern glacial sheet, accompanied by changes in sea level, exposed sandy deposits and what had once been coastal shelves. Wind pushed the sand into dunes and rippling plains; ocean storms added more sand; and coarse grasses covered everything. Early Britons used linksland mainly for livestock grazing, since the ground closest to the sea was usually too starved and too exposed for growing crops. When significant numbers of Scotsmen became interested in smacking small balls with curved wooden sticks, as they first did in 1400 or so, the links was where they went (or were sent), perhaps because there they were in no one's way. On South Uist, linksland is called *machair,* a Gaelic word. It's pronounced "mocker," more or less, but with the two central consonants represented by what sounds like a clearing of the throat.

The major design elements of a modern golf course are the synthetic analogues of various existing features of those early Scottish playing fields, and the fact that golf arose so directly from a particular landscape helps explain why, more than any other mainstream sport, it remains a game with a Jerusalem: it was permanently shaped by the ground on which it was invented. Groomed fairways are the descendants of the well-grazed valleys between the old linksland dunes; bunkers began as sandy depressions worn through thin turf by livestock huddling against coastal gales; the first greens and teeing grounds were flattish, elevated areas whose relatively short grass—closely grazed by rabbits and other animals and stunted by the brutal weather—made them the logical places to begin and end holes. ("A rabbit's jawbone allows it to graze grass lower than a sheep," Gordon Irvine told me recently, "and both those animals can graze grass lower than a cow.")

On the great old courses in the British Isles, the most celebrated holes often owe more to serendipity and to the vicissitudes of animal husbandry than they do to picks and shovels, since in the early years course design was more nearly an act of imagination and discovery than of physical construction. One of Old Tom Morris's best-known holes, the fifth at Lahinch, in southwestern Ireland, is a short par 3 whose green is concealed behind a tall dune, so that the golfer's target is invisible from the tee—a feature that almost any contemporary architect would have eliminated with a bulldozer. The greatest hole on the Old Course at St. Andrews is often said to be the seventeenth, a long par 4 called the Road Hole, which violates a list of modern design rules: the tee shot not only is blind but must be hit over the top of a tall wooden structure that reproduces the silhouette of a cluster of old railway sheds; the green repels approach shots from every direction and is fronted by a vortex-like circular bunker, from which the most prudent escape is often backward, away from the green; a paved public road runs directly alongside the green and is treated as a part of the course, meaning that golfers who play their way onto it must also play their way off. Over the centuries, every idiosyncratic inch of the Old Course has acquired, for the faithful, an almost numinous aura.

For Gordon Irvine, Askernish was in some ways an even more compelling historical artifact than the Old Course—so much so that shortly after his first visit to the course he called it "the holy grail." Unlike most other early links courses, Askernish had never been stretched to accommodate high-tech clubs and balls, and its original quirks had not been worn smooth, over the years, by motorized maintenance equipment. "Askernish was as Old Tom left it," Irvine told me. "Because the old holes were abandoned so early, there had been no real proactive maintenance done with machinery or chemicals, and it had never been revisited by other architects. The last time the old holes were played, the greens were probably cut with scythes."

In 2006, he enlisted the help of Martin Ebert, a golf architect whose specialty is links courses. No plan of Morris's Askernish layout was known to exist, so the men's first task was to identify eighteen likely green locations among the dunes. A round of golf consists of eighteen holes primarily because the Old Course ended up with that many in 1764, when four very short holes were combined to make two longer ones—although the number took a while to catch on. Prestwick, where the first dozen Opens were played, had twelve holes until 1883. Leith, where golf's first rule book was written, in 1744, had five. Montrose had twenty-five.

Finding a lost golf course isn't as simple as you might think: the creators of early layouts did so little in the way of earthmoving that unambiguous evidence of their work can be difficult to detect, even for someone who knows where to look. My hometown, in northwestern Connecticut, had a small golf course in the 1890s, contemporary with Askernish. I know exactly where it was and have seen old photographs of it, but during a long afternoon spent tramping over the area I was unable to find a single undeniable surviving feature. In the earliest days of the game, golfers created courses the way children do when they knock balls around a vacant lot, by devising interesting ways to go from Point A to Point B.

Ebert developed his restoration design by hiking over the *machair* and visualizing golf shots (Old Tom's method) and by studying satellite photographs, which helped him weigh various schemes for connecting the greens in a logical sequence. He also extrapolated from his knowledge of Morris's designs elsewhere, and from his own work in restoring old links courses. When I visited Askernish in 2007, he and Irvine had placed eighteen flags in the ground, denoting provisional green locations, and were taking readings with a laser range finder and a handheld GPS device, so that Ebert could enter accurate coordinates into his laptop—enabling him, among other things, to leave a clearer record of his thinking than Old Tom Morris did. Ebert told me that he and Irvine were fairly certain they had identified a number of the original greens, in some cases because the ground appeared to have been slightly flattened, most likely by hand, at some point in the past, and in other cases because particular formations simply looked like golf greens to them and so presumably would have looked like golf greens to Old Tom Morris too. One such site—the fourteenth green in Ebert's layout—occupied a plateau surrounded by dunes, which resembled ocean billows. "That green plays well from many different directions, but I think it plays best the way we've laid it out, as a par 3," Ebert told me. "It just seems like a par-3 green, set high on the dune with everything dropping away."

While Ebert and Irvine worked, Ralph Thompson, a couple of his friends, and I followed along, hitting golf balls into the marram grass, and losing many. At one point, we all hit shots toward the top of a distant dune directly above the beach, so that Ebert could get a sense of whether it was reasonable to expect golfers to hit such a long shot to such a small target and into the prevailing wind. Putting wasn't really possible yet, although a few of the proposed greens had been encircled by single strands of barbed wire, to keep sheep and cattle from wandering onto them.

The most vocal opponents of the Askernish project have been Gilbert Walker and William Macdonald, both crofters. I went to see them this past December at Walker's house, down the street from the Borrodale Hotel. Walker, who is seventy, went upstairs to find his hearing aid, and Macdonald rolled a cigarette and took a seat near the hearth, so that he could blow his smoke toward the flue. Macdonald is fifty-four but looks and sounds at least ten years older. He apologized for his hair, which was pointing in several directions, and explained that he'd fallen asleep in his chair, at home, while waiting for Walker to pick him up. When Walker returned, I asked the men if they could explain crofting to me, and Macdonald smiled and said, "It is complicated."

Most of northern Scotland used to be occupied by clans, whose leaders had a conception of real estate which Macdonald likened to that of American Indians before the arrival of Europeans. "The clan chieftain did not regard himself as the owner," he said, relighting his cigarette, which had gone out. "He regarded himself as the chief of his people, and he considered his wealth in terms not of the number of acres he occupied but of the number of fighting men he had, or the number of cattle, or these things combined." Beginning around the time of Macbeth, the Scottish government (and, later, the British) increasingly viewed the northern clans as military, political, cultural, and religious threats, and took various steps against them. In the mid-eighteenth century, the rule of the clans began to be replaced by a modern system of land tenancy—the beginning of the clearances.

South Uist was bought in 1838 by Colonel John Gordon of Cluny, who lived in a castle on the other side of Scotland. Most of the island's residents spoke only Gaelic and subsisted by growing potatoes, raising cattle and sheep, fishing, and collecting seaweed for fertilizer. Their cottages, which they often shared with their animals, usually lacked chimneys; smoke from smoldering peat fires inside seeped out through thatched roofs. Colonel Gordon— whose name in historical accounts is often preceded by "heartless," "brutal," or some similarly grim epithet—eventually transported more than two thousand of these people, perhaps half of South Uist's population at the time, to Quebec, and consolidated their plots into large livestock farms, which were more profitable. His treatment of his tenants was among the reasons that the government acted, in the late nineteenth century, to bring the clearances to an end, by giving small tenant farmers protection from arbitrary removal. Crofters continued to pay rent to their landlords, but eventually gained many of the powers of ownership, including the ability to bequeath their crofting rights. The system, with various modifications, remains in place today.

After Colonel Gordon died, South Uist passed to his son and then to the son's widow, Lady Emily Gordon Cathcart. It was she who commissioned the first Askernish golf course, in 1891. A major golf boom was under way, and her decision to hire the most famous golfer of the day probably reflected a hope of attracting sportsmen from the mainland. When Old Tom Morris traveled to South Uist at her behest, he was accompanied by Horace Hutchinson, who was both a champion golfer and one of the first golf correspondents. An account of their trip, probably written by Hutchinson, appeared in *The Scotsman* and reported, "On a stretch of beautiful links ten miles in length it was difficult to select the best site for a course, as half-a-dozen courses, each having special points of interest, could have been marked off on the available ground. After a survey, a part of the farm of Askernish was selected, principally on account of its proximity to the excellent hotel at Lochboisdale, which at this season is usually crowded with anglers."

In 1922, most of Askernish Farm was divided among eleven tenants, one of whom was William Macdonald's grandfather. Each of the Askernish crofters received the permanent right to occupy a portion of the old farm and to graze animals on common land near the sea, while Lady Gordon Cathcart, who still owned the farm and the rest of the island, retained the manor house, a portion of the arable land, and the right to play golf on the *machair.*

The meaning of that last stipulation was central to the golf-course dispute. Macdonald told me that the golf provision, in his opinion, expired with Lady Gordon Cathcart's death, and that the crofters on her former property tolerated continued golf-playing only as a favor. He and Walker said that they had no issue with the old nine-hole course, which didn't extend into the dunes, but that the new course was an outrage. Walker, rising from his seat, said, "What they have now is four times the size of what was there. The whole *machair* is four hundred and thirty-seven acres. What they've taken over is three hundred and forty!"

In 2003, new legislation enabled communities in Scotland's crofting regions to collectively purchase the land they occupied. Three years later, the people of South Uist, Eriskay, and Benbecula paid £4.5 million for their islands, which are now owned and managed by a community-run nonprofit company called Stòras Uibhist —Gaelic for "the treasure of Uist." In 2006, Stòras Uibhist confirmed the decision of the previous owner to allow the golf club to restore the course—a decision that the Askernish crofters contested. The vice chairman of Stòras Uibhist is Father Michael Macdonald, who is the priest of the Catholic parish at South Uist's northern end. When I asked him about the complaints, he shook his head. "I can't figure out what's behind it all," he said. "It's hugely expensive to go down this road. And for what benefit?"

Walker's and Macdonald's objections to the golf course are less straightforward than they may seem: although each man has a croft at Askernish, Macdonald doesn't graze animals there, and Walker owns only a few. In addition, the people who run the golf club, far from asking anyone to remove livestock, have said repeatedly that they wish the crofters would graze more animals on the course. Hungry sheep and cattle are good for a links course, Irvine and Ebert told me, because they fertilize the soil and help keep the rough under control.

Part of the difficulty may lie with crofting itself. Father MacDonald, when I asked, defined a croft as "a small piece of land surrounded by legislation." This is an old joke in Scotland, but it's apt. Crofting was devised to protect small tenant farmers from abusive landlords, but the system was already becoming an anachronism by the time it was put in place. The land on South Uist is so marginal and the plots are so small—an average of forty or fifty acres—that no one on the island today makes a living from crofting alone, despite substantial government grants and subsidies, and legally protected rents of less than a pound an acre. The system successfully preserves a sanitized form of medieval land tenancy, but it makes cost-effective agriculture impossible, since it divides the land among far too many tenants.

Perhaps for that reason, modern debates about crofting tend to focus more on symbols than on practicalities. The Askernish controversy has been portrayed as a class conflict, between struggling crofters and wealthy golfers, but the distinction makes no sense on South Uist, since virtually everyone on the island has at least one croft, including Ralph Thompson, the other local members of the golf club, and Father MacDonald. South Uist's economy—and therefore crofting itself—depends heavily on visitors from elsewhere, and has since at least the era of Lady Gordon Cathcart. Ralph Thompson has said that Askernish could eventually contribute as much as a million pounds a year to the local economy, a big deal on an island with a population of eighteen hundred and falling.

In early 2008, the protesting Askernish crofters asked the Lochmaddy Sheriff Court to halt the golf project. The court declined to intervene, and the crofters took their case to the Scottish Land Court, in Edinburgh. Meanwhile, construction of the golf course began. Actually, "construction" is the wrong word. At Askernish, Ebert and Irvine were determined to create golf holes the way Old Tom Morris and his contemporaries did, by doing virtually nothing beyond cutting the grass and filling in old rabbit burrows. (The 1891 article in *The Scotsman* about Askernish suggests that the first round of golf there was played within a few days of Morris's visit.) Modern golf-course designers usually work closely with contractors called shapers, who use heavy earthmoving equipment (and, often, explosives) to transform existing terrain to suit a designer's vision of what golf holes ought to be. For Askernish, Ebert didn't need a shaper, because he and Irvine intended to be no more aggressive than a nineteenth-century course builder would have been. Only a few small areas were subjected to more than trivial amounts of soil disturbance. One of those was the seventh green. Irvine and Ebert were both fairly certain that the seventh had been one of the original holes, because the valley in which it was situated looked so much like a fairway. But in what seemed to be the logical location for the green Irvine found virtually no organic matter beneath the grass. This led him to deduce that the old putting surface, if there was one, must be buried beneath six or seven decades' worth of windblown sand. He and a crew of local volunteers removed the beach grass from that spot and then raked away sand, looking for the original contours. A few feet down, they reached topsoil (or what passes for it on South Uist), confirming his hunch. Another green that required significant work was the eleventh — the target overlooking the sea which Ebert, in 2007, had asked several of us to hit shots to. Irvine and Ebert suspected that the original green (and most of the fairway leading up to it) had been lost to erosion, but they still wanted to use what remained of the dune, both because it formed an invitingly level plateau, and because the required shot, though challenging, had been so deeply appealing to all of us who had tried it. (Part of golf's addictiveness, for those who are hooked, arises from the thrill of effecting action at a distance — a form of satisfaction also known to anti-aircraft gunners.)

Ebert and Irvine used no pesticides or artificial fertilizers, and they didn't install an irrigation system. The entire cost of the golf-course construction was less than £100,000, a fraction of the usual bill for even a modest golf course nowadays. (Ebert helped to keep the price low by agreeing to work for Old Tom's fee, which was £9.) Ebert told me, "Askernish goes back to the roots of the game, where you're just sort of playing across the landscape." Modern golf-course architects have individually recognizable styles, but most of them adhere to certain hole-design conventions: that golfers should be able to see their targets, that hazards and other obstacles should not be arbitrarily punitive, that fairways and greens should be shaped to reward good shots. In Old Tom Morris's era, a designer's main function was not to recontour the ground in order to conform to golfers' expectations but to direct play over existing terrain in thought-provoking ways, and to capitalize on lucky topographical accidents. Because Ebert and Irvine did their work at Askernish in that spirit, some of the holes pose challenges of a type that most modern players are unaccustomed to meeting. "Golfers who have only experienced modern courses will find some of the Askernish greens very, very difficult to understand," Irvine told me. "Some of them look as if they were sloping the wrong way, but that's only because we've got so used to pandering to the golfer." The sixteenth hole, called Old Tom's Pulpit, has an elevated green whose rear half falls off severely, into a sort of bowl, where many players' approach shots are likely to come to rest. The green breaks any number of design rules, but the hole is both memorable and fun to play, as well as challenging—just like Old Tom's blind par 3 at Lahinch.

The restored Askernish course opened officially on August 22, 2008. The retired Scottish soccer legend Kenny Dalglish played in the first group and was named the club's honorary president. Five months later, the Land Court heard two days' worth of testimony from the attorneys representing the protesting crofters and Stòras Uibhist, and in late February it issued a ruling. It affirmed Stòras Uibhist's right to create golf holes anywhere on the *machair*, as well as to build a clubhouse and make other improvements, while stipulating that the golf club must not deprive the crofters of the right to graze their animals adequately. (If the crofters and Stòras Uibhist can't settle the grazing details on their own, the Land Court will hold a hearing in May.) Ralph Thompson had told me beforehand that Stòras Uibhist's attorneys were confident they would prevail, but, even so, the scope of the ruling surprised him. "It's miles above what we expected," he said.

Crofting remains an important part of life on South Uist, and many residents, Father MacDonald among them, believe that it serves a critical social function, by enabling the island to sustain a larger full-time population than would otherwise be possible. But crofting, because it spreads residents so thinly across the settled parts of the island, also undermines any deep sense of community: most of the houses on South Uist are widely scattered rather than clustered in true villages. The golf club, which is open to all and costs very little to join, has the potential to become a community anchor, and its junior golf program, which the club and Stòras Uibhist have both treated as a priority, may keep at least a few of the island's young people interested in hanging around instead of pursuing careers on the mainland. At any rate, it will give them something interesting to do on weekends while they wait for their chance to escape.

I got to play a couple of rounds at Askernish in December. Even though the course is farther north than Sitka, Alaska, the Gulf Stream keeps temperatures on South Uist mild through most of the winter and creates the possibility of a twelve-month golf season, at least for die-hards. I played one day with Ralph Thompson and Donald MacInnes, who is the club's captain, as well as a builder and a crofter. There was a film of frost on some of the beach grass when we began, but the sky was virtually cloudless, and I never needed the stocking cap that I had tucked in my golf bag. On the fifth hole, we passed a spot where an Askernish crofter had plowed a small potato plot up to the very edge of the fairway, most likely as a provocation. I expected Thompson to be angry, but he laughed. "We never would have got the course finished so fast if it hadn't been for the crofters," he said. "They turned Askernish into international news."

MacInnes had brought along his dog, which ran ahead of us over the dunes, pausing occasionally to enlarge a rabbit hole. The fairways and the greens were ungroomed, in comparison with a typical course at home, and we sometimes had to play around a rut or a bare spot or a half-buried skeleton of a sheep. But roughness is part of the course's charm. The bunkers looked like real hazards, rather than like oversized hotel ashtrays, and the slanting winter light made the beach grass glow. We were a little worried, when we began, that we wouldn't have time for eighteen holes, because the winter solstice was approaching and the sun had seemed to begin setting almost as soon it came up. But we finished with visibility to spare, and had time for a beer in the tiny clubhouse, which MacInnes had built. We were able to play quickly because we had the golf course to ourselves, except for a few cows.

JENNIFER KAHN

Flat

FROM OUTSIDE

WHEN SCOTT MACARTNEY entered the gate at the January 2008 World Cup downhill race in Kitzbühel, Austria, he gave the start referee a rare, brief smile. Positioned in the top twenty after his final practice run, Macartney was celebrating his thirtieth birthday, a coincidence that felt lucky. As he waited for the countdown, a coach told him, "Today's your day."

In fact, it was almost his last. Entering the final jump at eighty-nine miles per hour, he felt what he later described as a "pop" under one foot: a kick on the takeoff as one ski hit what was likely a raised patch of snow. This imbalance magnified in the air, and Macartney's body began a grim, inexorable rotation. For two seconds—180 airborne feet—he fought unsuccessfully to right himself. When he hit, facing sideways, the impact snapped both skis and fractured his inch-thick helmet, which broke off and ricocheted across the snow. Unconscious, Macartney tumbled gruesomely and slid down the rest of the hill. Finally drifting to a stop past the finish line, he lay still for a moment and then went into a seizure and convulsions.

Watching from the sidelines, Macartney's coach, Chris Brigham, judged the wreck "one of the worst I've seen." Macartney was airlifted to a hospital in Innsbruck, where he was put into a coma. It was unclear at first whether he would live.

Back on the course, news of the disaster propagated quickly. Macartney had had an early gate time—he was only the second skier to descend—and the accident had been broadcast live to the other racers, including his teammate Marco Sullivan, who was in the lodge at the top of the course. On the room's television, the crash replayed twice before the feed was cut, and Sullivan later told me he assumed Macartney had broken his neck. "The thing that freaked everybody out was the convulsions," he said.

At the hospital, Macartney spent thirteen hours unconscious while doctors tried to control the swelling in his brain. He was lucid when he woke up, although he had trouble remembering names and his vision was blurred in one eye.

Despite this, Macartney recovered, and soon announced his intention to return to competition—and to Kitzbühel. Over the summer of 2008, he met once with the Ski Team psychologist, Keith Henschen. Otherwise, he didn't discuss the accident in public and seemed to find the idea of dwelling on his feelings unpalatable. Though the science of fear therapy has burgeoned in recent years, Macartney's own plan for recovery remained decidedly old-school: he would keep his mouth shut and get back on the horse.

"In the end, it's about the amount of risk you're willing to take," he said when asked about the wreck. "Either you get used to it or you don't. The sport selects for the people who can." Not long after, he reclaimed his spot on the U.S. Ski Team, and in September 2008 he left for the squad's race camp at Portillo, a Chilean ski resort high in the Andes.

World Cup competition demands mental fortitude, and downhill racers can seem almost supernaturally resilient. Austria's Hermann Maier famously came back to win two gold medals at the 1998 Nagano Olympics just days after a horrifying seventy-mile-per-hour wreck. Following a crash that shattered her femur, American Picabo Street watched videos of her wipeout obsessively, then insisted that she'd forgotten about it. "I took what I needed from it and moved on," she said.

But for every skier who returns to winning form, there are others who never manage it. Not long after Macartney's crash, 2006 Olympic downhill champion Antoine Dénériaz, of France, quit the sport abruptly when he was unable to shake vivid memories of a 2006 wreck. Dénériaz's coach, Gilles Brenier, spoke frankly when he told a reporter, "Something was broken that day. Something . . . from which he could not recover."

Coming less than two months after Dénériaz's Olympic victory, his departure was startling. Or so it seemed. When I spoke with

Phil McNichol, who coached the U.S. men's alpine ski team for five years until his retirement in March 2008, he said Dénériaz stood out not so much because of his mental struggle but because he'd admitted it. "Most guys who quit lay it off to some other reason, like an injury," he said.

In fact, insiders knew that Dénériaz's problems were not uncommon. "It happens often enough that we have a term for it," said Lester Keller, coordinator of sports psychology services for the U.S. Ski and Snowboard Association. "We say they get the Fear."

Not surprisingly, the Fear afflicts athletes in almost any high-risk pursuit. One performance psychologist I spoke with had spent the past six months quietly assisting a Tour de France racer who'd lost his ability to descend at high speeds after a training crash. Another recalled a collegiate diver who'd developed a paralyzing reaction to reverse dives after watching a teammate fracture her skull on the edge of the platform. "It was a very physical reaction," he explained. "The minute this person stepped onto the board, her heart would start to race. And then, when she started her stride, it felt like all her joints were locking up."

Exactly what causes an athlete to develop a long-term feeling of dread is a mystery, but it's known that the process starts at the initial moment of calamity. During an accident or a dangerous near miss, a complex network in the body, including a portion of the inner brain called the amygdala—an almond-shaped mass of tissue that's found in creatures ranging from lizards to humans—takes in the information and sends out neurological alarm signals in the form of electrical impulses and a flood of chemicals like adrenaline, epinephrine, and cortisol.

When this happens, brain regions associated with higher-order mental functions, particularly the frontal cortex, receive the signals and coordinate a protective response, which varies depending on the level of threat. When the event is minor, the brain calms down fast. When it's serious, the effects are usually long-lasting.

Roger Pitman, a professor of psychiatry at Harvard Medical School who studies traumatic stress, said that once the amygdala connects the feeling of terror with a particular experience, that link is branded into the brain. "You see it all the time," he said. "The rational system says, 'There's nothing to be afraid of.' But that kind of argument doesn't penetrate to conditioned fear."

The more times a memory is replayed, the more crippling the

effect can be. Sean McCann, who worked as a sports psychologist with the U.S. women's ski team for fifteen years, recalled a skier who, having once crashed, would step out to inspect a race hill and be overwhelmed by visions of disaster. Because of this, she was unable to really let loose on the course. "The term we use is 'hyper-vigilant,'" McCann told me. "You're basically trying to survive the race instead of win."

According to McCann, this anxiety is particularly debilitating in athletes who obsess over their accident—a process, he says, that functions like "a neurochemical loop tape reinforcing the message 'Be scared of this.'" Interrupting that loop is difficult. The most widely used treatment is exposure therapy, in which patients confront their phobia by visualizing the same sequence of events but with a happy ending, the idea being to create an alternate "safe" neural pathway in the brain.

There are promising drugs that may help in the future—including D-cycloserine, an antibiotic with positive side effects in the treatment of phobias—but for Macartney, therapy and chemical aids weren't part of the equation.

At first, Macartney seemed strangely immune to the trauma. Back home in Washington State after the accident, he updated his website with a YouTube video of the crash and even appeared on a local TV news program, where he gamely watched a replay as the anchors bantered.

This toughness was a family tradition. In 2006, Macartney's mother, Laurie, had nearly died in a ski accident; she'd survived only because Macartney's dad happened to notice her boot sticking out of the snow near a tree well. At the time, Laurie was undergoing chemotherapy for breast cancer. Determined to watch Macartney compete in the Olympics, she flew to Turin two months later. The next year, still suffering from lymphatic edema—which results in painful swelling of the limbs—she motorcycled from Seattle to Mexico. Stung by a scorpion en route, she kept riding.

Macartney absorbed the same attitude early. Growing up in the Cascades, he entered his first downhill race at seven, placing third. Several years later, his parents climbed Mount Rainier with Scott and his brother in tow. "We did a lot of stuff that wasn't easy," Macartney recalled. "There was an undercurrent of expectation: That's what you did. You didn't just quit."

Up to this point, injuries hadn't slowed Macartney—he sustained a concussion in 2001—and, in public, at least, he seemed to treat his blowout like an interruption. "If, after Kitzbühel, I'd said, 'I just don't have it anymore,' no one would have questioned that," Macartney told me when we first spoke by phone, "but I never had any doubt that I wanted to come back."

The question was whether Macartney's determination would be enough. Studies of combat veterans suffering from post-traumatic stress disorder have found that vets who keep their fear to themselves tend to fare worse, but as Pitman pointed out, combat survivors aren't usually planning to return to the front lines; they just want to stop panicking every time a car backfires.

Macartney's case was different. Not only was he returning to competition; he was returning at a level that required him to operate at the very edge of his ability, under the most treacherous circumstances. Given all that, Pitman said, Macartney's brain arguably was doing exactly what it should: replacing bad associations with positive ones. "Learning what is likely to hurt you is very useful," Pitman observed dryly. "If you're a World Cup skier who nearly died, fear is normal. Returning to take the same risk after a bad crash—that might be what's abnormal."

Shortly before the team left for Portillo, I contacted Coach Brigham to discuss Macartney's return to competition. Since May 2008, Macartney had attended all of the team's dry-land fitness camps—grueling weeks of gym work and agility drills held at altitude in Park City, Utah—and Brigham confidently described his physical condition at the last one as "fantastic, even better than normal."

Even so, Brigham, who invited Macartney back onto the team and remained optimistic about his prospects, acknowledged that the Fear was unpredictable. "You see guys who've had a bad crash and that's pretty much the end of them," he said. "And then there are guys that you didn't think would come back who prove you wrong. It's a funny game."

Located at 9,500 feet in the Andes, the Portillo resort anchors a narrow valley abbreviated by abruptly rising sidewalls. For a training site of elite racers, the resort is surprisingly antique: a handful of old lifts feed the slopes, augmented, on the sheerest pitches, by steep Poma tows. The week I arrived, the U.S. team had staked out a super-G run on the resort's southeastern wall—a steep, off-camber corridor of gates set below softening cliffs that periodically sent large black rocks barreling down the course.

On the first day of practice, six skiers were in the lineup, including Macartney, his close friend Marco Sullivan, and Ted Ligety, the 2006 Olympic gold medalist in the alpine combined and 2008 world champion in the giant slalom. Also present was Bryon Friedman, who'd shattered his leg in a training crash in 2005 and endured eight surgeries. In the years since, Friedman had struggled with anxiety and had yet to regain his old speed. Cut from the U.S. team the previous spring, he paid his way to Portillo, where he was allowed to train with the team so long as his performance was deemed promising. "If it doesn't happen this year, it won't happen," he said.

Macartney appeared to be in a better position. Since entering World Cup competition in 2004, he had mostly placed in the top forty, and shortly before his crash had skied a breathtaking third-place run on the downhill course at Val Gardena: the best performance of his career. On the slopes, Macartney is known for being incredibly strong and, like all downhill racers, uncommonly agile. He was also mentally disciplined, displaying a level of concentration so intense that it could almost be frightening. Unlike many competitive skiers, who skip college in order to race professionally, he joined the World Cup circuit while working in semesters at Dartmouth, where he got a degree in economics.

"I used to tell him, 'You're too smart to race downhill,'" joked Peter Lavin, the team's amiable start coach. "Then he got second at Garmisch. I said, 'I guess you're not so smart.' He said, 'That's what comes from hanging out with all you dumbasses.'"

Good-natured and goofy, Lavin—known on the team as Baby Huey for his large, egg-shaped body and fluting voice—was bullish on Macartney's ability to bounce back. "He'll do it," Lavin said confidently as the racers towed to the start on a sheen of early-morning ice. "He's got the desire."

That day, Macartney seemed to struggle. As coaches with video cameras took up positions along the run, he cycled unsuccessfully through the short first pitch of the course, taking awkward lines that repeatedly left him out of position. With each missed gate, Macartney returned wordlessly to the lift.

The performance augured poorly. Fear makes an athlete tense, and that tension makes skis harder to control, in turn reducing confidence. Interrupting that cycle is difficult, and even a momentary fright can be enough to undo weeks of gradual desensitization. As one sport psychologist put it, "When you're confident, everything feels easy. But how do you get confident?"

That question is particularly critical in World Cup racing, where margins are so slight—roughly a hundredth of a second over a three-mile course—that victories are determined largely by a skier's ability to sustain a state of fearless abandon.

Shortly after one of Macartney's runs, Ligety kicked out of the start and demonstrated how it was done: cutting sharply through the top gates and rocketing over the roll with a zippering sound like the whine of rope running fast through a ring. "Ted's killing it," one coach remarked admiringly.

Talking about the episode later, Friedman described Ligety's descent on the steep first section as being "without fear." Friedman noted that Ligety had never been badly injured in a crash, and his descent was correspondingly assured. "You watch the guys on that pitch and you can tell who's been injured," he said. "You can just see it." Friedman seemed aware of a subtler loss: a shimmering, pure belief that had been irrevocably taken away. "It's like you know what you need to do, but you can't quite get there," he said at one point. "Your body won't let you, or your mind won't let you—at least, mine won't."

But if fearlessness is an ephemeral commodity, it also entails a rather complicated self-deception. This is particularly true in the speed events, the downhill and the super-G. Run on bulletproof ice, on courses riddled with high-compression turns and hair-raising drop-offs, these races leave no margin for error. To push the limits under such conditions requires a breathtaking repression of protective instinct.

Jim Taylor, a performance psychologist and former ski racer who specializes in recovery among elite athletes, believes that the Fear has become more severe in the past decade as advances in surgical repair have enabled competitors to come back from accidents that would have been career-ending thirty years ago. That has tipped the recovery burden onto the mind, he said. "An athlete's body may be rebuilt, but they can't always get back in the game at one hundred percent."

The results of the morning's super-G practice seemed to bear this out. In two of the five runs, Macartney failed to finish; in another two, he finished last—three seconds behind Ligety. "You know, he goes from having a good day to one where he struggles," Brigham said when we talked about it later. "He was struggling right away today." He paused, then added, "He'll turn it around."

That afternoon, I arranged to talk with Macartney in a hotel lounge. In person, he was wary, with a deliberate reticence that masked a sharp eye for detail.

Since the crash, Macartney had begun to closely manage media interviews. "In every conversation, there was this underlying tone of 'What if you never come back?'" he told me. "The frustrating part was that it started to affect my thinking. You start thinking, Well, maybe they're right."

At a video-review session later that day, he sat in silence, arms crossed, concentrating on the grainy footage of his runs. Video sessions are group events, and there's inevitably a fair amount of commentary, often self-deprecating. During the replay of one run, in which Macartney took a bizarrely wide line through a turn, he deadpanned, "Around there is when I start losing my mind." For the most part, though, he neither joked nor spoke, and his expression was tight. At the end, one of the coaches asked if he wanted to see another racer's tape, to compare lines through the top of the course. Macartney shrugged.

"Had enough?" the coach joked.

"I know what I have to do," Macartney said.

The capacity to re-create confidence after a psychological trauma is mysterious, and Macartney, who had already managed to come this far, seemed to offer a clue to how it was done. But the man himself was enigmatic. When I asked him about the prospect of injury, he grew brusque. "You're taking risks that you need to take," he said. "Such that most of the time it works out well." And while Macartney remembered the crash in detail, up until the moment of his concussion, he had little to say about it. During the frightening seconds in the air, he said, he was focused on keeping his ski tips down, so they wouldn't catch air. When I brought up the morning's super-G, his cool became even chillier.

"I'm not forcing it," he said tersely. "I'm a process person. I'm focused more on the execution than the results."

In Macartney's case, the challenge of moving beyond his crash had been compounded by the persistent curiosity of journalists like me. One day after practice, I casually asked him if we could arrange a time to watch a videotape of the crash together. We were seated at the hotel's afternoon tea, and in the pause that followed, he stared at the tablecloth. He seemed at once infuriated by the request and frustrated by the revelation of his own discomfort. When I tried to apologize the next day, however, he shrugged off the exchange. "The reason I wasn't so pumped to watch the video is that I'm trying to put it behind me," he said.

When I spoke to Macartney months later, he explained his frustration with a story. That winter, he told me, not long after Portillo, a reporter from an Austrian paper had approached him when he was racing in Wengen, requesting an interview and adding that he'd brought a gift.

Macartney agreed, with the provision that he wouldn't discuss his crash. "Two minutes later, the guy was asking me all this stuff—what I was thinking when I was in the air, whether I still had nightmares," Macartney recalled. "And his 'gift' was a bunch of still photos of me crashing, blown up to nine-by-eleven! He wanted to get a picture of me looking at them. I said, 'You do realize what I'm doing tomorrow?' And he said, 'Yeah, yeah, I'm really sorry—I can see how that would be tough.' And ten seconds later he's like, 'So . . . can we get the pictures?'"

This clash produces a strange dilemma. "There are a lot of things that you do subconsciously," Macartney told me at one point. "And it's confusing. You can be doing things in your opinion the same way and have totally different results from one day to the next." The result is that Macartney can, at times, seem eerily detached when discussing his own experience. When I pointed this out, he acknowledged that he was making a deliberate effort to disconnect. "There's a lot of . . . management in racing, is the best way to put it," he said. "I wouldn't say I've completely shut down my emotional side, but you have to be smart about what you let yourself believe."

Shortly after getting back from Portillo, I contacted Antoine Dénériaz, the downhill champion who lost his nerve after a wreck in Sweden. Unlike Macartney, Dénériaz was quite open about his psychological struggle. "To say that you are afraid, it is like you are not strong," he said from his home in the French Alps, "but when you have the real fear, you can't ski—it's not possible. It's already difficult when you're strong, when you have everything on your side. As soon as you're scared, it's too hard to fight for that last hundredth of a second."

Like Macartney, Dénériaz said that he originally felt confident about his ability to return. "I didn't have injuries—not big injuries, you know—so I was thinking that after a few weeks of rest, the feeling would come back and I would be okay."

Instead, he found himself battling a growing sense of dread. He consulted a mental coach, who recommended visualization. "I was really motivated, because I knew the feeling when you win a World Cup, or Olympic gold, and wanted to have that again. And it's strange because that winter I actually made a lot of progress technically. But parallel with that, it was growing more and more difficult to compete." He sighed. "And at the end, everything went bad."

Stefan Hofmann, a neuroscientist who studies fear in military veterans, speculated that Dénériaz's collapse could've been "a threshold issue": an accumulation of trauma that finally put the skier over the edge. Others pointed to Dénériaz's age (at thirty, relatively advanced) and the fact that his crash occurred late in the season, allowing more offseason time for the Fear to take hold.

Dénériaz had his own theory. When I asked what he thought had been different about the crash in Sweden, he described the fear he'd felt during the seconds in the air when he was falling. In that moment, Dénériaz said, he'd had a vivid vision of a wreck the previous year in Chamonix, where he'd severed the ligaments in his knee. He also remembered being struck by how much he stood to lose. "Three weeks before, I had won the Olympics and I was on top of the world: an Olympic champion with a gold. And then, in just a few seconds, I could have lost everything—maybe even lost my life." He paused. "The difference was so huge. It was too much."

Since Portillo, Macartney's own comeback has proceeded unevenly. Just one week before he was scheduled to race in January 2009, he crashed during a practice run, tearing a ligament in his left knee—an injury that ended his season. When I spoke with him recently, he called the accident "frustrating" but emphasized that he was looking ahead to his World Cup return in November, and to the Olympics in February, where he hopes to make both the downhill and super-G squads.

Whether he'll make it is unclear. Last year, Macartney's performance was patchy: he finished fifty-ninth at Lake Louise, twenty-fourth at Beaver Creek. But there were also moments of brilliance. On the last day of the downhill at Val Gardena, he seemed to hit his stride, posting fast times and soaring 180 feet on the course's biggest jump. That day, Coach Brigham told me, it was as though Macartney had never crashed. "He was right back in it," Brigham said, "flying like you know he can fly."

JOHN BRANT

Close to Home

FROM RUNNER'S WORLD

You'd see her running downtown along Lincoln Memorial Drive, by the futuristic ship of the Milwaukee Art Museum, by the white tents of Summerfest, by the marina where you can rent paddle-boats, by the oceanic plain of Lake Michigan, placid on a summer morning but in the winter subject to wolf winds that pile the spindrift into surreal ice sculptures along the frozen beach.

It was common to see Jenny Crain along the drive at just around sunrise, although there was nothing common about her. She was tall and wide-shouldered, and ran with a powerful, straight-backed stride, her long, dark hair sailing behind her. The top American female finisher in the 2004 New York City Marathon and a three-time Olympic Marathon Trials qualifier, Jenny stood out in the Milwaukee running community like an eagle amid a flock of starlings. Yet the city had always been her home, and she never wanted to live anyplace else.

Walkers, bikers, and runners access the drive and the lakefront trails by way of a pedestrian bridge at the end of Brady Street. It was just about 7:45 A.M., on August 21, 2007. Jenny was nearing the end of her workout, running across the bridge away from the lakefront and toward her downtown home, on a route she'd probably covered a thousand times. She remembers nothing about that day. She might have been thinking about the rapid heartbeat that had forced her to drop out of a 10-K the previous weekend. Or perhaps Jenny, who earned her living as a consultant to the insurance industry, was thinking about a phone call she had scheduled with a client for 9 A.M. But whatever filled her mind that summer morning, Jenny wasn't likely to feel frazzled or distracted.

"She was always rushing around, with a million projects, but she was able to focus totally on whatever was in front of her," says Marla Runyan, Jenny's former training partner and a two-time Olympic distance runner.

Peter Crain, Jenny's older brother, recalls his sister's discipline. "When I'm out on a ten-mile run, all I can think about is finishing. But Jenny always focused on the mile that she was running."

Cheryl and Bobby Neumann are two of Jenny's longtime friends in Milwaukee. "Jenny was always so *present*," Cheryl says. "Even for the simple things, like eating. During a meal, for instance, she would thrust her plate across the table and say, 'Here, you just have to taste this!' There was no way you could refuse her."

"Jenny," says Anne Marie Letko, who ran against Crain in the Olympic Trials and finished tenth in the marathon in the 1996 Games, "emanates a sense of being alive in the moment."

Standing slightly uphill from the bridge, at the same time of day that Jenny traversed it, you can envision the rush-hour traffic howling on the road beneath her and the cyclists and inline skaters flowing toward her on their way to the lakefront. You can imagine her breath chuffing and sweat dripping in the humidity, her brain seamlessly processing the sensory river, thinking and not thinking, seeing and not seeing, part of it automatically supervising the explosion of her muscles and another part, perhaps, rehearsing the pending phone call with her client.

Jenny ran across the bridge. Her condo was less than a mile away, in the city's historic brewery district, just a cooldown jog along Brady Street. She proceeded up from the bridge, passing a disc-shaped sculpture that she'd seen so many times that she probably barely registered it. Lines engraved on the base of the sculpture read like a prophecy:

> Inner time is limitless
> from past lives
> I can no longer remember
> only feel
> time flows,

and around me a continuum
moves and swirls
engulfing me . . .

Time flows until it slams up against a boulder, or freezes, or spurts out in a flood that scours the past and future into a depthless present. Two years since that August morning run, Marla Runyan's vibrant training partner now spends most of her day in a wheelchair. Peter Crain's irrepressible little sister, the girl with the iron work ethic, now complains about walking fifty feet. Cheryl and Bobby Neumann's exuberant old friend is now racked by morbid delusions, while Anne Marie Letko's old rival and new friend sometimes looks at her as if she were a stranger.

And yet, time also moves and swirls. Some days shards of the old Jenny resurface, searing her family and friends with grief at what has been lost, and kindling them with hope at what might be regained. To varying degrees and in their separate ways, her ordeal has transformed them. They are part of the continuum, at once detached and engulfed, changed and unchanging, and while sitting next to her, looking into her eyes, they remember this irreducible fact.

Jenny Crain went out for a run one morning in August 2007, and never came home.

Earlier that summer, Jenny Crain had accompanied Peter, his wife, Jeanne, and their three sons on a biking trip in central Wisconsin. One day during the trip she set out on a twenty-mile run, with her brother riding alongside on a mountain bike. "In the middle of this long, hot, hard run we come to this long hill with a three to five percent grade," Peter recalls. "Jenny was thrilled. 'What a great hill for speedwork!' she said. So I got out my stopwatch and she started knocking out intervals." Peter shakes his head. "When she was done, she picked up the run again."

After the biking trip, Jenny stayed with the family a few more days at their house in Edina, a suburb of Minneapolis. There, Peter says, his normally boisterous sister turned reflective. "Jenny knew that, approaching forty, this would be her last realistic shot at the Olympic Trials," he says of the women's Marathon Trials scheduled for the following April in Boston. "She also realized that if she was going to settle down into a stable long-term relationship, and have kids, then it would have to happen soon. She knew she was entering a period of transition. She and Jeanne would sit in the kitchen and talk for hours."

Peter, Jenny, and their younger brother, Scott, were all adopted as children. Peter was four when the infant Jenny became part of the family in 1968. Their mother, Donna, was a psychiatric social worker, and their father, Willard, was a systems analyst. The marriage was troubled, and ended when Jenny was in college. But that seemed like the lone dark spot in a sunny childhood.

"Early on you could tell Jenny was special," Peter says. "Even as a little girl, she had amazing leadership abilities." When she was ten, for instance, she organized an Olympic Games for the kids in their neighborhood in Franklin, Wisconsin, a suburb of Milwaukee. Along with planning the events, Jenny made prize medals, which she distributed to every participant. Later, Jenny served as the student representative on her church's parish council. She carried the Olympic torch in 1984 when it passed through the Midwest, and traveled to the Soviet Union as a student peace ambassador. "Everybody loved Jenny," Peter recalls with a smile. "So naturally I hated her."

Episodes of minor fraternal hazing ensued. Once, when they were small children, for instance, he cut off most of Jenny's hair. "But that all changed when I went to high school and started to run," says Peter, who would later compete for the University of Wisconsin–Stevens Point. "I became a mentor instead of a jealous big brother, and we grew very close."

Jenny decided to follow in her big brother's footsteps, and her talent for running emerged quickly. She was a consistent top-five finisher at state track and cross-country meets, which were usually dominated by Suzy Favor, the future Olympian who lived in Stevens Point. Jenny accepted a scholarship to Ohio University, but didn't enjoy the same level of success she'd had in high school. After graduating with a degree in communications, she returned to Milwaukee, where she eventually was hired by Northwestern Mutual Life Insurance Company to serve as a liaison between the main office and field representatives. She proved exceptionally effective at motivating the sales staff, and rose quickly through the company's ranks.

By the beginning of 1995, Jenny, then twenty-seven, seemed solidly launched on her professional and personal paths. She dated frequently, had a wide circle of friends, and kept in shape with bicycling and triathlons. Despite her success, she felt haunted by the Olympic dreams of her childhood, and made a New Year's resolution to qualify for the 1996 U.S. Olympic Marathon Trials. That December, at the Tucson Marathon, Jenny made good on her vow, barely meeting the Trials qualifying time with a 2:50:01 performance. Nine weeks later, she finished eighty-fourth in the Trials in Columbia, South Carolina.

She steadily improved over the next few years, running a 1:15:05 PR at the 1997 World Half-Marathon Championships. In 2000, she finished fourteenth in the U.S. Olympic Marathon Trials and four years later, at the 2004 trials, finished eleventh with a 2:37:36 PR. That race formed the first part of a trilogy of peak midcareer performances: in the fall of 2004, at age thirty-six, her 2:41:06 clocking at the New York City Marathon placed her fifteenth overall and first among American women; a year later at the World Championships in Helsinki, she finished thirty-sixth in 2:39:02.

In August 2007, at age thirty-nine, Jenny was beginning to focus on the next spring's Olympic Marathon Trials, and to look ahead to a career on the masters' circuit. "I think she was in the best shape of her life that summer," says Elva Dryer, a two-time Olympic distance runner and a close friend of Jenny's. "I remember seeing her at a 10-K and thinking, *Whoa, could that really be Jenny?*"

On Saturday, August 18, Jenny entered the Heart of Summer 10-K in Minneapolis. Four miles into the race she experienced heart palpitations and dropped out. She went to the hospital, where doctors could find nothing wrong. "She called me from the hospital, and she sounded relieved," says Mike DeWitt, the track and cross-country coach at the University of Wisconsin–Parkside, who helped guide Jenny's training. "She probably hadn't slept well the night before the race, or she'd had a little too much coffee. But naturally, the episode was on her mind."

Jenny and DeWitt agreed that until her follow-up doctor's appointment, which she'd scheduled for the afternoon of Tuesday, August 21, in Milwaukee, she should cut back on training. So early that morning, before her 9 A.M. phone consultation with a client, she headed out for what she assumed would be a routine bread-

and-butter run along the lakefront and back home via the Brady Street bridge.

Once she crossed the bridge, Jenny ran across quiet Prospect Avenue, then continued fifty meters on Brady Street to the corner of Farwell Avenue, a busy one-way, three-lane, southbound arterial. The intersection of Brady and Farwell forms the heart of the city's old Italian neighborhood, where most of the buildings consist of brick storefronts with apartments upstairs. Franchises anchor three of the corners: a Starbucks, a FedEx office, and a CVS pharmacy. It's a busy intersection with an intricate system of traffic lights, but one that Jenny had negotiated countless times in all types of weather and in all degrees of sunlight and darkness.

According to witnesses, she stopped when she reached the northeast corner of Brady and Farwell, waiting to cross Farwell. In the middle lane of Farwell, a car, heading in the direction where Jenny waited, was slowing to a stop as the traffic light turned yellow. She stepped off the sidewalk and into the crosswalk, apparently expecting other cars to either slow or stop as well. But then an Audi sedan veered left around the car that had stopped. The driver, a twenty-two-year-old man on his way to work, attempted to make it through the intersection, but struck Jenny in the crosswalk as she was about to start back on her run.

"The police didn't cite the driver for any violation," says Peter Crain, who has replayed that moment countless times, from every conceivable angle. "He wasn't talking on his cell phone, he wasn't text-messaging, and he wasn't impaired. He was probably rushing to make it through the light. And Jenny," Peter acknowledges, "might have jumped into the crosswalk a beat early—just a stride or two, the difference between first and second at the end of a close race."

The car was traveling at least thirty miles per hour. The post supporting the windshield on the driver's side, the connector between the roof and the hood, slammed into the right side of Jenny's unprotected skull. She was thrown over the hood and landed on the far side of the vehicle. The one piece of good luck was that the accident occurred in the heart of a major city; an ambulance arrived within minutes. Jenny was still conscious when she arrived in the emergency room of Milwaukee's Froedert Hospital, where doctors determined that the impact had fractured vertebrae, shattered her

jaw, bruised her aorta, and most grievously caused massive brain
damage. In the ICU surgeons opened her skull to drain the swelling from a blood clot. "If the accident had occurred in a more remote location," says Dr. Jeffery Cameron, Jenny's attending physi-
cian throughout most of her recovery and rehabilitation, "chances
are she wouldn't have survived."

The human brain is a miracle, a mystery, and a paradox. Intact, it
can process information faster than a supercomputer; damaged, it
can never fully heal, unlike other parts of the body. Each brain is
one of a kind, and so is each brain injury. This makes treatment simultaneously hopeful, fascinating, frustrating, and unending.

Sitting stiffly in a wheelchair on a warm morning this past May,
bundled in a heavy red-and-white-striped hooded sweater, Jenny
greets her brother and Jake, Peter's nine-year-old son, in the day
room of the brain-injury unit of Mt. Carmel Health and Rehabilitation Center in Milwaukee, where she's lived since April 2008. An
aide says that Jenny has just finished a hearty snack; due to perseveration, though, she still complains that she's hungry.

Perseveration is a common, bedeviling consequence of a severe
brain injury. It is the uncontrollable repetition of a phrase despite
the absence of a corresponding stimulus. In Jenny's case, damage
to her brain's frontal lobe produces morbid obsessions that im-
pede her recovery and at times test the patience of her caregivers.
The condition, however, only forms one of her challenges.

The trauma to Jenny's parietal lobe, located at the top of her
head, created a loss of spatial awareness; the onetime national-class
distance runner, who was also an accomplished cyclist and swimmer, now struggles to grasp a teacup. Injuries to Jenny's occipital
lobe, meanwhile, located at the back of her head, limit her ability
to read. Her short-term memory impairment results from her injured temporal lobes, while her difficulty with walking results from
the trauma to one whole hemisphere of her brain that integrates
sensory perception and motor skills. Damage to her brain stem, finally, restricts both her sense of balance and her ability to swallow.

"I'm hungry," she chants intermittently throughout the day in a
voice that, in the two years since the accident, has never varied
from a low monotone. "I'm cold. I don't want to die."

Peter and Jake try to distract her with family news, but without
much success. On her good days Jenny can be a delightful com-

panion. She questions visitors about their lives, and talks at length about events from her distant past. She checks her e-mail and beats all comers in games of Trivial Pursuit or Boggle. This morning, however, she can't shake her obsessions.

"I'm hungry. I'm cold. I don't want to die."

Eventually it's time for her physical therapy session, which today consists of a fifty-foot walk down a hallway. One therapist, Barb Foster, supports Jenny from the front, while another, Teri Mueller, supports her weight from behind. Both therapists murmur steady instruction and encouragement as they help Jenny maneuver her stiff, unresponsive limbs. Drained after his five-and-a-half-hour drive from Edina, Peter leans against a wall to watch. He'll make the return trip this afternoon, so he can be back at work tomorrow morning managing his home-building business. For the last two years, on an average of twice a month, he's repeated this round-trip. And yet he reports no burnout. "This is just how we live now," he says. "Jenny keeps improving — last week, for instance, she was only walking forty feet."

Peter pushes away from the wall. He moves to the end of the hall and turns to face his sister, spreading his arms and waving like a ground crewman guiding a jetliner into the gate. After a moment, Jake comes to stand shyly beside his father.

"The goal isn't just distance," Foster tells Jenny, sounding uncannily like a running coach. "It's also form."

"Get real tall, Jenny," Mueller says. "Lift that rib cage."

"This isn't a contest to see how tall I can get," Jenny mutters, breaking free of perseveration to employ her monotone to deadpan effect. Even on her toughest days, she shows glimmers of the wit that, in her previous life, entertained Marla Runyan and other training partners during long runs.

Peter grins. Jenny continues to work on her next step.

Two years have passed since Jenny's accident, and almost that long since Marla Runyan's debilitating back condition forced her to retire from elite distance-running competition. Over the last few months, Runyan has resumed running. On an overcast July morning in Eugene, Oregon, she tests her fitness, and remembers her friend, by running along the Willamette River, tracing a route that the two women often covered together.

The nine-mile run starts at the Downtown Athletic Club, referred to around Eugene as "the DAC." Earlier, Runyan, a member of the club, had dropped off her four-year-old daughter, Anna Lee, at preschool. "Jenny would say, 'Let's go do the DAC!'" Runyan recalls, imitating Jenny's goofy, infectious tone. "That girl was a demon for getting in her work, but at the same time she had this gift for transforming a chore into an escapade. She could also find fun in the oddest places."

Runyan cites the 2003 USA 20-K Championships in New Haven, Connecticut, as an example. "It was an important race for Jenny," she says, "part of her buildup for the upcoming Marathon Trials. The wheelchair division got a head start, and the leaders in the women's race caught up with them after two miles or so. When she saw the wheelchairs, Jenny started clapping and belting out the woo-woos." Eventually, Runyan pulled away and won the race while Jenny finished ninth.

Jenny had moved to Eugene in 2002 in order to focus her training on the 2004 Olympic Marathon Trials. She connected with Matt Lonergan, Runyan's husband and coach, and the two women quickly became training partners and close friends. Jenny enjoyed her stint in Oregon, Runyan says, but she missed her hometown, and at the end of 2004 moved back to Milwaukee.

"I was heartbroken when she left," Runyan says. "Sometimes I wonder, what if Jenny had stayed in Oregon? With Jenny, there are so many what-ifs."

Runyan sets out on her run, cutting through the heart of downtown, moving toward the river and the web of trails snaking through leafy Alton Baker Park. "This is a tempo run that Jenny and I must have done a hundred times," she says. "During some workouts I would ride the bike and cheer on Jenny, and sometimes vice versa. Either way, Jenny made a lot of noise. When she was running, she would always be spitting, and on the bike she would holler like a high school cheerleader. You could hear us coming from a mile away."

Now, Runyan's smile takes a quarter-mile to fade. "At the time, we had no way of knowing the charmed life we were living."

She filters through the busy streets and sidewalks, moving past an outdoor market. Runyan explains that Jenny kept in close touch after she left town. "Jenny came back to Eugene to put on my baby shower with Elva Dryer," she says. "Jenny visited here in July of

2007, not long before her accident. She was in great shape. She seemed happy. We went for a hike, and I showed her the house that Matt and I were buying. I took her up to the guest room. 'Here's where you'll stay when you visit,' I told her."

As she nears the edge of downtown, approaching a highway underpass, a pickup truck pulls out of a garage, moving a little faster than it should, given the crowded street. Runyan, for her part, is running a notch or two over the red line, lost in her mission and memories. She senses the truck a split second before the driver sees her. Stopping on a dime, like a point guard pulling up for a jump shot, she raises her right hand toward the truck in a half-commanding, half-pleading gesture for it to stop. The driver hits the brakes; tires squeal; passersby snap up their heads. But with no subsequent thud, they just as quickly continue on their way. A thousand similar routine near misses occur every day, in every city around the world. It's the reassuring scenario that every runner lives by: you always see the car in time, or the driver always sees you.

The driver turns onto Sixth Street, waving at Runyan in a gesture equal part relieved, apologetic, and angry. You can almost feel the adrenaline surging in his blood. Runyan, meanwhile, takes the fleeting episode in stride, running on toward the river without giving it another thought. You can almost see Jenny Crain running beside her.

For weeks after the accident Jenny hung precariously between life and death. The calamity shocked the local and national running communities. In Milwaukee, where Jenny was regarded as a minor celebrity, the story was covered heavily by the local media. In the online running-related message boards, people weighed in with stories about their own accidents and near misses involving careless drivers, while others inveighed against runners who, moving in traffic, took far too much for granted.

At home in Minnesota, Peter heard the news from John Lancaster, Jenny's boyfriend at the time, and made the drive to Milwaukee in four and a half hours, an hour less than normal. Cheryl Neumann saw the bulletin on the *Milwaukee Journal*'s website, and called her husband, Bobby. In Eugene, Marla Runyan learned of the accident as she and her husband were moving into their new house. Runyan sprinted back to her old house, and phoned Elva Dryer.

For that first grim month, while Jenny lay in a medically induced coma at Froedert Hospital, Donna Crain kept vigil over her daughter. Because Jenny was vulnerable to life-threatening infections, visitors had to put on antiseptic masks and suits that looked like something out of a bad science-fiction movie. Peter, meanwhile, had to deal with the doctors, the hospital bureaucracy, and the media. He established a website providing weekly updates on Jenny's condition, along with spaces for financial contributions to defray the cost of her long-term therapy.

Much of Jenny's care and treatment, which so far has totaled an estimated $1 million, has been paid for by disability insurance funds administered through the state. But with her care shifting from acute treatment to long-term care and with her own health insurance coverage soon expiring, the accident will increasingly strain the Crains' finances. The family has filed a lawsuit against the driver and his insurance company, based on the premise that he should have maintained control of his vehicle even though Jenny was in the crosswalk before she had a walk sign. Due to Jenny's seeming partial fault in the accident, Peter doubts that the suit will yield more than $500,000, with much of that sum going to attorney's fees. A trust fund composed of Jenny's liquidated assets, primarily money generated from the sale of her condo, amounts to $75,000.

Local and national running communities have stepped in to contribute support. Kristine Hinrichs, director of Milwaukee's Lakefront Marathon, led a campaign selling MAKE IT HAPPEN wristbands for five dollars apiece ("Make It Happen" was the phrase Jenny used to sign off every letter and e-mail). And Milwaukee-area runners, along with Jenny's friends and coworkers, raised $30,000 from a benefit concert; Peter recalls spilling the cash receipts out on the bed in his motel room and feeling like he'd just robbed a bank.

While these fundraising activities took place, Jenny gradually showed signs of coming back to life. A month after her accident, she was transferred from Froedert Hospital to the critical-care brain-injury center at Milwaukee's Sacred Heart Rehabilitation Institute. "Around December, just in time for the holidays, Jenny started making these leaping improvements and everybody was elated," says Mary Jean Fowler, who served as Jenny's massage therapist during her competitive running career and now donates her services to Jenny at Mt. Carmel.

A shunt was permanently implanted in Jenny's brain to relieve the pressure from fluids that had built up, her spine was fused to repair the broken vertebrae, and she underwent a series of operations on her broken jaw and other injuries. She started to recognize faces, track conversations, and ingest food. "We began to hope for a miracle-type recovery," Fowler says. "But brain injuries, we subsequently learned, show most of their improvement in the first six months. Then the rate of healing slows dramatically."

Such was the case with Jenny Crain. From Sacred Heart she moved to Mt. Carmel, where for the past year and a half she has filled her days with physical, occupational, speech, and massage therapy sessions, all part of a grueling, perhaps unending slog of rehab. Donna spends most days with her, supplementing Jenny's structured therapy with a range of activities that stimulate her body, mind, and memory. Donna also takes Jenny on visits to her house and to parks, restaurants, and malls. At her best moments, Jenny demonstrates the curiosity and empathy that characterized her before the accident. "Jenny never wanted to talk about herself," Runyan says. "She always wanted to know what was going on in your life. Her curiosity was never fake or forced. She was the most amazing listener I've ever met."

Jenny even worked this magic in the first months after the calamity, before she had regained any speech at all. One day, about four months after the accident, Hinrichs, the Lakefront Marathon director, visited Jenny; during the preceding days, Jenny had been showing on-and-off signs of coming out of her coma. "I sat down beside Jenny's bed and looked into her eyes," Hinrichs remembers. Earlier that week, Hinrichs had learned that her mother had been diagnosed with terminal cancer. "I told her the whole story about my mom. I talked for a long time. At one point Jenny opened her eyes and groaned. It took me a while to realize what was happening; Jenny was empathizing with me. Here was this young woman, this wonderful athlete, lying in a hospital bed, unable to say a word, and *she* was comforting *me*."

Cheryl and Bobby Neumann sit on the porch of their house in the Bay View neighborhood of Milwaukee on a warm June evening, eating ice cream and telling stories about the runners that have stayed with them over the last two years. The guests, such as Marla Runyan, are out-of-town friends of Jenny Crain, who continues to deliver excitement and meaning to the Neumanns' lives even while confined to a wheelchair at Mt. Carmel.

One of the top age-group runners in the Milwaukee area, with a 3:03 PR in the marathon, Cheryl, fifty-three, met Jenny in the mid-1990s, just as Jenny was recommitting to the sport. "We met in a downtown gym where I do my strength-training," Cheryl recalls. "Jenny asked me about my routine and I showed her a few things and we got to be friends. We would work out together, although it was laughable, the weights she could lift compared with what I could do."

Despite the two women's differences in age and athletic ability, their friendship deepened. "Jenny felt comfortable around Bobby and me," says Cheryl, who works as an administrative assistant for a Milwaukee law firm. "She would show up when she wanted to unwind. She always came to our big neighborhood party. Or sometimes she would just come over on a Friday night to relax, although relaxing for Jenny would exhaust a normal person. We would go out to dinner, then go to a movie, and after the movie she would rent another DVD and stay up into the middle of the night watching it. I would always fall asleep."

During the first month or so after the accident, Cheryl visited Jenny even though her friend was unresponsive. "And then a little later, after she came out of the coma, she couldn't speak at all," Cheryl says. The only way she could communicate was by blinking her eyes, once for yes and twice for no. But that was enough for her to express herself. We would have these amazingly long and intimate conversations, with me blabbing away, and her blinking every now and then."

Cheryl and Bobby continue to visit Jenny every Sunday afternoon, and continue to open their house to her friends. They drive their guests to Mt. Carmel to visit Jenny and pick them up when they are done. They show them the running routes along the shore of Lake Michigan, and take them downtown to the intersection of Brady and Farwell, to the spot where the tragedy began.

"I think that, on some level, Jenny understands everything that's happened to her, and what's going on around her," says Bobby, a machinist at a jet-engine parts factory. "One day she's going to sit up and say, 'Why the hell have you been acting so sad and creepy around me?'"

It is 3 P.M., a slow and quiet hour in the brain-injury rehab unit. After the draining PT session in which Jenny had struggled to walk fifty feet, she retreats to her room for a long nap. Peter and Jake settle at a table in Mt. Carmel's day room, joining a half-dozen patients, all of them younger men. "The majority of brain-injury patients are male," Peter says in a quiet voice. "It's the guys who tend to smash up motorcycles and snowmobiles, and who think they're too tough to wear seat belts and helmets."

Mary Smith, a recreational therapist who has worked with Jenny since she came to Mt. Carmel, joins Peter and Jake at the table. "Jenny might not be demonstrating any dramatic improvements at this point," Smith concedes, "but she's steadily showing flashes of her old self—the humor, the curiosity, the generosity. At the same time that we're seeing the old Jenny emerge, she'll never be quite the same as she was before the accident."

Smith pauses, choosing her words carefully. "Every brain injury is unique, and each brain-injury patient is one of a kind," she says. "At this point it's impossible to say how far Jenny can go."

During the conversation Jake sits quietly in his chair, shuffling an Uno deck. Earlier, Peter had explained that Jenny was close to all three of his sons, but had a special relationship with Jake, the youngest. When he'd first seen his aunt shortly after the accident, he'd been extremely upset—but quickly got used to her. Now, he looks forward to his visits to Mt. Carmel.

Today, however, there seems little payoff for Jake's long journey. When Jenny awakens from her nap, she still seems spacey and dissociated, unable to sustain a conversation. She can't seem to get out of herself, and exhibits none of the curiosity or energy that she displayed earlier in the day when she inquired about a visitor's own running, family, and professional career.

Peter and Jake stick around during Jenny's dinner, which consists mostly of soft foods due to her compromised swallowing function. (The starchy diet, combined with Jenny's immobility, voracious appetite, and water retention caused by her medications, has produced a significant weight gain over the last two years.) Efforts at conversation fizzle; Jake talks gamely about his baseball team, and his plans for the summer, but he can't quite divert Jenny from her perseveration.

"I'm cold. I'm hungry. I don't want to die," she repeats again and again.

Finally, it's time for Peter and Jake to start their long drive home. As Jake says goodbye, however, his aunt unexpectedly focuses. She looks up from her mashed potatoes. "Jake the snake," she says. They playfully bump fists. She fixes her nephew with an astonishingly clear and lucid look, like a beam of late-afternoon sunshine lancing through a daylong cloud cover. Then the moment passes. Jenny goes back to her dinner, and Jake and his father head for the parking lot.

During her prime, when Jenny returned home from a road race or track meet, she would often drop by the Neumanns' house. In the warm months they'd sit out on the front porch, and during the cold ones relax in the living room. Jenny would start talking about her race, then catch herself, worried that she was monopolizing the conversation. Cheryl and Bobby would say no, no, we love hearing these stories. So Jenny would continue, describing her contests against famous athletes like Marla Runyan and Deena Kastor. But she never mentioned Anne Marie Letko, one of the dominant female American distance runners of the 1990s.

That's because, though friendly with each other, the two women weren't friends. Letko respected Jenny as a competitor and admired the way she interacted with the public at races. But there were a lot of athletes on the circuit and Letko was so single-minded in those days that she didn't get friendly with many. Her focus and concentration delivered her the top-ten finish at the Atlanta Olympics, but also exacted a price.

After the Games, Letko discovered she had stress fractures in both feet. Then, once the fractures had healed, she developed symptoms of acute lethargy and painfully swollen joints. Doctors diagnosed Lyme disease, but could do little about it. She soldiered through these difficulties, managing a second-place finish at the 2001 national 10-K championships. But after that race, the wheels fell off, both personally and professionally. The effects of the Lyme disease intensified, forcing her to discontinue her training for the 2002 Boston Marathon. Later that year she decided to end her pro-

fessional running career. Around the same time, her marriage began to dissolve as well.

Letko entered a painful, unmoored period of introspection. She
read and thought and walked in the woods, figuring out along the
way that she wasn't the center of the universe. Having studied massage therapy years earlier, she started a new career. Her practice
built steadily, and by 2007 Letko had regained her equilibrium.
Then in August of that year she got a call from friends in Eugene
—Jenny Crain had been hit by a car in Milwaukee.

Letko was stunned. She didn't know why the news struck her so
hard. Maybe it was the fact that she and Jenny were around the
same age and, despite long and accomplished running careers,
hadn't received much attention. Now they had both learned how
quickly the sport they loved could disappear. Circles and conver-
gences: over the last few years, Letko had learned to heed them.
Late that fall she posted a note to the website that Peter Crain had
established.

> Dear Jenny, I don't know if you remember me? We used to compete
> against each other on the roads as well as the track in the 1990s through
> early 2000. I have since retired from professional running and spend
> my time in the healthcare field as a massage therapist. I heard about
> your terrible accident and the news has impacted me greatly . . . This
> may sound weird, but I'll voice it anyway. I can feel and sense your inner
> strength . . . Keep with it! "Persevere in gentleness and it will lead to
> resolution. Persevere in weakness and it will lead to strength." (Huai-
> Nan-Tsze) . . . I would love to visit you in the future . . . Even though I
> live in New Jersey, I would travel out your way in a heartbeat . . . Take
> care! Anne Marie Letko

Realizing that visitors representing Jenny's past would help stimulate her memory, Donna Crain replied immediately, inviting
Letko to visit. In early 2008, she made her first trip to Milwaukee.
Letko thought she was ready. In her massage practice she had
worked with terminally ill patients. But the scene at Sacred Heart,
where Jenny was then a patient, was foreboding and surreal; Letko
had to don the antiseptic suit to avoid inflicting Jenny with any
harmful germs. In this getup, she entered Jenny's room; the powerful athlete that Letko remembered was now appallingly frail, little more than skin and bones.

But for the first time since the accident, Jenny could whisper a
word or two. Moreover, she was awake, and making deep, luminous

eye contact. She was speaking with her eyes, Letko realized. Despite her shattered body, Jenny was intact inside.

Since that trip, Letko has returned to Milwaukee several times, including visits during a cross-country car trip she took during the summer of 2008. The two women have grown close, and yet even now Letko cannot precisely say what draws her to Jenny.

"To be honest, I go for selfish reasons," Letko says. "Visiting Jenny helps me. It teaches me to wake up each morning and consciously decide to live. I don't mean anything spooky or dramatic by that; you can decide to live in a very quiet way. Jenny just puts out these powerful and positive reverberations. It's kind of amazing." After a moment's thought, she adds, "It's also okay not to really understand it."

A few weeks after their previous trip to see Jenny, Peter and Jake hit the road again. At five in the morning Peter piles a half-asleep Jake into the back seat of the Suburban, kisses Jeanne, and then drives down the silent lanes of Edina to Interstate 94, beginning the long trek across the Minnesota River and state of Wisconsin.

Peter talks for hours, as the miles unreel and Jake sleeps in the back seat. He remembers road trips he took as a college runner, tells stories from his fifteen-year career as a high school art teacher, and acknowledges the gut-clenching anxiety of building high-end homes in the heart of the present economic scourge. It's only 9 A.M. when he reaches the Wisconsin Dells, the journey's halfway point, but the traffic is picking up. Reluctantly, Peter turns his thoughts to what lies ahead. The division of labor between Peter and his mother, he explains, has led to a difference of philosophy regarding Jenny's treatment.

Encouraged by her daughter's progress, Donna argues for spending the bulk of their money in an all-out, yearlong therapy blitz, which, she hopes, will lift Jenny over the hump and onto the path to living independently. Peter, by contrast, thinks that the family's limited resources should be meted out prudently, with the assumption that his sister will require lifelong care. Dr. Cameron shares this view.

"Jenny's biggest obstacle is her motor impairment," Cameron says. "Motor function is generated by the surface and frontal portion of the brain, which in Jenny's case suffered extensive damage.

Unfortunately, the brain doesn't recover well. It has limited ability to create new cells. Major gains in recovery usually occur in the first twelve to eighteen months following the injury. From here on out, short of a breakthrough coming in stem-cell research, I don't expect significant improvement."

Peter welcomes and appreciates the financial support the family has received from friends and strangers, but also realizes it doesn't go far. Jenny's need for therapy far exceeds the funds available for it. Her recovery, moreover, has been slow and undramatic, and the family understands that the public's interest will dwindle as time passes. "Jenny hasn't made the big jump," Peter acknowledges. "There is no feel-good hook to her story. Brain injuries need time. Long-term, it would be great to see her speaking for herself and telling her story in public. I think she would make an ideal spokesperson for understanding brain injuries."

In the meantime, which might stretch indefinitely, Jenny's family and friends make a point of living in the present. They rarely give way to exhaustion, or indulge in self-pity. "People assume that I must be angry," Peter says. "They tell me, 'You must be furious that one moment two years ago has led to all this misery, and messed up your sister's life—and your life—forever.' But I can honestly say that I don't feel that way. I can't afford to get angry because I'm too busy trying to figure my way through each day."

For a few minutes he drives in silence. "You know what bothers me the most?" he says. "Jenny used to be such an unbelievable worker, and now she won't reach for her own water glass. If it weren't for PT, she would never get out of that wheelchair. But then I realize that this is my problem, not Jenny's. She's a different person. Before her accident she would do hill repeats in the middle of a twenty-mile run, and now her goal is stand up by herself. It's the same degree of effort. My belief is that Jenny's working like crazy on the mile that she's running now."

Another summer has come to Milwaukee, the second since Jenny's accident, and Donna Crain accompanies her daughter to an occupational therapy session held outdoors in the Mt. Carmel courtyard. A group of five patients—four men and Jenny—play a memory-building game. The therapist lists categories on a white board: things you can drive, sports, and animals. She then asks the patients to cite examples of each category. Jenny appears alert, relaxed, and engaged. She is not perseverating. Today, clearly, is one of her good days.

When it's Jenny's turn in the "things you can drive" category, she cracks a joke. "You can drive people crazy," she says. Throughout the thirty-minute session she steadily encourages her fellow patients—"Good job, James! . . . Well done, Dave!"—in the way that, during tempo runs on the riverside trail in Eugene, she used to bellow encouragement to Marla Runyan.

Following the session, while the rest of the group goes back into the air conditioning, Jenny and Donna remain outside. Jenny opens a card that Elva Dryer has sent from Albuquerque. Jenny still has difficulty sustaining her attention for longer pieces of writing, but she fluently reads her friend's note aloud.

Dryer writes how much she'd enjoyed visiting Milwaukee the previous week and how excited she is by Jenny's rate of recovery. Dryer gives specific examples: Jenny's facility getting in and out of her wheelchair has improved; her grip of a teacup is firmer. The trip was vastly different from Dryer's first journey to Milwaukee after the accident, in December 2007, when she was accompanied by Marla Runyan.

At the time Jenny was being treated at Sacred Heart. She still couldn't talk or move. As was the case with Letko's visit, Runyan and Dryer had to wear the antiseptic suits and masks. The gear looked and felt strange, and the two women were frightened to encounter Jenny in her stricken state. As they put on the suits, they had to laugh to keep from crying. They then entered the hospital room where Jenny lay immobilized on a specially equipped bed beneath a high window.

Overcoming their initial rush of grief, Dryer and Runyan looked into their good friend's eyes and saw a familiar glint. They also noticed something new. "Jenny's whole being—all her intelligence, vitality, curiosity, generosity—was concentrated in her eyes," Runyan says. "I sat there kind of awestruck. I kept thinking, *This is it; this is life.*"

Now, on this sunny summer morning, a similar sense of life—fleeting, repetitive, frustrating, funny, paradoxical, tragic, and precious—reverberates from the simple way that Jenny carefully replaces the note in its envelope. Time flows around her, a continuum of a past increasingly remembered and a future in the making.

Jenny Crain went out for a run one morning in August 2007, and she's on her way home.

(Still) Life

FROM TEXAS MONTHLY

COMPARED WITH THE GLISTENING two-story mansions that surrounded it, the house looked like something from another time. It was only 2,180 square feet. Its red-brick exterior was crumbling, and its gutters were clogged with leaves. Faded, paint-chipped blinds sagged behind the front windows. Next to the concrete steps leading to the front door, a scraggly banana plant clung to life.

Built in 1950, it was one of the last of the original single-story homes on Northport Drive, in Dallas's Preston Hollow neighborhood. The newer residents, almost all of them affluent baby boomers, had no idea who lived there. Over the years, they'd see an ambulance pull up to the front of the house, and they'd watch as paramedics carried out someone covered in a blanket. A few days later, they'd see the paramedics return to carry that person back inside. But they'd never learned who it was or what had happened. Some of the local kids were convinced that the house was haunted. They'd ride their bikes by the lot at dusk, daring one another to ring the doorbell or run across the unwatered lawn.

None of the neighbors knew that mailmen once delivered boxes of letters to the front door and that strangers left plates of food or envelopes stuffed with money. They didn't know that high school kids, whenever they drove past the house, blew their horns, over and over. They didn't know that a church youth group had stood on that front yard one afternoon, faced the house, and sung a hymn.

In fact, it wasn't until the spring of last year that they learned that the little house used to be one of Dallas's most famous residences, known throughout the city as the McClamrock house. It was the home of Ann McClamrock and her son John, the boy who could not move.

On the morning of October 17, 1973, John McClamrock bounded out of bed; threw on bell-bottom jeans and a loud, patterned shirt with an oversized collar; jumped into his red El Camino with a vinyl roof; and raced off to Hillcrest High School, only six blocks away. He was seventeen years old, and according to one girl who had dated him, he was "the all-American boy, just heartbreakingly beautiful." He had china-blue eyes and wavy black hair that fell over his forehead, and when he smiled, dimples creased his cheeks. Sometimes, when he sacked groceries at the neighborhood Tom Thumb, Hillcrest girls would show up to buy watermelons so that he'd carry them out to their cars. On weekend nights, they'd head for Forest Lane, the cruising spot for Dallas teenagers, hoping to get a look at him in his El Camino—or better yet, catch a ride. One cute Hillcrest blonde, Sara Ohl, had been lucky enough to go out with John on her first-ever car date, to play miniature golf. After he took her home, she called all her friends and told them she had had trouble breathing the entire time they were together.

That morning, John sat restlessly through his classes. When the lunch period bell rang, he drove to the nearest Burger King to grab a Whopper. He pushed buttons on the radio until he found the Allman Brothers' "Ramblin' Man," turned up the volume, and pressed down on the gas pedal to get back to school. He walked past the auditorium, where the drama club was rehearsing Neil Simon's *Plaza Suite;* made a left turn; and then walked on toward the boys' locker room to put on his football uniform. John—or "Clam," as he was known among his friends—had a game that afternoon.

Earlier that summer, John had quit playing for the Hillcrest Panthers so he could work extra hours at Tom Thumb to pay off his El Camino. When he tried to rejoin the team at the start of his junior year, the coaches had ordered him to spend a few weeks on the JV squad. He was five feet eleven inches tall and weighed 160 pounds. He played tackle on offense, linebacker on defense, and he was the wedge buster on the kickoffs, assigned the task of breaking up the other team's front line of blockers. That afternoon, the junior varsity was playing Spruce High School, and John was determined to show the coaches what he could do. This was the week, he vowed to his buddies, that he would be promoted to varsity.

On Hillcrest's opening kickoff, he burst through the Spruce blockers and zeroed in on the ball carrier. He lowered his head, and as the two collided, John's chin caught the runner's thigh. The sound, one teammate later said, was like "a tree trunk breaking in half."

John's head snapped back, and he fell face-first to the ground. For the next several seconds, another teammate recalled, "there was nothing but a terrible silence." Because there were no cell phones in that era, a coach had one of the players run to the high school's main office to call an ambulance. When it arrived fifteen minutes later, John was still on the ground, his body strangely still. "You've got some pinched nerves," a referee told him, speaking into the ear hole of his helmet. "You'll be up in no time."

But as soon as he was wheeled into Presbyterian Hospital, doctors knew he was in trouble. They gave him a complete neurological exam, scraping a pencil across the bottoms of his feet and taking X-rays, then ordered that his head be shaved and two small holes be bored into the top of his skull. Large tongs, like the ones used to carry blocks of ice, were attached to the holes, and seventy pounds of weight was hung from the tongs in an attempt to realign his spine.

A Hillcrest administrator called John's mother at her office at a local bank. Ann McClamrock was fifty-four years old, a striking woman, green-eyed with strawberry-blond hair. She was, as her niece liked to say, "perpetually good-natured." She always had extra food in the refrigerator for the neighborhood kids who came running in and out of the house, and on weekends she loved to throw boisterous dinner parties, most of them ending with her exhorting everyone around the table to sing corny old songs like "Skinnamarink." When she arrived at the hospital, a doctor took her aside and quietly asked if she had any religious preference.

"I'm Catholic," Ann said, giving him a bewildered look.

"Maybe you should call your priest, in case you need to deliver your son his last rites," the doctor said. "We're not sure he's going to make it through the night."

The doctor told Ann that John had severely damaged his spinal cord and was paralyzed from his neck down. He was able to swivel his head from side to side, but because his circulatory system had been disrupted, causing his blood pressure to fluctuate wildly, he could not lift his head without blacking out. "It couldn't be any worse," the doctor said.

At least outwardly, Ann seemed to take the diagnosis rather calmly. Or maybe, she later told her friends, she had simply been unable to comprehend the full meaning of what the doctor was saying. She stood at her son's bedside until her husband, Mac, who had been out of town that day—he worked for a company that insured eighteen-wheelers—arrived with the McClamrocks' other child, Henry, a quiet boy who was a freshman at Hillcrest. It was right then, with the family all together, that Ann felt the tears coming.

She slowly turned to the doctor, her hands trembling. "My Johnny is not going to die," she said. "You wait and see. He is going to have a good life." And then, her voice choking, she fell into Mac's arms.

John made it through the night and then through the next day. His friends flocked to the hospital, many of them dropped off at the front door by their parents. One night, nearly one hundred kids were in the ICU waiting room, all of them signing their names on a makeshift guest register—a legal pad—pinned to a wall. There were so many phone calls coming into the hospital about John that extra operators were brought in to work the switchboard.

The local newspapers jumped on the story, and soon just about everyone in Dallas was following John's struggle to stay alive. Dallas Cowboys coach Tom Landry and star defensive back Charlie Waters came to see him. The owner of the local Bonanza steak-house chain held a Johnny McClamrock Day, donating 10 percent of all the restaurants' sales to a medical fund. "Buy a Drink for Johnny" booths were set up at shopping malls all over the city, with proceeds from the one-dollar soft drinks going to the family. And at Hillcrest alone, there was a bake sale, a benefit basketball game, a bowl-a-thon, a fifties dance, and even a paper drive conducted by the Ecology Club.

After one of the national wire services ran a story about John,

letters began pouring in from all over the country. A group of
North Carolina women who attended Sunday school together
mailed John a card with an encouraging Bible verse. A faith healer
from Michigan sent a note to let John know that "healing sensa-
tions" were coming his way ("You will begin to feel sensation . . .
KNOW you are going to be UP and around very SOON"). John received hand-drawn get-well cards from Texas schoolchildren and
sentimental notes from teenage girls who had never met him. (A
girl named Patti wrote to let him know that she had played "Bad,
Bad Leroy Brown" on her record player in his honor.) Then, in
November, a letter arrived at the hospital from the most unlikely
place of all: the White House. President Richard Nixon, who was in
the midst of his spectacular downfall from the Watergate scandal
—he was only ten days away from delivering his "I am not a crook"
speech—had read about John and stopped what he was doing to
write him a sympathetic note.

"Mrs. Nixon and I were deeply saddened to learn of the tragic
accident which you suffered," he began, "but we understand that
you are a very brave young man and that your courage at this difficult time inspires all who know you. You have a devoted family and
many friends cheering for you, and we are proud to join them in
sending warm wishes to you always."

In December doctors suggested that John be moved to the Texas
Institute for Rehabilitation and Research, in Houston, which specialized in spinal injuries. Maybe someone down there could figure
out a way to get him to move, they said. When he left Presbyterian,
there were nearly four thousand names listed on the guest register.
Students stood by the hospital's exit and held up signs that read
GOOD LUCK, CLAM!

While Ann lived in an apartment near the rehabilitation center
and Mac and Henry visited on weekends, John stayed in a ward
with other paralyzed men, going through two hours of physical
therapy every day. The following March, when forty of his high
school friends showed up to surprise him on his eighteenth birthday—they gave him the new albums by Elton John and Chicago—
he was too weak to blow out the candles on his cake. But he assured
them that the therapy was working. Speaking into a telephone receiver held by his mother, he told a *Dallas Morning News* reporter

that he would walk again and "probably" would go back to playing football. "I will never give up," he said in as firm a voice as he could muster.

But late that spring, doctors met with Ann, Mac, and Henry in a conference room. Staring at their notes, they said that not a single muscle below John's neck had shown any response. He still couldn't raise his head without losing consciousness, they added, which meant there was almost no chance he would be able to sit in a wheelchair.

One of the staffers took a breath. "We've found that ninety-five percent of the families that try to take care of someone in this condition cannot handle it," she said. "The families break up." She handed them a sheet of paper. "These are the names of institutions and nursing homes that will take good care of him."

Ann nodded, stood up, and said, "We will be taking Johnny home, thank you." A relative arrived with a station wagon, John was loaded into the back, and the McClamrocks returned to Northport Drive, where a newspaper photographer and some friends were waiting. Mac, Henry, and a couple of others carried John, who was wearing his Hillcrest football jersey, into the house. They twisted him into a sort of L shape as they turned down the hall and turned again into the guest bedroom, where they laid him on a hospital bed with a laminate headboard.

To make everything look as normal as possible, Ann redecorated the bedroom, hanging photos on the wall of John in his uniform. On a set of shelves she displayed footballs that had been autographed by members of various NFL teams, and she also placed the football from the Spruce game, which had been signed by his teammates. Because she had heard John tell his friends that he was determined to go hunting again, she had Mac buy a Remington twelve-gauge shotgun, which she hung on another wall. Then she told her son, "Here we are. Here is where you are going to get better."

Every morning before sunrise, she got out of bed, did her makeup and hair, put on a nice dress or pantsuit, dabbed perfume on her neck, and walked into John's room. She shaved him, clipped his nails, brushed his teeth, gave him a sponge bath, shampooed his hair, and scratched his nose when it itched. She fed him all his meals, serving him one bite of food after another, and she taped a straw to the side of his glass so that he could drink on his own. She changed his catheter and emptied the drainage bag when it filled up with urine, and she dutifully cleaned his bottom as if he were a newborn whenever he had a bowel movement. To prevent bedsores, she turned him constantly throughout the day, rolling him onto one side and holding him in place with pillows, then rolling him onto his back, then rolling him to his other side — over and over and over.

From Monday through Saturday, she almost never left the house. On Sunday mornings, she went to Mass at Christ the King Catholic Church, lit a candle for John, and put a $10 check in the collection box. Afterward, she drove to Tom Thumb, the same one where John used to work, to buy groceries. Once a month she'd treat herself to a permanent at the hair salon at JC Penney. But that was it: every other minute was devoted to John.

Perhaps Ann kept up such a schedule because she thought he didn't have long to live. Within weeks after their return from Houston, he developed a kidney infection so severe it caused blood poisoning. An ambulance pulled up to the house. Paramedics ran inside, picked up John from his bed, and drove him to Presbyterian Hospital. Somehow he recovered, and when the paramedics brought him home, Ann kissed him on the forehead and said, "I'm so proud of you." A few weeks later, he developed pneumonia, which forced another trip to the hospital. Once again, he made a comeback, and once again, as he was returned home, Ann went through her ritual, kissing his forehead and saying how proud she was.

For the next few months, his friends constantly dropped in to visit. Driving past the house on their way to and from school, they always honked their horns. When John's friend Jeff Brown bought a classic 1939 Chevy Coupe, he drove it onto the McClamrocks' front yard so John could see it from his window. And because the newspapers in those days printed the home addresses of people they wrote about, strangers did indeed show up with food and gifts. At least five well-wishers gave him copies of *Joni,* the autobiography of a young woman who was paralyzed at the age of seventeen but became a skillful artist, using only her mouth to guide her brush.

One Saturday night in May 1975, Ann left home for a few hours with Mac so that they could accept John's diploma at Hillcrest High School's graduation ceremony. When his name was announced and Ann began to walk across the stage, the cheers were so loud that people put their hands to their ears. The reporters wrote about his graduation; "Gridder Scores" was the *Dallas Times Herald*'s headline. When one journalist came to see him, John remained upbeat, saying he might take business law courses and someday try to pass the bar exam. "I really appreciate all the help everyone has given me and my family," he said. "Tell everyone thanks." But when the reporter asked him about his dream of walking again, he simply said, "Oh, I don't know."

Later that summer, before heading off to college, John's friends came over to say their goodbyes. In September the sound of the crowds cheering at the Hillcrest football games on Friday night began drifting across the neighborhood. Although John's window was always shut — his mother didn't want pollen coming into the house because it might congest his already weak lungs — the sound slipped in anyway. John would listen to the band play the school fight song, and he knew exactly the place in the song where the cheerleaders would kick their long, beautiful legs. "Right there," he'd softly say. "Right there."

"Come on, Johnny, we can get through this," Ann would say when she saw that look of despair cross his face. She would often read to him her favorite lines from a Catholic book of devotions she owned: "You can find the good in what seems to be the most horrible thing in the world . . . God tells us that in all misfortunes we must seek the good . . . Acting hopeless is easy. The real challenge is to hope."

She would also show him a small, well-worn card, titled "Prayer of Thanksgiving," which she kept on her bedside table. The prayer ended with the lines "Lord Jesus, may I always trust in your generous mercy and love. I want to honor and praise you, now and forever. Amen." She told John that she read that prayer every night. "We must pray for God's mercy," she said. "That's all we can do."

But a lot of people who knew the McClamrocks could not help but wonder if God had abandoned them. In 1977, during Henry's senior year at Hillcrest, doctors found cancerous lymph nodes in his neck. After removing them, the doctors told Ann and Mac that there was no guarantee the cancer was gone. A few months later, after paying his own visit to the doctor, Mac came home and told Ann that his nagging cough had been diagnosed as acute emphysema. Ann couldn't believe what she was hearing. She had been married once before, right out of high school, and she had given birth to a son'named Cliff, who was now grown. But her first husband had died of liver disease before she turned thirty, and now here was Mac — "the genuine love of my life," she liked to say — telling her he too was going to die.

As Mac's breathing worsened, oxygen tanks piled up in their bedroom. In January 1978 he walked down the hall to sit with John. Wheezing, he patted his son on the shoulder and said he was going to need to spend a little time in the hospital. He walked out of the house and died four days later.

The funeral was held on a frigid afternoon. Ann dressed John in a suit he hadn't worn in five years and had him driven in a van to Christ the King Catholic Church. Other than his emergency trips to the hospital, it was the only time he had been out of the house. As he was pulled from the van and placed onto a stretcher outside the church, he exhaled heavily. "I can see my breath," he said, his eyes widening. "I can see my breath." He was pushed to the front of the sanctuary, next to the family's front-row pew, and he turned his head so that he could watch a priest swing a burner of incense over his father's casket. When John started to sob, Henry wiped the tears from his eyes with a tissue.

Incredibly, just two years later, Cliff called to say he had been diagnosed with lung cancer. He died in 1981, at the age of thirty-nine. At that funeral, people looked at Ann, convinced she was at the breaking point. Two husbands and one of her sons were dead. Another son was battling cancer. And, of course, there was John. Her niece, Frances Ann Giron, who always called her "Pretty Annie," told her to take a vacation. "Go someplace you've always wanted to go, like New York City," Frances Ann said. "I'll take care of John. A long weekend. That's all."

But Ann shook her head. She drove home from the funeral, walked into John's room, and put on her best smile for her son. "We're going to keep fighting," she said. "That's all I ask — just keep fighting."

They lived on Social Security disability benefits and a little insurance money. To help make ends meet, Ann, who had never gone back to her bank job after John's injury, found part-time work with an answering service, taking after-hour phone calls for a Dallas heating and air-conditioning company that were forwarded to the McClamrock house. To save money, she ordered inexpensive clothes for herself from catalogs, and she continued to wear the same clip-on earrings she had bought when she first met Mac.

She and John developed a daily routine. In the mornings, either she read to him, mostly stories out of *Reader's Digest,* or he read alone, using a page-turning device that he could operate with a nod of his head. They watched game shows and *Guiding Light.* They watched all the news broadcasts and movies on a VCR. Henry, who by then was living in his own apartment and working as a car salesman, would come over to sit with John on Sundays so that Ann could go to church and the grocery store. When she returned, she would fix a huge meal, usually chicken or pot roast with potatoes. Finally, at the end of each night, she would kiss John on the forehead and go off to her own bed, always reading her prayer of thanksgiving before falling asleep.

At least once a year, John came close to dying. He developed a urinary tract infection that nearly caused renal failure. Bladder stones clogged his catheter. His lungs filled with fluid, nearly drowning him. During his stays at the hospital, the doctors would say to Ann, "It's touch and go." But he always recovered, and as he was brought back into the house, Ann would always kiss him on the forehead and say, "I'm so proud of you."

One afternoon, as paramedics carried him back into the home, he looked at his mom and Henry and said, "Here I am, still kicking." He grinned and added, "Well, maybe not kicking."

Ann was delighted. "That's the spirit," she said.

Although John had found it impossible to get through a college correspondence course because he couldn't write anything down, he began watching all the history documentaries on PBS, he studied encyclopedia entries in hopes that someday he would be able to answer all the questions on *Jeopardy,* and he carefully read the newspaper (his mother folding the pages and putting them in front of him) so that he could have a better chance at guessing who would be the Person of the Week on ABC's Friday evening newscast.

Sometimes, he'd blow into a specially designed tube that allowed him to turn off the radio or television, and he'd stare at the ceiling, letting his mind wander. He kept a mental list of places he wanted to see: Alaska, the Swiss Alps, and the Colosseum, in Rome. He imagined himself taking a trip down the Nile or exploring Yellowstone National Park in the winter. And he spent hours thinking back on his life before his injury: the street baseball games he played with neighborhood kids in the fourth grade, the time he put twenty pieces of bubble gum in his mouth in junior high school, the students who passed by him in the halls, the Saturday nights cruising in his El Camino. He seemed to remember some days at Hillcrest in their entirety, right down to the food he ate in the cafeteria. "It's like everyone else has all these new memories filling up their brains," he told one of his closest friends, Mike Haines, a former lineman on the football team who had become a lawyer. "All I've got are the ones before October 1973."

In March 1986, to nearly everyone's surprise, he made it to his thirtieth birthday. Ann threw one of her old-fashioned dinner parties, inviting relatives and friends. At the end of the meal she made everyone sing "Skinnamarink." Then she sang the ballad "How Many Arms Have Held You?" The dining room got strangely quiet. Everyone stared at Ann, this woman in her sixties who refused to be broken. At the end of the song, they turned to look at the motionless John, who was smiling at his mother, cheerfully telling her she still sang off-key. "You simply could not fathom how they were able to do it, day after day," Ann's niece, Frances Ann, later said. "I'd say to Pretty Annie, 'Don't you ever feel overwhelmed? Aren't you ever bitter at what has happened to you?' And she'd say, 'Frances Ann, we can either act hopeless or we can make the best out of the life we have been given.' And she'd show me that prayer of thanksgiving card and she'd say, 'God will provide. I know he will.'"

Another year passed, and then another. Around the neighborhood, older residents began to sell off their little houses to a new generation of wealthy Dallasites, who would almost immediately tear them down to build mansions with high-ceilinged foyers and impressive "great rooms." Ambitious young real estate agents would knock on the front door of the McClamrock home, and when Ann answered, they'd tell her that they could get her a large amount of money if she'd sell too. But she would quickly turn them away, their business cards still in their hands. "I'm sorry," she'd say politely, "but this is our *home*."

It was perfectly understandable that the new residents knew nothing about the McClamrocks. By then, John was no longer being written up in the newspapers: reporters, predictably, had found other senseless tragedies to write about. In fact, by the time the nineties rolled around, a lot of people in Dallas who had once followed John's struggles had forgotten all about him. Many of John's classmates—the very ones who had flocked to the intensive-care waiting room so many years ago—had also lost touch with him. They'd certainly meant to visit, but one thing or another had gotten in the way, and now, after so many years, they were no longer sure how to restart the friendship they'd once had.

But in 1995, the organizers of the twentieth reunion festivities for Hillcrest's class of '75 put out the word that John, his mother, and Henry would be more than happy to entertain visitors. (Henry had moved back home after a divorce and undergone two more cancer surgeries on his already scarred neck.) During the reunion weekend, fifty or so classmates went by the house, and they were stunned at what they saw. Perhaps because he had not spent a day in the sun since 1973, John hardly seemed to have aged. His skin was perfectly smooth and his hair was still jet-black and long over the ears, exactly the way all the guys used to wear their hair in high school. And except for the shotgun—John had told Henry years earlier to take it down and give it to someone who could use it —nothing in his room had changed. The photos of John in his football uniform were still on the wall, and his clothes from high school, including his jersey, his bell-bottom jeans, and his loud, patterned shirts with oversized collars, were still in the closet. Even the same shag carpet covered the floor.

A couple women who had once dated him blinked back tears when they saw him. Another classmate, Sara Foxworth, a Dallas housewife and mother, gasped when she walked into his room and he called her name.

"But I thought you didn't know who I was," she exclaimed. "I was too shy to talk to you."

"You sat three seats behind me in English," he said. "And your locker was over by the cafeteria." He gave her a gentle smile. "I remember," he said.

Several of his old teammates, still muscular and narrow-waisted, had no idea what to say to him. They certainly didn't want to make John feel worse about his plight by telling him about all the things they had done since high school. But John asked them about their careers, their wives and children, and where they went on vacations. He also assured them that he was doing just fine—that he even watched football on weekends and didn't flinch when he saw a jarring tackle. "I'm the same person I've always been—only I don't move," he joked. And when each of his visitors told him goodbye, he said cheerfully, "Come on back, anytime you want. Believe me, I'm not going anywhere."

Some of his classmates did come back around. A few of them brought along their children to meet John so they could learn about courage. (As soon as they got back to their homes, the kids would go lie in their beds, trying to see how long they could stay still.) Bill Allbright, a trainer on the junior varsity team who had become a successful financial adviser, found himself driving over to see the McClamrocks after he lost his wife to cancer, knowing they would understand his loss. And when Sara Foxworth was diagnosed with leukemia, she too showed up at the McClamrocks'. After she left, John asked his mother to come into his room with some stationery so that he could dictate a letter for Sara. He had his mom write the lines "You can find the good in what seems to be the most horrible thing in the world. Take good care of yourself. Sincerely, John McClamrock."

Ann was then in her late seventies, and she was still maintaining her daily schedule, changing John's catheter, cleaning his bottom, and turning him every couple hours, refusing any help. A few years earlier, after reading an article about exercise and a healthy heart, she had ordered a cheap stationary bicycle from a catalog, which she put in her bedroom and faithfully pedaled each night. Wearing ancient, cracked tennis shoes, she had also been taking quick walks around the block, pumping her arms back and forth.

But she knew that time was catching up with her. It wasn't long after the twentieth reunion that she began adding a single sentence to the end of her prayer of thanksgiving. She asked God to let her live one day longer than John—only one day, she fervently prayed—so that she could always take care of him. "I'm not going to leave him," she told Henry. "He's hung on for me. I'm going to hang on for him."

John did continue to hang on. He came down with another urinary tract infection. His intestines suddenly twisted, which forced doctors to push a tube down his throat and pump everything out of his stomach to provide him some relief. He got a bedsore so severe that plastic surgery was required to mend it. His lungs again filled up with fluid. But each time, he bounced back. As paramedics carried him inside the house, he would say, "Still kicking," and his mother, following her ritual, would kiss him on the forehead and say, "I'm so proud of you."

One afternoon, a pretty brunette named Jane Grunewald, who had been a classmate of John's, called and asked if she could visit. Jane had married soon after graduating from Hillcrest and spent twenty years trying to be what she described as "the perfect PTA mom," raising two children in the suburbs. But her marriage had fallen apart, and she was struggling. On that first visit, she and John talked for two hours. She began returning once a month, often wearing a lovely black dress, always bringing along Hershey's Kisses for John. Before she arrived, John would have his mother wash his hair, comb his mustache, dab some cologne on his neck, and then pull his bedsheet up to his chin so she wouldn't see his painfully thin body. Sometimes, Ann would fix them cocktails, carrying them into John's room on a tray (with a straw always taped to the side of John's glass). Then she'd leave them alone.

During one visit, Jane told him that he was the kind of man she longed for—someone who genuinely appreciated her. "And you're always there for me," she said.

"That's true, you never have to worry about me running around on you," John replied. He told Jane to look in the top dresser and pull out his old Saint Christopher pendant. "It's yours," he said. "I never did get the chance to give it to someone in high school." She leaned down and kissed him on the cheek, leaving a thick red lipstick print.

He later told Henry that his monthly visits from Jane were his version of a love affair. "Not that we are going to have sex," he said with a sort of resigned smile. "You know, I never had sex. I'll never make love to a woman." He gave his brother a look. "Is there any way you can tell me what it feels like?"

For Ann's eighty-second birthday, on January 12, 2001, Henry brought home a gift, along with a takeout chicken-enchilada dinner from El Fenix and a bag of red licorice, her favorite candy. "To Mom, still kicking," John said as she opened her present, a small bottle of perfume that Henry had bought at Dillard's. Five years later, on her eighty-seventh birthday, Henry again brought home takeout enchiladas and a bag of red licorice, and John again said, "To Mom, still kicking."

By then, it was obvious she was slowing down. Instead of getting dressed as soon as she got out of bed, she spent her mornings in her nightgown and her favorite green terrycloth bathrobe. She was having trouble hearing, and her eyesight was weakening. She began to wobble when she walked and once fell while cooking breakfast. A doctor told her that she had a type of vertigo and that she needed to stay off her feet. "Absolutely not," she replied.

But in the fall of 2007, she fell again, breaking a bone in her right shoulder and tearing her left rotator cuff. It was the first time she had been admitted to the hospital since Henry's birth, in 1959. Still, she left a couple days earlier than the doctors wanted so that she could get back to John. "I have to keep going," she said when Henry came to take her home, and she suddenly burst into tears. "Henry, I can't leave him."

Only then did she allow Henry to take over the task of turning John in his bed. She let him make the instant coffee in the morning for the three of them. Because of her eyesight, she also agreed to let Henry drive her to Christ the King and the grocery store on Sundays. But she still had precise rules for their excursions. She told Henry that as soon as he dropped her off at the church, he had to immediately return to the house to sit with John. He then could pick her up at the end of the service and take her to the grocery store, but he had to drive right back to the house again to sit with John, and he could return to the store only when she called.

In January 2008, Ann, John, and Henry celebrated her eighty-ninth birthday with another takeout meal from El Fenix and another bag of licorice. A few weeks later, in the middle of the night, she thought she heard the sound of bedsprings squeaking in John's room. She heard footsteps and then a hesitant cry.

"Mom . . ."

She sat up, pulled her green terrycloth bathrobe over her gown, and headed down the hall. Because she could barely see in the darkness, she kept one hand on the wall to keep herself from falling. When she reached John's bedroom doorway, she stepped forward and peered toward his bed, in the corner of the room.

"Johnny?" she asked. "Johnny?"

She was nearly out of breath. She turned on a lamp and there he was, fifty-one years old, lying on his back in his bed just as he had been for the past thirty-four years. He turned his head a few inches to the side and looked at her.

"Mom, are you okay?"

She took a breath and said, "I thought . . ." And then she paused for a moment.

"I thought you had . . ." But she paused again, unable to bring herself to say the words.

It was the first time, she later said, that she had ever dreamed that John could walk again. "What does it mean?" she asked Henry. "What do you think it means?"

Not long after the dream, two new bedsores appeared on the backs of John's knees. In late February, he was taken to Presbyterian. The doctors, realizing the tissue of his skin was wearing out and unable to withstand the constant pressure from the bed, suggested that he be admitted to a nearby rehabilitation facility, where a wound-care specialist could treat him.

Within days, he developed a fever, and because he could not cough with any strength, he was unable to expel any dust or mucus from his lungs. His weight dropped to ninety-eight pounds. "You have to admit, my body held up for a long, long time," he said when Henry dropped by to check on him.

"Come on now, you can get through this," Henry said, using one of their mother's phrases. "All you have to do is keep fighting."

"Why don't you bring Mom over?" John said. "Have her look pretty. She'd like for me to see her that way."

"John, are you giving up?"

There was a long silence. A food cart rattled down the hall and a nurse's sneakers squeaked on the hallway floors. From other rooms came the beeps of heart monitors and the deep whooshing sounds of ventilators.

"We know about her prayer," John finally said. "We know she doesn't want to go first." He looked at Henry and said, "I need to go so she can go."

*

On March 18, Henry drove Ann to JC Penney to get her hair done before he took her to the rehabilitation facility. Because she was so feeble, Henry put her in a wheelchair. He pushed her into John's room, where she immediately began to check his catheter and inspect the bandages on his bedsores. "Mom, it's okay," John said.

She smoothed John's hair along the temples. She touched his forehead, and she slowly ran her hand down one side of his face, past his cheekbones and the curls of his hair. She said, as if she knew what was about to happen, "Johnny, we'll be back together soon."

"I know we will," John said.

Then he told his mother something he had never said before. "I know how hard it's been for you."

"Hard?" Ann asked. "Johnny, it's been an honor."

Henry took her home, helped her into her bed, and made sure she had her prayer of thanksgiving card. After she fell asleep, he drove back to the rehabilitation facility to check on John one last time. A nurse greeted him at the door. John had died about thirty minutes earlier, she said. He had closed his eyes and quietly drifted away, not making a single sound.

It was standing room only for the funeral. Some of John's childhood friends had flown in from around the country. Jane Grunewald, of course, arrived in one of her black dresses, and Sara Foxworth, less than a year away from death herself, was also there, gingerly taking a seat at the end of a pew. John's schoolmate Jeff Whitman, a prominent Dallas eye surgeon, came straight from a hospital, still wearing his scrubs, and Dave Carter, the former Hillcrest swimming coach, who had named his dog after John, already had tears in his eyes when he walked into the sanctuary.

The mourners looked toward the front rows to get a glimpse of Ann. But just before the service began, a priest walked up to the pulpit to announce that she and Henry would not be there. Earlier that morning, the priest said, Ann had collapsed while getting dressed for the funeral and Henry had rushed her to Presbyterian Hospital.

The organist launched into the opening hymn, and John's casket was rolled down the main aisle. He was dressed in the suit he'd worn to his father's funeral. The priest waved a burner of incense over John's casket and said, "May the Lord bless this man who is finally freed of the binds that have held him. May he run over fields of green."

Ann returned home a couple of days later. Clearly disoriented, she wandered through the house, always holding on to a wall, not sure what to do. At one point, she picked up the phone and asked Henry for the number of a Dallas department store that had been closed for decades. She asked to talk to her father, who had been dead for fifty years. She then stood in the doorway of John's bedroom, staring blankly at his bed. "Johnny?" she said. "Johnny, are you walking?"

Eight weeks after John's death, Ann died in her bed, her prayer of thanksgiving card on the bedside table. Henry was sitting beside her, holding her hand. He had her cremated and her ashes put in an urn, which he decided to bury in the ground directly over John's casket, at a cemetery near Love Field. At her service, the same priest who had presided over John's funeral said, "We send off Ann today to be with the son she loved. We send her to the mansions of the saints." The priest was about to say something else about Ann, but he saw Henry holding his hands to his face. "And may God bless Henry, who gave his life to his family," the priest said. "God bless Henry."

For days, Henry just sat in the little house on Northport Drive, not sure what to do. He finally got rid of John's hospital bed and, except for his mother's terrycloth robe, donated her clothes to charity. He then planted a FOR SALE sign in the front yard. Many of the neighborhood's residents were no doubt relieved: the old house was finally going to be demolished so that a new mansion could be built.

But one afternoon, when he was in the front yard watering the banana plant, two young mothers on their power walk slowed down and waved at him. They said they had read a sports column in the newspaper eulogizing the McClamrocks. "We're sorry we never got a chance to meet your mother and brother," one of the women said, grabbing Henry's hand. A few days later, a man got out of a luxury car, rang the doorbell, and told Henry he lived down the street. "If there's anything we can do for you, let us know," he said.

In March, a year after John's death, Henry still hadn't accepted any offers to sell. "I know I need to move on and get my life started again," he recently told a visitor while the two of them sat in John's room. "But I keep hearing Mom's and John's voices. In the mornings, I keep making three cups of instant coffee. When I go to the grocery store, I drive back home as fast as I can, thinking someone might need me."

The visitor noticed that Henry had started remodeling, pulling out the old shag carpet and repainting the walls. Henry shrugged. "I don't know if I can ever leave," he said. "This has been a good home. It's been a very good home."

ALEXANDER WOLFF

The NFL's Jackie Robinson

FROM SPORTS ILLUSTRATED

THE ACTORS TOOK THEIR MARKS, director Stanley Kubrick stood at the ready, and Woody Strode turned on the one-hundred-yard stare he had deployed so effectively a decade earlier on the football field. By then, in late 1959, Strode had largely moved on from the frustration of his single season in the NFL. He and Kenny Washington, his teammate at UCLA, had broken the league's color barrier with the Los Angeles Rams in 1946, and since then Strode had cashed in on the physique that once made Leni Riefenstahl beg him to model for her. He had gone to Canada and won a Grey Cup and spent offseasons barnstorming as a good-guy pro wrestler. Now he was in the movies, preparing for the scene in *Spartacus* in which he and Kirk Douglas are ordered to fight to the death. Suddenly Strode heard the voice of another actor in the cast.

"Woody Strode!" said Laurence Olivier.

"Yes, sir?"

"I'm a fan of yours and Kenny Washington's."

"I don't know what I'm doing here in your business," Strode said.

"What you're about to do," Olivier replied, "I could never do."

What Strode does in *Spartacus*—he subdues a fellow slave in one of cinema's epic one-on-one battles but refuses to kill him and is instead finished off by a Roman general, played by Olivier—emblemizes the ferocious, tragic grace with which Strode and Washington made history. Today those feats go essentially unremembered. Their NFL careers were brief and, in Strode's case, personally unfulfilling; both men had passed their primes when the league finally admitted them. But together they were to the NFL what their UCLA football teammate Jackie Robinson would be to Major League Baseball one year later: pulling guards in the sweep of history.

Baseball, bless its pastoral soul, offers a tidy and reassuring desegregation narrative. It's a story that reflects how we like to think of ourselves, as a society forever improving if not perfecting itself, and it offers ennobling roles for whites as well as blacks. We know the archetypes: commissioner Kenesaw Mountain Landis, overtaken symbol of the bigoted past; Brooklyn Dodgers general manager Branch Rickey, patron of a new day; Robinson, who fulfills his potential once given the chance. Robinson is one of the first men we see when we visit Cooperstown, at the very portals of the Hall of Fame, in life-sized bronze paired with the words CHARACTER and COURAGE.

By rights the NFL should be able to celebrate a history of abiding enlightenment. Whereas organized baseball began excluding African Americans in 1898 and kept them out for the next five decades, pro football's Shelby (Ohio) Athletic Club paid a black man, Charles Follis, to play for it in 1904. In 1920 the Akron Pros' black quarterback, Fritz Pollard, was the first great star of the league that would two years later rename itself the NFL, and he even served as his team's player-coach. (Not just a black NFL quarterback, not just a black NFL coach, but *both at the same time!*) At the peak of African American participation, in 1923, six players suited up in the NFL. But as the pro game grew in popularity, the ranks thinned to just two in 1933. The following year the league began a stretch of twelve all-white seasons that, Arthur Ashe writes in his survey of the African American athlete, *A Hard Road to Glory,* has to be "one of the blackest spots on the record of American professional sports . . . All NFL records should properly show asterisks beside any records made during this era."

How did the league come to bleach itself white? No single explanation entirely satisfies. Pro football had no strong commissioner like Landis, who categorically barred blacks. But in 1933 the NFL restructured itself into two divisions of five teams each, with a season-ending title game, which led to more media attention and presumably a desire to emulate baseball and its commercially successful formula of large markets and all-white rosters.

Paul Schissler coached the Chicago Cardinals' Joe Lillard, one of the last two blacks to play before the ban, and after the 1933 season Schissler told the *Brooklyn Eagle* that the Cardinals had let Lillard go in the best interests of both club and player. "He was a marked man, and I don't mean that just the southern boys took it out on him either," the coach said. "After a while whole teams, northern and southern alike, would give Joe the works." But Ashe and others speculate that owners were just as likely favoring white players in a shrinking labor market. The NFL had shed franchises as the Depression wore on, and surviving teams carried fewer and fewer players.

Whatever the reasons, the period from 1934 to '46 is a stain on the names of the NFL's founding families. "Among the NFL's decision makers during those 12 years were some of the most storied individuals in the history of the game," writes Andy Piascik in his recently released book, *Gridiron Gauntlet*. "Their commitment to apartheid was seemingly stronger than their commitment to winning championships. The Bears under [George] Halas did not employ a single black player in their first 32 seasons. The Giants began play in 1925 and did not sign any blacks until 1948. The Steelers were all-white from the day Ray Kemp was released [in 1933] until 1952." As for George Preston Marshall, owner of the Washington Redskins, Piascik writes: "He at least did not pretend there were no blacks good enough to make his team. Unlike the others, he was honest enough to admit that he simply didn't want them around."

Halas claimed to journalist Myron Cope in 1970 that "no great black players were in the colleges then," but such protestations are disingenuous and even slanderous. During the period of the NFL's segregation, a time when it was hard for them to win the favor of white selectors, no fewer than nine black players earned All-America honors, and not one got an NFL tryout. Northwestern coach Dick Hanley called Ozzie Simmons, a back at Iowa from 1934 to '36, "the best I've ever seen." In 1937 Grantland Rice named Jerome "Brud" Holland of Cornell a first-team All-America end. Other African American stars included Julius Franks, a guard at Michigan; Bernie Jefferson, a running back at Northwestern; and Wilmeth Sidat-Singh, a quarterback at Syracuse. Scores more played in obscurity at historically black colleges.

The league instituted a twenty-round draft in 1939, yet no team chose an African American until 1949. Even with the advent of World War II, when the NFL was so shorthanded that a desperate Halas coaxed Bronko Nagurski out of a five-year retirement and owners considered signing high school players, blacks needed not apply.

The snubbing of Kenny Washington indicts the football establishment more than any other exclusion. Though he led the nation in total offense as a senior in 1939, and played 580 of a possible 600 minutes by doubling as the anchor of the defensive secondary, Washington was relegated to second-team All-America by Hearst, the AP, the UP, and Grantland Rice, while the East-West Shrine Game passed him over entirely. Yet when *Liberty* magazine polled more than 1,600 collegians on the best player they had faced on the field, Washington was the lone man named on the ballot of everyone he played against. It is only fitting that Washington — of whom former UCLA teammate Ray Bartlett once said, "He could smile when his lip was bleeding" — gouged the first bricks out of the NFL's all-whites wall.

The story of the NFL's integration offers no comfort to the league, which would prove notoriously slow to trust blacks with the positions of greatest responsibility, on the field, along the sideline, or in the front office. Nor does the story offer the angels or redemptive moments we'd like or expect. "Integrating the NFL was the low point of my life," Strode told *SI* in an unpublished interview before his death. "There was nothing nice about it. History doesn't know who we are. Kenny was one of the greatest backs in the history of the game, and kids today have no idea who he is.

"If I have to integrate heaven, I don't want to go."

Woody Strode grew up not far from the L.A. Coliseum, in what's now known as South Central Los Angeles but was then called the East Side. Just as he entered Jefferson High, his father, a mason with Native American blood, moved the family to Central Avenue, which ran like a high-tension line through the black community. As a high school freshman Woody spread only 130 pounds over a six-foot-one-inch frame, but he soon filled out enough for the *Los Angeles Examiner* to rave, "He haunts his end like a departed spirit, taking out four men on one play if need be."

Kenny Washington hailed from Lincoln Heights, where his was

the rare black family among mostly working-class Italians. A woman who lived next door would regularly drag six-year-old Kenny to early-morning mass. His father, Edgar "Blue" Washington, was a rolling stone, playing Negro leagues baseball between intermittent jobs in Hollywood. He would collect from a studio, then disappear until his pockets went light. Kenny would write him out of his life and credit two others with raising him: his grandmother Susie, a grammar school custodian beloved for vetting the suitors of the daughters of her Italian neighbors; and his uncle Rocky, who would become the first black uniformed lieutenant in the Los Angeles Police Department.

"I had a black principal in my grammar school when I was a kid," Strode would recall. "On the Pacific Coast there wasn't anything we couldn't do. As we got out of the L.A. area we found these racial tensions. Hell, we thought we *were* white."

The two met in 1936 as freshmen at UCLA, which welcomed black football players. In the idiom acceptable at the time, a local sportswriter called them the Goal Dust Twins, a play on the two black children featured on the box of Fairbank's Gold Dust, a popular soap powder. "When I met Kenny, I swear he was nothing but a nice Italian kid," Strode wrote in his 1990 memoir, *Goal Dust*. "He had an accent that was half-Italian."

Washington—aka the Kingfish, after a character in the radio comedy series *Amos 'n' Andy*—stood astride the Westwood campus. During two seasons of varsity baseball he hit .454 and .350, far better than Robinson. Rod Dedeaux, the longtime USC baseball coach who scouted for the Dodgers, believed that Washington also had a better arm, more power, and more agility than Robinson.

Though pigeon-toed and knock-kneed, Washington ran with power and a prodigious straight-arm. "He had a crazy gait, like he had two broken legs," Tom Harmon, a teammate with the Rams, told *SI* before his death in 1990. "He'd be coming at you straight, and it would look like he was going sideways." As a tailback in the single wing, Washington passed as much as he ran. In 1937, with five minutes to play and the Bruins trailing USC 19–0, he threw for two touchdowns in twenty-nine seconds, then added what could have been the winner if Strode had held on to his pass at the one-yard line. The first scoring pass traveled sixty-two yards in the air. Afterward UCLA coach Bill Spaulding went by the USC locker room to congratulate his counterpart, Howard Jones. "It's all right to come out now," Spaulding called through the door. "Kenny's stopped passing!"

When the Washington State coach taunted him from the sideline with the *n* word, Washington went after him. Opposing players would sometimes pile-drive Washington's face into the lime used to line the fields; Strode and other Bruins would take names and settle scores on subsequent plays. But Strode remembered Washington's reluctance to play the same game: "If Kenny knocked a guy down, he'd pick him up after the play was over."

As the wingback in motion during Washington's senior season, Robinson helped free up Washington, who led the Bruins to an undefeated 6–0–4 season, including a scoreless tie with USC, which ended as UCLA's final drive stalled inside the Trojans' four-yard line. Years later it would be easy to read a pattern into both those dramatic games with USC: they seemed to prefigure a fate in which Washington would fall just short or lose out to the clock. When he left the Coliseum field as a Bruin for the final time, Washington received an ovation that sounded, as Strode put it, as if "the pope of Rome had come out."

Robinson, writing for *Gridiron* magazine in 1971, called Washington "the greatest football player I have ever seen . . . I'm sure he had a deep hurt over the fact that he never had become a national figure in professional sports. Many blacks who were great athletes years ago grow old with this hurt."

Anticipating the snubs that would inflame the black press, *Pittsburgh Courier* columnist Wendell Smith wrote, "When the All-American teams are selected this year, the one with Washington's name missing can be called the 'un-American' team." Washington did play in the College All-Star Game at Soldier Field, scoring a touchdown, and afterward Halas asked him to stick around Chicago, saying he would "see what he could do," Washington recalled. A week later the Bears owner told Washington that he couldn't use him.

Similarly, *New York Daily News* columnist Jimmy Powers appealed to Giants founder Tim Mara and Brooklyn (football) Dodgers co-owner Dan Topping to sign him. Yet Washington went unselected in the NFL draft, prompting NBC Radio commentator Sam Baiter to blast league executives in a broadcast *j'accuse:* "You know . . . he would be the greatest sensation in pro league history with any one of your ball clubs . . . [yet] *none* of you chose him."

Washington spent the next year coaching the UCLA freshmen and finishing up his degree, then joined the LAPD. As undergraduates he and Strode had earned spending money as porters on Warner Brothers movie sets, and Washington picked up several film roles. In the meantime Strode took a job serving subpoenas and escorting prisoners for the L.A. County DA's office, and after Pearl Harbor he joined an Army football team at March Field in Riverside, California. When they could, Washington and Strode played in a pro league that would have them, the Pacific Coast Football League (PCFL).

Washington never failed to earn all-league recognition during his four minor league seasons, despite several knee injuries, including one in 1941 that kept him out of the service. Legend had it that he once stood in one end zone of Hollywood's Gilmore Stadium and heaved a football clear to the other. ("It was really ninety-three yards," Washington would confess.) By 1945, when he and Strode played for the Hollywood Bears, Washington found his former Bruins teammate with a touchdown pass that covered sixty-two yards, and he surpassed that with sixty-five- and sixty-seven-yard strikes to another black NFL *refusé*, Ezzrett "Sugarfoot" Anderson. 'You'd have thought it was a revival for black people," Brad Pye Jr., the longtime sports editor of the *Los Angeles Sentinel*, says of those PCFL games. "People would come on Sundays after church, all dressed up. Thirty to forty percent in attendance were black. Kenny was like a god. He did everything, and Sugarfoot Anderson could catch anything Kenny put up."

By the end of 1945 the future of the Hollywood Bears—indeed, the fate of the entire PCFL—hung on two developments. One was a vow by the fledgling All-American Football Conference (AAFC) to plant a flag in Los Angeles with a team owned by actor Don Ameche and called the Dons. The other factor was the decision by NFL owners, eager to checkmate the new league, to grant Cleveland owner Dan Reeves permission to move his Rams to L.A.

That city, however, was no longer the one Washington and Strode had known upon leaving Westwood. The war had fed the East Side's growth as blacks poured into southern California to work in the defense industries that FDR barred from discriminatory hiring. Restrictive covenants kept blacks from settling in much of the L.A. basin, but the Double V campaign waged by the *Courier*—"victory over fascism abroad and segregation at home"—elevated expectations, especially among returning African American troops.

Meanwhile, policies barring blacks from downtown hotels and Hollywood clubs had touched off a flowering along Central Avenue. Film stars lit out for the 4200 block, which included the Dunbar Hotel, the Club Alabam, and the Last Word Café, to drink in the music and the vibe. "They had to come down there because we couldn't go over *there*," jazz pianist Gerald Wiggins would recall in 1993, savoring the irony. One night Stepin Fetchit pulled up in front of the Dunbar in a yellow Rolls-Royce with Mae West riding shotgun. Swing had given way to bebop, and the result was an empowering headiness among black Angelenos.

Operating along "the black Sunset Strip," as Central Avenue was known, L.A.'s African American reporters now worked to secure the second V, targeting whites-only unions and bigoted housing policies. Edward "Abie" Robinson of the *Sentinel* and later the *California Eagle* was one of the most prominent of these crusaders. Herman Hill, West Coast bureau chief of the *Courier*, could count some two million readers of thirteen editions nationwide. But the most fearless, outspoken, and tenacious of all was a former pro athlete who served as sports editor of the *Los Angeles Tribune*.

William Claire "Halley" Harding wrote in a voice that jumped off the page. Sarcastic, conversational, self-congratulatory, and self-aggrandizing, he never lacked for an opinion or a provocation. Harding called his *Tribune* column "So What?" and the contrariness in the title captures him perfectly. "He was a loudmouth," remembers the *Sentinel*'s Pye, who as a junior high schooler in 1946 made pocket change emptying wastebaskets in the *Courier*'s West Coast bureau. "I used to pass by [his] office and hear him through the door. There was a boxing gym down the street and a pool hall around the corner—I could always hear him in there too. With ninety thousand people in the Coliseum you could still hear Halley Harding."

As a kid in Rock Island, Illinois, Harding would have known of Robert "Rube" Marshall, the second black pro footballer, who played for the local team, the Independents, as would two other pioneers, Sol Butler and Fred "Duke" Slater. Harding himself played football at historically black colleges Wilberforce, Wiley, and Fisk. At Wiley he overlapped with Melvin B. Tolson, the renowned English professor and debate coach—played by Denzel Washington in the 2007 film *The Great Debaters*—whose team memorably defeated national debate champion USC in 1935. Tolson served as an assistant coach of the Wiley football team, which went 8–0–1 in 1928 with Harding at quarterback.

Through the late '20s and '30s, Harding was a kind of black sports Zelig, playing Negro leagues baseball after the college football season ended and basketball for Abe Saperstein's Savoy Big Five, the Chicago-based forerunner of the Globetrotters. When the NFL drew the color line, all-Negro pro football teams popped up, and Harding spent the mid-1930s with Pollard's Chicago Black Hawks and New York Brown Bombers. By the end of the decade he had landed in Los Angeles. In 1939 and 1940 he appeared in a couple of films with all-black casts, including *Gang War,* in which he throws a mean right cross during a barroom brawl.

On the afternoon of January 15, 1946, representatives of the Rams and the Dons appeared before the L.A. Memorial Coliseum Commission to lobby for leases to a stadium that had never before hosted pro football. Commission president Leonard Roach, an L.A. County supervisor who enjoyed broad black support, had tipped off the black press that the meeting was open to the public. Just off a plane from Cleveland, Rams GM Charles "Chile" Walsh surely had no idea what the black man seated beside him had in store.

While minutes of the Coliseum Commission note that "Hally Hardin [*sic*], representing 30 colored newspapers," was present and delivered one of a number of "short talks" that day, they don't record exactly what he said. But from surviving accounts we do know that Harding set his sarcasm aside and stood and delivered like a Wiley College debater. He walked the commissioners through the NFL's early, integrated history. He highlighted pioneers like his old teammate Pollard. He invoked the Double V campaign and the contributions of black soldiers during World War II. He fingered Marshall as the handmaiden of Jim Crow pro football and appealed to southern Californians' tradition of tolerance. And he declared it "singularly strange" that no NFL team had signed Kenny Washington.

After Harding sat down, the *Sentinel*'s Abie Robinson told Ron

Bishop, a Drexel communications professor, in 2002, "you could have heard a rat piss on cotton."

"Walsh was really shook up," the *Courier*'s Hill later reported. "He turned pale and started to stutter. He denied any racial prejudice on the part of the Rams or the NFL. He even went to the league's rulebook. Halley and I answered by charging [that the rule barring blacks] was *unwritten*. The old supervisor [and commission member] Roger Jessup got up and asked whether the Rams would dare bar Kenny Washington."

"Of course not," said Walsh.

"I just want you to know," Jessup said, "if *our* Kenny Washington can't play, there will be no pro football in the L.A. Coliseum."

Attorney Lloyd Wright, representing the Rams, pledged at length that Washington or any other qualified African American could play with the Rams. Roach urged the Rams and the black newsmen to further discuss the issue on their own. So a week later Walsh and Rams publicity man Maxwell Stiles ventured to Central Avenue to the Last Word, where at least a dozen black journalists lay in wait. Here the names of Washington and several other Hollywood Bears came up, but Walsh expressed concern that they were all under contract to the PCFL club. Harding replied that if the Bears wouldn't stand in their way, what impediment could possibly remain? The Rams conceded as much. Walsh promised to try to sign Washington and also expressed interest in Strode and another Bears end, Chuck Anderson.

Most historical accounts say the Coliseum Commission forced integration on the Rams. But in her forthcoming book, *The Lost Championship Season,* historian Gretchen Atwood makes the case that Harding deserves the primary credit. "Harding pushes Roach to put in writing the promise not to discriminate, and Roach does," Atwood says.

Both in the commission meeting and at the Last Word, every time Walsh says something vague like, "We'll try out all qualified players regardless of race," Harding responds with a demand for specifics, such as, "O.K., when will Washington's tryout be?" Then when the Dons don't hire any blacks, Harding goes back to the commission and asks it to enforce the written nondiscrimination agreement. Roach isn't at this meeting, but the commission now says it has no record of any such agreement and won't tell a team who it can or can't hire. If it was the Coliseum Commission that forced the Rams to integrate, then how do you explain that the Dons had a lease in 1946 when they hadn't even given a black player a tryout? So in sports terms, Harding gets the goal and Roach the assist, not the other way around.

Atwood believes a comment made years later by Rams backfield coach Bob Snyder—that the team signed Washington at the insistence of the Coliseum Commission—is a convenient official story. "I think Snyder believed that, but I also think Chile Walsh was sick of Harding's constant pressure. And because of the public statements Roach and Jessup made against racial bias, Walsh and the Rams could pass the buck if anyone objected to the signing—basically, shrug and tell other NFL owners, 'Hey, our hands were tied, we needed the lease to the stadium.'"

The Rams' press release on March 21, 1946, announcing Washington's signing includes this disclaimer: "The National [Football] League has never had a rule against the use of Negro players and no precedent is being set in the signing of Washington." But that's belied by the reaction of other NFL owners. "All hell broke loose," Snyder told Mike Rathet and Don R. Smith, authors of *The Pro Football Hall of Fame Presents: Their Deeds and Dogged Faith*, in 1984. "There was objection to it—you can bet your butt on that."

The *Tribune* gloried in the news of Washington's signing. One article exulted, "Yesterday *Tribune* sports editor Halley Harding's one-man crusade against the National Football League's patent, if unwritten, law against Negro players paid off in full."

In his column Harding wrote, "Of course Kenny hasn't got a whole lot of years on the gridiron ahead of him, but we'll string along with him for our money's worth, never having been robbed yet. Another Negro is about to sign on the dotted line in the same office, but while the details are being worked out, mum's the word."

That other black player, Strode, came to terms a couple of months later. The Rams had asked Washington to choose someone to room with on the road, and he nominated his old running mate. The Rams grumbled about Strode's marriage to Luana Kalaeola, a descendant of Hawaiian royalty, Strode said later, "but Kenny had power at that point, and he said, 'I want my buddy.'"

*

Kenny Washington had already undergone five knee operations when he made his NFL debut at age twenty-eight. Now a running back on a T formation team, he could no longer mystify defenses as a tailback who might run or pass. He fared best in the second of his three seasons, when he finished fourth in the NFL in rushing yardage, led the league with 7.4 yards per carry, and ran 92 yards from scrimmage for a score shortly after being knocked unconscious by a Chicago Cardinals linebacker.

"Kenny was just a shell of himself when he played for the Rams," says the *Sentinel*'s Pye. "If you could have seen him with the Hollywood Bears . . ." Angelenos seemed to know that. Upon his retirement in 1948, the eighty thousand fans who came out for a tribute did so to honor his entire career.

When the Rams hit the road that first season, management checked the white players into one hotel and peeled off a hundred dollars for each of the black players to find lodging elsewhere. This wasn't always because of Jim Crow; Washington and Strode liked the autonomy. "In the black section of Chicago, we'd never seen so many black people in our whole lives," Strode recalled. "Bob Waterfield and about five players came down looking for us because they'd made arrangements for us to move back to their hotel. We're in a cellar [of the Persian Hotel] where Count Basie's playing, it's integrated and all the white people are having a ball. We're sipping Tom Collinses, and Waterfield said, 'You sons of bitches!' The team was too embarrassed to bed-check us because we'd been shoved out of the family. And when the white players came to get us, we said, 'No way, we're gonna stay segregated.' That's why I say it was never [an issue among] the athletes."

On offense, Strode, then thirty-two, played only enough to catch four passes; on defense, he was put "in the butcher shop on the defensive line at two hundred pounds," Strode said. "It was a joke."

Harmon, his old teammate, confirmed this. "Woody was one of the greatest defensive ends I ever saw, but he never got a chance to prove it because of that fool coaching staff. In practice you could never get near him. You never saw a man in better shape."

Strode learned of his release while lying in bed one morning, when several of Washington's mob-connected friends from Lincoln Heights came by with the news. One of the wiseguys—"the biggest bookie in Hollywood," Strode said—reported overhearing Reeves and Snyder in a bar on Sunset Boulevard ("drunk on their asses," in Strode's telling) bragging about how they'd let Strode go. "[The bookie] said, 'We don't like the way they did it. We want to know if you want to fight it.' I could have started a war."

Both Chile Walsh and his brother Adam, the L.A. coach, resigned after the Rams, NFL champions in 1945, went 6–4–1 in 1946. But even if the season had been a disappointment on the West Coast, to a man watching from Brooklyn it had been a triumph. As a teammate of Charles Follis's with the Shelby Athletic Club at the turn of the century, Branch Rickey had been impressed by Follis's even temper in the face of taunts and cheap shots. Now, Rickey said to himself, if blacks and whites could play a game of violent collisions in close quarters without major incident, the Dodgers could surely call up Jackie Robinson to the majors. Robinson made his debut with the Dodgers the following season.

Strode went on to play two seasons in Canada and spent five years in Italy doing spaghetti Westerns and action films. On screen he exuded an equipoise that one critic praised as "an effective counterpoint to the noise and confusion around him." By the time he died of lung cancer in 1994, he had made more than one hundred movies, including *Sergeant Rutledge* and *The Man Who Shot Liberty Valance.* His last film, *The Quick and the Dead,* was released in 1995.

After retiring, Washington worked as a distributor for a grocery chain and a whiskey distillery. He served as a part-time scout for the Dodgers, in whose system his son, Kenny Jr., played several seasons. In 1971, after Washington became ill with congestive-heart and lung problems, Strode hurried back from Italy to his old friend's hospital room in the UCLA Medical Center. He wanted to take Washington to Rome, to show him a place full of people like the neighbors back in Lincoln Heights. But Washington was too far gone and knew he was best left to contemplate the Bruins' football practice field, which he could see from his window.

Washington was fifty-two when he died. In his obituary in the *Los Angeles Times,* Waterfield said, "If he had come into the National Football League directly from UCLA, he would have been, in my opinion, the best the NFL had ever seen."

In what kind of peace is that supposed to leave a man? Pastor

L. L. White addressed the question in his eulogy, invoking Saint Paul's Epistle to the Philippians: "You live in a world of crooked and mean people. You must shine among them like stars lighting up the sky."

Pete Fierle oversees education programs for the Pro Football Hall of Fame in Canton, Ohio. He knows well the obscurity that shrouds the story of the game's reintegration in the modern era. "My eleven-year-old son could tell you Jackie Robinson's name but not Kenny Washington's or Marion Motley's," Fierle says. Thus, the Hall hangs most of the tale of pro football's desegregation on Paul Brown's addition of Motley and Bill Willis to the Browns in 1946. Those events came after the Rams' signings of Washington and Strode, but they are stories of principle, vision, and courage. It's a narrative more in the Rickey-Robinson mold and, Fierle points out, easier for visitors to get a handle on.

Problem is, Motley and Willis didn't integrate the NFL. They integrated the AAFC. Washington and Strode integrated the NFL. League owners remained reliably reactionary even after the NFL champion Minnesota Vikings lost Super Bowl IV to the AFL's Kansas City Chiefs, who fielded more black starters than white. Not until Doug Williams led the Redskins to a Super Bowl title in 1988 did a starting black NFL quarterback become less than remarkable. And not until a renegade owner, Oakland's Al Davis, hired Art Shell in 1989 did the NFL get its first black head coach since Pollard.

The sad fact is, the NFL's journey to integration didn't have to take place at all. If only the league had left well enough alone, its history would be a proud one. Instead those thirteen years of segregation—ended only when the NFL gave ground grudgingly to a howling sportswriter and a public servant—diminish the league to a level of a small-minded steward of some waiting room or lunch counter.

That gracelessness wasn't lost on the key players. "They didn't take Kenny because of his ability," Strode said. "They didn't take me on my ability. It was shoved down their throats."

NBA Leads This Race

FROM THE BOSTON GLOBE

THIS JUST IN: the president of the United States is a man of color.

What? You knew this already? That's good. So does this mean we are all now postracial?

Of course, we're not yet quite postracial, and we may never become an ideally color-blind society, but if we truly want to get there, we do have a working institutional model.

Professional football (1946) and baseball (1947) integrated in the competition area first, and hockey doesn't really enter into this discussion, for rather obvious reasons, but the fact is the National Basketball Association is the most egalitarian major institution in our society. In fact, the NBA is so infused with black power that it is the only significant American institution I know of where the white man is inherently perceived to be inadequate to the task.

But put the topic of playing ability to the side for a moment. Where the NBA laps and relaps the field is in the area of authority. All this discussion about the paucity of black coaches and managers in football and baseball is so much Sanskrit to those of us who follow the NBA, where black coaches have been coming and going and coming and going and coming and going for forty-plus years.

Unless there's been a change in the last five minutes (you'd be wise to check), the NBA has nine black head coaches. Two of them replaced fired black head coaches, something that has been going on in this league since the Detroit Pistons fired Earl Lloyd and replaced him with assistant Ray Scott in 1972, when Barack Obama was eleven years old and living in Honolulu.

Entering the 2008–2009 season, there had been seventy-five

black coaching appointments in the history of the league covering forty-seven individuals. The list includes familiar names such
as Lenny Wilkens (the all-time winningest NBA coach), Al Attles,
K. C. Jones, Nate McMillan, Doc Rivers, Bernie Bickerstaff, Mo
Cheeks, and, of course, Bill Russell, the man who started it all when
he took over the Celtics in 1966.

It also includes such names as Gene Littles, Darrell Walker, Sid-
ney Lowe, Butch Carter, Leonard Hamilton, and Randy Ayers. In
other words, men whose names aren't quite so recognizable to the
casual NBA fan.

And that's without mentioning the previous interim coaches.
I've counted twelve of them, ranging in fame from Magic Johnson
to Draff Young.

Black coaches are such a matter-of-fact way of life in the NBA
that the Lakers and Heat are the only teams that have not yet hired
one, although each has had a black interim mentor. Black coaches
are so entrenched in the NBA that this spring we will celebrate the
thirty-fourth anniversary of the first all-black coaching matchup in
the NBA Finals (Golden State's Attles versus Washington's Jones).

Look, the NBA has plenty for which to apologize. When Chuck
Cooper, Nat "Sweetwater" Clifton, and Lloyd entered the league in
the 1950–51 season, it did not trigger some tsunami of talent washing into the NBA. Rosters were small and there were unofficial
quotas that lasted well into the '70s. It was well understood that a
black player was going to have to be substantially better to the point
of being irreplaceable to beat out a white player for a job. There
weren't any black journeymen sitting at the end of NBA benches.

Race was a major issue for a long, long time. It was quite a big
deal when both the Celtics (Russell, Satch Sanders, Willie Naulls,
Sam Jones, K. C. Jones) and 76ers (Wilt Chamberlain, Chet Walker,
Luke Jackson, Hal Greer, Wally, later Wali Jones) shattered convention by starting five black players in the 1965–66 season. Everyone
understood that the reason the St. Louis Hawks, located in America's "northernmost southern city," moved to more progressive Atlanta in 1968 was race, just as everyone understood that the reason
the Hawks would later trade potential star Paul Silas to Phoenix for
white stiff Gary Gregor a year later was the desire to whiten the
lineup a little. A few years later, there was quite a stir when the
Knicks finalized the first all-black twelve-man roster.

No team was more in the hurricane's eye than our own Celtics, who, after winning sixteen championships, found that some people wished them to apologize for having employed such white stars as John Havlicek, Dave Cowens, Larry Bird, Kevin McHale, Danny Ainge, Scott Wedman, and Bill Walton. The team that drafted the first black player, hired the NBA's first black coach (the first of five, at last count), and whose franchise icon insisted on black-white roommate pairings (I can bear personal testimony to this) found its image threatened by being regarded as too white in an increasingly black-oriented league. In retrospect, I guess this was an enormous compliment for the NBA itself.

But the NBA's embrace of color doesn't stop with players and coaches. At present, there are four blacks calling the organizational shots as either general managers or vice presidents of operations, or whatever. In addition, Elgin Baylor, in charge of the Clippers' personnel affairs since 1986, was let go earlier this season. But who should be surprised? Wayne Embry was given control of the Bucks in 1971.

The only major professional sports league with black ownership? The NBA, of course (Charlotte Bobcats).

Referees? Plenty of those have come and gone, including some of the best (Hugh Evans, Danny Crawford) and, yup, some of the worst (as with their white counterparts, far too many candidates to enumerate). And that is what's so important to note about the NBA.

There have been plenty of failed black head coaches, and isn't that the point? All anyone, black, white, Asian, whatever, can ask for is a fair chance. There's no inherent barrier in the NBA, and there's no condescension either. It's produce or get out, which is as it should be.

The NBA is the land of administrative fairness and opportunity, and on the playing front, the days are long gone when a black man must be twice as good as a white man to secure a job. There are countless examples of black journeymen, men who bounce from team to team as glorified Kelly Girls.

Ever hear of Kevin Ollie? Since entering the league in 1997, the former University of Connecticut star has played for eleven teams, one of them (Philadelphia) three times and another (Orlando) twice. It is a journey that would have been unimaginable for someone such as Cleo Hill, a great black player of the late '50s and through the '60s who could not get a job in the league even though he was, by all anecdotal evidence, one of the top ten guards alive. It's not unlike telling people in Honolulu thirty-six years ago that in their midst was a mixed-race eleven-year-old who would grow up to be president.

But no less significant is the coaching résumé of a Bernie Bicker-staff, who was no big basketball star, no household name, but who, after being introduced to the professional basketball world by a mentor named K. C. Jones, would find himself coaching four NBA teams and running another one.

It's an only-in-the-NBA saga.

Barack Obama has to know all this. I'm not saying he has made basketball his sport of choice for this reason, but I don't know that he hasn't.

MICHAEL SOKOLOVE

Allonzo Trier Is in the Game

FROM THE NEW YORK TIMES MAGAZINE

AFTER SCHOOL ON A RECENT AFTERNOON, Allonzo Trier, a sixth-grader in Federal Way, outside Seattle, came home and quickly changed into his workout gear—Nike high-tops, baggy basketball shorts, and a sleeveless T-shirt that hung loosely on his five-foot-five, 110-pound frame. Inside a small gymnasium near the entrance of his apartment complex, he got right to his practice routine, one he has maintained for the last four years, seven days a week. He began by dribbling a basketball around the perimeter of the court, weaving it around his back and through his legs. After a few minutes, he took a second basketball out of a mesh bag and dribbled both balls, crisscrossing them through his legs. It looked like showboating, Harlem Globetrotters kind of stuff, but the drills, which Trier discovered on the Internet, were based on the childhood workouts of Pete Maravich and have helped nurture his exquisite control of the ball in game settings—and, by extension, his burgeoning national reputation.

One of the websites that tracks young basketball prospects reports that Trier plays with "style and punch" and "handles the pill" —the ball—"like a yo-yo." He is a darling of the so-called grass-roots basketball scene and a star on the AAU circuit—which stands for Amateur Athletic Union but whose practices mock traditional definitions of amateurism.

All youth sports now operate on fast-forward. Just about any kid with some ability takes road trips with his or her team by the age of twelve, flying on planes and staying in hotels. That used to happen, if at all, only after an athlete was skilled enough to play in college. Now it occurs in just about any sport organized enough to form into a league. But basketball operates at a level beyond other sports, and in recent years, the attention, benefits, and temptations that fall on top high school players have settled on an ever-younger group.

Trier has his own line of clothing emblazoned with his signature and personal motto: "When the lights come on, it's time to perform." His basketball socks, which also come gratis, are marked with either his nickname, Zo, or his area code, 206. He's expecting a shipment of Under Armour gear soon, thanks to Brandon Jennings, last year's top high school point guard and now a highly paid pro in Italy. He is flown around the country by AAU teams that want him to play for them in tournaments—and by basketball promoters who use him to add luster to their events. A lawyer in Seattle arranged for Trier's private school tuition and academic tutoring to be paid for by the charitable foundation of an NBA player, and the lawyer also procured free dental care for Trier.

Many of the top competitors in this month's NCAA basketball tournament, and most of the young NBA players, have emerged from the culture that Trier inhabits. They made their reputations at all-star camps, where team play is hardly encouraged. To have any hope of establishing winning squads, college coaches must try to deprogram their young stars—but only after first flattering them and granting them scholarships.

Marcie Trier is a single mother who makes a modest salary as a social worker at a shelter for victims of domestic violence. The two-bedroom apartment she shares with her son is Section 8, federally subsidized housing. What accrues to Allonzo because of his basketball exploits leaves Marcie feeling dazzled, bewildered, seduced, and wary. "They're doing nice things for my son, things that he needs and I can't afford," she told me. "So how can I say no?" But she knows the reason for the largesse. "If his game falls off, they will kick him to the curb. That's what makes me nervous, and I don't want it to happen."

Marcie, who is thirty-three, said she has "obsessive tendencies, and I think Allonzo's sort of the same way." To ensure that his basketball skills will keep evolving and he won't be cast aside, Trier practices obsessively. After about ten minutes of ball-handling at the gym, he moved on to what makes up the bulk of his daily workout—shooting. He must make (not just try) 450 shots a day from various spots on the floor, beginning with short- and midrange attempts, then on to shots from beyond the three-point line. His mother, who works an early shift so she can get home for these sessions, does the rebounding and keeps the tally of made shots. When he misses two in a row, which rarely happens, she subtracts one from his total. Shots that bounce off or roll around the rim before going in are not counted, which was Allonzo's idea a couple of years ago in response to his mother's belief that he should strive to "control his own destiny." He figured he should train to be a dead-eye shooter rather than one who hopes for some kind of luck.

As Allonzo practiced, Marcie, who was a gymnast and ballet dancer through her teens, wore a pink warm-up suit and flip-flops, which clattered against the gym floor when one of his shots missed so badly that she had to chase it down. Mostly she just caught the ball after it came through the net and then quickly passed it back to him. The sound in the otherwise quiet gym was rhythmic and mesmerizing—the repeated swish of the ball as it rippled through the net, followed by a smack when the return passes hit Allonzo's hands. I could have closed my eyes and tallied the made shots just by listening.

At one point, after Allonzo uncharacteristically missed three of four, Marcie said, "Put more arc on it." He made the correction and hit the next eleven in a row. Mother and son appear to be in almost perfect sync. She never has to push him to practice, and he does not have to convince her why basketball should be at the center of their lives. They rarely disagree or argue, but a continuing point of contention is that Allonzo wants to take instruction only from his coaches. "They know the game," Marcie said, "but I see him shoot three thousand shots a week, so I think I know his shot better than they do."

Putting up so many shots is a hard workout, especially since Trier releases many of them on the move, after a couple of dribbles and a juke—as if he were trying to elude a defender. He stopped several times for short breaks and a few gulps of a sports drink. Each time, his mother rubbed an herbal ointment on his knees, which, not surprisingly, were aching.

But this was only the beginning of his basketball day. After he made his quota of shots, which took about ninety minutes, Marcie drove Allonzo to another gym nearby, where a local high school coach who moonlights as a private basketball tutor put him through an hourlong workout that included more ball-handling and shooting, followed by a vigorous session of one-on-one play. (These workouts occur twice weekly.) From there, they drove about twenty minutes into downtown Seattle, where he practiced for another two hours with his AAU team.

As that session was coming to an end, at about 9:30 P.M., and after he had been practicing or traveling between practices for nearly seven hours, a player pulled Trier down with an arm across the neck as he drove toward the basket. In football parlance, he was "clotheslined." In the NBA, such a foul would be considered flagrant and the offender ejected from the game and fined. Trier picked himself up and kept playing. Marcie, watching the practice with other parents, explained to me that her son's fame makes him a marked man, even among some teammates. She felt that the perpetrator in this case was not a friend to her son and might have acted with malice.

When Trier came over for a water break a few minutes later, he said: "He didn't even tell me he was sorry. Don't you think he should have apologized?" He had tears in his eyes and said his neck hurt, but mostly he just seemed like an exhausted little boy who needed to go home to bed.

Elite basketball stands apart for two main reasons. First, prodigies do exist, and the game's cognoscenti like to believe they can identify them. If a kid is lavishly skilled, athletic, and looks as if he'll grow tall enough—and seems to possess the artistry and imagination that are the components of true basketball genius—he may be anointed by the wise men of hoops. And some of the time, they will even be right. (Scouts are less tempted to project greatness in football and baseball, where it is often just the biggest, fastest, or most coordinated kids who excel early.)

The other reason for basketball's difference has to do with economics and incentives. Many of the best players come from poor neighborhoods and single-parent homes. The shoe companies, Nike and Adidas most prominently, along with apparel makers like Under Armour, pour money into the system, hoping to win the loyalty of kids who might become the next LeBron James. They finance the best AAU teams and find ways to funnel gear to the most promising players. It's a relatively small investment for these companies, even if they make bets on hundreds of kids, but to the families it can seem like a lot—not just the material goods but also what the attention and gifts seem to foreshadow. Think of it this way: youth soccer may seem out of control, and here in the United States there's no big pot of money at the end of the rainbow, and few suburban families believe their kid's talent is going to get them to a better class of subdivision.

Basketball has a different DNA. It's a city game, an intimate sport dense with colorful characters, some of whom invariably turn out to be nefarious. Going back to the 1940s, and as recently as the mid-1990s, college basketball has survived periodic point-shaving, or gambling, scandals orchestrated by insiders with connections to top players. Last year, an NBA referee began serving a fifteen-month prison term for criminal charges related to gambling on games.

Nor do college coaches as a group distinguish themselves through their ethics. Technically, they are not allowed to talk with prospective high school recruits until June of a player's sophomore year. But in the last two years, coaches at major schools have offered scholarships to highly regarded *eighth*-graders, which has put an even greater focus on players in Trier's age group. Tim Floyd, head coach at USC, made two such offers in the last two years, and he hired the father of one recruit to be on his staff. ("College Basketball Coaches Are Now One Step Away from Recruiting Embryos," the website FanIQ headlined an article after the Kentucky coach Billy Gillispie offered a scholarship to another eighth-grader last spring.)

In January, the NCAA expanded its recruiting rules to more explicitly cover seventh- and eighth-graders, putting them largely off-limits to college coaches. Jim Haney, the executive director of the National Association of Basketball Coaches, explained to me why coaches were aggressively dipping into the lower grades. "You can talk all you want about 'coaching players up,'" he said, using the phrase for improving players through intense instruction. "But you can only get so far with that." To qualify for the NCAA tournament, and certainly to advance through the regionals and into the Final

Four, he said, requires "the top talent, and you go out and find it where you can. It's a competitive business."

NCAA recruiting rules tend to be arcane, with mystifying exceptions. For example, college coaches cannot make calls or write personal letters to players before the end of their sophomore year of high school. But they can signal their interest by sending "questionnaires," without personal letters, to players of any age. When I was with Trier in Seattle, he was excited to have just received a questionnaire from Memphis, one of the premier college teams, which conformed to the rules because it did not include a personal letter. It's possible that Trier could have been a recipient of a random mass mailing, but considering his reputation, he was probably right to assume that the school's head coach, John Calipari, or someone on his staff, knew something about him. (Marcie Trier told me that she receives regular text messages from a coach with another college team, which would be an NCAA violation.)

The recent agreements with young players lead to the question of how you offer a scholarship to a kid, and have it accepted, when you're not really allowed to communicate with him. The answer: while college coaches and their assistants cannot mix with underage recruits at all-star camps, they can host players of any age at their own on-campus summer camps. If one of the really heralded players shows up, coach and player—even, in theory, a second-grader—can make a deal (though it has to happen after the camp is over).

Trier has already attended a couple of camps where he was sought out by on-campus coaches and asked if he was considering the school. At one, he told me, a coach took him aside for a private, behind-the-scenes tour of the team's locker room and then upstairs to a pavilion above the court that contained trophies and other memorabilia. "It caused some resentment," according to his mother, "because other campers saw it. Parents got upset."

None of this was necessarily against the rules, because these were coaches' private camps. Floyd, the USC coach, explained in an interview posted on a college-sports website two years ago how such innocent-seeming encounters can quickly lead from point A to point B and all the way to "S"—a scholarship offer to a kid who has not yet begun high school. "I think that we all recognize that young people can have great talents, and if those players have dreamed about going to your school, they tend to ask you if they're being offered a scholarship by your school," he said. "And if you don't tell them that you are, then you offend them. If you tell them you've offered, sometimes you have to be prepared for them to accept it."

The scholarship offers are not binding on either party because they cannot be put in writing until a player's senior year. But Haney, of the coaches' association, and others say they are unwise because they bring the hurly-burly and distractions of recruiting to kids too young to handle them, and they bind parties to each other, at least verbally, well before either can know if it's a good match. The early recruiting also brings what Haney calls the "nonscholastic influences" to children — shoe company representatives and others who have a commercial interest in befriending young talent.

I asked Haney if the rule against recruiting middle-schoolers, which he termed a "new line of demarcation," will be respected. "In this business," he said, "you have people who follow the rules, you have those who want to follow them but struggle sometimes, and you have a third group that sees every rule as a little speed bump. They slow down and then navigate over it."

In the upper tiers of elite youth basketball, it is common for fathers, if they are present, to be highly involved. They pester coaches, camp directors, and scouting services for greater exposure for their sons, and they videotape games and splice together the best moments for display on YouTube. (No player on YouTube has ever missed a shot.) Those with absent fathers tend to accumulate father figures along the way — men who may genuinely want to help, along with others who may hope to broker scholarships, share in endorsement deals, or just remain part of the entourage if a player strikes NBA gold.

Steve Goldstein, general counsel in the United States for Tokio Marine, the Japanese insurance company, is a former small-college basketball player who spends much of his free time coaching youth basketball in New York and leading a foundation called Beyond Basketball. It offers academic assistance to players who excel at their sport but without help might fall short of the classroom standards needed to qualify for a college scholarship. Goldstein first met Trier at a basketball camp last summer in Chantilly, Virginia. "I saw him play and noticed his swagger," says Goldstein, who has become an adviser to Marcie Trier (one of many). "There's just something about the way he carries himself on the court. But the way I got to know him was that one morning in the hotel, he came up to me and said, 'Excuse me, sir, can I have a ride to camp?' And I just took him every morning after that."

Trier has never met his father, who Marcie says was her first boy-friend. She has lost touch with him. All Trier knows is that he was African American and about six foot three. Right now, Trier is five foot five, slightly above average for his age, but short for a youngster with elite-basketball ambitions. "I guess I'll be at least six-three," he told me, "but I'm hoping for maybe six-five." (His mother is about five foot four. She was born in the Pacific Islands but does not know much more than that because she and her twin sister were in foster care before being adopted by a family in the Midwest. She has no other children, and her only close family nearby is her sister.)

Marcie herself has become immersed in grassroots-basketball culture. She worries that her son does not encounter sufficient challenges close to home, expresses her opinions to his coaches, and is open to opportunities for him beyond Seattle. In recent years, several players who have come through Trier's AAU pro-gram, Seattle Rotary Style, have gone on to the NBA. But Daryll Hennings, the senior athletic director at the Rotary Boys and Girls Club, which sponsors the team, told me that Trier is flying at a higher altitude—traveling more, competing for a greater number of teams, mixing with more out-of-town coaches and promoters, creating more buzz. "Every year, everything gets bigger, the whole scene, and he's caught up in it," Hennings said.

In just three months last summer, Trier flew on four separate oc-casions to the East Coast to play in events in New York, New Jersey, Pennsylvania, and Virginia—in addition to making shorter excur-sions to Los Angeles and San Diego. When I was with him in Janu-ary, his mother took a call from a coach in southern California who wanted to fly him down for a tournament the following weekend. (She declined; he was already committed to play in Texas one week after that.) She showed me a text from an AAU parent who wanted Trier's e-mail address for his son. "I would like my son to branch out and build relationships with some of the top guards out there," he wrote.

The father of a top player in New York, Jerron Love, had also been in touch and was hoping to lure Trier to a new team, one that would not practice together but rendezvous in various cities for big tournaments. I had met Jerry Love, Jerron's father, who is well known in New York basketball circles for his zealous advocacy on behalf of his son. He posts Jerron's highlights on YouTube, sends out a promotional DVD ("Just 10: Jerron Love, aka the Golden Child"), and communicates in e-mail blizzards.

We sat together one evening at the bar at Londel's, a soul-food restaurant in Harlem, as he scrolled through a BlackBerry on which he had seemingly downloaded the entirety of known basketball knowledge, which he was doling out to his son in their private training sessions. "You see this right here," he said, showing me one of the entries. "It tells you the three options you have on a secondary fast break—pull up for a jump shot, find a player spotted up for a three-pointer, or hit the trailer for a lay-up. Jerron knows this stuff, but other kids his age, they're not there yet. I put this stuff into him like a computer chip."

When Love got to a page describing how a defender should squeeze between a player setting a screen and the ball-handler, he became animated as he demonstrated proper positioning, bumping my shoulder and nearly toppling me from my bar stool. Other patrons were talking quietly over after-work drinks; I noticed a couple of them glance our way with looks of mild alarm.

Marcie Trier told me she had participated in conference calls with Jerry Love, other parents, and a coach about this proposed new team, but it didn't look as if it was going to come together. In my conversations with her, she occasionally relayed information that, at first, seemed beyond belief. For example, she told me she had heard that her son might be recruited to play for an AAU team in Texas that travels by private jet and stays in luxury hotels. A team of sixth-graders? I checked up on it: the Texas Titans, backed by Kenny Troutt, the billionaire founder of Excel Communications (and father of a team member), have traveled by private jet. At a tournament in Las Vegas, they stayed at Caesars Palace.

Hennings told me he assumes that Trier at some point will be lured away from the Seattle Rotary program. "I swear," he said, "every time his mom takes him on a road trip, I'm waiting for that call that he's not coming back, that he's going to play for this team or that team that's gonna fly him around and all that. I wish him the best. He's a hard worker. I want him around for the duration, but I don't see it happening."

I met Allonzo Trier for the first time last summer, at the Adidas Junior Phenom Camp in San Diego, the premier annual gathering for pre–high school talent. I already knew that he was considered a star among stars, and I watched a couple of his games before seeking him out. When we shook hands, he held on to mine for what seemed like ten or fifteen seconds as we began to talk, only letting go after the father of another camper tapped him on the shoulder and asked if he would pose for a picture with his son. "Thank you," he said to Trier after snapping the photo. "You're a role model, brother."

The Junior Phenom Camp was grassroots basketball in distilled form—a caldron of ambition, networking, gossip, and backbiting. The players had been identified and invited to San Diego after attending regional camps. Most of the 360 campers were being charged $450 to participate. All kinds of merchandise was available for purchase, including a camp program for $25 that listed the participants and their heights, hobbies, hometowns, and nicknames, which made for interesting reading. There was a G-Money, a K-Money, a Cash-Money, and one young man who simply called himself Money. Two campers went by Sir, while others—Da Truth, Superstar, Big Dog, the Chosen One—selected handles that seemed to demand respect. (Trier's listed nickname was Zo, which is what just about everyone but his mother calls him.)

There were plenty of middle-class kids at the camp whose families paid their way. Other players raised money to attend from individuals or businesses in their communities. Seven of the campers came from an AAU program called Houston Select, coached and bankrolled by Steve Trauber, a managing director and head of global energy investment banking for UBS. "I've got a great job," Trauber told me, "so I'm lucky enough to be able to sponsor the whole team."

Trauber's sixth-grade team traveled to tournaments two weekends a month and played 118 games in 2008—36 more than an NBA team does in the regular season. He estimated that he spent more than $200,000 on travel and other expenses. The star among his sixth-graders was Jesse Pistokache (White Chocolate), a six-footer who lives all the way down in the Rio Grande Valley and travels most weekends to Houston to practice with his team-mates—or join them on another flight to a tournament. "This is our life," his mother, Teri Mata-Pistokache, a college professor, told me. "You've just got to give in to it. If he wants to meet his goals in basketball, this is what we've come to understand is necessary."

Nearly everyone in the camp was there either to defend a high national ranking—as was Trier, who for two years has been the top-ranked player in his class—or to improve a ranking. The idea is to "be on the radar," as one parent put it, in order to be among the players whom college coaches will want to scout. The level of cynicism among parents and even some of the kids was extreme. I heard talk that the biggest stars among the high school players attend these kinds of camps only if they are paid—that is, they demanded cash in addition to free travel and camp tuition. Trier himself named a New York–area high school star who is rumored to play that game. "He doesn't go anywhere unless he gets a minimum of $15,000," he said. I don't know if that's true, but it says a lot about this whole business that people believe it is and talk so openly about it.

The campers were put on teams that played twice a day, on one of six full courts, in a cavernous gymnasium at Alliant International University that looked as if it had been an airplane hangar. Presiding over everything was Joe Keller, a former AAU coach in southern California and the president of the company that runs this camp—as well as, he said, 277 regional camps for different age groups, for both boys and girls, in the United States, Canada, Puerto Rico, Japan, and China.

Keller is an imposing man, broad-shouldered and barrel-chested. Baseball was his sport as a kid, but with his big frame and goatee, he looked more like an NFL middle linebacker. Keller and his staff consistently tell the kids that they are at the beginning of a long journey and should just focus on learning to play proper basketball because, after all, no one at their age can really be projected as a pro or even as a college prospect. In private, everyone lapses.

"Have you seen number 109?" Keller asked me, referring to Pistokache. "He's a monster, isn't he?" At a different point, he said, "And 106?" He was referring to another sixth-grader, a skilled, smaller player but one who everyone seemed to know had a six-foot-eleven father. "Going to be a pro," Keller said. "You mark my word."

As I was talking with Keller just inside the gym's front door, an angry-looking man, the coordinator of referees at the camp, came rushing his way, and they quickly got into a loud, profane argument. Apparently, some officials had not shown up for their assigned games, and Keller wanted to fire the coordinator. Their dispute escalated, and Keller shouted: "You want to take this outside? C'mon, let's go, I'll kick your [expletive]! I'll beat the [expletive] out of you." They marched out to the parking lot, where the other man took off his shirt and wristwatch and laid them on the hood of a car, but before they could brawl, one of Keller's other employees grabbed his arm and led him back toward the gym.

When Keller got back inside, he muttered to me, "You won't see him again," and described him with a vulgarity. Then he resumed telling me about his business. "This camp in particular is branded nationally," he said. "It sells out six months in advance. We've got nine hundred kids on the waiting list."

When I asked how much money he made from his basketball endeavors, he replied: "Not much. Not as much as you might think." Then he added that to the extent he does turn a profit, he pours most of it back into a charity he says he is affiliated with that benefits abused children. "It's not about money to me," he went on. "I just try to create an avenue so the kids can learn things and be something in life. It's about character, integrity, hard work, knowing the difference between right versus wrong. If they get that down, they'll have a good life."

The Junior Phenom event is categorized as an "exposure camp" to distinguish it from camps whose primary mission is teaching. But the sixth-, seventh-, and eighth-graders who attend are really performing for an audience of one: Clark Francis, the editor of *Hoop Scoop*, an online tout sheet, many of whose subscribers are either college coaches or parents who want to see how their kids measure up.

Without the presence of Francis, the camp would lose much of its edge and a chunk of its paying clientele. "They all know that Clark Francis is going to be here," Keller explained. "They know coming in: you're going to get evaluated, you're going to get ranked. That's part of the branding. Without it, we wouldn't get players. But we get the best players, and they get what they pay for."

The *Hoop Scoop* editor is a man of strong opinions and snap judg-
ments. "It's not PC what I do, ranking young kids," Francis told me.
"I know that. Some people like it, some people don't. But if you're
playing at an event and I'm not scouting it, nobody knows and nobody cares."

Francis, who is a short and plump forty-nine-year-old, never
played the game at even the high school level, but he has managed
to turn his passion into a vocation. He has attended thirty-six consecutive Final Fours, and he told me that his apartment in Louisville contains so much college-basketball memorabilia that visitors
get lost in it for hours, as if it were a museum exhibit. He speaks in
a torrent of words that consist almost entirely of basketball refer-
ences. "Did you hear about the Long Island Lightning?" he asked
me as we sat having lunch at an In-N-Out Burger near the gym in
San Diego. I thought he was alerting me to a weather event, perhaps some unlucky weekenders struck down on a beach in South-
ampton. But he meant an AAU team from Long Island that had
just won an important tournament in Orlando.

I walked from court to court with him at the camp as he made
notes on a clipboard. His method was to see each of the dozens of
teams and rank each player against his teammates, from best to
worst, before working up campwide rankings. The frenetic nature
of play made it difficult for me to discern quality, but Francis exuded the confidence of a handicapper who makes his bets after
casting his eye on the Thoroughbreds in the paddock. "The more
times you have to keep going back and looking at a kid, the less
likely it is he can play," he said. "I can usually pick them out in
warm-ups. Just how they carry themselves. Does the guy pass the
look test? That's the first thing."

I asked what attributes he looks for. "Size, athleticism, outside
shooting," he answered. "Bottom line is, if you don't have one of
those things, forget it. Go play soccer. Have a nice life."

In Major League Baseball, players from the Dominican Republic, many of them raised in poverty, have a reputation as free swing-
ers who will chase almost any pitch rather than work a base on
balls. When the former Atlanta Braves shortstop Rafael Ramirez
was asked during the 1986 season about why he had gone some
forty games without drawing a walk, seemingly an impossibility, he
famously replied, "A walk won't get you off the island."

A similar line of thinking prevailed at the Junior Phenom camp. The young players may not have known Francis's precise methods, but they seemed to have a sense that they had better do something pretty spectacular, and quickly. One morning, I watched a game involving Billy Clark III, a quick and slippery twelve-year-old guard from the Bedford-Stuyvesant section of Brooklyn who had the speed and moves to evade his defender and get off a shot at any time. Which he did—just about every time he touched the ball. In a thirty-two-minute game, of which he played just a little more than half, he put up thirty-four shots by my count.

His father, Billy Jr., sat in the bleachers and exhorted him on. He explained to me, "What I told him is, in this setting, you've got to establish your dominance."

Billy's shooting, while certainly excessive, was pretty much emblematic of how most of the young players approached their mission. They passed only as a last resort. They played indifferent defense, or none at all. To watch this up close was to gain an understanding of the roots of the decline of team play in American basketball.

I talked to Billy Clark III after his game. He had an oddly adult way of speaking. I didn't really need to ask questions; he had things he wanted me to know, as if he had been expecting to be interviewed and rehearsed his lines. "I just want to stay humble," he said. "If my head gets too swollen, I'm not going to be that good anymore."

He told me that he was thankful to his father, who had risked his job at an events-planning company to accompany him to this camp. His father asked him, "What are we striving for?" and Billy replied, "Free education!" Billy then added a thought that sounded like a fragment of dialogue from a 1970s after-school special: "I'm just trying to get my family out of the ghetto," he said.

One afternoon, after Francis grew irritated at having to observe too much middling talent, he said, "C'mon, let's go watch Allonzo Trier." Much of his job is a chore, but Francis really enjoys watching Trier, whom he always refers to by his first and last names. "Allonzo Trier is going to make it no matter what," he told me. "And that's what makes Allonzo Trier fun to watch. He just does things right."

A certain kind of sports aficionado likes to feel in the know—

that he has seen, or even just heard of, some up-and-coming player before the rest of the world has caught on. A whole industry has grown up around so-called NFL "draftniks"—men (well, 99.9 percent of them are men) who keep track of, say, the offensive lineman from West Texas A&M who might be selected in a late round of the spring draft.

In basketball, the real discoveries must be found among those still in middle school. LeBron James's first high school game, in ninth grade, was eagerly anticipated by insiders, and the televising of high school games took off during the four years he was prepping for the NBA at St. Vincent–St. Mary High School in Akron, Ohio. "The explosion in grassroots basketball is directly related to LeBron James," Francis said. "People were on him early, so everything moves back a couple of years."

On the court in front of us, Trier was playing for a team designated "Michigan State" with teammates who ranged from four foot eight to six foot one. At first, I didn't really get all the hubbub. He was clearly a good shooter and deft passer, but the chaos of these games, with everyone desperately trying to make an impression, didn't really cast glory on anyone. The quality of play was appalling, a crime against basketball.

But on the final day of camp, watching Trier participate in the all-star game, involving those deemed the camp's best players, I finally did start to see. The game was more organized. His teammates could anticipate his passes and move to the right spots to receive them. At one point, he sped up the court with the ball, lost a defender at half-court with a crossover dribble, reached the foul line, and, without picking up his dribble, shoveled a pass with his left hand to a cutting teammate. The whole sequence, and especially the method of delivery—off-hand, off the dribble—was highly sophisticated.

"That," said Francis, "is classic Allonzo Trier."

A smallish basketball player at the pro or major college level—say, six foot two or shorter—has to be extraordinarily fast to become a star. Someone like the NBA's Allen Iverson, or the budding superstar Chris Paul, may have never encountered anyone as quick as they were until they reached the pros, and even then they will meet just a handful of similarly supercharged little men. Trier looked fast to me, but there were a few others who seemed just as quick. His superiority lay more in the realm of his ball-handling, shooting ability, and feel for the game, what coaches call "basketball IQ."

Clark Francis did not express any doubts about Trier's gifts. He referred several times to "the Allonzo Trier phenomenon," as if it existed apart from him. At the close of the camp, he ranked Trier number one in his class, just as he had in 2007.

Francis posts rankings for players all the way through high school, and he was an enthusiastic advocate of Brandon Jennings, who opted last year to play in Italy rather than in college; Jennings is expected to be a coveted NBA prospect whenever he chooses to return. Francis often likens Trier to Jennings. "You know what Brandon Jennings's potential is, right?" he asked me. I didn't, actually. "Top-five point guard ever to play the game. Does that put it in perspective for you, what I'm saying about Allonzo Trier?"

Late in January, not long after I visited him in Seattle, Trier attended the U.S. Superior Skills Camp in Fort Worth, where, according to *Hoop Scoop,* he excelled again. Francis's account gushed about "the continued dominance" of Allonzo Trier. "If you will recall, Trier is the jet-quick point guard that reminds us in so many ways of 6–2 Brandon Jennings, who was the consensus No. 1–ranked high-school player in the nation a year ago and is currently averaging 8.2 ppg in 10 games for Lottomatica Virtus Roma in the Euroleague and . . . just like Jennings, Trier has a flair for the spectacular . . ."

Comical as the overheated rhetoric may be, it's hard to imagine that it wouldn't lead a basketball-loving child to believe he is on a straight course to the NBA. Trier and his mother consider Francis an authority, and he praises her as "a smart lady, not your typical nettlesome parent."

In San Diego, Francis counseled Marcie about the challenge Allonzo faces in living up to a top *Hoop Scoop* ranking. "Brandon had to be the best player all the way through, just like LeBron James, Kevin Garnett, and Sebastian Telfair," he said, referring to Jennings and three high school phenoms who went straight to the NBA. "That's the challenge. How do you stay up there?"

I often hear from parents of young athletes that their kids "started late," even if they joined an organized team at age seven. That's a defining element of the modern youth-sports culture, the feeling that there is always someone who has a head start or is doing more, and that there is ground to be made up. This drives the profession-alism that permeates childhood sport: paid coaches leading teams that were once coached by volunteers; expensive sports tutoring; all the travel; even genetic testing to determine a child's ideal sport. The culture demands lodestars, young sports luminaries like Allonzo Trier, to show what is possible with early attention, extreme effort, and money.

The hype over Trier makes him a much-anticipated prospect in the far-off basketball future. But it also certifies him as someone due concrete benefits right now—for example, the free, person-ally branded clothing he receives from the label NYICE, a Seattle-area start-up. As he travels the AAU and camp circuit, Trier serves as a billboard for the company. It is a form of viral marketing, the hope being that he will attract paying customers.

Seattle has in recent years been a hotbed for young basketball talent. Several highly ranked high schoolers, including a girl, are also wearing NYICE gear. Gerald Wright, a Bronx native who played college basketball in Seattle, owns the company. "It's a win-win for the kids and my brand," he told me. "We want other people to say, 'If Zo's wearing it, I want to wear it.' Meanwhile, he's got some-thing unique. I don't think LeBron had a logo in middle school. I don't think Kobe did. To the young man, it's a way of saying, you've worked hard, so good things will come to you. I don't see it as ex-ploitative or taking advantage, and the moment I did, I would get out of it."

(Active NCAA athletes cannot accept gear and other items, but athletes who are in high school or younger can take just about any-thing but cash without endangering their college eligibility. Steve Mallonee, the NCAA's managing director for academic and mem-bership affairs, said even if his organization wanted to, it couldn't enforce rules at below the college level because it would have a hard time disseminating its guidelines.)

The more important benefits flowing to Trier concern his aca-demics. Over the summer, tests revealed why he had been reading at well below grade level: he is dyslexic. In AAU ball, he competes as a seventh-grader, but academically, he's in sixth grade because he was held back a year. (Francis includes him in the class of 2014, the age group in which he plays, but he's really the class of 2015, the year he should graduate from high school.)

Rich Padden, the Seattle lawyer and investor who arranged for

Trier's schooling, said he set about addressing his educational
needs after hearing from Steve Goldstein and another coach in
New York who had taken an interest in Trier's basketball and academic progress and had flown him in to play tournaments. Padden
arranged for Trier's testing, private tutoring, and tuition to be paid
for by the charitable foundation established by Brandon Roy, a star
with the Portland Trail Blazers. Padden served as a mentor to Roy
in high school, as well as to another NBA player from the Seattle
area, Martell Webster. (Padden is also an investor in one of the major manufacturers of basketballs, so Trier, who goes through a lot
of balls, has a reliable source for more.)

"Allonzo is the first beneficiary of the Brandon Roy Foundation,
hopefully the first of hundreds or thousands," Padden said. "He fit
our criteria. We would have supported him even if he were not a
basketball player."

Trier's tutor wants to work with him three days a week, but so far
Trier has been able to fit in only two sessions a week because of
his busy basketball schedule and his limited enthusiasm for them.
When his mother asked what would motivate him to be more excited about the tutoring, he answered: more basketball instruction. Private coaches were hired to teach him to play "lockdown
defense" and to further refine his shooting. He made ninety-five of
one hundred foul shots for his new shooting coach, who identified
flaws in his form and said that if they were fixed, Trier could consistently make ninety-eight out of one hundred.

When I asked Trier about school, he said, "It's hard for me because
I'm not the smartest kid." But that was not my impression of him at
all. Whenever we talked, he displayed a lively curiosity. He had an
ease in dealing with people, adults as well as kids. But basketball is
clearly easier for him than school.

Marcie Trier, in her travels through the male-dominated world
of youth basketball, gets a lot of unsolicited advice. People have
told her to take her son out of the Pacific Northwest and go to New
York or Texas, where he'll get better competition and more exposure—which seems to be particularly poor counsel since he's already the most heralded player in the history of sixth-grade basketball, and Brandon Roy and others have already proved that being
from Seattle is no barrier to becoming an NBA multimillionaire.

Others suggest that she should pull Trier away from the spotlight and pare back his basketball schedule. Trier is already being circled by men whose motivations must be constantly assessed. In the coming years, dozens more will come around, and Marcie and Allonzo will have to make some keen character assessments.

"I worry about him," says Hennings, the athletic director at the Rotary Boys and Girls Club in Seattle. "I worry about injuries. I worry about his knees. I worry about all the people around him. I tell his mom all the time, 'No one does something for nothing.' I'm sorry, but some of these people are going to want something down the line. Some of this stuff could come back to bite him. I'm trying to stay in Allonzo's life and give him the team thing, but I've said to them, if you want to explore all that stuff, you're on your own."

How much is too much is an unanswerable question in sports. The childhood training routine maintained by Michael Phelps would have driven nearly any other promising swimmer back to dry land. The laserlike focus of the young Tiger Woods was a singular gift, and his practice routine with his father may be replicable, if at all, once in a generation.

It could be that for Trier, taking 450 shots a day, seven days a week, along with the rest of his arduous schedule, is a terrific undertaking that will pay dividends in basketball success and happiness. His joints and spirit will hold up, and he'll attain his dreams. It is just as likely that he would be as good and have as bright a future by taking 200 shots a day, with Sundays off.

His current lofty status does not confer future success—or protect against the consequences of being a great player at thirteen who, by nineteen, is perceived as having failed to live up to expectations. If becoming a coveted college prospect and signing with a big-time NCAA program is an endpoint of sorts, Trier has a long time to maintain his standing. By the time he starts playing college basketball, a second Obama administration could be winding down.

Marcie Trier is correct in thinking that his game must not fall off. Her son might not be "kicked to the curb," but the smart basketball set would move on and find other objects of affection. He has to grow taller. And he has to avoid being swallowed up within the netherworld of grassroots basketball.

Trier, steely in competition, otherwise exudes a sweetness and a concern for others that is rare among top-level teenage athletes. As I watched him one day going through his workout in the gym at his apartment complex, he caught sight of a younger child in an adjacent room who was swinging dangerously from a piece of weight-training equipment. "Mom!" he yelled as he abruptly let the basketball fall to the floor. "You've gotta go over there and make her get off of that." She went over and told the little girl to climb down.

For the rest of his practice, Trier kept glancing in the direction of the weight room, worried that the girl would climb back up and lose her grip.

BOB HOHLER

Failing Our Athletes

The Sad State of Sports in Boston Public Schools

FROM THE BOSTON GLOBE

Missed Opportunities

THEY FEEL like the forgotten ones: football teams training on hazardous turf, soccer teams practicing on fields without goals, track teams running in school hallways for lack of access to training facilities.

They are players who share uniforms because there are too few to go around, players who yearn for more qualified coaches on the sidelines and a few fans in the empty stands, players who never make it to the field because of academic woes and the scourge of deadly street violence.

In a golden age of professional sports in Boston, they are portraits of a bleak reality for student-athletes in the city's public schools.

Consider the baseball players at Burke High School in Dorchester who were forced this spring to practice in an alley strewn with broken glass three days before their season opener because their field —a mile-plus walk from school through one of the city's most dangerous neighborhoods—had yet to be prepared. Outfielder Augusto Ceron spoke for many of his fellow athletes when he said of city leaders, "They treat us like second-class citizens. It's like nobody cares."

City leaders point to a few splendid new fields and facilities and offer promises of better days. But as students like Ceron know all too well, Boston's high school athletic program languishes in chronic distress. A system that could inspire greater achievement on the field and in the classroom while providing a vital alternative to the hazards of the streets is failing because of inadequacies in funding, facilities, equipment, coaching, oversight, and vision, according to a nine-month review by the *Globe*.

Mayor Thomas M. Menino has trumpeted "the true value of sport" for Boston's youth and frequently appears at neighborhood sports events. But by many measures, the educational system the mayor oversees has severely shortchanged children in the schools who long for a chance to play, to compete, to succeed.

The first measure of failure is financial. City leaders allocated just under $4 million this year for athletics, less than one-half percent of the total budget of $833 million. That's far less than the statewide average of 3 to 4 percent, according to the Massachusetts Interscholastic Athletic Association. The national average is 1 to 3 percent, according to the National Federation of State High School Associations.

Boston dedicates a smaller percentage of its school budget to athletics than neighboring cities such as Cambridge and Somerville and similarly sized urban centers, including San Francisco and Atlanta. Boston's athletic budget has not increased in more than six years.

"The inequality is stark," said Stanley Pollack, executive director of the Boston-based Center for Teen Empowerment. "There is a real dearth of athletic opportunities in the city schools, and it contributes to a persistent achievement gap and much higher dropout rates."

The second measure is opportunity. Only about three thousand students participate in Boston's struggling sports system, as countless others are effectively deprived of the opportunity to play because the programs are not available to them. While 68 percent of students statewide play interscholastic sports, a mere 28 percent participate in the Boston Public Schools, according to an MIAA survey last year.

Scarcer Opportunities

It's not that many Boston students don't want to play. It's because, for a host of reasons, they can't. At Charlestown High School, for instance, girls have the option of playing only five sports all year —volleyball, basketball, softball, and indoor and outdoor track— and they turn out in small numbers to participate. By comparison, girls in neighboring Everett enjoy many more sports options, including field hockey, ice hockey, soccer, tennis, and swimming, and they participate at much higher levels.

In Boston, many sports are delivered in a two-tier system that disenfranchises the fourteen thousand students who cannot gain entry to the city's three exam schools: Boston Latin, Latin Academy, and O'Bryant School of Mathematics and Science. Only Boston Latin students can compete in sailing and crew. Only students at the two Latin schools can participate in girls' ice hockey and girls' varsity soccer.

And though the city claims to offer every athlete access to interscholastic tennis, golf, and cross-country through co-op programs at exam schools, only one of the fourteen thousand students outside the exam schools—a female tennis player—opted to participate.

Of the eighteen thousand public high school students in Boston, none have access to the fast-growing sport of lacrosse. Nor can they compete in field hockey or gymnastics, which are offered in neighboring communities.

The situation is even bleaker at Boston's twenty-two middle schools. The only interscholastic sports available to those children are basketball and spring track.

Other *Globe* findings underscore the scope of the problem:

- The city employs only one athletic director to oversee eighteen high schools that field teams, and he is chronically overwhelmed. The vast majority of other athletic directors in the state oversee a single high school.
- Boston has just one part-time athletic trainer under contract for all of its schools, which results, coaches say, in some players competing with undiagnosed or inadequately treated injuries.

- The city faces a shortage of qualified coaches, even though its coaching stipends rank among the highest in the state. Boston's contract with its teachers union also makes it hard to root out lackluster or incompetent coaches because it renders the athletic director powerless to hire and fire coaches.
- The coaching shortage also deprives some student-athletes of proper instruction and increases their risk of injury. Coed track teams with fifty or more athletes, for instance, are led by a single coach, making it impossible for the coach to monitor players competing in track's multiple disciplines.
- The athletic department's limited equipment budget has stagnated for years, while the cost of necessities such as football helmets has ballooned. Boston, for example, spends $1,700 a year to equip each high school football team, compared with $4,800 in Lincoln-Sudbury.
- Widespread academic ineligibility contributed to low participation levels in many sports. Five teams with too few players for various reasons were shut down during their seasons, and more than thirty other games were forfeited for reasons ranging from ineligible players to transportation snafus.
- With Boston largely considered a wasteland by college recruiters, only two of the city's 3,500 graduating seniors—a distance runner at Charlestown and a boys' basketball player at English —received full Division 1 college athletic scholarships, though English catcher Nelfi Zapata was the first Massachusetts high school player selected in this year's Major League Baseball draft, in the nineteenth round by the New York Mets.

  By comparison, more than twenty students in the smaller Atlanta school district received full athletic scholarships this year.

  "Boston is an underrecruited league at every level," said Juan Figueroa, O'Bryant's boys' basketball coach. "The perception, unfortunately, is that kids in Boston can't qualify academically."
- Other than the Charlestown boys winning a Division 2 indoor track title, the Boston schools were so overmatched by suburban opponents that thirty-nine of the city's fifty-two teams that qualified for postseason tournaments failed to win a game. (Boston's baseball and softball teams were outscored in the playoffs, 158–25.)

Pleas for Assistance

In a city where school spirit, neighborhood pride in athletics, and a sense of personal security among students have plummeted, it's no wonder that most of Boston's best athletes have abandoned the public schools for private and parochial schools, and that others have enrolled in suburban schools through the Metco program, according to many coaches, parents, and advocates.

"I know people want to be optimistic," said Latin football coach John McDonough, "but if you look at the situation and think about whether the glass is half-full or half-empty, I want to say, 'It's half-empty. Fill the damn thing, would you?'"

A city whose high school teams once were envied by suburban rivals now fosters a system that inspires little more than pity.

"My heart goes out to those folks," said Nancy O'Neil, the athletic director at Lincoln-Sudbury High School, which competes against Latin in the Dual County League. "There's no question that across Massachusetts you have the haves and the have-nots, and the Boston schools clearly fall into the category of the have-nots. It's such a tragedy."

Menino said he is committed to improving the city's high school athletic system.

"Can we do better? We sure can," the mayor said. "It's a work in progress. We're making some gains, but the issue is resources. We need to find a way to do more in these difficult financial times."

Boston School Superintendent Carol R. Johnson said she is strongly committed to building an athletic system that provides excellence, access, and equity for every student.

"We're not there yet, but we're working toward that goal," she said. "Because of the challenges we have with our budget, we have not expanded as rapidly as we would like, but we do consider sports part of our effort to reduce the dropout rate, and we understand how important athletics are in helping students learn about teamwork and sportsmanship."

Johnson said she has dedicated a $20,000 donation from Red Sox pitcher Manny Delcarmen, who graduated from West Roxbury High in 2000, to help pay a new administrator to upgrade athletics in middle schools. She said Boston Public Schools athletic director Ken Still is working with Boston University to provide more athletic trainers. The city also has funded six artificial turf fields for Boston schools and built a new gym as part of a $49.5 million project at Burke.

But with a proposed 2.5 percent cut in Boston's school budget, the prospects of upgrading athletics appear grim. Unlike most communities in the state, Boston does not charge students a user fee to play sports. The fee to play football at Hamilton-Wenham, for example, was $969.

Meanwhile, the state of Boston school athletics is such that maintaining the status quo is viewed as unthinkable by numerous coaches, students, and advocates.

"Things are bad enough already," said Dennis Wilson, the boys' basketball coach at Madison Park Technical Vocational High School. "We need to get the word to the bigwig politicians that they need to add to the sports budget. We need more equipment, more resources, more opportunities for students to participate."

In Hyde Park, the football team dodges manhole covers on its practice field. In West Roxbury, the football team practices on a field so rutted that players regularly injure ankles. The Brighton team works out on an uneven field so littered with dog feces and goose droppings that players call it "the toilet bowl."

In South Boston, football coach Sean Guthrie turned away nearly twenty players because he lacked enough equipment. A shortage of uniforms forced members of Charlestown's champion track team to swap sweat-soaked jerseys during meets. Guthrie and other coaches scavenged for equipment and reached into their pockets for thousands of dollars to outfit their teams.

Stranded on the sidelines were scores of students who hanker to compete in lacrosse, field hockey, tennis, golf, cross-country, and gymnastics but have little or no chance to pursue them in the Boston schools.

"You need to offer these activities if you want to keep kids engaged in the classroom," said Matt Knapp, who persuaded administrators to let him launch a wrestling program last winter at Burke. "A lot of kids are quitting the Boston schools because the schools offer nothing to them."

Alternative to Crime

The need for a vibrant high school athletic system has never been greater, according to administrators, coaches, and advocates who said experience has shown that students who participate in sports are more likely to stay out of trouble and achieve better grades.

"When I step on the field, it's the one place where I don't think about all the craziness," said Alex Munoz, a Dorchester High baseball player. For him, the "craziness" is this: a lender threatening to foreclose on his mother's home, a personal dilemma involving his girlfriend, the shooting deaths of several friends, the escalating gang violence in his Roxbury neighborhood.

Many student-athletes in Boston this year were victims of crimes, from assault and armed robbery to murder. Others were perpetrators.

"The way things are going, probation and parole officers are the new guidance counselors," said Guthrie, who teaches math at South Boston's Monument High.

Numerous students said that, but for sports, they might well have succumbed to the lure of the streets. Boston Police Superintendent Paul Joyce, who helped secure wrestling mats for the Burke team and volunteered as an assistant coach for the Charlestown boys' basketball team, said high school sports are crucial in the fight against crime, particularly gang violence.

"There's nothing easy about playing sports in the city schools," Joyce said. "There's a lot these kids have to endure, but we've found that sports can help them gain the confidence and self-esteem they need to say no to picking up a gun."

Boston's struggle to sustain competitive athletic programs is also made more difficult by the city's surge of immigrant students who have never been exposed to numerous sports, most notably football and hockey. Coaches in those sports routinely struggle to recruit enough athletes to field teams.

The challenge is particularly acute at Burke, which has a large number of Cape Verdean immigrants; Hyde Park, which enrolls an abundance of newcomers from Haiti; and Madison Park, where English is a second language for 51 percent of the students. Coaches often rely on bilingual players to translate their instructions.

"The nationalities of our players go from A to Z," said Madison Park football coach Roosevelt Robinson. "When I ask everybody who is American to stand up, nobody does."

Shortcomings in the system are less extreme at the exam schools, particularly Latin, which enjoys most of the privileges of its suburban counterparts thanks to generous financial support from alumni. But coaches and students in the non-exam schools consider the disparity between Latin's programs and theirs a form of de facto discrimination.

"The city treats the big three exam schools like real schools," Robinson said. "They get special privileges. It's a shame the rest of the schools aren't treated that way."

Latin's McDonough could do little more than express sympathy.

"I know what some of my peers have to deal with to make ends meet," he said. "It's extremely difficult for them. I wish it could be better. Unfortunately, it's not right now."

Competing Under Fire

Gunshots rang out—at least six rounds in rapid fire—as girls played softball last month at Madison Park Technical Vocational High School, just blocks from Boston police headquarters. Only a few girls flinched at the gunfire, and none ducked for cover as a pack of youths sprinted from the shooting site amid the scream of sirens and screech of tires from approaching police vehicles.

For student-athletes across the city, the chilling cacophony of violence has become part of the soundtrack of their lives.

"It's something we hear every day," said Madison Park baseball catcher Jeffrey Santana. "Sometimes we don't even notice it."

Like never before, the challenges of staying alive and staying out of jail have become as crucial for athletes in the Boston schools as honing their sports skills, according to coaches, players, and youth advocates. It's a disturbing reality that complicates efforts to develop a comprehensive high school athletic system in a city that, a *Globe* review shows, shortchanges its student-athletes on funding, facilities, equipment, coaching, and other services.

Two days before Thanksgiving, Charlestown High's senior shortstop Sergio Ibanez, eighteen, was shot dead outside his grandmother's house. Less than six months later, Soheil Turner, fifteen, who planned to play basketball next season at Charlestown, was killed waiting for a school bus. Numerous other student-athletes told the *Globe* they have been robbed or assaulted going to or from school, games, or practice.

"When they leave us at six o'clock, we don't know if we will see them the next morning," said Ibanez's coach, George Farro.

Fifteen teenagers, most Boston school students, were killed this school year in the city. Boston school police logged more than 740 crimes against individuals and seized more than 625 weapons, including three firearms, reinforcing the fear among many coaches that one of their athletes could be the next to die.

"We've been to more funerals than graduations," Madison Park football coach Roosevelt Robinson said of himself and Dennis Wilson, the basketball coach.

"Snitches Get Stitches"

It was a gun crime at Madison Park that led Ibanez to Charlestown. A mild-mannered church keyboardist, Ibanez was walking to Madison Park's music school two years ago when a gun-wielding gang stole his cell phone and the $3 in his pocket. Police arrested one suspect, and Ibanez's parents, Jean and Ignacio Diaz, feared their son would be exposed to retaliatory violence.

"The boy who robbed Sergio knew who he was, so we needed to get him out of that school," Jean Diaz said.

Rules of the street required they fear for the victim's safety, as Madison Park basketball player Andre Mascoll reminded his mother after a gang jumped him in January, returning home from practice. Just days after a student survived a shooting outside Madison Park, Mascoll — two blocks from his Dorchester home — was confronted by thugs. One grabbed his arm, another reached in his pocket and stole the $12 his mother gave him, another punched him in the face.

"That's when I went down, and they all started kicking me," Mascoll said.

He suffered lacerations and bruises. Yet Wilson expressed relief when he heard the news.

"Andre was alive," said Wilson, mindful that one of his ex-players was killed for a gold chain.

Mascoll's mother urged her son to call police, but he warned her, "Snitches get stitches."

Which is why Ibanez transferred from Madison Park to Charlestown. A versatile athlete, Ibanez played two years of baseball at

Charlestown and one year of hockey. He also scored high enough on MCAS tests to earn an Adams Scholarship, a four-year scholarship to any public college in Massachusetts.

Ibanez had no criminal or school disciplinary record. Though he lived across from the gang-beset Bromley-Heath complex in Jamaica Plain, no evidence linked him to gangs. But he made a fatal mistake late November 24, responding to a plea from his cousin, William "Chino" Santos, to pick him up at their grandmother's Roslindale apartment.

"If I knew it was [Santos], I would have told Sergio, 'Don't do it,'" his mother said.

Santos, she said, is a former convict who runs with the notorious Latin Kings. A little after 1 A.M., just after Santos slipped into the back of Ibanez's girlfriend's car—Ibanez sat in the passenger's seat—a gunman approached, by all accounts intending to kill Santos. Instead, he wounded Santos and killed Ibanez. The crime remains unsolved.

For Farro, the news was chillingly familiar. In 2005, one of his football players, Kevin Walsh, sixteen, was stabbed to death in Charlestown's Bunker Hill projects.

Fear of Gang Violence

Gang-related gun crimes are prevalent near many Boston schools and sports facilities. Police Superintendent Paul Joyce said gangs are recruiting children as young as twelve to wield guns.

"We're coaching a lot of kids who have been traumatized by the violence," said Paulo De Barros, the boys' soccer coach at Burke High School in Dorchester.

Many student-athletes in Boston grew up with gang members. Some are gang-affiliated for their own safety. Others try making it on their own, sometimes walking blocks out of their way to avoid gang-controlled turf.

"It doesn't matter if you're not a troublemaker," said Johan Rosario, a senior baseball player at Burke who was attacked by a gang on his way home. "If you're wearing certain colors, or they don't like the way you look, they're coming after you."

The fear of gang violence was so high when Madison Park played O'Bryant for the city boys' basketball title in February that police dispatched a mobile command center and dozens of officers to the game.

With several officers monitoring metal detectors and many others stationed throughout the gym—a number of youths were denied entry or escorted out—Madison Park won the championship without an off-court incident.

For many coaches, saving children from the streets involves trying to keep them out of criminal trouble. Burke baseball coach Paul Duhaime said he refrained from reporting one student who told him he kept a gun, hidden outside school, for his protection. Duhaime said he visited two other players in jail. At Dorchester High, baseball coach Ed Toto was trying to help three players this spring who had criminal histories.

In Charlestown, basketball coach Edson Cardoso dropped two players caught carrying knives or box cutters into school, and he struggled to save several younger players with criminal records from further trouble.

"With some kids, honestly, I've dealt more with their probation officers and judges than I have with their teachers or guidance counselors," Cardoso said.

South Boston football coach Sean Guthrie went to the playoffs last fall without his best linebacker, Sir Warrior Greene, who was locked up late in the season on an armed robbery charge and probation violation.

One of the Lucky Ones

Dorchester basketball star Darius Carter was more fortunate. He was nearly expelled as a freshman, was later wounded in a drive-by shooting, and then locked up for three months in a youth detention center for gang-related activity. He appeared on track to follow his older brother, who has spent most of his adult life behind bars. But as a junior at Dorchester's TechBoston Academy, Carter repudiated the gang life, and as a senior he became the leading boys' scorer in eastern Massachusetts.

"I realized I didn't want to die," he said. "I wanted to go to college, so I started focusing on school and left the streets alone."

With his coaches, John Evans and Justin Desai, as mentors, Carter became one of his school's best students and most popular leaders, earning him some goodwill when he needed to clear up his final brush with the law. On January 16, a game day, Carter was excused from school while a jury in Suffolk Superior Court convicted him of aggravated assault as a youthful offender against a teenage rival in 2007.

The same afternoon, Torey Evans, sixteen, was shot dead in the street a mile from the Dorchester complex and a fifteen-year-old boy was caught minutes later entering the school with a gun. By the time Carter arrived at the gym from the courthouse, he had missed the first half of Dorchester's game against O'Bryant. He played the rest of the game, scored twenty points, but Dorchester could not overcome a twenty-six-point halftime deficit and lost, 94–79.

Carter, who received probation for the assault conviction, epitomizes the student-athletes in Boston who find ways to excel despite long odds against them. He plans to attend Brandeis in the fall.

It is teens like Carter, whose love of basketball helped motivate him in school and turn him away from the street life, who are testament to the social and economic benefits of high school athletics in the inner city. As numerous coaches said, it costs much less to educate students than to later incarcerate them.

To help keep others from losing their way, Wilson enlisted Greg Simpson, a former Madison Park star and NBA prospect, as a volunteer assistant this year. Simpson, forty-five, is on parole after serving fourteen and a half years for robbing convenience stores at gunpoint to feed his cocaine addiction. He told Wilson's players how he made it from Bromley-Heath to the threshold of his NBA dream, only to squander it all.

"I worry about these kids because of all the gang violence," said Simpson, who recently joined the Boston Foundation's StreetSafe outreach team. "It's very tough to make it in high school sports in this city because of all the obstacles. If you make it, you've done something great."

Eligibility a High Hurdle

He was the golden boy, a football captain and student leader hand-picked by the headmaster of Burke High School to appear on stage with Mayor Thomas M. Menino of Boston last September as a symbol of hope at the start of a new school year. But Brandon Cook was headed for a fall.

Presented as a college-bound senior, Cook beamed as Menino unveiled his pride and glory, a $49.5 million upgrade to the long-embattled school in the gang-plagued Grove Hall section of Dorchester. Student-athletes such as Cook, who received a commemorative basketball from Menino, were expected to especially benefit from the project, which featured a gleaming new gymnasium and a finely equipped fitness and weight-training facility.

Haunted by previous heartaches—his older brother suffering a gunshot to his face and his homeless father being brutally beaten in the street—Cook's landlord threatened to evict him and his mother from their apartment, raising the frightening prospect that he may be forced to return to living in his mother's car. He fell through Burke's safety net as his grades tumbled, and by November he joined scores of other Boston school students who had been stripped of their academic eligibility to play interscholastic sports.

In a city where high school sports can save vulnerable teenagers from dangerous streets, Cook found himself on the sideline with the many who for various reasons failed to perform as well in the classroom as they do in the athletic arena. This crisis in academic eligibility, by itself, forced several teams to shut down for lack of players, stripped many teams of their best athletes, and underscored the city's reputation among recruiters as a virtual wasteland for college prospects.

The loss of students to poor grades and various other hardships —many need to help support their impoverished families—has all but ended the days of competitive tryouts for teams. Now, coaches scramble to find enough students to field a team, competitive or otherwise.

"It's the same struggle everywhere," said West Roxbury track coach Hugh Galligan. "Talk to anybody across the city, and they'll tell you the biggest challenge is getting kids to come out and keeping them eligible."

Athletic director Ken Still shut down eight programs this year for lack of players, up from four the previous year. Among the casualties:

The Charlestown football team lost nearly ten players, including its starting offensive line, to poor grades. The girls' basketball team did not field a junior varsity squad for the first time in years. The Burke indoor track team lost ten athletes to grades, the football team at least six. The school's volleyball team went to the playoffs with only one reserve on the bench. The South Boston hockey team forfeited a city playoff game because the coach wanted to send a message to players who had squandered their eligibility during the season. The Brighton boys' basketball team lost its two big men to academics.

The roll of lost opportunities goes on and on.

"I see talent in this building that you would probably never find elsewhere," said Charlestown track coach Kristyn Hughes. "The trick is trying to coax it out of them, trying to get them to believe in themselves, and trying to get them eligible."

"Feeling of Helplessness"

Cook's downfall was particularly stunning because he had posted one of the highest SAT scores (1660 out of 2400) in his senior class. Witty and engaging, and with a gift for music production, he was preparing his college applications when he began to buckle under his family-related stress. With his brother jobless after being badly injured in a gang-related shooting and his mother unable to make ends meet despite working two jobs, Cook scrambled to find a job after school and football practice. He found nothing, even at several fast-food restaurants.

"That's when everything started to hit me and my grades started falling," he said.

In a panic, he said, he enlisted in the Marines.

"I signed up out of a feeling of helplessness that plagues so many youths in the city," Cook said. "I did it without really consulting anybody, out of fear of what they would say."

His football coach, John Rice, said he was unaware of Cook's plunging grades or his enlistment.

"Brandon was the best kid in our school and one of the most intelligent," Rice said. "I said, 'Brandon, we're in two wars right now. Why are you signing up for the Marines?' He told me more people die in Roxbury than in Iraq."

With Rice's help, Cook has tried to rescind his enlistment. But nothing could be done about his grade point average, which slipped below the minimum (1.67, or C-minus) required by the Boston Public Schools to compete in athletics. When report cards were issued in mid-November, Cook's GPA was 1.43. He missed the final games of the football season, including the Thanksgiving game, and his senior basketball season.

"Part of me wanted to hide and cry," he said.

Boston School Superintendent Carol R. Johnson said she is exploring and planning to attack the eligibility problem by requiring all student-athletes to attend regular study halls.

"It's all about helping scholar-athletes achieve their goals," she said.

Cook managed to regain his eligibility to compete on the spring track team. He was accepted at the Art Institute of Boston and hopes to attend if he can work out the finances.

Extra Burden on Needy

But struggles like Cook's are far from uncommon at schools such as the Burke, where only 40.2 percent of the students graduated in four years and 42.1 percent dropped out, according to a 2008 BPS report. Citywide that year, only 59.9 percent of Boston's students graduated in four years and 21.5 dropped out.

Some coaches say the school system is partly to blame for the problem.

"Some kids are legitimately struggling in some of these courses," said South Boston football coach Sean Guthrie, who teaches math at the school. "But a kid can fail Algebra 1 and they will still put him in geometry. He can fail geometry and they will still put him in advanced algebra. He can fail advanced algebra, and they will still put him in precalculus, because if they held back as many kids that needed to be held back, there would be a logjam."

Juan Figueroa, the boys' basketball coach at O'Bryant School of Mathematics and Science, said he struggles to field teams in part because so few African Americans pass the school's entry exam. Only seventeen black males were invited to attend O'Bryant next fall from the eighteen middle schools with basketball programs, he said, and not a single black male was invited from nine of the schools, including two of the largest: the Curley School in Jamaica Plain and Orchard Gardens in Roxbury.

"The city and the schools are failing when those schools cannot send us even one black male," Figueroa said.

Still, in a city where nearly 75 percent of the students are classified as low-income, with thousands living in single-parent homes, some of the success stories are remarkable. And, for those students, athletics is often a key part of the picture.

Jean Raphael, a junior running back and track star for Hyde Park High School, has not seen his mother since he left Haiti for America when he was seven. He has since lived in New York, Florida, California, and Massachusetts with relatives or his father's acquaintances. He lived briefly with his father in Boston until his father evicted him last fall during the football season. He has since lived with his father's ex-girlfriend in Roslindale.

Raphael, like Cook, has no criminal history and credits sports with helping to keep him in school. In his backpack, he carries recruiting letters from Sacred Heart University and Springfield College. But Raphael has also had his ups and downs academically as external pressures buffet him.

He was leading Hyde Park to an undefeated season in the South Division of the Boston City League in May when the woman he lives with told him to find a job. While he looked for work, competed in track, and tried to keep pace in school, he flunked chemistry and lost his eligibility to finish the track season.

"I never flunked anything before," Raphael said. "Raising myself all these years finally caught up with me."

Personal Touches

A number of coaches make special efforts to keep their players eligible. In Hyde Park, football coach Adilson Cardoso needed to send about 300 letters and make 150 phone calls to recruit enough athletes to field a team this year; he ended the season with 20 players in uniform. He provided tutoring for his players, many of them Haitian immigrants, and the incentive of a weekly Italian dinner for those who maintained their eligibility and regularly attended practice.

Charlestown boys' basketball coach Edson Cardoso is sending all nine of his seniors to college next fall in part because he roused some of them on school days with wake-up calls and transported a number of them to school from their homes across the city. He also sacrificed practice time for two-hour daily study halls, checked weekly progress reports, and required tutoring for struggling students.

"We have a lot of at-risk kids," Cardoso said. "It's not easy in the inner city to make it out. We try to do whatever we can to help them survive."

Ill-Equipped to Compete

Every new sports season in the Boston public schools starts with a reminder to all coaches: an athletic trainer is available for injured players.

Trouble is, there is only one trainer for thousands of student-athletes in eighteen high schools scattered over nearly fifty square miles of the city. To no one's surprise, only a small fraction of injured players receive treatment from the trainer, Flo Russo, because of the trouble reaching her office at the Reggie Lewis Track and Athletic Center in Roxbury.

Imagine telling kids on crutches in distant corners of the city to ride the T alone to Roxbury and find their way to Russo's office.

"It doesn't make sense," said Charlestown football coach George Farro, echoing the sentiments of several coaches.

Even worse, said East Boston headmaster Mike Rubin, are the number of students whose injuries go undiagnosed or are inadequately treated because of the shortage of trainers.

"I had one kid with a broken ankle and another with a broken clavicle, and I didn't realize it," said Rubin, the school's former basketball coach.

That's life for students in Boston's high school athletic system, many of whom practice in substandard conditions with too little gear and too few services. All too often, they are left to get by with the help of strangers, from physical therapists who contribute free care to grocery shoppers who donate spare change to help them buy equipment the city does not provide.

"The lesson the kids get is that the adults don't care about them," said Ben Okiwe, who recently resigned as boys' basketball coach at Lincoln-Sudbury to help Boston's disadvantaged youths through his nonprofit organization, Young Savants.

In February, Okiwe attended a boys' basketball playoff game between his alma mater, Boston Latin Academy, and Belmont, and watched a Latin Academy player hobble to the bench in pain. With no athletic trainer on site, Okiwe attended to the player, who was suffering from leg cramps.

"If there was a problem like that in the suburbs," Okiwe said of the trainer shortage, "it would be fixed."

Russo, who also serves Roxbury Community College, said she does the best she can. But she almost never treats injured players from distant schools such as West Roxbury and East Boston, and the vast majority of her high school patients attend nearby Madison Park and O'Bryant.

"It would be nice if the city paid for a full-time assistant so we could get out there and help more kids," Russo said, "but I don't think that's going to happen because of the budget cuts."

The city's athletic director, Ken Still, is working with Boston University to try to enlist more trainers through a grant program. Meanwhile, Kennedy Brothers Physical Therapy fills some of the gap by providing free care to Boston's injured student-athletes.

"We do it because of the incredible have-nots in the city," said owner Jake Kennedy, who chaired the urban subcommittee of the Governor's Committee on Physical Fitness and Sports. "It's unbelievable what the city kids don't have, and their facilities are horrible."

Budget Disparity

Across the city, from the Charlestown football team training on a secondhand blocking sled spattered with bird droppings under the Tobin Bridge to the Hyde Park team trying to compete without weight-training equipment, many other needs remain unmet. Many coaches try to make do by dipping into their personal savings, organizing fundraising drives, or asking students to solicit spare change.

"We can't run teams on what the city gives us," said Robert Anthony, who coaches hockey at East Boston and has spent thousands of his own dollars on equipment, facility upgrades, and ice time.

The city allots high school football programs $1,700 a year to equip their varsity and junior varsity teams, while the annual budgets for other athletic programs range from $400 for cross-country to $900 for hockey. By contrast, Lincoln-Sudbury spends more than $4,800 a year just to equip its football team.

Most school districts in Massachusetts, like Lincoln-Sudbury, rely on user fees and boosters to support their athletic programs. Boston, whose student population is overwhelmingly low-income, funds its sports programs through the city budget, and few teams have enough to go around.

"Every coach at every school has to do some kind of fundraising to meet their team's needs," said Michael Viggiano, whose Madison Park baseball team last month won the city championship. "It makes you wonder where athletics are on the totem pole in the Boston schools."

Boston's high school equipment budget has not increased during athletic director Ken Still's six years on the job. During that time, the price of basic football helmets has more than doubled to $150 from $60, while the cost of other essentials has mushroomed.

"Steady doesn't work," Still said of the budget. "Things cost more, so the kids have less."

One exception is the girls' basketball team at English High School, whose coach, Ernie Green, said he considers the program's $800 annual budget generous. In past years, Green said, he shared his leftover equipment money with the school's football team.

Other Boston high schools try to make ends meet with external support. Boston Latin's athletic programs have received more than $100,000 annually from the school's alumni association, while East Boston's sports teams have received more than $20,000 a year from the Massport-funded East Boston Foundation.

"We definitely have an advantage because of it," Rubin said. "It has been a huge part of our success in athletics."

Alumni groups at Boston English, Latin Academy, and O'Bryant have helped their sports programs. But Latin is the only Boston school that can match suburban athletic programs in booster support. Canton's community supporters, for example, donated $180,000 last year to high school sports, while booster clubs at Lincoln-Sudbury and Walpole each gave more than $100,000.

The disparity was stunning when Martha's Vineyard eliminated South Boston from last fall's football tournament. The Vineyard team, bolstered by $50,000 in booster support, dressed more than forty players in the finest gear, while Southie fielded only seventeen players, some of them in ragged uniforms and cleats. The Vineyard coaches, whose touchdown club pays for their scouting trips, communicated through headsets against their ill-equipped Southie counterparts and won the game, 42–14.

"A lot of times, we feel like second-class citizens," South Boston coach Sean Guthrie said.

Forced to Improvise

The nonprofit Good Sports has eased some of the hardship by donating nearly $200,000 worth of athletic equipment to the Boston schools since 2005. Other charities have helped, including the Mark Wahlberg Youth Foundation, which has donated to Dorchester High.

"Unfortunately, we can only do so much for the Boston schools," said Christy Pugh Keswick, the chief operating officer of Good Sports. "We can give them equipment, but we can't solve their other issues."

There is little Good Sports can do about the Hyde Park and Brighton football teams practicing on poor fields without goalposts. The Snowden basketball team plays in a cramped gym in the South End without seats for spectators.

Numerous outdoor teams have trained at remote sites without restrooms, including the Brighton football team, which routinely trudged to bathrooms at a restaurant in Cleveland Circle until City Councilor Mark Ciommo helped unlock a field house that had been shuttered for years. The decrepit facility has no running water, however, so the city last fall delivered a portable toilet to the field.

At Franklin Park, the four soccer teams from Latin Academy— varsity and JV boys and girls—share a practice field that has no soccer goal.

"That adds insult to injury," said boys' varsity coach Dennis Allen. "If nothing else, it would be nice if our kids could practice shooting at a proper goal."

At least Allen's team had enough uniforms. Members of the Latin Academy track team, like Charlestown and others, have so few uniforms that they need to share them during meets. "It's pretty gross," said Latin Academy coach Brian Leussler.

Troubling too was a maintenance snafu that caused the city to temporarily close a number of pools during the high school swim season, prompting swimmers to drop off several teams.

"The city kicked us to the curb like yesterday's rubbish," said East Boston swim coach Dave Arinella, who logged his 250th career victory in the shortened season. "We had no pool for three and a half weeks, and all we could do was watch DVDs about swimming."

Many outdoor teams have benefited from the construction of artificial turf high school fields at Charlestown, English, South Boston, and East Boston, as well as Madison Park and O'Bryant, which share a field. However, the scoreboards have not worked for years at South Boston and Madison Park/O'Bryant, significantly diminishing the game experience.

One major benefit for Boston high school athletes is the Reggie Lewis Center, a premier indoor track venue. Most of the city's high school track teams train and compete there. But because the center is available to the Boston schools only from 2 to 4 P.M., teams at schools with late release times like Boston English (3:35 P.M.) are relegated to practicing in school hallways.

English's disadvantaged athletes finished no better than third in the twenty-two individual events in the Boston City League championships in February.

"We would be a much better team if we weren't practicing on the fifth floor of our school," said English captain Abel Burgos. "If we could train on a track, we would have more endurance and learn more strategies, like how to run in lanes and pace ourselves."

Charlestown track coach Kristyn Hughes said much of her job involves hunting for equipment that colleges or suburban schools plan to discard so she can meet her program's basic needs. Despite the deprivation, though, her boys' team won the state outdoor title last year and the indoor championship this year.

"Because of everything we have to go through, it feels like such a sense of accomplishment when we win," Hughes said. "It's like, 'Wow, we beat the system. We beat the odds. We overcame all the negativity surrounding inner-city schools and did something positive.'"

Coaches in the Crossfire

Number of years Keith Parker has coached football at English High School: twenty-nine.

Number of times Parker's teams have defeated Boston Latin in the nation's oldest continuous high school football rivalry: two.

To some of Parker's critics, even those who witnessed English's 36–0 loss last Thanksgiving to a winless Latin team, the won-lost record is excusable. What's not acceptable to them is how Parker has presided over the decline of English's once-formidable football program. Winners of divisional Super Bowls in 1993 and '97, Parker's teams have since gone 42–76 and struggled for respectability.

Parker's critics said he no longer exerts the energy, enthusiasm, and innovation to sustain a competitive program in an era when city coaches need to work harder than ever to overcome a multitude of challenges. Parker, sixty-four, kept his coaching job after he retired last year from teaching at English.

"I love the man, but his time has passed," said Clarzell Pearl, who starred for Parker's teams in the 1980s and served as his assistant for several years, including last season. "It's time for him to go."

Pearl and numerous other critics, including former NFL draftee Erle Garrett, who has coached against Parker and officiated his games, have expressed their views to Ken Still, the city's athletic director. Still shares their opinion.

"Parker is a friend of mine, but it's time for him to go," Still said. "He's still in the same mold he was thirty years ago, running the same stuff, and it doesn't work."

Still said he would remove Parker if he could. But in a city where the best coaches routinely complain about ill-prepared, uncommitted, and underqualified colleagues failing their student-athletes, the hiring and firing of coaches is controlled by each school's headmaster rather than the athletic director, who may be better suited for the task.

English headmaster Jose Duarte recently appointed Parker to coach his thirtieth season.

"I don't know who's trying to do Keith Parker in, but I'm not," Duarte said. "Keith Parker is a gentleman who cares deeply about our kids. Some people only care about winning, but high school football is about developing young men to work as a team and developing them to understand the hard work it takes to achieve success. Keith Parker has done that."

Parker said he continues to give everything he has to the job.

"For twenty-nine years at English High School, I have been the best I can be and I have helped the kids be the best they can be," he said. "I understand that we all need to move aside one day for the younger guys, but I want to go out on my terms and I think I've earned that right."

As for Parker's record against Latin, the coach described the rivalry as a monumental mismatch. Latin's enrollment is three times the size of English's, and while Latin is predominantly white (31 percent) and African American (28 percent), English is mostly Hispanic (52 percent). As a result, English is far more competitive in baseball and soccer than football.

"I can win if I have the talent," Parker said, "but I can't wave a magic wand and make it happen."

Lucrative Side Job

Parker will coach another year because headmasters are empowered under the city's contract with the Boston Teachers Union to hire and fire coaches. The policy, which gives union teachers preference for coaching positions, grants the final hiring authority to headmasters.

"The process is working well," union president Richard Stutman said.

A number of other coaches disagree.

"Let our athletic director function like other athletic directors by hiring and firing his coaches," said Garrett, the Brighton High basketball coach. "He has the expertise. Let him take the ball and run with it."

Under the system, coaching candidates are first interviewed by Still, who sends the headmaster a written evaluation and recommendation. Still said Parker is one of numerous coaches who have been hired or retained against his written or verbal recommendations.

"There are a whole lot of people who are coaching in the city who shouldn't be," Still said. "In a system of this magnitude, with 275 coaches, you would like to have 80–90 percent who are committed to the job and know what they're doing. We're not there yet."

Boston coaches rank among the highest-paid in the state, with salaries ranging from $2,777 for wrestling and tennis to $10,414 for head football coaches. There are too few coaches, however, and some of them see an inequity in the salaries.

Soccer coaches, for instance, earn $4,947, less than the assistant coaches in football ($6,147), basketball ($5,456), and baseball ($5,205). And soccer coaches have no paid assistants.

"My [former] principal told me to get an assistant and pay him five hundred dollars out of my salary," Brighton boys' soccer coach Matt Krebs said. "I find it absurd that I was asked to do that."

Another problem, according to Still and others, is that too many teachers become coaches only for the extra check. The additional salary can boost a teacher's pension.

"I know there are coaches who do it only for the money," said East Boston High hockey coach Robert Anthony, a Boston police officer. "You hate to see it."

Paul Duhaime, the head baseball coach and assistant football coach at Burke High School, said he could tolerate colleagues enhancing their pensions if they were committed to coaching.

"We make very good money," he said, "but some people just aren't doing their jobs."

That was news to Stutman.

"I know a lot of coaches, and not one of them does it for the money," he said.

The city can take pride in many of its coaches. But the *Globe* received numerous accounts of others selling short their athletes. The accounts ranged from coaches routinely calling off outdoor practices at the slightest forecast of rain to others showing so little interest in the job that they read newspapers or chat on cell phones during games and practices. Other coaches were criticized for failing to teach students the fundamentals of their sports.

"Just because you're a teacher doesn't mean you're a coach," said Burke boys' soccer coach Paulo De Barros, whose team won the city championship last fall. "Some coaches just throw the kids out on the field."

Filling Voids

A number of coaches said headmasters have asked teachers to take over teams simply to fill voids. West Roxbury girls' volleyball coach Margaret Hoyt has coached several sports throughout the city during a lengthy teaching career.

"When they needed a cheerleading coach, I did it because they needed a cheerleading coach, not because I was any kind of a cheerleading coach at all," Hoyt said.

Some headmasters were said to prefer appointing trusted allies rather than the most competent coaching candidates.

"You have headmasters who don't know anything about sports and it doesn't make any difference to them who's running the program as long as somebody is running it," said Turi Lonero, who coached boys' soccer at East Boston High School for twenty years and has coached the men's teams at Northeastern and Salem State. Lonero said he was not referring to East Boston's current headmaster, Mike Rubin, the school's former basketball coach.

Still said he would welcome hiring and firing coaches, but he is unlikely to get the opportunity because of opposition from the teachers union and headmasters.

"Headmasters should have the say about who coaches at their schools," Duarte said. "We know the kids in our schools and we know what they need to develop and be successful."

East Boston's Rubin, a director of the Massachusetts Interscholastic Athletic Association, also defended the hiring policy, although he acknowledged problems may arise when headmasters lack expertise in sports.

"Those headmasters need to reach out for help from people in the community who have some experience in athletics," Rubin said.

Most headmasters assign teachers to serve as their athletic coordinators for a small stipend or as volunteers. Yet most coordinators have little influence, according to some, including Charlestown's coordinator, Steve Cassidy, who called the job "kind of a joke."

The best coaches commit year-round to the job, enriching their knowledge of their sports, tracking the grades of their players, encouraging students to join their programs. Many reach deep into their pockets to provide uniforms and equipment players need to compete.

Personal Investment

As for Parker, Duarte said the veteran coach has made invaluable contributions to many at-risk youths by steering them away from the streets toward brighter futures. Duarte also suggested that some of Parker's critics have personal agendas. Pearl, for instance, has made no secret he would like to succeed Parker.

"To have somebody take a shot at that man, after all he has done to turn the boys in our school into men, is really sad and unfair," Duarte said.

The challenge for Parker and most other coaches in the city is making the best of what they have. For many, like Margaret Cash, who retired last year as a science teacher at Snowden International School and remains the school's girls' volleyball coach, it means investing extra hours and personal savings in their student-athletes.

Cash estimated she has spent about $5,000 a year on her students. She bought a winter coat for a player. She took another player and her siblings for a meal after she visited them and found their refrigerator empty. She also counseled the family of a girl who showed up at practice with her suitcase because her immigrant mother told her she needed to live with the coach.

"The idea is to keep their morale up," Cash said. "I tell them all they are champions in their own way."

Many of her colleagues said the challenge for city leaders is finding more coaches who care.

"Unfortunately," said Madison Park football coach Roosevelt Robinson, "we have a lot who need to go."

That Awful Empty Feeling

It was senior night, South Boston High School's final home football game of the 2008 season, and coach Sean Guthrie wanted to make it memorable for the players who were ending their high school careers. Unable to find anyone in city government to switch on the public-address system, Guthrie rented a generator, hauled a pair of speakers to Saunders Stadium at Moakley Park, and asked a fellow teacher to serve as the announcer for a ceremony honoring the seniors.

Forget that the scoreboard had not worked for seven years and that the new artificial turf had drained poorly from a recent storm. Everything else seemed in order as South Boston ran up a comfortable lead against Charlestown, clearing the way for a once-in-a-lifetime halftime ceremony for the team's ten seniors.

The only problem: almost no one bothered to show up.

As Guthrie's colleague called the roll of South Boston's seniors, he shared the grandstand with eleven spectators.

It was *Friday Night Lights,* Boston-style: eleven supporters for more than sixty players, coaches, and cheerleaders. As thousands of commuters rolled past on the nearby expressway and downtown financial towers twinkled in the distance, the expanse of empty bleachers in the football stadium looked like the aftermath of a fire drill.

The scene is common at high school sports events across the city, where athletes rarely hear the roar of a crowd, see their parents, schoolmates, or teachers turn out to support them, or simply know that someone is taking note of special moments in their lives.

"It's pitiful," said Sandra Redish, the mother of a West Roxbury High cheerleader who has witnessed similar scenes at other competitions. "There should be a lot more parents here. What's going on?"

Guthrie, who played football for Boston College and in NFL Europe, was so dismayed by the empty stands that he changed the start of his Friday home games last season from 3:30 to 7:00 P.M., believing it would boost attendance. No such luck, even though admission was free.

"I don't know where everybody is," he said. "It's a shame."

The turnout was no better for many events at White Stadium, the city's premier high school stadium in Franklin Park, where football, soccer, and track teams compete.

"I love White Stadium, but it's a sin when you play a game on a beautiful, sixty-degree Friday afternoon and you turn around and there are only ten people there," said Paul Duhaime, Burke's assistant football and head baseball coach.

Preoccupied Parents

Coaches say it is heartrending to watch the efforts some students make to commute to schools and games through dangerous neighborhoods, maintain their academic eligibility, and dedicate themselves to their teams, only to play their games in virtual anonymity. Longtime coaches said attendance has faded as poverty has risen in the school population. Working parents who have no time to attend teacher meetings have even less time to attend sports events.

"The parents will never be there," said Paulo De Barros, the Burke boys' soccer coach who founded the Teen Center at St. Peter's Church in Dorchester. "They are working two or three jobs so their families can survive."

Not a single parent turned out to support Burke in its tournament soccer game on a balmy Sunday afternoon last November against Wayland in Dorchester. In fact, De Barros benched several top players because they arrived late for a pregame meeting for reasons that reflected the hard demands of home. The benched players included Dory Vicente, one of the city's best goalkeepers.

While more than fifty supporters cheered Wayland to its 2–0 victory, Vicente sat on the sidelines with his aunt, Maria DePina, a former BC track star who teaches at the Burke. With DePina translating his Cape Verdean Creole, Vicente said he arrived late because he needed to watch his siblings until his mother returned from her job as a hairdresser. His father was in Cape Verde.

"In the suburbs, God forbid if a parent doesn't go to a game," DePina said. "The problem in Boston is that nobody comes."

Charlestown track coach Kristyn Hughes, who competed before ample crowds as an athlete at Woburn High School before she pole-vaulted for BC, was struck by the contrast to her own experience. Her Charlestown teams have won state championships the last two years with nationally competitive athletes, yet in her six years of coaching, she said, she has met only one parent at a meet.

Some of that is economic pressures. Some of the Charlestown players' families are so needy, Hughes said, that when her students take home their medals, their parents ask, "How much can we get for them?"

But some of it seems more like simple absenteeism.

"A lot of parents aren't a big part of their children's lives anymore," said Madison Park football coach Roosevelt Robinson.

"One of the saddest things is that I might see a parent at graduation, and I think, 'I've had your child for four years and I've met you once or twice, or maybe not at all.'"

School Spirit Is Lacking

It is a situation exacerbated, at some schools, by teachers and administrators who show scant commitment to their schools' athletes. Numerous coaches said their schools rarely, if ever, stage pregame rallies. Some coaches said they are rebuffed when they ask for team news to be broadcast on the school's public-address system. And only Boston Latin rallies its teams with a band.

"When I went to Latin in the seventies, we had rallies and plenty of school spirit," said Hyde Park softball coach Bruce Collotta as he rooted for the school's football team against English. "But we've never had school spirit here."

Many coaches attribute the problem in part to the splintering of large education complexes into smaller schools. West Roxbury, Hyde Park, South Boston, and Dorchester each has been divided into at least three schools, each occupying a different section of the building. Lunch hours are separate, and interaction between students and teachers in the schools is extremely limited.

"Breaking up the school has really hurt us," said West Roxbury football coach Brian Collins. "There's not the same kind of pride. I went to the Walpole game one night and there were five thousand people. We're lucky if we get fifty."

Boston School Superintendent Carol R. Johnson acknowledged the problem, though she commended three schools in Brighton —Brighton High, Another Course to College, and Boston Community Leadership Academy—for rallying together in Brighton High's 2007 Division 4 Super Bowl victory.

"We have some schools that don't really understand yet how to work together and promote athletics," Johnson said, "but we know that it's possible."

No Sense of Community

A lack of neighborhood ties also hurts. More than thirty years after the city began busing vast numbers of students out of their neighborhoods in an effort to achieve racial integration, so few students attend schools in their own geographic areas that local interest in sports teams has plummeted. The problem is especially acute in areas such as West Roxbury, South Boston, and Charlestown.

"I only have one kid from West Roxbury on my roster, so you can see why there's no real community support," Collins said.

Attendance is typically better for basketball, the city's most popular high school sport. The crowds also are generally larger when teams from East Boston, Brighton, and a couple of exam schools are involved because their headmasters actively promote sports. But athletes at other Boston schools struggle for recognition.

When South Boston advanced to the eastern Massachusetts football tournament last fall for the first time in a decade, its opponent, Martha's Vineyard, rolled into the stadium in Taunton with busloads of fans, dwarfing the number of Southie supporters. South Boston's crowd could have been much larger, but school administrators denied a request for a bus to shuttle students to the game.

South Boston lost, 42–14, after winning the city's North Division championship. The experience left Guthrie with a bitter taste.

"Most schools, when you win a championship, they put up a banner in front of the school," Guthrie said. "We haven't seen one."

Brighton boys' basketball coach Erle Garrett, who also officiates city football games, said he was "gravely disappointed" by the turnout at many high school games. He plans to send letters to parents next fall asking them which time slots would best enable them to attend their children's contests.

"I don't care when it is, I'll change the schedule," Garrett said. "They need to understand it's part of being a parent. To save your kids, you've got to be around your kids."

The problem may not be easily solved, said Ken Still, Boston's athletic director. He said it demands the community's attention.

"This is the kind of thing that needs to change if we are going to get high school sports in the city going again," Still said. "It's going to take a lot of work."

City Seeks Heroes to Rescue School Athletics

With local school athletic systems in crisis, professional sports teams in some American cities have rushed to the rescue.

In Denver, charitable arms of the Avalanche, Broncos, Nuggets, and Rockies have contributed more than $1 million over the last five years to improve sports in the public schools. In Cleveland, the Browns donated $300,000 to the city's school athletic department, and the Indians kicked in $250,000.

In San Francisco, the Giants and 49ers agreed to a ticket tax—25 cents for every Giants ticket, 75 cents for every 49ers ticket over $27—to help fund the city's athletic programs. The fees have generated about $1 million a year for sports in the schools.

"The teams were heroes," said Don Collins, the San Francisco district's athletic director. "They made us viable again."

Will there be similar heroes in Boston? After a *Globe* review found the city's high school athletics program plagued by serious inadequacies in funding, facilities, equipment, coaching, and oversight, city leaders were scrambling for answers this week to problems that have festered for years and have cost countless students opportunities to make the most of their athletic abilities.

The cash-strapped Boston School Department has routinely allocated less than a half percent of its total budget to athletics, far below state and national averages.

"It really would help us a heck of a lot if the professional teams stepped up to the plate and contributed," said School Committee member Alfreda Harris, long an advocate for youth sports.

Boston's professional teams expressed preliminary interest this week in helping the city's struggling school athletic program. The teams already contribute to urban programs aimed at improving health care, education, and recreational opportunities for needy children.

A high-ranking city official said the Red Sox are weighing a significant contribution after the *Globe* series. The Red Sox Foundation already contributes $200,000 a year for summer baseball and softball for Boston youth and $325,000 annually for Red Sox Scholars in the city's schools.

"In a time of great need, there is always more we can all do, and we're happy to work with the mayor, the School Department, other sports teams and supporters to try to provide young people in our community with more healthy, active, and safe programs that serve their needs," said Meg Vaillancourt, the foundation's executive director.

Celtics president Rich Gotham said, "If the city of Boston were to approach the Boston sports teams with a program that demonstrated how assistance provided by the teams could benefit school athletic programs in a way that positively impacts the lives of students, it's something we would carefully consider, along with the many other causes we support through the Shamrock Foundation."

The Bruins too are poised to field a request for help.

"If the Boston public schools were to apply for a grant to help the city's scholastic athletic programs, the Boston Bruins Foundation's board would certainly be willing to give them consideration," said Bruins executive vice president Charlie Jacobs.

Examples of Support

While the long-standing problems in Boston's athletic program raise questions about whether city leaders have the political will to make the necessary improvements — the problems will take more than money to fix — no one disputes that major financial contributions from private sources would address many needs.

"In an era of shrinking revenues, we would welcome any additional assistance," School Superintendent Carol R. Johnson said of the prospect of the city's professional teams helping to save sports in the schools.

The Denver Public Schools Foundation, which supports both academic and athletic programs, has grown from giving $2 million to the school system in 2004 to more than $6 million last year. The city's athletic department has received more than $250,000 a year, helping to fund a vibrant middle school sports league in which youths compete in football, soccer, basketball, baseball, softball, volleyball, and cross-country.

The only interscholastic sports programs offered at Boston's twenty-two middle schools are basketball and spring track.

"We're very fortunate that all of Denver's professional sports teams have been incredibly supportive of the athletes in the Denver public schools," said Kristin Colon, the foundation's president.

Cleveland's pro teams responded to a deeper crisis than Boston's. They stepped up after budget cuts in 2005 threatened the future of the city's high school football and baseball teams.

The story was similar in San Francisco, with the Giants and 49ers rushing in after budget writers in 1988 zeroed out funding for high school sports. The ticket tax has helped fund programs since 1991, but it never has been enough to fully support the city's school sports teams. To help, San Francisco voters in 2004 approved a $20 million annual enrichment fund for chronically underfunded programs, of which about $2.4 million a year goes to athletics.

The San Francisco school district allocates only $600,000 a year to high school sports.

"In a properly run system, the district would fully fund athletics," Collins said. "Without the two other pots of money, we would be out of business."

The additional support allows San Francisco to provide high school students a broader range of athletic opportunities than Boston provides. Students attending at least half of San Francisco's twelve high schools can participate in interscholastic fencing, badminton, golf, and tennis, as well as the traditional sports, which all twelve schools offer.

Boston athletic director Ken Still said he would welcome aid from Boston's pro sports teams. Together, they sell about 4.5 million tickets a year.

"I would take five cents a ticket," he said, referring to a version of San Francisco's ticket fee.

The prospect of the Massachusetts Legislature approving such a tax is highly unlikely, which means that Boston needs either to increase public funding for athletics or seek additional aid from private sources.

Considering the enormous financial capital in Boston, the resources exist to support school athletics across the city on a much larger scale. For example, Boston Latin's alumni generated more than $100,000 a year for sports.

In New York, by contrast, Loews executive Robert Tisch raised $140 million before he died in 2005 to renovate more than forty athletic fields for public school students.

"It would be great if somebody donated $150,000," Still said. "We could really establish goals and have some outside consultants do the fundraising for us."

Building on Partnerships

Community leaders, meanwhile, have indicated they need to strengthen the links between the schools and public and private groups that provide opportunities, facilities, services, and transportation for children to play sports, particularly at a younger age. Boston's high school teams generally fare poorly against suburban competition because they lack dynamic feeder programs.

Dan Lebowitz, executive director of Northeastern's Center for the Study of Sport in Society, said a recent study showed that Boston's youth have one-third the opportunities to participate in sports as their suburban counterparts. "The situation in Boston's high schools is an outgrowth of the youth sports participation problem," he said.

Many youth sports groups are trying to fill the void, some through partnerships with the schools. Boston-based Tenacity, for one, helps run a pilot program at Umana Middle School in East Boston in which the school day is extended until 4:15 P.M. and students receive extra help with academics and tennis instruction. The program also reaches out to parents, which is vital to improving children's academic and athletic lives.

"It's critical that the school system, the state legislature, and everyone involved be willing to take some risks and try these new innovative approaches to the problem," Tenacity president Ned Eames said.

Youth advocates said the city needs to build on partnerships with organizations such as Young Savants, which helps Boston high school students develop learning, basketball, and character skills. Young Savants founder Ben Okiwe, a probation officer who recently stepped down as boys' basketball coach at Lincoln-Sudbury to focus on his nonprofit, said working with children is only part of the challenge.

"Moving forward, the parental support is key," he said. "So are the coaches. We need to create an atmosphere that will help them be the best they can be, and Boston school athletics will be better for it."

City leaders said this week that they are considering ways to improve the quality of coaches in the city. They also plan to address the equipment shortage and said they expect to continue working with Boston University to provide more athletic trainers for the city's high school athletes. Currently, there is only one trainer for eighteen high schools.

No one wishes city leaders greater success than the shortchanged athletes. Brighton High football player Alex Tisme said, "In the future, I hope the younger kids get something better than we had."

MICHAEL LEWIS

The No-Stats All-Star

FROM THE NEW YORK TIMES MAGAZINE

OUT OF Duke University . . . A six-foot-eight-inch forward . . .

He had more or less admitted to me that this part of his job left him cold. "It's the same thing every day," he said, as he struggled to explain how a man on the receiving end of the raging love of 18,557 people in a darkened arena could feel nothing. "If you had filet mignon every single night, you'd stop tasting it."

To him the only pleasure in these sounds — the name of his beloved alma mater, the roar of the crowd — was that they marked the end of the worst part of his game day: the eleven minutes between the end of warm-ups and the introductions. Eleven minutes of horsing around and making small talk with players on the other team. All those players making exaggerated gestures of affection toward one another before the game, who don't actually know one another, or even want to. "I hate being out on the floor wasting that time," he said. "I used to try to talk to people, but then I figured out no one actually liked me very much." Instead of engaging in the pretense that these other professional basketball players actually know and like him, he slips away into the locker room.

Shane Battier!

And up Shane Battier popped, to the howl of the largest crowd ever to watch a basketball game at the Toyota Center in Houston, and jumped playfully into Yao Ming (the center "out of China"). Now, finally, came the best part of his day, when he would be, oddly, most scrutinized and least understood.

Seldom are regular-season games in the NBA easy to get worked up for. Yesterday Battier couldn't tell me whom the team played three days before. ("The Knicks!" he exclaimed a minute later. "We played the Knicks!") Tonight, though it was a midweek game in the middle of January, was different. Tonight the Rockets were playing the Los Angeles Lakers, and so Battier would guard Kobe Bryant, the player he says is the most capable of humiliating him. Both Battier and the Rockets' front office were familiar with the story line. "I'm certain that Kobe is ready to just destroy Shane," Daryl Morey, the Rockets' general manager, told me. "Because there's been story after story about how Shane shut Kobe down the last time." Last time was March 16, 2008, when the Houston Rockets beat the Lakers to win their twenty-second game in a row—the second-longest streak in NBA history. The game drew a huge national television audience, which followed Bryant for his forty-seven miserable minutes: he shot 11 of 33 from the field and scored 24 points. "A lot of people watched," Morey said. "Everyone watches Kobe when the Lakers play. And so everyone saw Kobe struggling. And so for the first time they saw what we'd been seeing." Battier has routinely guarded the league's most dangerous offensive players—LeBron James, Chris Paul, Paul Pierce—and has usually managed to render them, if not entirely ineffectual, then a lot less effectual than they normally are. He has done it so quietly that no one really notices what exactly he is up to.

Last season, in a bid to draw some attention to Battier's defense, the Rockets' public relations department would send a staff member to the opponent's locker room to ask leading questions of whichever superstar Battier had just hamstrung: "Why did you have so much trouble tonight?" "Did he do something to disrupt your game?" According to Battier: "They usually say they had an off night. They think of me as some chump." He senses that some players actually look forward to being guarded by him. "No one dreads being guarded by me," he said. Morey confirmed as much: "That's actually true. But for two reasons: (a) they don't think anyone can guard them and (b) they really scoff at the notion Shane Battier could guard them. They *all* think his reputation exceeds his ability." Even as Battier was being introduced in the arena, Ahmad Rashad was wrapping up his pregame report on NBA TV and saying, "Shane Battier will try to stop Kobe Bryant." This caused the co-host Gary Payton to laugh and reply, "Ain't gonna happen," and the other co-host, Chris Webber, to add, "I think Kobe will score fifty, and they'll win by nineteen going away."

Early on, *Hoop Scoop* magazine named Shane Battier the fourth-best seventh-grader in the United States. When he graduated from Detroit Country Day School in 1997, he received the Naismith Award as the best high school basketball player in the nation. When he graduated from Duke in 2001, where he won a record-tying 131 college basketball games, including that year's NCAA championship, he received another Naismith Award as the best college basketball player in the nation. He was drafted in the first round by the woeful Memphis Grizzlies, not just a bad basketball team but the one with the worst winning percentage in NBA history—whereupon he was almost instantly dismissed, even by his own franchise, as a lesser talent. The year after Battier joined the Grizzlies, the team's general manager was fired and the NBA legend Jerry West, aka the Logo because his silhouette is the official emblem of the NBA, took over the team. "From the minute Jerry West got there he was trying to trade me," Battier says. If West didn't have any takers, it was in part because Battier seemed limited: most of the other players on the court, and some of the players on the bench too, were more obviously gifted than he is. "He's, at best, a marginal NBA athlete," Morey says.

The Grizzlies went from 23–59 in Battier's rookie year to 50–32 in his third year, when they made the NBA playoffs, as they did in each of his final three seasons with the team. Before the 2006–2007 season, Battier was traded to the Houston Rockets, who had just finished 34–48. In his first season with the Rockets, they finished 52–30, and then, last year, went 55–27—including one stretch of twenty-two wins in a row. Only the 1971–72 Los Angeles Lakers have won more games consecutively in the NBA. And because of injuries, the Rockets played eleven of those twenty-two games without their two acknowledged stars, Tracy McGrady and Yao Ming, on the court at the same time; the Rockets player who spent the most time actually playing for the Rockets during the streak was Shane Battier. This year Battier, recovering from offseason surgery to remove bone spurs from an ankle, has played in just over half of the Rockets' games. That has only highlighted his importance. "This year," Morey says, "we have been a championship team with him and a bubble playoff team without him."

Here we have a basketball mystery: a player is widely regarded inside the NBA as, at best, a replaceable cog in a machine driven by superstars. And yet every team he has ever played on has acquired some magical ability to win.

Solving the mystery is somewhere near the heart of Daryl Morey's job. In 2005, the Houston Rockets' owner, Leslie Alexander, decided to hire new management for his losing team and went looking specifically for someone willing to rethink the game. "We now have all this data," Alexander told me. "And we have computers that can analyze that data. And I wanted to use that data in a progressive way. When I hired Daryl, it was because I wanted somebody that was doing more than just looking at players in the normal way. I mean, I'm not even sure we're playing the game the right way."

The virus that infected professional baseball in the 1990s, the use of statistics to find new and better ways to value players and strategies, has found its way into every major sport. Not just basketball and football, but also soccer and cricket and rugby and, for all I know, snooker and darts—each one now supports a subculture of smart people who view it not just as a game to be played but as a problem to be solved. Outcomes that seem, after the fact, all but inevitable—of course LeBron James hit that buzzer beater, of course the Pittsburgh Steelers won the Super Bowl—are instead treated as a set of probabilities, even after the fact. The games are games of odds. Like professional card counters, the modern thinkers want to play the odds as efficiently as they can; but of course to play the odds efficiently they must first know the odds. Hence the new statistics, and the quest to acquire new data, and the intense interest in measuring the impact of every little thing a player does on his team's chances of winning. In its spirit of inquiry, this subculture inside professional basketball is no different from the subculture inside baseball or football or darts. The difference in basketball is that it happens to be the sport that is most like life.

When Alexander, a Wall Street investor, bought the Rockets in 1993, the notion that basketball was awaiting some statistical reformation hadn't occurred to anyone. At the time, Daryl Morey was at Northwestern University, trying to figure out how to get a job in professional sports and thinking about applying to business schools. He was tall and had played high school basketball, but otherwise he gave off a quizzical, geeky aura. "A lot of people who are into the new try to hide it," he says. "With me there was no point." In the third grade he stumbled upon the work of the baseball writer Bill James—the figure most responsible for the current upheaval in professional sports—and decided that what he really wanted to do with his life was put Jamesian principles into practice. He nursed this ambition through a fairly conventional academic career, which eventually took him to MIT's Sloan School of Management. There he opted for the entrepreneurial track, not because he actually wanted to be an entrepreneur but because he figured that the only way he would ever be allowed to run a pro sports franchise was to own one, and the only way he could imagine having enough money to buy one was to create some huge business. "This is the 1990s—there's no Theo," Morey says, referring to Theo Epstein, the statistics-minded general manager of the Boston Red Sox. "Sandy Alderson is progressive, but nobody knows it." Sandy Alderson, then the general manager of the Oakland Athletics, had also read Bill James and begun to usher in the new age of statistical analysis in baseball. "So," Morey continues, "I just assumed that getting rich was the only way in." Apart from using it to acquire a pro sports team, Morey had no exceptional interest in money.

He didn't need great wealth, as it turned out. After graduating from business school, he went to work for a consulting firm in Boston called Parthenon, where he was tapped in 2001 to advise a group trying to buy the Red Sox. The bid failed, but a related group went and bought the Celtics—and hired Morey to help reorganize the business. In addition to figuring out where to set ticket prices, Morey helped to find a new general manager and new people looking for better ways to value basketball players. The Celtics improved. Leslie Alexander heard whispers that Morey, who was thirty-three, was out in front of those trying to rethink the game, so he hired him to remake the Houston Rockets.

When Morey came to the Rockets, a huge chunk of the team's allotted payroll—the NBA caps payrolls and taxes teams that exceed them—was committed, for many years to come, to two superstars: Tracy McGrady and Yao Ming. Morey had to find ways to improve the Rockets without spending money. "We couldn't afford another superstar," he says, "so we went looking for nonsuperstars that we thought were undervalued." He went looking, essentially, for underpaid players. "That's the scarce resource in the NBA," he says. "Not the superstar but the undervalued player." Sifting the population of midlevel NBA players, he came up with a list of fifteen, near the top of which was the Memphis Grizzlies' forward Shane Battier. This perplexed even the man who hired Morey to rethink basketball. "All I knew was Shane's stats," Alexander says, "and obviously they weren't great. He had to sell me. It was hard for me to see it."

Alexander wasn't alone. It was, and is, far easier to spot what Battier doesn't do than what he does. His conventional statistics are unremarkable: he doesn't score many points, snag many rebounds, block many shots, steal many balls, or dish out many assists. On top of that, it is easy to see what he can never do: what points he scores tend to come from jump shots taken immediately after receiving a pass. "That's the telltale sign of someone who can't ramp up his offense," Morey says. "Because you can guard that shot with one player. And until you can't guard someone with one player, you really haven't created an offensive situation. Shane can't create an offensive situation. He needs to be open." For fun, Morey shows me video of a few rare instances of Battier scoring when he hasn't exactly been open. Some large percentage of them came when he was being guarded by an inferior defender—whereupon Battier backed him down and tossed in a left jump-hook. "This is probably, to be honest with you, his only offensive move," Morey says. "But look, see how he pump-fakes." Battier indeed pump-faked, several times, before he shot over a defender. "He does that because he's worried about his shot being blocked." Battier's weaknesses arise from physical limitations. Or as Morey puts it, "He can't dribble, he's slow, and hasn't got much body control."

Battier's game is a weird combination of obvious weaknesses and nearly invisible strengths. When he is on the court, his teammates get better, often a lot better, and his opponents get worse—often a lot worse. He may not grab huge numbers of rebounds, but he has an uncanny ability to improve his teammates' rebounding. He doesn't shoot much, but when he does, he takes only the most efficient shots. He also has a knack for getting the ball to teammates who are in a position to do the same, and he commits few turnovers. On defense, although he routinely guards the NBA's most prolific scorers, he significantly reduces their shooting percentages. At the same time he somehow improves the defensive efficiency of his teammates—probably, Morey surmises, by helping them out in all sorts of subtle ways. "I call him Lego," Morey says. "When he's on the court, all the pieces start to fit together. And everything that leads to winning that you can get to through intellect instead of innate ability, Shane excels in. I'll bet he's in the hundredth percentile of every category."

There are other things Morey has noticed too, but declines to discuss as there is right now in pro basketball real value to new information, and the Rockets feel they have some. What he will say, however, is that the big challenge on any basketball court is to measure the right things. The five players on any basketball team are far more than the sum of their parts; the Rockets devote a lot of energy to untangling subtle interactions among the team's elements. To get at this they need something that basketball hasn't historically supplied: meaningful statistics. For most of its history basketball has measured not so much what is important as what is easy to measure—points, rebounds, assists, steals, blocked shots—and these measurements have warped perceptions of the game. ("Someone created the box score," Morey says, "and he should be shot.") How many points a player scores, for example, is no true indication of how much he has helped his team. Another example: if you want to know a player's value as a rebounder, you need to know not whether he got a rebound but the likelihood of the *team* getting the rebound when a missed shot enters that player's zone.

There is a tension, peculiar to basketball, between the interests of the team and the interests of the individual. The game continually tempts the people who play it to do things that are not in the interest of the group. On the baseball field, it would be hard for a player to sacrifice his team's interest for his own. Baseball is an individual sport masquerading as a team one: by doing what's best for himself, the player nearly always also does what is best for his team. "There is no way to selfishly get across home plate," as Morey puts it. "If instead of there being a lineup, I could muscle my way to the plate and hit every single time and damage the efficiency of the team—that would be the analogy. Manny Ramírez can't take at-bats away from David Ortiz. We had a point guard in Boston who refused to pass the ball to a certain guy." In football the coach has so much control over who gets the ball that selfishness winds up being self-defeating. The players most famous for being selfish—the Dallas Cowboys' wide receiver Terrell Owens, for instance—are usually not so much selfish as attention-seeking. Their sins tend to occur off the field.

It is in basketball where the problems are most likely to be in the game—where the player, in his play, faces choices between maximizing his own perceived self-interest and winning. The choices are sufficiently complex that there is a fair chance he doesn't fully grasp that he is making them.

Taking a bad shot when you don't need to is only the most obvious example. A point guard might selfishly give up an open shot for an assist. You can see it happen every night, when he's racing down court for an open lay-up, and instead of taking it, he passes it back to a trailing teammate. The teammate usually finishes with some sensational dunk, but the likelihood of scoring nevertheless declined. "The marginal assist is worth more money to the point guard than the marginal point," Morey says. Blocked shots—they look great, but unless you secure the ball afterward, you haven't helped your team all that much. Players love the spectacle of a ball being swatted into the fifth row, and it becomes a matter of personal indifference that the other team still gets the ball back. Dikembe Mutombo, Houston's forty-two-year-old backup center, famous for blocking shots, "has always been the best in the league in the recovery of the ball after his block," says Morey, as he begins to make a case for Mutombo's unselfishness before he stops and laughs. "But even to Dikembe there's a selfish component. He made his name by doing the finger wag." The finger wag: Mutombo swats the ball, grabs it, holds it against his hip, and wags his finger at the opponent. Not in my house! "And if he doesn't catch the ball," Morey says, "he can't do the finger wag. And he loves the finger wag." His team of course would be better off if Mutombo didn't hold on to the ball long enough to do his finger wag. "We've had to yell at him: start the break, start the break—then do your finger wag!"

When I ask Morey if he can think of any basketball statistic that can't benefit a player at the expense of his team, he has to think hard. "Offensive rebounding," he says, then reverses himself. "But even that can be counterproductive to the team if your job is to get back on defense." It turns out there is no statistic that a basketball player accumulates that cannot be amassed selfishly. "We think about this deeply whenever we're talking about contractual incentives," he says. "We don't want to incent a guy to do things that hurt the team"—and the amazing thing about basketball is how easy this is to do. "They *all* maximize what they think they're being paid for," he says. He laughs. "It's a tough environment for a player now because you have a lot of teams starting to think differently. They've got to rethink how they're getting paid."

Having watched Battier play for the past two and a half years, Morey has come to think of him as an exception: the most abnormally unselfish basketball player he has ever seen. Or rather, the player who seems one step ahead of the analysts, helping the team in all sorts of subtle, hard-to-measure ways that appear to violate his own personal interests. "Our last coach dragged him into a meeting and told him he needed to shoot more," Morey says. "I'm not sure that that ever happened." Last season when the Rockets played the San Antonio Spurs Battier was assigned to guard their most dangerous scorer, Manu Ginóbili. Ginóbili comes off the bench, however, and his minutes are not in sync with the minutes of a starter like Battier. Battier privately went to Coach Rick Adelman and told him to bench him and bring him in when Ginóbili entered the game. "No one in the NBA does that," Morey says. "No one says put me on the bench so I can guard their best scorer all the time."

One well-known statistic the Rockets' front office pays attention to is plus-minus, which simply measures what happens to the score when any given player is on the court. In its crude form, plus-minus is hardly perfect: a player who finds himself on the same team with the world's four best basketball players, and who plays only when they do, will have a plus-minus that looks pretty good, even if it says little about his play. Morey says that he and his staff can adjust for these potential distortions—though he is coy about how they do it—and render plus-minus a useful measure of a player's effect on a basketball game. A good player might be a plus 3—that is, his team averages three points more per game than its opponent when he is on the floor. In his best season, the superstar point guard Steve Nash was a plus 14.5. At the time of the Lakers game, Battier was a plus 10, which put him in the company of Dwight Howard and Kevin Garnett, both perennial All-Stars. For his career he's a

plus 6. "Plus 6 is enormous," Morey says. "It's the difference between forty-one wins and sixty wins." He names a few other players who were a plus 6 last season: Vince Carter, Carmelo Anthony,
Tracy McGrady.

As the game against the Lakers started, Morey took his seat, on
the aisle, nine rows behind the Rockets' bench. The odds, on this
night, were not good. Houston was playing without its injured superstar, McGrady (who was in the clubhouse watching TV), and
its injured best supporting actor, Ron Artest (cheering in street
clothes from the bench). The Lakers were staffed by household
names. The only Rockets player on the floor with a conspicuous
shoe contract was the center Yao Ming—who opened the game by
tipping the ball backward. Shane Battier began his game by grabbing it.

   Before the Rockets traded for Battier, the front-office analysts
obviously studied his value. They knew all sorts of details about his
efficiency and his ability to reduce the efficiency of his opponents.
They knew, for example, that stars guarded by Battier suddenly
lose their shooting touch. What they didn't know was why. Morey
recognized Battier's effects, but he didn't know how he achieved
them. Two hundred or so basketball games later, he's the world's
expert on the subject—which he was studying all over again tonight. He pointed out how, instead of grabbing uncertainly for a
rebound, for instance, Battier would tip the ball more certainly to
a teammate. Guarding a lesser rebounder, Battier would, when the
ball was in the air, leave his own man and block out the other
team's best rebounder. "Watch him," a Houston front-office analyst
told me before the game. "When the shot goes up, he'll go sit on
Gasol's knee." (Pau Gasol often plays center for the Lakers.) On
defense, it was as if Battier had set out to maximize the misery Bryant experiences shooting a basketball, without having his presence
recorded in any box score. He blocked the ball when Bryant was
taking it from his waist to his chin, for instance, rather than when it
was far higher and Bryant was in the act of shooting. "When you
watch him," Morey says, "you see that his whole thing is to stay in
front of guys and try to block the player's vision when he shoots.
We didn't even notice what he was doing until he got here. I wish
we could say we did, but we didn't."

People often say that Kobe Bryant has no weaknesses to his game, but that's not really true. Before the game, Battier was given his special package of information. "He's the only player we give it to," Morey says. "We can give him this fire hose of data and let him sift. Most players are like golfers. You don't want them swinging while they're thinking." The data essentially broke down the floor into many discrete zones and calculated the odds of Bryant making shots from different places on the court, under different degrees of defensive pressure, in different relationships to other players—how well he scored off screens, off pick-and-rolls, off catch-and-shoots, and so on. Battier learns a lot from studying the data on the superstars he is usually assigned to guard. For instance, the numbers show him that Allen Iverson is one of the most efficient scorers in the NBA when he goes to his right; when he goes to his left he kills his team. The Golden State Warriors forward Stephen Jackson is an even stranger case. "Steve Jackson," Battier says, "is statistically better going to his right, but he *loves* to go to his left—and goes to his left almost twice as often." The San Antonio Spurs' Manu Ginóbili is a statistical freak: he has no imbalance whatsoever in his game—there is no one way to play him that is better than another. He is equally efficient both off the dribble and off the pass, going left and right and from any spot on the floor.

Bryant isn't like that. He is better at pretty much everything than everyone else, but there are places on the court, and starting points for his shot, that render him less likely to help his team. When he drives to the basket, he is exactly as likely to go to his left as to his right, but when he goes to his left, he is less effective. When he shoots directly after receiving a pass, he is more efficient than when he shoots after dribbling. He's deadly if he gets into the lane and also if he gets to the baseline; between the two, less so. "The absolute worst thing to do," Battier says, "is to foul him." It isn't that Bryant is an especially good free-throw shooter but that, as Morey puts it, "the foul is the worst result of a defensive play." One way the Rockets can see which teams think about the game as they do is by identifying those that "try dramatically not to foul." The ideal outcome, from the Rockets' statistical point of view, is for Bryant to dribble left and pull up for an eighteen-foot jump shot; force that to happen often enough and you have to be satisfied with your night. "If he has forty points on forty shots, I can live with that,"

Battier says. "My job is not to keep him from scoring points but to make him as inefficient as possible." The court doesn't have little squares all over it to tell him what percentage Bryant is likely to shoot from any given spot, but it might as well.

The reason the Rockets insist that Battier guard Bryant is his gift for encouraging him into his zones of lowest efficiency. The effect of doing this is astonishing: Bryant doesn't merely help his team less when Battier guards him than when someone else does. When Bryant is in the game and Battier is on him, the Lakers' offense is worse than if the NBA's best player had taken the night off. "The Lakers' offense should obviously be better with Kobe in," Morey says. "But if Shane is on him, it isn't." A player whom Morey describes as "a marginal NBA athlete" not only guards one of the greatest—and smartest—offensive threats ever to play the game. He renders him a detriment to his team.

And if you knew none of this, you would never guess any of it from watching the game. Bryant was quicker than Battier, so the latter spent much of his time chasing around after him, Keystone Cops–like. Bryant shot early and often, but he looked pretty good from everywhere. On defense, Battier talked to his teammates a lot more than anyone else on the court, but from the stands it was hard to see any point to this. And yet, he swears, there's a reason to almost all of it: when he decides where to be on the court and what angles to take, he is constantly reminding himself of the odds on the stack of papers he read through an hour earlier as his feet soaked in the whirlpool. "The numbers either refute my thinking or support my thinking," he says, "and when there's any question, I trust the numbers. The numbers don't lie." Even when the numbers agree with his intuitions, they have an effect. "It's a subtle difference," Morey says, "but it has big implications. If you have an intuition of something but no hard evidence to back it up, you might kind of *sort of* go about putting that intuition into practice, because there's still some uncertainty if it's right or wrong."

Knowing the odds, Battier can pursue an inherently uncertain strategy with total certainty. He can devote himself to a process and disregard the outcome of any given encounter. This is critical because in basketball, as in everything else, luck plays a role, and Battier cannot afford to let it distract him. Only once during the Lakers game did we glimpse a clean, satisfying comparison of the efficient strategy and the inefficient one — that is, an outcome that reflected the odds. Ten feet from the hoop, Bryant got the ball with his back to the basket; with Battier pressing against him, he fell back and missed a twelve-foot shot off the front of the rim. Moments earlier, with Battier reclining in the deep soft chair that masquerades as an NBA bench, his teammate Brent Barry found himself in an analogous position. Bryant leaned into Barry, hit a six-foot shot, and drew a foul. But this was the exception; normally you don't get perfect comparisons. You couldn't see the odds shifting subtly away from the Lakers and toward the Rockets as Bryant was forced from six feet out to twelve feet from the basket, or when he had Battier's hand in his eyes. All you saw were the statistics on the board, and as the seconds ticked off to halftime, the game tied 54–54, Bryant led all scorers with sixteen points.

But he required twenty possessions to get them. And he had started moaning to the referees. Bryant is one of the great jawboners in the history of the NBA. A major league baseball player once showed me a slow-motion replay of the Yankees' third baseman Alex Rodriguez in the batter's box. Glancing back to see where the catcher has set up is not strictly against baseball's rules, but it violates the code. A hitter who does it is likely to find the next pitch aimed in the general direction of his eyes. A-Rod, the best hitter in baseball, mastered the art of glancing back by moving not his head, but his eyes, at just the right time. It was like watching a billionaire find some trivial and dubious deduction to take on his tax returns. Why bother? I thought, and then realized: this is the instinct that separates A-Rod from mere stars. Kobe Bryant has the same instinct. Tonight Bryant complained that Battier was grabbing his jersey, Battier was pushing when no one was looking, Battier was committing crimes against humanity. Just before the half ended, Battier took a referee aside and said: "You and I both know Kobe does this all the time. I'm playing him honest. Don't fall for his stuff." Moments later, after failing to get a call, Bryant hurled the ball, screamed at the ref, and was whistled for a technical foul.

Just after that, the half ended, but not before Battier was tempted by a tiny act of basketball selfishness. The Rockets' front office has picked up a glitch in Battier's philanthropic approach to the game: in the final second of any quarter, finding himself with the ball and on the wrong side of the half-court line, Battier refuses to heave it honestly at the basket, in an improbable but not impossible attempt to score. He heaves it disingenuously, and a millisecond after the buzzer sounds. Daryl Morey could think of only one explanation: a miss lowers Battier's shooting percentage. "I tell him we don't count heaves in our stats," Morey says, "but Shane's smart enough to know that his next team might not be smart enough to take the heaves out."

Tonight, the ball landed in Battier's hands milliseconds before the half finished. He moved just slowly enough for the buzzer to sound, heaved the ball the length of the floor, and then sprinted to the locker room—having not taken a single shot.

In 1996 a young writer for the *Basketball Times* named Dan Wetzel thought it might be neat to move into the life of a star high school basketball player and watch up close as big-time basketball colleges recruited him. He picked Shane Battier, and then spent five months trailing him, with growing incredulity. "I'd covered high school basketball for eight years and talked to hundreds and hundreds and hundreds of kids—really every single prominent high school basketball player in the country," Wetzel says. "There's this public perception that they're all thugs. But they aren't. A lot of them are really good guys, and some of them are very, very bright. Kobe's very bright. LeBron's very bright. But there's absolutely never been anything like Shane Battier."

Wetzel watched this kid, inundated with offers of every kind, take charge of an unprincipled process. Battier narrowed his choices to six schools—Kentucky, Kansas, North Carolina, Duke, Michigan, and Michigan State—and told everyone else, politely, to leave him be. He then set out to minimize the degree to which the chosen schools could interfere with his studies; he had a 3.96 GPA and was poised to claim Detroit Country Day School's headmaster's cup for best all-around student. He granted each head coach a weekly fifteen-minute window in which to phone him. These men happened to be among the most famous basketball coaches in the world and the most persistent recruiters, but Battier granted no exceptions. When the Kentucky coach Rick Pitino, who had just won a national championship, tried to call Battier outside his assigned time, Battier simply removed Kentucky from his list. "What seventeen-year-old has the stones to do that?" Wetzel asks.

"To just cut off Rick Pitino because he calls outside his window?" Wetzel answers his own question: "It wasn't like, 'This is a really interesting seventeen-year-old.' It was like, 'This isn't real.'"

Battier, even as a teenager, was as shrewd as he was disciplined. The minute he figured out where he was headed, he called a sensational high school power forward in Peekskill, New York, named Elton Brand—and talked him into joining him at Duke. (Brand now plays for the Philadelphia 76ers.) "I thought he'd be the first black president," Wetzel says. "He was Barack Obama before Barack Obama."

Last July, as we sat in the library of the Detroit Country Day School, watching, or trying to watch, his March 2008 performance against Kobe Bryant, Battier was much happier instead talking about Obama, both of whose books he had read. ("The first was better than the second," he said.) He said he hated watching himself play, then proved it by refusing to watch himself play. My every attempt to draw his attention to the action on the video monitor was met by some distraction.

I pointed to his footwork; he pointed to a gorgeous young woman in the stands wearing a Battier jersey. ("You don't see too many good-looking girls with Battier jerseys on," he said. "It's usually twelve and under or sixty and over. That's my demographic.") I noted the uncanny way in which he got his hand right in front of Bryant's eyes before a shot; he motioned to his old high school library. ("I came in here every day before classes.") He took my excessive interest in this one game as proof of a certain lack of imagination, I'm pretty sure. "I've been doing the same thing for seven years," he said, "and this is the only game anyone wants to talk about. It's like, Oh, you can play defense?" It grew clear that one reason he didn't particularly care to watch himself play, apart from the tedium of it, was that he plays the game so self-consciously. Unable to count on the game to properly measure his performance, he learned to do so himself. He had, in some sense, already seen the video. When I finally compelled him to watch, he was knocking the ball out of Bryant's hands as Bryant raised it from his waist to his chin. "If I get to be commissioner, that will count as a blocked shot," Battier said. "But it's nothing. They don't count it as a blocked shot. I do that at least thirty times a season."

In the statistically insignificant sample of professional athletes

I've come to know a bit, two patterns have emerged. The first is, they tell you meaningful things only when you talk to them in places other than where they have been trained to answer questions. It's pointless, for instance, to ask a basketball player about himself inside his locker room. For a start, he is naked; for another, he's surrounded by the people he has learned to mistrust, his own teammates. The second pattern is the fact that seemingly trivial events in their childhoods have had huge influence on their careers. A cleanup hitter lives and dies by a swing he perfected when he was seven; a quarterback has a hitch in his throwing motion because he imitated his father. Here, in the Detroit Country Day School library, a few yards from the gym, Battier was back where he became a basketball player. And he was far less interested in what happened between him and Kobe Bryant four months ago than what happened when he was twelve.

When he entered Detroit Country Day in seventh grade, he was already conspicuous at six foot four, and a year later he would be six foot seven. "Growing up tall was something I got used to," he said. "I was the kid about whom they always said, 'Check his birth certificate.'" He was also the only kid in school with a black father and a white mother. Oddly enough, the school had just graduated a famous black basketball player, Chris Webber. Webber won three state championships and was named national high school player of the year. "Chris was a man-child," says his high school basketball coach, Kurt Keener. "Everyone wanted Shane to be the next Chris Webber, but Shane wasn't like that." Battier had never heard of Webber and didn't understand why, when he took to the Amateur Athletic Union circuit and played with black inner-city kids, he found himself compared unfavorably with Webber: "I kept hearing 'He's too soft' or 'He's not an athlete.'" His high school coach was aware of the problems he had when he moved from white high school games to the black AAU circuit. "I remember trying to add some flair to his game," Keener says, "but it was like teaching a classical dancer to do hip-hop. I came to the conclusion he didn't have the ego for it."

Battier was half-white and half-black, but basketball, it seemed, was either black or white. A small library of PhD theses might usefully be devoted to the reasons for this. For instance, is it a coincidence that many of the things a player does in white basketball to prove his character—take a charge, scramble for a loose ball—are more pleasantly done on a polished wooden floor than they are on inner-city asphalt? Is it easier to "play for the team" when that team is part of some larger institution? At any rate, the inner-city kids with whom he played on the AAU circuit treated Battier like a suburban kid with a white game, and the suburban kids he played with during the regular season treated him like a visitor from the planet where they kept the black people. "On Martin Luther King Day, everyone in class would look at me like I was supposed to know who he was and why he was important," Battier said. "When we had an official school picture, every other kid was given a comb. I was the only one given a pick." He was awkward and shy, or as he put it: "I didn't present well. But I'm in the eighth grade! I'm just trying to fit in!" And yet here he was shuttling between a black world that treated him as white and a white world that treated him as black. "*Everything* I've done since then is because of what I went through with this," he said. "What I did is alienate myself from everybody. I'd eat lunch by myself. I'd study by myself. And I sort of lost myself in the game."

Losing himself in the game meant fitting into the game, and fitting into the game meant meshing so well that he became hard to see. In high school he was almost always the best player on the court, but even then he didn't embrace the starring role. "He had a tendency to defer," Keener says. "He had this incredible ability to make everyone around him better. But I had to tell him to be more assertive. The one game we lost his freshman year, it was because he deferred to the seniors." Even when he was clearly the best player and could have shot the ball at will, he was more interested in his role in the larger unit. But it is a mistake to see in his detachment from self an absence of ego, or ambition, or even desire for attention. When Battier finished telling me the story of this unpleasant period in his life, he said: "Chris Webber won three state championships, the Mr. Basketball Award, and the Naismith Award. I won three state championships, Mr. Basketball, and the Naismith Awards. All the things they said I wasn't able to do, when I was in the eighth grade."

"Who's they?" I asked.

"Pretty much everyone," he said.

"White people?"

"No," he said. "The street."

*

As the third quarter began, Battier's face appeared overhead, on the Jumbotron, where he hammed it up and exhorted the crowd. Throughout the game he was up on the thing more than any other player: plugging teeth-whitening formulas, praising local jewelers, making public-service announcements, telling the fans to make noise. When I mentioned to a Rockets' staff member that Battier seemed to have far more than his fair share of big-screen appearances, he said, "Probably because he's the only one who'll do them."

I spent the second half with Sam Hinkie, the vice president of basketball operations and the head of basketball analytics in the Rockets' front office. The game went back and forth. Bryant kept missing more shots than he made. Neither team got much of a lead. More remarkable than the game were Hinkie's reactions — and it soon became clear that while he obviously wanted the Rockets to win, he was responding to different events on the court than the typical Rockets (or NBA) fan was.

"I care a lot more about what ought to have happened than what actually happens," said Hinkie, who has an MBA from Stanford. The routine NBA game, he explained, is decided by a tiny percentage of the total points scored. A team scores on average about one hundred points a game, but two out of three NBA games are decided by fewer than six points — two or three possessions. The effect of this, in his mind, was to raise significantly the importance of every little thing that happened. The Lakers' Trevor Ariza, who makes 29 percent of his three-point shots, hit a crazy three-pointer, and as the crowd moaned, Hinkie was almost distraught. "That Ariza shot, that is really painful," he said. "Because it's a near-random event. And it's a three-point swing." When Bryant drove to the basket, instead of being forced to take a jump shot, he said: "That's three-eighths of a point. These things accumulate."

In this probabilistic spirit we watched the battle between Battier and Bryant. From Hinkie's standpoint, it was going extremely well: "With most guys, Shane can kick them from their good zone to bad zone, but with Kobe you're just picking your poison. It's the epitome of, Which way do you want to die?" Only the Rockets weren't dying. Battier had once again turned Bryant into a less-efficient machine of death. Even when the shots dropped, they came from the places on the court where the Rockets' front office didn't mind seeing them drop. "That's all you can do," Hinkie said, after Bryant sank an eighteen-footer. "Get him to an inefficient spot and contest." And then all of a sudden it was 97–95, Lakers, with a bit more than three minutes to play, and someone called time-out. "We're in it," Hinkie said, happily. "And some of what happens from here on will be randomness."

The team with the NBA's best record was being taken to the wire by Yao Ming and a collection of widely unesteemed players. Moments later, I looked up at the scoreboard:

Bryant: 30.

Battier: 0.

Hinkie followed my gaze and smiled. "I know that doesn't look good," he said, referring to the players' respective point totals. But if Battier wasn't in there, he went on to say, "we lose by twelve. No matter what happens now, none of our coaches will say, 'If only we could have gotten a little more out of Battier.'"

One statistical rule of thumb in basketball is that a team leading by more points than there are minutes left near the end of the game has an 80 percent chance of winning. If your team is down by more than six points halfway through the final quarter, and you're anxious to beat the traffic, you can leave knowing that there is slightly less than a 20 percent chance you'll miss a victory; on the other hand, if you miss a victory, it will have been an improbable and therefore sensational one. At no point on this night has either team had enough of a lead to set fans, or even Rockets management, to calculating their confidence intervals—but then, with 2:27 to play, the Lakers went up by four: 99–95. Then they got the ball back. The ball went to Bryant, and Battier shaded him left —into Yao Ming. Bryant dribbled and took the best shot he could, from Battier's perspective: a long two-point jump shot, off the dribble, while moving left. He missed, the Rockets ran back the other way, Rafer Alston drove the lane and hit a floater: 99–97, and 1:13 on the clock. The Lakers missed another shot. Alston grabbed the rebound and called time-out with fifty-nine seconds left.

Whatever the Rockets planned went instantly wrong, when the inbound pass, as soon as it was caught by the Rockets' Carl Landry, was swatted away by the Lakers. The ball was loose, bodies flew everywhere.

Fifty-five . . . fifty-four . . . fifty-three . . .

On the side of the court opposite the melee, Battier froze. The moment he saw that the loose ball was likely to be secured by a teammate—but before it was secured—he sprinted to the corner.

Fifty . . . forty-nine . . . forty-eight . . .

The three-point shot from the corner is the single most efficient shot in the NBA. One way the Rockets can tell if their opponents have taken to analyzing basketball in similar ways as they do is their attitude to the corner three: the smart teams take a lot of them and seek to prevent their opponents from taking them. In basketball there is only so much you can plan, however, especially at a street-ball moment like this. As it happened, Houston's Rafer Alston was among the most legendary street-ball players of all time—known as Skip 2 My Lou, a nickname he received after a single spectacular move at Rucker Park, in Harlem. "Shane wouldn't last in street ball because in street ball no one wants to see" his game, Alston told me earlier. "You better give us something to ooh and ahh about. No one cares about someone who took a charge."

The Rockets' offense had broken down, and there was no usual place for Alston, still back near the half-court line, to go with the ball. The Lakers' defense had also broken down; no player was where he was meant to be. The only person exactly where he should have been—wide open, standing at the most efficient spot on the floor from which to shoot—was Shane Battier. When Daryl Morey spoke of basketball intelligence, a phrase slipped out: "the IQ of where to be." Fitting in on a basketball court, in the way Battier fits in, requires the IQ of where to be. Bang: Alston hit Battier with a long pass. Bang: Battier shot the three, guiltlessly. Nothing but net.

Rockets 100, Lakers 99.

Forty-three . . . forty-two . . . forty-one . . .

At this moment, the Rockets' front office would later calculate, the team's chances of winning rose from 19.2 percent to 72.6 percent. One day some smart person will study the correlation between shifts in probabilities and levels of noise, but for now the crowd was ignorantly berserk: it sounded indeed like the largest crowd in the history of Houston's Toyota Center. Bryant got the ball at half-court and dribbled idly, searching for his opening. This was his moment, the one great players are said to live for, when everyone knows he's going to take the shot, and he takes it anyway. On the other end of the floor it wasn't the shooter who mattered but the shot. Now the shot was nothing, the shooter everything.

Thirty-three . . . thirty-two . . . thirty-one . . .

Bryant—12 for 31 on the night—took off and drove to the right, his strength, in the middle of the lane. Battier cut him off. Bryant tossed the ball back out to Derek Fisher, out of shooting range.

Thirty . . . twenty-nine . . .

Like everyone else in the place, Battier assumed that the game was still in Bryant's hands. If he gave the ball up, it was only so that he might get it back. Bryant popped out. He was now a good four feet beyond the three-point line, or nearly thirty feet from the basket.

Twenty-eight . . .

Bryant caught the ball and, 27.4 feet from the basket, the Rockets' front office would later determine, leapt. Instantly his view of that basket was blocked by Battier's hand. This was not an original situation. Since the 2002–2003 season, Bryant had taken 51 three-pointers at the very end of close games from farther than 26.75 feet from the basket. He had missed 86.3 percent of them. A little over a year ago the Lakers lost to the Cleveland Cavaliers after Bryant missed a three from 28.4 feet. Three nights from now the Lakers would lose to the Orlando Magic after Bryant missed a shot from 27.5 feet that would have tied the game. It was a shot Battier could live with, even if it turned out to be good.

Battier looked back to see the ball drop through the basket and hit the floor. In that brief moment he was the picture of detachment, less a party to a traffic accident than a curious passer-by. And then he laughed. The process had gone just as he hoped. The outcome he never could control.

JEANNE MARIE LASKAS

This Is Your Brain on Football

FROM GQ

ON A FOGGY, STEEL GRAY SATURDAY in September 2002, Bennet Omalu arrived at the Allegheny County coroner's office and got his assignment for the day: perform an autopsy on the body of Mike Webster, a professional football player. Omalu did not, unlike most thirty-four-year-old men living in a place like Pittsburgh, have an appreciation for American football. He was born in the jungles of Biafra during a Nigerian air raid, and certain aspects of American life puzzled him. From what he could tell, football was rather a pointless game, a lot of big fat guys bashing into each other. In fact, had he not been watching the news that morning, he may not have suspected anything unusual at all about the body on the slab.

The coverage that week had been bracing and disturbing and exciting. Dead at fifty. Mike Webster! Nine-time Pro Bowler. Hall of Famer. "Iron Mike," legendary Steelers center for fifteen seasons. His life after football had been mysterious and tragic, and on the news they were going on and on about it. What had happened to him? How does a guy go from four Super Bowl rings to . . . pissing in his own oven and squirting Super Glue on his rotting teeth? Mike Webster bought himself a Taser gun, used that on himself to treat his back pain, would zap himself into unconsciousness just to get some sleep. Mike Webster lost all his money, or maybe gave it away. He forgot. A lot of lawsuits. Mike Webster forgot how to eat too. Soon Mike Webster was homeless, living in a truck, one of its windows replaced with a garbage bag and tape.

It bothered Omalu to hear this kind of chatter — especially about a dead guy. But Omalu had always fancied himself an advocate for the dead. That's how he viewed his job: a calling. A forensic pathologist was charged with defending and speaking for the departed—a translator for those still here. A corpse held a story, told in tissue, patterns of trauma, and secrets in cells.

In the autopsy room, Omalu snapped on his gloves and approached the slab. He noted that Mike Webster's body was sixtynine inches long and weighed 244 pounds. He propped up the head and picked up his scalpel and sliced open the chest and cracked open the ribs. He took out the heart and found everything he expected of a man who was believed to have died of a heart attack, as was the case with Webster. Then he made a cut from behind the right ear, across the forehead, to the other ear and around. He peeled the scalp away from the skull in two flaps. With the electric saw he carefully cut a cap out of the skull, pulled off the cap, and gently, like approaching a baby in the birth canal, he reached for the brain.

Omalu loved the brain. Of all the organs in the body, it was easily his favorite. He thought of it sort of like Miss America. Such a *diva!* So high-maintenance: it requires more energy to operate than any other organ. The brain! That was his love and that was his joy, and that's why his specialty was neuropathology.

Omalu stared at Mike Webster's brain. He kept thinking, *How did this big athletic man end up so crazy in the head?* He was thinking about football and brain trauma. The leap in logic was hardly extreme. He was thinking, *Dementia pugilistica?* "Punch-drunk syndrome," they called it in boxers. The clinical picture was somewhat like Mike Webster's: severe dementia—delusion, paranoia, explosive behavior, loss of memory—caused by repeated blows to the head. Omalu figured if chronic bashing of the head could destroy a boxer's brain, couldn't it also destroy a football player's brain? Could that be what made Mike Webster crazy?

Of course, football players wear helmets, good protection for the skull. But the brain? Floating around inside that skull and, upon impact, sloshing into its walls. Omalu thought: *I've seen so many cases of people like motorcyclists wearing helmets. On the surface is nothing, but you open the skull and the brain is mush.*

So Omalu carried Mike Webster's brain to the cutting board and turned it upside down and on its side and then over again. It appeared utterly normal. Regular folds of gray matter. No mush. No obvious contusions, like in dementia pugilistica. No shrinkage like you would see in Alzheimer's disease. He reviewed the CT and MRI scans. Normal. That might have been the end of it. He already had a cause of death. But Omalu couldn't let it go. He wanted to know more about the brain. There had to be an answer. People don't go crazy for no reason.

He went to his boss, pathologist Cyril Wecht, and asked if he could study the brain, run special tests, a microscopic analysis of the brain tissue, where there might be a hidden story.

There was nothing routine about this request. Another boss might have said, "Stick with the protocol," especially to a rookie such as Omalu, who had not yet earned a track record, who was acting only on a hunch. But Wecht was famously never one to shy away from a high-profile case—he had examined JFK, Elvis, Jon-Benét Ramsey—and he said, "Fine." He said, "Do what you need to do."

A deeply religious man, Omalu regarded Wecht's permission as a kind of blessing.

It was late, maybe midnight, when Bob Fitzsimmons, a lawyer working in a renovated firehouse in Wheeling, West Virginia, got a call from the Pittsburgh coroner's office. It was not unusual for him to be at the office that late; he was having a bad week. He struggled to understand the man's accent on the phone, jutted his head forward. "Excuse me? You need *what?*"

The brain. Permission from the Webster family to process Mike Webster's brain for microscopic examination.

Oh brother was Fitzsimmons's initial thought. As if the Webster case wasn't already complicated enough.

Fitzsimmons had first met Webster back in 1997, when he showed up at his office asking for help untangling his messed-up life. Webster was a hulk of a man with oak-tree arms and hands the size of ham hocks. Fitzsimmons shook his hand and got lost in it, mangled fingers going every which way, hitting his palm in creepy places that made him flinch. It seemed like every one of those fingers had been broken many times over. Mike Webster sat down and told Fitzsimmons what he could remember about his life. He had been to perhaps dozens of lawyers and dozens of doctors. He really couldn't remember whom he'd seen or when. He couldn't remember if he was married or not. He had a vague memory of divorce court. And Ritalin. Lots of Ritalin.

"With all due respect, you're losing your train of thought, sir," Fitzsimmons said to Webster. "You appear to have a serious illness, sir." Not a pleasant thing to tell anyone, and here was a hero, a famous football player Fitzsimmons once bowed to, as did all young guys worth the Terrible Towels they proudly waved in the 1970s. The Dynasty! The black and the gold! It fueled optimism here, up and down the rivers, mill towns held tight in the folds of the Allegheny Mountains. And here was Iron Mike himself.

As a personal-injury lawyer, Fitzsimmons thought what he saw in Webster was an obvious case of a man suffering a closed-head injury — the kind he'd seen plenty of times in people who had suffered through car crashes and industrial accidents. No fracture, no signs of physical damage to the skull, but sometimes severe psychiatric problems, memory loss, personality changes, aggressive behavior.

"Please help me," Mike Webster said.

It took Fitzsimmons a year and a half to hunt down all of Webster's medical records, scattered in doctors' offices throughout western Pennsylvania and West Virginia. He sent Webster for four separate medical evaluations, and all four doctors confirmed Fitzsimmons's suspicion: closed-head injury as a result of multiple concussions.

Fitzsimmons filed the disability claim with the NFL. There are several levels of disability with the NFL, and Mike Webster was awarded the lowest one: partial, about $3,000 a month.

Fitzsimmons said, "Oh, please." He said if ever there was a guy who qualified for the highest, it was Mike Webster. The highest level was "total disability, football-related," reserved for those who were disabled as a result of playing the game. It would yield Webster as much as $12,000 a month. Fitzsimmons said to the NFL, "Four doctors — all with the same diagnosis!"

The NFL said no. Four doctors were not enough. They wanted Webster seen by their own doctor. So their own doctor examined Webster . . . and concurred with the other four: closed-head injury. Football-related.

The NFL pension board voted unanimously for partial disability anyway.

Fitzsimmons said, "You have got to be kidding me." He filed an appeal with the U.S. District Court in Baltimore, where the pension board is headquartered. The judge reversed the decision of the NFL pension board—the first time in history any such action had been taken against the NFL.

And yet still the NFL fought. They took the case to federal court. They said Mike Webster—who had endured probably twenty-five thousand violent collisions during his career and now was living on Pringles and Little Debbie pecan rolls, who was occasionally catatonic, in a fetal position for days—they said Mike Webster didn't qualify for full disability.*

Mike Webster and Bob Fitzsimmons grew close during those days. In fact, Mike Webster clung to Fitzsimmons like a baby to his mamma. He took to sleeping in the parking lot, waiting for Fitzsimmons to show up for work. He would stay there all day, just watching, waiting, and when Fitzsimmons would go home, Mike Webster would go back to his truck and write him letters. Hundreds and hundreds of letters. "Dear Bob, Thank you for helping me. We've got to keep up the fight. We have to see this thing through." And then he would start talking about wars. And blood splattering. The letters would inevitably trail off into the mutterings of a madman.

And now he was dead.

Bob Fitzsimmons did not know what in the world to say, in 2002, to the man with the thick accent who called from the Pittsburgh coroner's office, four days after Mike Webster died of a heart attack, asking to study Webster's brain. Fitzsimmons was, in truth, grieving his client's death deeply; Mike Webster had been living for nothing but the case, the appeal, the last victory against a multibillion-dollar entertainment industry that seemed to have used him, allowed him to become destroyed, and then threw him away like a rotten piece of meat.

And now he was dead.

"Yes," Fitzsimmons said. And he gave Omalu the brain.

Days and nights went by. Weekends. Slicing, staining, ordering slides. It got so Omalu was embarrassed in front of his cowork-

---

* On December 13, 2006, seven years after the initial filing and four years after Webster's death, the U.S. Court of Appeals for the Fourth Circuit upheld the ruling that Webster had been totally and permanently disabled as a result of brain injuries from playing professional football. The ruling, a 3–0 decision, resulted in an award of more than $1.5 million to Webster's four children and former wife.

ers at the morgue. "He's gone mad!" he imagined them reasonably thinking. "He won't stop looking at that brain! He's here at two A.M.!"

So Omalu put Mike Webster's brain in a plastic tub and took it home to his condo in the Churchill section of Pittsburgh. He put it in the corner of his living room, where he set up a table, a cutting board, some knives, and a microscope, where he could work without shame as long as he wanted and as hard as he wanted, no one looking over his shoulder except Prema, his sympathetic wife. "What the mind does not know, the eye cannot see," he would say to her, explaining the piles of books and journal articles cluttering the house, the sheer volume of research on trauma, on football, on helmets, on Alzheimer's disease, on concussions, on impact, on g-force, on protein accumulation, on dementia pugilistica. He had to learn more so he could see more so he could learn more so he could see. For months it's all he thought about. It became for him a calling. He was after all a spiritual man, and he came to know Mike Webster in the most personal way. "Help me" is what he heard Mike Webster say.

One day he started on a new set of slides, prepared for him by a lab at the University of Pittsburgh where he had ordered specialized staining. He was ordering so many slides, he had to start paying for this out of his own pocket. He put the first slide from the new set under his microscope and looked in.

"What is this?" he said out loud. "Geez. Gee! *What is this?*"

Brown and red splotches. All over the place. Large accumulations of tau proteins. Tau was kind of like sludge, clogging up the works, killing cells in regions responsible for mood, emotions, and executive functioning.

This was why Mike Webster was crazy.

Omalu showed the slides to Wecht and to scientists at the University of Pittsburgh. Everyone agreed: this was a disease, or a form of it, that no one had ever seen before. Omalu wondered what to call it. He wanted a good acronym. Eventually, he came up with CTE, chronic traumatic encephalopathy. He wrote a paper detailing his findings. He titled it "Chronic Traumatic Encephalopathy in a National Football League Player" and put it in an envelope and sent it to the prestigious peer-reviewed journal *Neurosurgery.* He thought NFL doctors would be pleased when they read it. He really did. He thought they would welcome a finding as important as this: scientific evidence that the kind of repeated blows to the head sustained in football could cause severe, debilitating brain damage. He thought they could use his research to try and fix the problem.

"I was naive," he says now. "There are times I wish I never looked at Mike Webster's brain. It has dragged me into worldly affairs I do not want to be associated with. Human meanness, wickedness, and selfishness. People trying to cover up, to control how information is released. I started this not knowing I was walking into a mine-field. That is my only regret."

Nothing was welcoming, nothing was collegial, about the NFL's re-action to Omalu's article that appeared in the July 2005 edition of *Neurosurgery*. In a lengthy letter to the editor, three scientists, all of whom were on the NFL payroll, said they wanted Omalu's article retracted.

"We disagree," they said.

"Serious flaws."

"Complete misunderstanding."

The scientists, Ira Casson, Elliot Pellman, and David Viano, were all members of the NFL's Mild Traumatic Brain Injury Committee. In tone their letter to the editor struggled to remain calm, but eve-ryone could read the subtext: *We own this field. We are not going to bow to some no-name Nigerian with some bullshit theory.*

The attack against Omalu was that he had misinterpreted his own neuropathological findings. In his calmer moments, Omalu considered the fact that neither Casson, Pellman, nor Viano were neuropathologists. He wondered, *How can doctors who are not neuro-pathologists interpret neuropathological findings better than neuropatholo-gists?*

But mostly Omalu did not remain calm. In fact, he sweated pro-fusely when he heard that the NFL had written demanding a re-traction. It took a couple of shots of Johnnie Walker Red before he could even summon the courage to read their letter, after which he tore it up in disgust.

Omalu began to question the integrity of the MTBI committee. It was one thing to not even put a neuropathologist on the commit-tee, quite another to have the committee headed by . . . a rheuma-tologist, as was the case with Pellman.

A rheumatologist? You picked a joint guy to lead your brain study?

What the NFL couldn't have known then, of course, is that by the time Omalu's article was published, he had already gotten a second brain, that of former Steelers guard Terry Long, who died at forty-five after drinking antifreeze.

Same morgue. Same slab. Same story. Terry Long had a clinical history similar to Webster's. Depression. Memory loss. Crazy behavior. In and out of psych wards. He was bankrupt, living destitute and alone. He tried rat poison. He tried other cocktails. Nothing worked until finally he got it right.

Omalu took Terry Long's brain home, sliced it, sent it in for stains, ran the same tests, found the same splotches, the same tau proteins. "This stuff should not be in the brain of a forty-five-year-old man," he said. "This looks more like a ninety-year-old brain with advanced Alzheimer's."

So Omalu wrote another paper. He called it "Chronic Traumatic Encephalopathy in a National Football League Player: Part II" and put it in an envelope and sent it to *Neurosurgery*, the prestigious peer-reviewed journal that did not, in the end, accept the NFL's request to retract the first one and went ahead and published the second.

The news of CTE, of retired athletes possibly suffering debilitating brain damage, was now hitting the mainstream press. The NFL responded with denial and attack against the young pathologist in Pittsburgh, who surely had no idea what he was talking about.

"Preposterous," they said to reporters.

"It's not appropriate science."

"Purely speculative."

Omalu did not like the education he was receiving. He felt he was learning something very ugly about America, about how an $8 billion industry could attempt to silence even the most well-intentioned scientist and in the most insidious ways. He was becoming afraid. Friends were warning him. They were saying, "You are challenging one of the most powerful organizations in the world. There may be other things going on that you're not aware of. Be careful!"

Then came a bright spot. Maybe the best day of his life. Omalu got a phone call from Julian Bailes, a neurosurgeon of considerable renown who had for a decade worked as a Steelers team doctor. Bailes, chairman of neurosurgery at West Virginia University

Hospitals, had known Mike Webster well, was friends with the family. And he knew Terry Long. He knew brains. He knew concussions. In his lab in West Virginia he was concussing rats, examining the resulting damage to brain tissue. He knew retired football players, was co-chairing a study at the University of North Carolina's Center for the Study of Retired Athletes, suggesting a link between concussions and clinical depression. Bailes had experience that touched and intersected and paralleled Omalu's research in the way of all fascinating coincidences.

On the phone, Bailes introduced himself. He said, "Dr. Omalu, I'm calling to tell you I believe you."

It was the first time anyone who ever had anything to do with the NFL had validated Omalu's work. He ran home and told his wife. She said, "How do you know? It could be a trick!" They were becoming increasingly fearful. From his village in Nigeria, Omalu's father would call. "Stop doing this work, Bennet. I have heard not nice things about the NFL; they are very powerful, and some of them not nice!" It didn't much help that one day Omalu got a visit from a sports reporter who had come for some quotes, who saw Webster's and Long's brains sitting in tubs in the living room and had said, "Get these out of your house! Someone could come in and kill you and steal these brains! Do you know what you're dealing with?"

In the end, Omalu sent all his brain tissue to Bailes to store in his lab in West Virginia. Bailes met Fitzsimmons, and that became the team, a kind of brotherhood with a mission: to learn more about the disease, to understand the NFL's obstinate, perilous denial, and to break them of it.

The third case was Andre Waters—hard-hitting safety for the Philadelphia Eagles—who was denied disability under the NFL retirement plan despite numerous concussions, constant pain, and crippling depression. On November 20, 2006, at forty-four, he shot himself in the mouth.

Omalu got the brain, examined it, and found CTE.

The fourth case was Justin Strzelczyk, the youngest of all, just thirty-six when he died a most dramatic death. Offensive lineman for the Steelers through most of the 1990s, Strzelczyk was popular in the locker room, a big mountain man of a guy with a banjo at the ready. Just a few years after his retirement, the downward spiral began. He started hearing voices from "the evil ones," who he believed were in constant pursuit. He stopped at a gas station on a highway outside Buffalo, New York. He tried to give some guy three thousand bucks, told him to head for the hills! *The evil ones are coming!* Then he got in his truck and sped away, ninety miles an hour, eventually with the cops chasing him for forty miles. The cops threw metal spikes, blew out his tires, but he kept going and kept going, until finally he swerved into opposing traffic and smashed into a tanker carrying corrosive acid, and everything, everything, exploded.

Omalu got the brain, examined it, and found CTE.

Why these guys? Omalu and Bailes wondered. *Why not other guys?* Not every retired NFL player, after all, goes crazy and kills himself. How many had died young and had never been diagnosed? Why were so many retired players suffering from depression and signs of Alzheimer's? Omalu and Bailes would sit and think and talk and think. Head trauma, sure. But what else? Did these guys take steroids? Other drugs? Were there genetic markers? Did it matter when the head injuries occurred? It was a fascinating puzzle from a medical point of view—and they thought it would have been fascinating from the NFL's point of view too. Omalu had, in fact, asked. Way back after diagnosing Webster, he'd sent a letter to the Hall of Fame proposing a comprehensive, longitudinal study—take every Hall of Famer, get his genetic profile, get a baseline, monitor him every six months for depression and other neuropsychiatric symptoms, and look at his brain when he died.

Omalu did not get a response to that letter. So he sent a follow-up six months later. No answer.

Omalu, Fitzsimmons, and Bailes formed an organization, the Sports Legacy Institute, with the intention of studying CTE, furthering the science. They were joined by a fourth, Chris Nowinski, who had been helping broker brain deals with families—getting brains for Omalu to study. Nowinski was not like the others. He seemed to be on a different mission. It was hard to put your finger on it exactly. "We must not go running to the press with every new case!" Omalu would tell him. "We need to study, we need to learn." Nowinski had bigger ideas. He said CTE was a public health issue and the public had a right to know. He believed the Sports Legacy Institute—SLI—could and should make headlines.

No one could blame Nowinski, really, if he was on some sort of crusade. He was not a scientist. He was a former WWE wrestler who had fought under the stage name Chris Harvard—the only Harvard-educated wrestler in the WWE. He had played football in college, but it was the head bashing as a wrestler that did him in, especially that last one, at the Pepsi Center in Albany, when a Dudley Death Drop ("3D") engineered by the Dudley Boyz sent poor Chris Harvard's head smashing through a table to the cheers of thousands.

Vision loss, ferocious migraines, loss of balance, memory problems; he was twenty-four years old and feeling some days like a feeble old man. He went to eight doctors before anyone took the time to tell him what was going on. Those were *concussions.* All those times. Not just the times he had become unconscious. But all those times, perhaps one hundred times, that he saw stars, suffered a "ding"—any loss of brain function induced by trauma was a concussion, and all of them were serious, all of them were brain injuries, all of them required attention, not the least of which was the time to heal before suffering another one. No one had ever told him that. No one had ever told him that the job he returned to each day was potentially brain-damaging. No one until Nowinski met a world-renowned concussion expert who explained it all, and so Nowinski quit the WWE.

He wrote a meticulously researched book, *Head Games: Football's Concussion Crisis,* got himself on a lot of TV shows, and took the Chris Nowinski CTE show on the road.

Omalu did not understand what was happening. Bailes and Fitzsimmons did. They would look at each other and say, "Uh-oh."

In the summer of 2007, Roger Goodell, the new NFL commissioner, convened a meeting in Chicago for the first league-wide concussion summit. All thirty-two teams were ordered to send doctors and trainers to the meeting. It would be a chance for the NFL to talk about this and hear from independent scientists, many of whom they also invited to the meeting—three hundred participants in all.

They asked Bailes to come. They did not ask Omalu.

"Why did they not invite me?" Omalu said to Bailes. "Why does the NFL not want to speak to Dr. Omalu?"

Bailes had no easy answer. He knew those guys. He knew who

was in and who was out and how dirty the politics could get. "They were trying to blackball him, lock him out, marginalize him," Bailes says. "He was the whistle-blower."

"You will present my work, then," Omalu said to Bailes. "You will take my slides. You will take my research. You will show them what Dr. Omalu has found!" Not that it was news. He had already published the papers. Why weren't they listening?

So that's what Bailes did. Packed up Omalu's slides and downloaded his PowerPoint presentation and headed to Chicago.

By this point, the NFL had made some progress in admitting to a concussion problem. For one thing, Pellman, the rheumatologist, had stepped down as chair of the committee. Also, the committee announced a new concussion study that would blow everyone else's out of the water. (It involved a battery of clinical testing on 120 retired NFL players and would take at least until 2012 to finish. Bailes, in fact, was already working on a similar study, due out in 2010.)

But there was real, actual progress. The NFL instituted standards for concussion management: "Medical decisions must always override competitive considerations." They would do neuropsychological baseline testing on all NFL players—use that as a tool to assist in determining when, after a head injury, a player could return to the field.

(On hearing of the NFL's concussion guidelines, Omalu said: "You mean they never had any concussion guidelines before now? Geez.")

Perhaps most encouraging was the 88 Plan, a display of humanity on the part of the NFL and its treatment of retired players suffering dementia. The 88 Plan grew out of a letter written by Sylvia Mackey, wife of Hall of Famer John Mackey, who wore number 88 for the Colts. His existence, she said, had become a "deteriorating, ugly, caregiver-killing, degenerative, brain-destroying tragic horror," and the $2,450 per month pension he was receiving from the NFL could not begin to cover the institutionalization he needed. And so the 88 Plan, which offered up to $88,000 per year to former players with dementia.

Not that the NFL accepted any actual responsibility for this mess. Its MTBI committee published scientific studies claiming that repeated head bashing did not cause brain damage. On a 2007 HBO special, co-chair Casson was asked six different ways if repeated football-related concussions could result in brain damage, dementia, or depression. Six times he said no.

In Chicago, Bailes stood up there with evidence to the contrary. Scientific proof. Tissue damage in the brain. He saw guys rolling their eyes. He heard the exasperated sighs. He thought about Omalu and why he was doing this—how he had nothing against the NFL, how he had barely known what the NFL *was* before he looked at Webster's brain. He thought about how Omalu was about as pure a scientist as anyone could bring into this equation, and how he had spent $100,000 of his own money to get to the bottom of this.

So Bailes stood up there and he showed slides of Webster's seemingly perfect brain on the cutting board. He showed the slices. He showed the tau, that sludge that did him in. He showed Long, and he showed Waters, and he showed Strzelczyk. He showed that he believed in Omalu's work.

The meeting was closed to media, but Bailes remembers it well. "They didn't say, 'Thanks, Doc, that's great.' They got mad at me. We got into it. And I'm thinking, 'This is a new disease in America's most popular sport, and how are its leaders responding? Alienate the scientist who found it? Refuse to accept the science coming from him?'"

At a press briefing afterward, Omalu's name kept coming up, and so Casson responded: "The only scientifically valid evidence of chronic encephalopathy in athletes is in boxers and in some steeplechase jockeys. It's never been scientifically, validly documented in any other athletes."

A total dismissal of Omalu's work.

And what about the other studies? What about Bailes's report in 2003 out of the University of North Carolina with Kevin Guskiewicz, a leading expert in sports medicine, which, based on surveys of thousands of retired players, found that players who had suffered multiple concussions were three times more likely to suffer clinical depression?

The NFL concluded that that study was "flawed."

And what about the UNC follow-up study in 2005 that showed that repeatedly concussed NFL players had five times the rate of "mild cognitive impairment," or pre-Alzheimer's disease? That study showed retired NFL players suffering Alzheimer's disease at an alarming 37 percent higher rate than the average guy walking down the street.

"Flawed."

The only experiments that were not flawed, then, were the studies conducted by the scientists paid by the NFL, which just happened to disagree with a growing number of researchers. "That's just unprecedented in science," says Bailes. "That would be like the American Heart Association saying, 'Hey, if it's not our sponsored research, we don't acknowledge it or comment on it. Only *we* can figure out heart disease!'"

Or it would be like the tobacco industry in the 1980s — everyone saying cigarettes caused cancer except for the people making money off cigarettes.

It would have been laughable, if it weren't so irresponsible.

At stake, after all, were people's lives. Athletes suffering head injuries, pressured anyway by a culture of machismo that says: *Get back in the game! Man up! Don't ever show it hurts.* To say nothing of the college football players, the high school football players, the Pee Wee Leaguers, who dreamt of going pro.

On this point alone Bailes goes ballistic:

"Here we have a multi*billion*-dollar industry. Where does their responsibility begin? Say you're a kid and you sign up to play football. You realize you can blow out your knee, you can even break your neck and become paralyzed. Those are all known risks. But you don't sign up to become a brain-damaged young adult. The NFL should be leading the world in figuring this out, acknowledging the risk. They should be *thanking us* for bringing them this research. Where does their responsibility begin?

"Look, there was a seminal study published by the University of Oklahoma two years ago. They put accelerometers, which measure acceleration, in the helmets of University of Oklahoma players. And they documented the g-force. So we know the g-force for a football player being knocked out is about sixty to ninety g's. To compare, a fighter pilot will pass out at five or six g's, but that's over a long period of time. These football g-forces are just a few milliseconds, very brief — *boom!* And they found that in the open field, the dramatic cases of a receiver getting blindsided is about one hundred g's. It knocks them out. Very dramatic, everybody sees it. But the linemen? They were actually getting twenty to thirty g's on *every play*. Because they start out and they bang heads. Every play.

"Helmets are not the answer. The brain has a certain amount of play inside the skull. It's buoyed up in the cerebral spinal fluid. It sits in this fluid, floats. When the head suddenly stops, the brain continues, reverberates back. So when I hit, *boom,* my skull stops, but my brain continues forward for about a centimeter. *Boom, boom,* it reverberates back. So you could have padding that's a foot thick. It's not going to change the acceleration/deceleration phenomenon. And a lot of these injuries are rotational. The fibers get torn with rotation. You've got a face mask that's like a fulcrum sitting out here: you get hit, your head swings around. That's when a lot of these fibers are sheared—by rotation. A helmet can't ever prevent that.

"And have you seen helmets lately? In the old days of football, you had this leather cap to protect your ears. That was it. You'd never put your head in the game. You'd be knocked out after the first play! Even in the '60s, the helmet was a light shell. The modern helmet is like a weapon.

"So I told the NFL, I said, 'Why don't you take the head out of the game? *Just take it out of the game!* Let the linemen start from a squatting position instead of getting down for head-to-head. Have them stand up like they do on pass protection. So there's not this obligatory head contact.'

"Nothing. They had nothing to say. Who am I? I'm only a guy who has concussed hundreds of rats in the lab, a player for ten years, and a sideline doctor for twenty years. What do I know? Some stupid neurosurgeon.

"Instead of answering anything we bring to them, the NFL is ducking and shooting arrows at us. Criticizing us. Saying our work is a bunch of bunk. They have only attacked us."

The sixth case was Tom McHale, offensive lineman for nine seasons, most of them with the Tampa Bay Buccaneers. Depression and chronic pain in his joints had led him to discover oxycodone and cocaine. On May 25, 2008, at age forty-five, he died of a lethal combination of both.

Omalu got his brain, examined it, and found CTE.

He decided not to release the McHale case to the press. The

NFL was already plenty pissed off. They had refused to acknowledge CTE or any of Omalu's research or, really, Omalu himself. It seemed they wanted to simply pretend Omalu did not exist, and he was sick of it, sick of insisting that *yes, Bennet Omalu is a real person who has discovered a real disease that is really damaging real people even as you sit there denying it.* The public debate with the NFL was a distraction from his research. He would continue his work quietly, examining brains. He would set his sights on curing the disease. He would prepare scientific papers; the proof would be in the science.

Ideas like that caused the Nowinski connection to crumble. *Continue the work quietly?* But Nowinski was building SLI; he was making a name for himself. The split was abrupt, ugly, and to this day neither side agrees on what happened. Nowinski took SLI and teamed up with the Boston University School of Medicine to create the Center for the Study of Traumatic Encephalopathy. He started a brain bank under the direction of Ann McKee, an expert in neurodegenerative diseases, and they went on to do important work, diagnosing more cases of CTE and starting a registry of over one hundred athletes who have agreed to donate their brains for study after they die.

Indeed, the casual observer who wants to learn more about CTE will be easily led to SLI and the Boston group—there's an SLI Twitter link, an SLI awards banquet, an SLI website with photos of Nowinski and links to videos of him on TV and in the newspapers. Gradually, Omalu's name slips out of the stories, and Bailes slips out, and Fitzsimmons, and their good fight. As it happens in stories, the telling and retelling simplify and reduce.

History gets written. People shout and claim turf. Heroes get invented.

The Boston group wanted to see the Tom McHale brain, and at the request of the family Omalu agreed. So he sliced the brain in two and sent one half via UPS to Boston. He said please don't release the diagnosis to the press; he was preparing a scientific paper identifying CTE subtypes. Nowinski remembers this conversation very differently. He says Omalu never returned calls, and to this day he vehemently defends his decision to go ahead and announce the McHale diagnosis anyway, in Tampa, during the week of the 2009 Super Bowl. He made national headlines announcing that the Boston group, and not Omalu, had diagnosed CTE in yet another NFL player. (Nowinski says he was acting on behalf of the McHale family.)

"Geez," Omalu said, watching the CNN coverage. "That's my brain! They are lying about who diagnosed that brain!"

It was enough to tempt a man to become wicked, to lead him to thoughts of lawsuits and vengeance.

But Omalu did not become wicked. He reminded himself of who he was. "I perform autopsies on dead people every day, so every day I'm reminded of my mortality. It has made me become very religious. I know I'm going to die someday, I know I'm going to be judged by God, and I have work to do while I am here on the earth."

Morgantown, West Virginia, is surrounded by blue firs and green hardwoods, a town tucked in the folds of the Appalachian Basin, where coal still moves sleepily in and out on barges along the slim Monongahela River. The university—and its world-class health care complex—is by far the biggest thing going.

In Bailes's office, Becky, his secretary, just accepted a package and is digging through Styrofoam peanuts. It used to disturb her to reach into a cardboard box and pull out a jar full of brains, but by now she is used to it.

In the jar is Omalu's fifteenth confirmed case of CTE—the most dramatic he's seen. He is not ready to release it to the press.

"Your brain made it," Becky says to Omalu, who has himself just arrived. He doesn't like traveling with brains. He trusts UPS. "You had a good trip?"

"Sure, sure, sure," Omalu says. His face is walnut dark and boyishly round. His movements are smooth, calm, and efficient; the overall effect is of a nattily dressed man who might at any moment start whistling. "But my tailor was not in!" he tells Becky. Omalu moved to California two years ago—where he accepted a post as chief medical examiner of San Joaquin County—but he still buys all his suits from one tailor in Pittsburgh. Nearly all of them are wide blue pinstripe, vaguely flashy, with impeccable fit. Custom-made. Shirts too. He does not like pockets. If you have a shirt with a pocket, you run the risk of lint collecting at the bottom of the pocket. That is his position. Do away with the pocket—no lint. This is simply logical.

Fitzsimmons arrives, slim with a broad grin and quiet attire.

"How you doing, buddy?" he says to Omalu. "Got the red tie going today, huh?" The two men embrace, slap each other's backs.

Eventually, Bailes comes flying in, still in scrubs, just out of surgery, his mask hanging half off. He is carrying a Diet Coke. "You guys want nuts? Something to eat? Crackers? I haven't eaten."

They stretch out in the conference room, visit like country people, tell jokes, and forget about time.

"And so this guy, he calls from some smart-guy science magazine," Omalu is saying. "And he says, 'Dr. Omalu, you are a brilliant man! Why did you fizzle?' And I told him, I said, 'Dr. Omalu did not fizzle!'"

"Fizzle," Bailes says, shooting a grin at Fitzsimmons. The admiration the two share for Omalu is protective and fatherly. Even his vocabulary is raw innocence.

Then they get down to business, and Fitzsimmons pulls out the papers.

"Do I need to read it?" Bailes says.

"I'm your lawyer, and I say sign it," Fitzsimmons says, and all three men get out their pens and find their names, which together are "hereinafter referred to as 'The Brain Injury Group.'"

A brain bank. The Rockefeller Foundation. A brand-new $30 million research facility. The Blanchette Rockefeller Neurosciences Institute opened a year ago across the street from Bailes's office—a slick building, 78,000 square feet of state-of-the-art laboratory space. It's the only nonprofit independent institute in the world exclusively dedicated to the study of human memory and memory disorders, a partnership with West Virginia University and Johns Hopkins University. Senator Jay Rockefeller named it after his mom, Blanchette, who had Alzheimer's and died in 1992. And now, on the first floor, will be Webster's brain and Long's brain and all the rest—a whole laboratory dedicated to brain injuries and the study of CTE. They are gathering more brains, and more still; they would like to get Steve McNair's brain, and the boxer Roy Jones Jr. just signed on to donate his brain when he dies. The new center launches this month.

Omalu has set his sights on curing CTE. And why not? "You pop a pill before you play, a medicine that prevents the buildup of tau," he says. "Like you take an aspirin to prevent heart disease." *Why not?* "This is how we now need to talk. Not this back-and-forth of human selfishness. Not this NFL politics and meanness. Anybody still denying the disease is out of his mind. The issue now is treatment. That is my next step, now that I understand the pathology."

The Brain Injury Group is preparing seven new scientific papers. New findings. Subcategories of CTE. A possible genotype. Omalu has anything but fizzled. He took the conversation out of the public domain, got to work, and Fitzsimmons got to work on the Rockefeller deal, and Bailes on the scientific papers, and really, what they want is the NFL to join them in trying to figure this thing out.

It appears highly unlikely. The last they heard from the NFL was when the NFL called in 2008 in what seemed like a final attempt to disprove Omalu's work. *We have been speaking to a scientist. The world's leading authority on tau proteins. We would like to send him to West Virginia to look at your work.*

Bailes agreed.

Neuropathologist Peter Davies of the Albert Einstein College of Medicine in New York has been studying Alzheimer's and tau proteins for more than thirty years. He receives no money from the NFL, not even parking fare. He was more than a little doubtful about what he would find in West Virginia. He had examined thousands of brains, and he'd never seen anything even close to the degree of tau accumulation that Omalu was describing in his papers. He believed that Omalu was well intentioned but naive and mistaken. "I was very skeptical," he says. "I didn't think there was anything there."

So when Davies got to West Virginia in October 2008, he smiled politely and walked into Bailes's lab, and Omalu handed him the first slide, and he looked in the microscope, and he said, "Whoa." He said, "Wow." He said, *"What the hell is this?"*

It went on like this for two days, slide after slide. It got to the point where the only doubt Davies had left was on the staining of the slides themselves. Perhaps the technicians were not using state-of-the-art equipment and solutions. He asked Omalu if he would give him tissue samples, pieces of brain to take back to his lab in New York, where he could make new slides with his own equipment, his own technicians, his own sophisticated stains.

"Sure, sure, sure," Omalu said. "You take some pieces home, talk to your guys, see what you think."

In his lab in New York, Davies ran his tests, and when he looked in the microscope, he was stunned. The tau pathology was even worse—even more pronounced—than what he'd seen in West

Virginia. "Come look at this!" he said, calling in his team of researchers. "What the hell am I looking at? This will blow your socks off! And it's not just in one case. I have three separate cases here. Bucket loads of tau pathology, and the one guy wasn't even forty years old . . ." It was far more severe than anything they'd ever seen in the most advanced Alzheimer's cases — and in completely different regions of the brain.

"My God, this is extraordinary," Davies said. "We have to get involved." He wrote to Bailes and Omalu. He said Omalu was right.

"The credit must go to Bennet Omalu," he says today, "because he first reported this and nobody believed him, nobody in the field, and I'm included in that. I did not think there was anything there. But when I looked at the stuff, he was absolutely right. I was wrong to be skeptical."

The NFL never released Davies's report, never made it public. And they never talked to Omalu, Bailes, or Fitzsimmons again.

They called another meeting, much smaller than the Chicago summit, in May 2009, to talk again about concussions and the progress of the MTBI committee's work. They invited researchers from the Boston group. They invited Davies, who told them about what he saw in West Virginia.

"There is no doubt there is something there," Davies said. But he differs on the conclusion. He does not believe the main cause of CTE is concussion or trauma. He has even designed studies, principally on rats, to test his own hypothesis that the main cause is steroid use. He admits freely, however, that he is not a trauma expert, like Bailes, that he has not spent his career, like Omalu, looking at brains that have suffered repeated trauma. He's an Alzheimer's guy who believes that there has to be some reason he's never seen brains like this, and he believes the reason is steroid use. Plenty of people, after all, suffer concussions — not just athletes. Wouldn't he have seen *some* evidence of CTE in brains of regular folks over all these years? But only athletes take steroids, and so that is the link he is following.

Bailes, who co-authored a book on steroids and sports, does not rule out steroids or any other contributing factor to CTE, but points out that synthetic steroids were not even invented until 1959 — thirty years after brain changes were first identified in boxers in the form of dementia pugilistica.

Either way, the steroid theory is not, in itself, a cheerful hypothesis for the NFL to consider. What of its vaunted drug-testing policy? What of the way fans have been coaxed to blithely accept that the reason these big fast guys keep getting bigger and faster every year is . . . natural? Not because of performance-enhancing drugs.

Whether it's concussions or steroids or a combination of both, the NFL has a problem to solve that is becoming impossible to deny.

Ira Casson, co-director of the MTBI, was at the May meeting, and he came away from it still committed to the NFL's talking points — the ones he had first put out in 2005 when he co-authored the letter asking for the retraction of Omalu's article in *Neurosurgery.*

Has Casson's position changed, now that scientists from across the country have come to accept the research as sound?

"No," he says. "Nothing has happened that has changed any of our opinions about what we wrote in those letters. Is there a relationship between professional football, a career in the NFL, and changes in the brain? Well, we don't know. Maybe."

So why does he think so many independent scientists are saying there is?

"I think there are a lot of . . . gaps," he says. The main problem, as he sees it, is that all scientists have really looked at, after all, are dead people. There has been very little clinical data, he says, collected on living people — which is what the MTBI committee's study is designed to do.

"Essentially," he says, "if you look at the cases that have been reported in the medical literature — and I don't include the *New York Times* as medical literature — for the most part, the clinical data was collected posthumously: interviews with families, 'people told me this,' and so forth. You don't see any data that says, well, here's what a *doctor* found when they examined him; here's what their psychiatric evaluation showed; here's what their neurologist found. There's none of that!

"To me that creates a question of what exactly is the clinical picture? I don't think it's fair to jump from a couple cases that were suicides to assume that some of the others that, well, the guy was driving fast down the highway, it must have been a suicide. Well, we don't know that. I don't think anybody can tell you that unless you had a psychiatrist who was treating the person. I think there's a lot of people jumping to conclusions."

*

"Very little clinical data."

Fitzsimmons and Bailes and Omalu are silting in Bailes's conference room in West Virginia, contemplating what Casson has said.

"Very little clinical data?" Fitzsimmons says. But he had five doctors, including one from the NFL, who examined Mike Webster and concluded he had a closed-head injury. "I had a file *this thick* of clinical data."

"Why is he doing this?" Bailes says. "I just don't understand why the NFL is doing this. You know, pick up a textbook." He picks up a textbook, the kind you'd find in any neurosurgery department of any medical school. "Here's *The Neuropathology of Dementia*. It describes, in great detail, tau pathology. There's a whole chapter here about trauma causing dementia. That's why this is very quixotic to me that's there's even any resistance. It's well known that brain trauma is a risk for dementia. Why are we arguing this? Why can't we accept this and move on and try to prevent it?"

"Clinical data?" Omalu says. "*Clinical* data? Pardon me, but what is the gold standard for diagnosis? Autopsy! That is the gold standard for diagnosis. Only when you open up the body, look at the tissues, do you find proof of disease."

They have proof of the fifteenth case right here, sitting in a jar, a story still to tell.

And then there is the sixteenth case: Gerald Small, Dolphins cornerback in the 1980s. He was found dead at fifty-two in Sacramento, California, where he was unemployed, living with an aunt, drunk. The Sacramento coroner sent the brain to Omalu, who is by now well known on the coroners' circuit.

Omalu got the brain, examined it, and found CTE.

The seventeenth case is Curtis Whitley, center for the Chargers, Panthers, Raiders, in the 1990s. He was just thirty-nine when he was found facedown in the bathroom of a rented trailer in West Texas, shirtless, shoeless, wearing blue warm-up pants.

Omalu got his brain, examined it, and found CTE.

"You would think that sooner or later, like most things in life, you have to deal with the truth," says Bailes. "I think that was part of the NFL's intent on sending their expert to Morgantown. Maybe they're planning their strategy now, I don't know."

ROBERT SANCHEZ

This Is Ted Johnson's Brain

FROM 5280

TED JOHNSON IS FLAT on the turf of Boulder's Folsom Field.

From a bleacher seat on the 35-yard line, Ted Johnson Sr. had seen his son run headlong into a University of Miami running back on that warm, fall afternoon in 1993 and disappear into a tangle of pads and helmets as Johnson's University of Colorado teammates piled on. Now, Ted Senior strains his eyes and waits for his name-sake to pop back up. *Where are you, Junior?* Ted Senior repeats qui-etly to himself. *C'mon, Junior. C'mon.*

The players peel themselves off the heap slowly, pulling their bodies, one by one, off the green turf, until they are all stand-ing—every one of them, except number 46.

Johnson's CU teammates have formed a protective barrier by the time a trainer arrives at the linebacker's side. The man kneels down and looks closely at Johnson's face: his boyish, upturned nose and strong, fierce features. Johnson is unconscious, but he's hardly still, and the man almost instantly realizes that he's choking on something. The trainer opens Johnson's mouth and pulls his tongue from his throat.

In all the football games Johnson had played—from high school up to this point as a junior at CU—never once did he need to be carried off the field. It was a simple, almost trivial, fact, but one from which Johnson derived a great deal of pride. While others fell and rolled on the field in pain, Johnson always got up, went back to the huddle, and prepared for his next hit. Not this time, not to-day.

As he cranes his neck to get a better view of the field, Ted Senior sees, finally, that his son is sitting up, then standing, then is helped

off the field. He looks sick, glassy-eyed, empty. Players clear a path
to the bench where Johnson sits, face in his hands.

All at once, the stadium sounds began to crystallize in the young
man's head: the roaring crowd, the barking coaches, and a voice
calling to him from the railing above the Buffaloes' bench.

"Junior! Junior!" his father yells. "Are you okay?"

Johnson turns his head and tries to focus his eyes. His face is
long and worn.

"Yeah, Dad," he says. "I'm okay."

"Bro, where's my car?" Johnson asked me last fall after lunch at a
central Boston sandwich shop. "I thought I parked it right here."

I shrugged. Johnson pushed the horn button on his keychain
and listened for his Range Rover. Nothing.

"It's gotta be somewhere, bro, we parked right here," he said in
his surfer-dude drawl. Johnson slumped his enormous shoulders
and again pushed the button. "Bro, I feel like I'm going crazy. But
you don't remember where we parked either, so maybe that means
I'm not losing it. Right?"

We walked the street, searching for the SUV. Johnson's forehead
furrowed. He pushed the button again and again with no response
—until, finally, the Range Rover's horn sounded. A look of relief
washed across Johnson's face. "See," he said with a smile, pointing
to his skull, "not losing it."

It was one of my first meetings with Johnson, who was less than
two months out of Spaulding Rehabilitation Hospital in Boston. In
August of last year, the thirty-six-year-old former CU All-American
and star NFL linebacker had checked himself into the center at
the urging of his doctor, Heechin Chae, an expert on pain and rehabilitation medicine. Since retiring from the NFL three years earlier, Johnson's life—or perhaps, more precisely, his mind—had
gone completely to hell.

His list of troubles was ever-growing, and he ticked them off with
the sort of matter-of-factness that one might use to recount a grocery list. He was divorced. Johnson had been addicted to amphet-
amines. And he suffered from debilitating headaches, depression,
and fatigue, the result, he says, of dozens of concussions during a
ten-year career as the middle linebacker for the New England Patriots.

For much of his retirement up to this point, he had spent his time inside Room 801 of the Ritz-Carlton residences and in a rented two-story townhouse in Boston, where he locked the door, closed the blinds, and rarely left his bed unless he needed to eat, use the bathroom, or collect one of the four prescriptions he'd become dependent upon. His once-robust list of friends had dwindled—folks simply stopped calling because Johnson stopped answering. It was a painful fall from grace for a man who once seemed in the center of it all, with a wife and kids and a job that every American boy who'd ever strapped on a helmet longed to have.

Since leaving Spaulding, which was behind the townhouse where he'd sequestered himself for the previous year, Johnson had stopped using Concerta and Provigil (both stimulants), started an exercise regimen, and had been assigned to a psychologist who'd given Johnson a road map that would, hopefully, guide him back to some semblance of normality.

The idea of having to reattach training wheels to his life was embarrassing for Johnson. At CU, he'd grown from a shy, self-conscious California high schooler into one of the most important cogs in a defense that helped the Buffs to thirty-four wins and four bowl-game appearances. During his four years as a starter, from 1991 to 1994, Johnson developed into a concrete block of a kid: six foot four and 240 pounds of pure linebacker who had the unique talent of dispatching offensive linemen seventy pounds heavier and then brutally nailing running backs. The New England Patriots took him in the second round of the 1995 NFL draft. At twenty-two, Johnson became a millionaire overnight.

During a decade with New England, Johnson helped the Patriots to four Super Bowls, three of which they won, and was a defensive captain for three seasons. Over a career that spanned 125 regular-season games, he built a reputation as one of the league's most ferocious run-stoppers. Johnson shattered helmets and bones; he hit running backs so hard that, even surrounded by thousands of raucous fans, the players could hear the runners whimper upon contact. "He looked like a warrior coming off the field," former Patriots linebacker Larry Izzo once remembered of his teammate, "blood splattered on his pants."

But with each hit, Johnson may have been killing himself. "Sometimes I wish Junior would have just blown his knees out and couldn't walk," Ted Johnson Sr. told me earlier this year. "But his brain? Oh boy."

Since 2002, at least five NFL players have committed suicide or died following years of rapidly deteriorating mental health. Dozens, perhaps hundreds, of others have suffered quietly, victims of a particularly sinister trauma called post-concussion syndrome (PCS). In its most serious form, PCS can lead to Alzheimer's disease, dementia, and early death. When a player absorbs a blow to the head, the sloshing of the brain and subsequent banging against the interior skull can tear blood vessels, twist the brain stem, and compress tissue. With each successive concussion, the chance for a more devastating concussion—and the long-term effects that come with it—multiplies massively.

Although the exact number of professional football players who suffer concussions during a given season is up for debate—the NFL only recently created rules on how to address the injury—researchers at the University of North Carolina reported in 2006 that retired players faced a 37 percent higher risk of Alzheimer's disease than other males of the same age. Retired players with three or more concussions also had a five times greater chance of being diagnosed with mild cognitive impairment and a threefold greater prevalence of significant memory problems, compared to players without a concussion history.

The most noteworthy case of PCS is that of Mike Webster, who died of a heart attack in 2002. A Hall of Fame center with four Super Bowl–champion Pittsburgh Steelers teams, Webster, nicknamed "Iron Mike," played nearly two decades in the NFL, after which he literally lost his mind.

After his retirement in 1990, Webster wasted millions of dollars on ill-advised investments, got divorced, and lived out of his black Chevrolet truck with a garbage bag taped over a broken window. His diet consisted mostly of potato chips and dry cereal, and those who saw him in his final years said he suffered severe headaches, showed signs of dementia, and had the glassy-eyed look of a boxer who had taken too many shots to the head; he used a stun gun to shock himself into unconsciousness. By his fiftieth birthday, he was dead.

Bennet Omalu, then a neuropathologist at the Allegheny County

(Pennsylvania) medical examiner's office, examined Webster's brain after he died. Omalu was shocked at the microscopic red flecks—a telltale sign of irreversible damage. Webster's brain was shredded from repeated blows to his head over the years.

Webster wasn't the only NFL vet who had serious health issues after retirement. In 2005, former Pittsburgh Steelers offensive lineman Terry Long killed himself after a fifteen-year retirement marked by bouts of significant depression. In 2006, Omalu studied the brain of Andre Waters, a forty-four-year-old former hard-hitting Philadelphia Eagles safety who shot himself eleven years after his retirement. Waters suffered at least fifteen concussions during his twelve-year career. After viewing Waters's brain, Omalu said the former football player would have been "incapacitated" had he lived fifteen more years because of the damage to his brain. In 2007, Omalu examined the brain of Justin Strzelczyk, a thirty-six-year-old former Pittsburgh Steelers offensive lineman who died three years earlier during a high-speed police chase. Omalu saw four red splotches in the brain. And last year, Boston University doctors discovered signs of "chronic traumatic encephalopathy"— loosely known as "punch-drunk syndrome"—in former Houston Oilers and Miami Dolphins linebacker John Grimsley, forty-five, who accidentally shot himself and died earlier in the year. (Johnson has said that he will donate his brain to Boston University for research upon his death.)

In 2007—a few months after the *New York Times* and *Boston Globe* printed stories about Ted Johnson's head injuries, in particular two concussions he suffered within days of each other in 2002 from which Johnson said he had never fully recovered—I attended the National Concussion Summit in Marina del Rey, California. The event was among the first to address concussions in sports, particularly in the NFL, where the league was mounting a full-throated refutation of Omalu's findings. Omalu and other doctors who supported his research, the NFL argued, had cherry-picked a handful of players, massaged statistics, and passed off the worst-case scenario as typical of the average football player. Omalu defended his work, saying the league had failed to protect its most valuable assets in favor of television contracts and ticket sales. NFL officials were invited to the conference, but none attended. The league now is conducting its own study, which NFL officials say will "deter-

mine if there are any long-term effects of concussion in NFL athletes." The findings, the league has said, likely will be published in
2010.

Omalu spoke at the Concussion Summit. He had Webster's post-
mortem photo stored on his laptop, and he projected it onto a
large screen at the front of the room. The Hall of Famer's thinning
hair was tousled; his head and neck rested on a Styrofoam brace.
There was a slight upturn in the corners of Webster's lips, as if he
were smiling. Omalu left the photo on the screen for several moments. Dozens of us stared at it. The room was silent, perhaps because we could not believe what we were seeing—or maybe because of what Webster seemed to be telling us. After spending his
last decade trapped in a tortured mind, Iron Mike looked relieved
to be gone.

Ted Johnson was on the ground—again. On a muggy Saturday
night in August 2002, the New England Patriots were playing the
New York Giants at the Meadowlands in a meaningless preseason
game. One of the Giants' running backs, Sean Bennett, caught a
ball in the flat, and Johnson did what he'd done a thousand times
before: he charged, then lunged. His helmet hit Bennett's thigh,
taking him down. Everything went foggy after that. Almost immediately, trainers diagnosed Johnson with a concussion.

But four days later, Johnson returned to the Patriots' training
camp. He had something to prove that summer: a few months earlier, the Patriots, his second family, had offered him to the Houston Texans. After the Texans passed, Johnson threatened to hold
out. Instead, he decided to take a pay cut to stay with New England—then learned, when he arrived at summer camp, that he
had lost his starting slot. All of which explained the brutal hit on
Bennett in the exhibition game: Johnson wanted to show the team
that he still had it, that he was still ready to sacrifice for the team.

The team, however, appeared ready to sacrifice Johnson. A few
days after Johnson had his brain scrambled, coach Bill Belichick
had the linebacker in full-contact practice drills. On his first play
back, Johnson hit a fullback. His head snapped back, and a sensation cascaded from the top of his skull to the bottom of his toes. Its
warmth was comforting and sickening, like a blanket of fire. Johnson's mind slowed; he felt woozy. It was his second concussion in

less than a week. Despite lingering grogginess that season, Johnson slowly worked his way back and finished second on the team in tackles.

But Johnson continued to be lethargic, dizzy, and confused, and by the time the 2004 season began, he had started taking Adderall, which is usually prescribed for children with attention deficit hyperactivity disorder (ADHD) and patients with narcolepsy. Adderall countered the lingering effects of the concussions; it quieted Johnson's mind and allowed him to focus on subtle offensive shifts, to direct the human traffic flashing before his eyes. Johnson ripped off one of his most productive seasons, starting fifteen games and finishing third on the team in tackles. The Patriots won their third Super Bowl, beating the Philadelphia Eagles 24–21.

A few months later, in the spring of 2005, Johnson was driving to a movie. In the quiet of the vehicle, Johnson thought about the upcoming training camp. He remembered the warm sensation that accompanied the concussions, and how that first tackle in practice surely would bring the feeling. The idea of another hit sickened him. Johnson turned to his wife, Jackie, whom he'd met a few years earlier at a party, and said, simply: "I'm done."

Ted Johnson Jr. was born in 1972, the only son of Ted Senior and Patrice Johnson, a striking brunette who'd grown up poor in Iowa and was on her fourth marriage. As a boy in Houston, Ted Junior used to watch Oilers games at the old Astrodome, while his father, Ted Senior, extolled the virtues of Earl Campbell, the Oilers' star running back. Father and son marveled at Campbell's power and skill, the way he'd run up on a guy and mow him down, like he was a linebacker playing offense. Ted Senior liked to watch the runs. Ted Junior liked to watch Campbell limp back to the huddle and smash someone in the face on the next play.

Johnson's half-sister, Elyse, was thirteen years older and moved out when she went to college. (She eventually became an Oilers cheerleader.) In 1979, Patrice and Ted Senior divorced. Mom kept the house and took six-year-old Junior.

Patrice and Ted moved around for the next few years, first to Iowa, then to Carlsbad, California, and finally settled in Vista, California, where they lived in a tract-style house not far from the beach.

For much of her life, Johnson's mom did not have a regular job, though she flipped houses for a time while living in southern California. Slim, six feet tall, and beautiful, she instead relied on the men who bought her clothes and jewelry. The men visited often and sometimes stayed the night. When they didn't, sometimes she disappeared to faraway places, one time Las Vegas, the next some exotic island. Ted was shuttled to friends' homes, to couches and bedroom floors, where he lay awake at night, worried about whether his mother was going to pick him up the next morning. "Ted had a beautiful home, he had food, he had everything," Patrice told me. "Do I wish things would have been different? Yes, some things."

If a rift had developed in Johnson's relationship with his mother, he also reaped the benefits of being related to her. He'd inherited the size of his maternal grandfather — a six-foot-four, 350-pound bear of a man — and his mother's all-American looks. One night in 1984, one of Patrice Johnson's friends, a football coach, was at the house and called Ted to his side. He put his hands around the kid's wrists. Had the boy ever considered playing football?

Johnson joined the Carlsbad High School team that fall as a tight end. At a time when most boys were getting their first razors, Johnson was six foot one and 200 pounds. He dreamed of leaving his mother's house and over the years made local weight rooms his second home. "The process of building his body was an escape," his sister Elyse says now. "He could focus on something else. He worked hard to make his way out."

Former Colorado head coach Bill McCartney, whose recruiters first saw Johnson in 1990, saw him as the total package. "Looking at him, you could see that he was going to grow into his size," McCartney says. "I mean, in regular clothes he looked like a football player." Four schools — including CU — sent recruiters to the Johnson home. Colorado offered Johnson a scholarship, and he accepted immediately. Less than a month later, CU won its first football national championship. Now emboldened and with a destination, he graduated high school, moved out of his mother's house, and headed to Boulder.

"I was pretty overwhelmed," Johnson says of his arrival at college. Even when he blew up a runner, smashed a tight end coming through the middle, Johnson lamented that he had been too slow, that his technique was off, that anyone could have made the same play. "Nothing was ever good enough. Ted was emotionally damaged from the relationship he had with his mother," says Johnson's former linebacker coach, Brian Cabral. "In my coaching career, he's probably the most insecure player I've ever met."

Johnson, however, would find his calling in fall practices with "stun and separate," a technique that Cabral had mastered while winning a Super Bowl with Chicago in the mid-1980s. Under Cabral's tutelage, Johnson learned to drop larger offensive players with a single hit: forehead to the chinstrap, grab the breastplate of the shoulder pads and shove, a viciously lethal movement that cleared the way into the backfield.

The technique opened Johnson's world. "He was a beast," Cabral said one afternoon this past winter in an office overlooking the Folsom Field turf. On Cabral's wall were photos of his former linebackers, guys who'd won national awards, who went on to glory on fields in Detroit and Oakland and Foxboro, Massachusetts. He leaned back in his chair. "It was like he was created to do that one thing," he told me. "You know—" Cabral suddenly stopped, and the room went silent. For nearly a minute, Cabral had a pained look on his face. "You know," he said in a small voice, his right index finger pressed to his lips, "sometimes I wonder if [stun and separate] isn't to blame for this mess. I wonder sometimes if I didn't help do this to him."

After he retired from the NFL, Johnson still felt dizzy and fatigued. His short-term memory was shot. He continued to take Adderall. If, during his pro days, he had been using the drug to get up for the next play, he now was abusing it to get up in the morning. Johnson visited five different doctors, making sure the symptoms he described to them closely matched those of ADHD. Each prescribed Adderall as a remedy. "I became a pretty effective liar," Johnson recalls. "I just had to remember what story I told to what doctor; who was giving me fifty milligrams, who was giving me seventy-five. As long as I kept the stories straight . . ." At one point, his now ex-wife, Jackie, remembers, Johnson consumed a month's worth of pills in two days.

He got a job as a football analyst at a local television station shortly after his retirement, but he had to quit because the lights were too bright and gave him headaches and made him feel dizzy. Worried that his addiction had gotten out of control, in 2005 Johnson checked himself into the first of three rehabilitation centers, where he planned to kick the pills and get answers to the headaches and lethargy that were plaguing him. Treatments, including twelve-step addiction programs, and diagnostics, such as an inconclusive brain scan, failed, leaving Johnson feeling depressed and agitated.

In February 2006, Johnson entered McLean Hospital, ten miles west of Boston. For two weeks, Johnson shuffled from one darkened room to another and met a host of doctors and therapists each day, but, still, he didn't get any answers.

A few months after leaving McLean, Johnson and his wife argued about the prescriptions he was taking. According to police records, Johnson twisted Jackie's arm behind her back and pushed her into a bookcase. She fought back, punching and scratching him. She called the cops, who showed up at the couple's home. The two were arrested, but the charges were dropped when the pair declined to testify against each other.

Regardless of the legal outcome, the damage was done. The pair divorced late in 2006; Jackie took the kids—their oldest, Samantha, was two; their son, Charlie, was less than a year old—and Johnson moved into the Ritz-Carlton in downtown Boston. There, in the darkness of his room, he continued abusing Adderall and briefly used Ecstasy, which he purchased from strangers who immediately recognized him on the street. "I didn't hide who I was," Johnson recalls. "I just didn't care."

Johnson blamed his life's ugly turn on his head injuries, but his closest friends weren't totally buying the story. "There's fallout from his years of playing and the injury, but there became a cloudy area of how much of that was because of the misuse of drugs," his friend Barry Kolano says. "Ted knew and led us to believe it was all from the head injuries. I think he was being dishonest with himself and to us that he needed [the drugs] because of how badly he felt. It became a self-fulfilling prophecy."

Eventually, even Johnson grew tired of the game. He hired his friend Barbara Rizzo to help organize his life, and he planned to detox alone. "For a few months, I was ordering room service three times a day," Johnson recalls. "I wondered what those guys answering the phone thought about me. I was pathetic." Rizzo checked phone messages, returned calls to Johnson's friends and family, and kept in contact with lawyers who were finalizing his divorce. When Johnson didn't answer his door, she'd use a master key, rush to the bedroom, and make sure he was still breathing.

In April 2006, Johnson met Chris Nowinski, a then twenty-seven-year-old Harvard-educated former college football player and professional wrestler whose career had been cut short by concussions. Nowinski made fast friends with Johnson, in part because of their shared fear of what the future might bring. In the darkness of his room, Johnson confided to Nowinski his worries about dying young, about not knowing his kids' faces as he grew older, of living alone, drugged and depressed. Nowinski, who had found something of a mental clearing—a respite from the same worries that consumed him—consoled Johnson. Neurologists, Nowinski said, helped diagnose his own concussion problems. Nowinski now wanted the same relief for his friend, and he recommended several doctors.

One of them, Dr. Robert Cantu, the chief of neurosurgery and director of sports medicine at Emerson Hospital in Concord, Massachusetts, ran film of Johnson's brain. After years of questions, Cantu's work seemed definitive—and frightening. Johnson, the doctor said, had suffered several concussions at the end of his career that grew so devastating in severity that Johnson now had post-concussion syndrome and showed signs of early brain damage that might be permanent. Johnson's symptoms, the doctor told him, were so relentless that by his fifties Johnson could have severe Alzheimer's.

The diagnosis was both liberating and terrifying. Johnson was referred to Dr. Heechin Chae, who eventually directed his patient to the Spaulding Rehabilitation Hospital. Johnson wasn't prepared for what he was about to see. Inside Spaulding, the walls, the floors, everything in the clinic was dull and white and made him uneasy. Some rooms smelled like urine and feces. Most of the patients wore gowns, but Johnson did not. Even if the doctors didn't consider him normal, he at least wanted to look the part. Patients mumbled to themselves in the hallway; one man wore a bicycle helmet. Johnson's roommate was a Marine who'd had an RPG explode next to his head while he was on a mission in Iraq. The man didn't talk and had forgotten how to walk.

Johnson was embarrassed. He was nothing like these guys. Their minds had been wrecked in battle, in car crashes, in things that were far beyond their control. He was just a football player who'd taken too many hits to the head.

Before he began his therapy, Johnson's first task was to run on a treadmill until he became exhausted. The former world-class athlete lasted two minutes.

On a sunny fall morning, two months after he left Spaulding, Johnson and I walked to the Suffolk University campus in Boston where Johnson had an appointment with a career coach/assistant professor. Johnson had had his prescriptions taken away by his doctors and — at the urging of his therapist — had set out to find a job that would give him a reason to get up in the morning. The search was remarkably easy: Johnson had offers to do everything from working for insurance companies to playing golf with high rollers. The only thing that appealed to him was teaching; a friend who taught at Suffolk suggested to the dean that Johnson teach a course on sports crisis management.

As we walked, Johnson seemed nervous. He was dressed in slacks, a white dress shirt, a red tie, and a blue blazer, with the collar unintentionally flipped up in the back. Sweat poured down his face. "Bro, I'm dying here," he told me. We stopped, and he pulled out his wallet. There, from behind his driver's license, he removed a creased index card. He read it quietly. "Number one, go slow. Number two, get the gist. Number three, check your work. Number four, make necessary changes."

Johnson's Spaulding therapist recommended that he keep the card with him at all times, lest he inadvertently sabotage his progress. Two months out of rehab, he'd embraced the changes in his life with the spirit he once used to study his playbook.

"I even have a mission statement," Johnson told me. "My therapist said I needed one. Wanna hear it?" Johnson took a deep breath: "To be a devoted warrior whose love for his family is unmatched and who strives for authenticity at all costs, with the hopes that in my final act I can look back to say I've had a life well lived." With that, he patted my back. "For me, bro, that's *powerful*." The word lingered in the morning air.

Inside one of the brick buildings on the campus, the career coach met us as we got off the elevator and ushered us into a room where another assistant professor was seated at a desk. She was short with graying hair; Red Sox and Patriots pennants hung from the walls.

"You look familiah," the woman said in a thick Boston accent.

"This gentleman is Ted Johnson," the career coach said. "He played for the Patriots."

The woman jumped from her chair. "Oh my gawd! I knew it was you!" She charged, open-armed, toward Johnson. The embrace knocked him backward.

"My sistah was the biggest Pats fan in the world," she said.

"That's great," Johnson said, smiling.

"She was diagnosed with cancer the year before your first Super Bowl win; boy she woulda loved to see that. And you know what? That Super Bowl parade was on the first anniversary that she died. I just know she was smiling that day. Boy, she woulda loved to meet you."

The woman opened her arms again and embraced the linebacker.

"This isn't from me," the woman said. "This is from my sistah."

Johnson gathered the woman in his arms. He turned and wiped away a tear.

Back at his townhome later that afternoon, Johnson hung up his jacket and said he needed a nap. "All that work has my head spinning, bro."

The door opened to a small foyer, and beyond that to a family room and a kitchen with granite counters and a stainless-steel refrigerator. A tin Kokopelli swung a golf club from a windowsill; there was a glass coffee table with sports books, and the walls were lined with dozens of remnants from Johnson's playing career — photographs, footballs, and helmets, one of which was chipped and dented across the reinforced forehead, like a worm had chewed its way through the plastic.

Before he went to his room upstairs, he sat in his leather chair and turned on the television. He pushed some buttons on his remote, and in a few seconds there was Ted Johnson, number 52, taking down running backs and smashing quarterbacks in their ribs. A smile washed across his face. It was a tribute video the Patriots had played on the jumbo screen a few months after Johnson retired.

He settled in. "When I was lying around the house, I'd put this on so I could remember who I used to be. I know that guy is in here somewhere," Johnson said, pointing to his heart. He studied his old self on the screen, breaking through offensive lines and making tackle after tackle. Television Ted blasts a running back—a face full of Johnson's forehead under the chin. "That's what fucked me up," he told me. Johnson watched the hits, staring at the television. The smile evaporated.

In that moment, he was looking back but found himself again faced with his future, with the creeping uncertainty of a life and a mind that had veered terribly off-track. Regardless of his work, his improvements, and the friends who stuck with him, there is a fear —a gripping, stomach-twisting agony—that one day he will not recognize those people, and, maybe even more devastating, that he won't remember the man he now sees on his television screen.

Johnson paused the video. He sat forward, his shoulders square. He pushed Play and watched the hit. Each time he unfroze the video, he'd say, "Boom."

Another running back entered the screen. Johnson paused again before the hit. "Boom." He started and stopped the video for several minutes, again and again and again. "Boom," he said.

Boom.

Boom.

Boom.

Scout's Honor

FROM THE LOS ANGELES TIMES

THE OLD SCOUT doesn't shake hands. The old scout can't shake hands. Phil Pote's sun-baked right fist is so twisted from fifty years of clutching a lineup card and pen that he no longer opens it in greeting. You don't shake hands with the old scout, you bump fists — high, low, head-on — in a three-pronged routine that is only one of the scars.

The old scout has a shuffling gait from years of chasing prospects, deep wrinkled skin cancer from doing it in the sun, declining vision from describing it all in tiny handwritten notes on crumpled paper.

Even more compelling is what he doesn't have.

No wife, no children, no air conditioning in his cluttered, ancient house on a hill near Dodger Stadium, and no more expense account from his bosses with the Seattle Mariners.

During the middle of this week's national high school showcase Area Code Games at USC, the old scout excuses himself from his folding chair to return to his battered convertible parked on a nearby street.

Unable to afford the campus lot, he has to feed the meter.

In what might be his last summer of work, while chasing what might be the last player he signs, the old scout has a warning.

"I'm beat up and broke down," Phil Pote says, laughing. "If you don't slow down, you will end up like me."

You will end up like me.

At first glance, a sad thing, there being nothing more forgotten in baseball than an old scout.

Despite the celebrated baseball practice of collecting, rating, and bartering prospects, the world ignores the guys who sign them.

There are no scouts in baseball's Hall of Fame. There are no old-timers' days for scouts, no midgame video tributes for scouts, no first pitches or last hurrahs.

Once a scout reaches the age of seventy-six like Southland legend Pote, there is no way to retire gracefully, so they simply don't retire.

When you offer to meet Pote at his home, he sets up two folding chairs down the left-field line of a prep baseball game.

"This is my home," he says.

While other scouts are ensconced in bleacher seats in the shade, Pote opts for a better view under the sun.

"It's not about seeing better, it's about hearing better," he says. "I want to hear the ball off the bat. I want to hear the players talk. I want to hear the game."

Yet he says this with a giant hearing aid in each ear.

With a plastic pen, he scribbles. With the greatest of hope for that one final big star, he scouts. With each at-bat, he slowly disappears.

"The game goes on, and everyone forgets the old guys," says Greg Whitworth, the Mariners' area scouting supervisor who works with Pote. "They give their heart and soul and . . . nothing."

Nothing given, it seems, and everything taken.

Pote is asked, even with the added expense, why couldn't you have just talked your way into the campus parking lot?

"Like any old scout, I'm full of b.s.," Pote says. "But I think I dispelled enough of it over the years that there isn't any left."

You will end up like me.

At first glance, a sad thing, then you listen to Phil Pote's encouragement to take a deep breath, sit in one of his cheap folding chairs, and just watch.

Scout the scout, he urges, and so you do.

First thing you notice is, it's tough for Pote to watch a game from his spot down the left-field line because his view is increasingly blocked.

Stretched golf shirts everywhere, scouts leaving the stands and lining up to say hello to him, to thank him, to pump that fist.

And it's never Phil. It's always "Mr. Pote." That, or "the Ancient Mariner."

"If the baseball scouts around here were a city, Phil would be the mayor," Whitworth said. "He has left a lasting impression on all of us."

The second thing you notice is that some of these protégés remember Pote not only for his baseball eye, but his baseball embrace.

Like many scouts, he not only found prospects, he groomed them, spending more than thirty years coaching inner-city Los Angeles baseball in places like Fremont High, Locke High, and Los Angeles City College.

"He would go places nobody else would go," remembers Derrel Thomas, a longtime major leaguer who went to Dorsey High. "He was a great baseball man who wasn't afraid to come in there and help us, and we never forgot him."

During Pote's fifty years scouting for the Oakland Athletics, Dodgers, and Mariners, he signed several notable major leaguers, including Matt Keough, Chet Lemon, and Wayne Gross.

But during that time, he is also proud of the kids he coached, which included Bob Watson, Bobby Tolan, and the late Willie Crawford on Fremont's 1963 City champions.

"This is a man who has spent his life standing up for Los Angeles City baseball," says Shannon Williams, coach of Compton College.

The third thing you notice is that Phil Pote does all of this the hard way.

Unlike virtually every other scout alive, he doesn't use a computer, he has no e-mail address, he has never accessed the Internet. Unlike most scouts, he also doesn't use a radar gun or video camera, nothing but a stopwatch and a stare.

"I came into this world without all that technology, I will leave without it," says Pote.

Also, unlike everyone in all areas of baseball, Pote doesn't work from sundown Friday to sundown Saturday, as he observes his Sabbath as a Seventh-Day Adventist.

"It is a tribute to baseball's tolerance that I've been allowed to hang around so long with such a restriction," Pote says. "I've been very blessed."

Hang around the old scout long enough and realize that it's baseball that has been blessed.

Listen to the story of how Crenshaw's Darryl Strawberry signed his first contract with the New York Mets only after Pote — who didn't even work for the Mets—assured him that he was being treated fairly.

Listen to the story of how Pote's Fremont team wore uniforms with giant numbers because he wanted them to walk into hostile suburban schools with oversized pride.

Listen to how Pote was the voice for local baseball fixture Dennis Gilbert's philanthropic mission to build a stadium at L.A. Southwest College. It is no coincidence that Gilbert also founded the Professional Baseball Scouts Foundation, the leading benefactor of needy scouts everywhere.

Finally, listen to John Young, the founder of the first and most successful national inner-city baseball movement in history, the twenty-year-old Reviving Baseball in Inner Cities (RBI) program.

"Phil Pote was my inspiration for that program," says Young, a former major leaguer from south Los Angeles. "I remember I signed my first contract and I bought a new car and I was cruising around when I ran into Phil."

Pote encouraged Young to give back to the community, Young listened, and the rest is a wondrous bit of baseball history.

"I saw the impact Phil was making, and I realized I could make the same impact, so I went for it," Young says. "None of it would have happened without Phil."

The old scout is still pushing his causes, pushing for scouts to be allowed in the Hall of Fame, pushing for someone to make his baseball movie, pushing for a national council of athletes designed to guide youngsters as he did.

"I don't have much time left," Pote says. "I'm just an old beat-up guy, but I'm hoping somebody will still listen."

On a bright Saturday afternoon at Griffith Park, there is hard evidence that somebody has.

Tacked to the backstop of a green gem of a baseball field is a square wooden sign

POTE FIELD, it reads.

The diamond was dedicated to him about fifteen years ago after city fathers realized the old scout would already be remembered forever.

"The kids come from everywhere to play here, they love this place," a security guard says.

You will end up like me.

One can only hope.

KARL TARO GREENFELD

Stay in the Moment (with Doctor Baseball)

FROM MEN'S JOURNAL

THE PLANE BEGINS ITS DESCENT into western North Carolina. The jet may be private, the flight chartered, and the passenger secluded in maple and leather opulence, but inside he is hurting. He is a ballplayer, a superstar slugger, a master of the diamond, and a statistical monster whose projected totals have his plaque landing in Cooperstown one day if he can somehow regain his form. So now he's making this journey to figure out the source of his pain, his humiliation, his unforgivable fucking up, his letting down his teammates and disappointing his fans: his utter, complete, total, unredeemable, one-million-and-ten-percent suckitude.

The slugger — who when he is right inspires intestine-clenching fear in opposing pitchers — is unused to admitting to anyone his weaknesses, his fears, his dark past, or his depraved present, the psychosis that keeps him up at night, the terror that still has him using Ambien to put himself to sleep. But Harvey Dorfman, the fellow who answered the phone when the star finally mustered the courage to call a couple of weeks ago, said he could help. He told him to come see him.

How long do I gotta stay?
Two days.
How long do we gotta talk?
Six hours a day. But one thing?
What?
You have to be totally honest with me.

When the player enters the terminal, he lays eyes on a narrow, hunched, gimpy-legged little guy with hips soon to be replaced, wearing an oversize U.S. Navy sweatshirt, sunglasses, and a baseball cap. He has thick ridges of forehead wrinkles, jowly cheeks, and a little wattle of skin beneath his chin that flaps as he says hello. When he takes off his sunglasses, his eyes are green and his eyebrows, unlike his hair, are still black. His ears are like bats' wings. He looks like a cross between George McGovern and Mr. Magoo.

This is Harvey Dorfman, baseball's top psychologist, who dishes out common sense, cognitive therapy, and hard-headed discipline to the sport's fragile egos and powerful bodies. He virtually invented sports psychology, though he will insist that he considers some aspects of the field to be, basically, a load of shit. He created the discipline almost by accident, so he is entitled to his opinions. His clients, and there are dozens of them, athletes you watch and cheer for every day as a baseball fan—A-Rod, Halladay, Ibanez, Maddux, to name just a few—say the complete opposite. They say that Dorfman made them who they are today. They say that this journey, this man, saved them.

In the early 1980s, Harvey Dorfman, the one who fixed all these stars, was not exactly a fancy shrink on the Upper East Side of Manhattan, or some psychoanalytic Ivy League hotshot. He was a high school teacher. He lived in Manchester, Vermont, wrote for a local paper, taught English, and coached basketball at Burr and Burton Academy (formerly Seminary). He was, however, a legend in Manchester for having won a state championship, and for his popular sports columns in the *Rutland Herald*. While writing an article on the local minor league baseball team, he became friends with Roy Smalley, then a prospect with the Rangers playing for their local Pittsfield affiliate.

After reaching the big leagues, Smalley kept in touch with Harvey. In 1979 he introduced Dorfman to Karl Kuehl, a coach with the Twins who wanted to write a book about baseball. Kuehl had noticed that players benefited if they were able to push aside their doubts and anxieties about game situations and concentrate on executing, on being completely in the moment, thinking only about the next pitch or swing. Yet almost no one in baseball was looking at this subject. He persuaded Dorfman to join him, and Harvey began to research the psychology of baseball players and how they can get their mojo back.

Dorfman began to visit Montreal and Boston regularly to interview dozens of major league players as they passed through town. It was during this period that he began to formulate his ideas. "I was talking to players about their strategies and their deficits, and I noticed that other players were hanging around, eavesdropping . . . I'm talking to Wade Boggs, and as soon as I'm finished, Bruce Hurst says, 'Hey, I heard what you're talking about. Can you spend time with me?' I sensed there was this hunger, it was suppressed . . . I knew I was on to something."

He began to apply it with Hurst, the left-handed Red Sox pitcher who, after beginning his talks with Dorfman, blossomed into an All-Star. "With Bruce, what I saw was more what he was doing to himself. He would be dealing, keeping it small, executing his pitches, and then the Red Sox would take a three-run lead, and then he would begin thinking, *Two more innings and I've got a win, a shutout,* instead of thinking about the next pitch. Concentration is prepotent. You have to focus on what you are doing right now."

The Mental Game of Baseball, the book that Harvey wrote with Karl Kuehl, is the single volume most likely to be found on a minor league baseball bus. But it makes for slow going for the casual reader. More than once I found myself bogged down in its steady repetition of self-help and Zen platitudes applied to baseball. The philosophy of the book can be summed up in one cliché: it's the journey, not the destination. Players should stay in the moment, focus on process, and let the results take care of themselves. It is *Zen and the Art of Baseball,* with supporting quotes from the likes of Pete Rose, Tom Seaver, and Wade Boggs. Yet players swear by it. Since its first printing in 1989, the book has inspired Talmudic reading and rereading by ballplayers who dog-ear the pages and buy new copies to replace worn-out editions. "Young players today still read that book, the same as when I was a young player," says four-time Cy Young Award winner and longtime Dorfman client Greg Maddux. "I see them and I think, Well, hopefully these guys won't have to repeat the same mistakes I did."

But if all Harvey had to offer was in that book, then he would never have become the go-to guy for diamond-related psychosis.

"The book is great, but it's only a part of it," says sixteen-game winner and current World Series champ Jamie Moyer. "You have to go see Harvey to get the full benefit."

Sports psychology, informally, has been around a long time, probably since some unnamed friend of David lied and said that Goliath was actually terrified of little guys with slings. It has been an academic field since the 1940s, when European psychologists began the formal study of the nexus of emotion and performance. Myriad performers, from Olympic athletes to bicyclists to golfers, have long made use of mental coaches who offered a variety of techniques designed to finesse their charges into the often-described Zen-like state known variously as "flow" or "in the moment." But the insular world of baseball remained, predictably, resistant to such ideas well into the national couch trip that America embarked on during the 1960s and '70s, a golden era of psychotherapy. It was Harvey's genius to meld the then-fashionable ideas of visualization and actualization, of human growth and potential, some aspects of the various Zen-of-sports and Tao-of-sports ideas that were swirling around, with baseball. He understood that ballplayers, like people, sometimes needed to be told that they were good enough, smart enough, and dammit, they should like themselves.

The method he conceived, however, was in direct opposition to the Freudian notion that the way to deal with a person's demons was to bring him back to the source of those fears through psychoanalysis. Dorfman practices a version of Semantitherapy, believing that coming up with behaviors and tools — specific, real actions — to address a subject's fears is more important than the Freudian method of seeking the root cause and then talking about those fears. If a player is, say, afraid of his father, Harvey will urge the player to call his father and tell him to leave him alone. The vast majority of the issues, however, have to do with players getting ahead of themselves in game situations. So Harvey will establish an actual mental and physical routine, starting in practice, so that the player can stay in the correct mental state.

One component of his method is that players be able to visualize their own correct actions and movements in a game situation. Roberto Clemente did this naturally as part of his pregame ritual. "How do you understand through visualization?" Harvey asks rhetorically. "You don't. But you remember . . . Visualization is a picture. When I visualize, I am telling my muscles to remember so that I can make the next appropriate action."

By the time Karl Kuehl was named the Oakland A's farm director in 1983, he and Dorfman already had a good idea of how they might implement their mental approach, and Karl persuaded general manager Sandy Alderson to hire Dorfman as a special instructor. Dorfman recalls the meeting: "They told me, 'Players will run away from you, they will say bad things about you, they'll be afraid of you.'"

Alderson, now the CEO of the San Diego Padres, remembers his decision to bring Dorfman to Oakland: "I was a departure from baseball myself—I was an attorney—so it didn't take much to convince me there were two elements to success: mental and physical. Still, there were people in the organization who were wary of Harvey, especially among the major league coaching staff."

"In those days, you didn't talk about the mental part," Harvey says. "Everything was mechanics. Because if you talked about the mental part, it made you sound vulnerable, because it wasn't macho . . . But anything above the neck, including breathing, was my business."

The forty-nine-year-old cut a curious figure on the major league diamond, with his baggy uniform, sunglasses, and fingerling potato nose. He looked like a middle-aged man who might have wandered off a golf course yet he was ready to challenge a young player with salty talk or to reassure him with fatherly advice. "I had to create a persona," Harvey remembers. "One of not being a Caspar Milquetoast. I had to be a credible figure who was aggressive enough to confront athletes who weren't used to being confronted like that. I blended into the woodwork, and of course, it gave me access to the dugout. I could hear everything that they were saying."

His purview was the entire Oakland organization, major league club, and farm system, which had Harvey traveling throughout the United States, mentoring the players who would eventually form the nucleus of the dominant Athletics teams of the late '80s: McGwire, Canseco, Eckersley, Stewart, Welch, Honeycutt, Weiss, Javier, and others. (One player he didn't work with was Rickey Henderson. "Certain guys don't need my help," Harvey explains. "Rickey has rocks in his head. You can't mess with his approach.") By the time these players had arrived in Oakland, some of them knew and trusted Harvey better than manager Tony La Russa. "Tony was a little suspicious of me, of my relationships with the guys, until it became obvious I would never undermine his authority," Harvey says. "For one thing, it was clear I wasn't in it for fame. To me, invisibility is one of the components to my being successful. I have this line: if any reporter asks me who I am, I just say, 'I'm nobody,' and keep walking." During the season, he traveled with the team and spent a lot of his time with the major league players, taking off for the farm system from time to time to help younger players. During the spring and offseason, he would work throughout the organization, ensuring that struggling players were given a chance to succeed to the best of their abilities, to "get out of their own way."

He was in uniform as a special instructor for four World Series and became an integral part of two World Championship teams, with Oakland in 1989 and, after moving on, with Florida in 1997. His last major league stint was with the Tampa Bay Devil Rays in 1998. He joined superagent Scott Boras's firm, the Boras Corporation, the following year and is still an employee, though he works independently with repeat clients and with players who are referred to him.

His method is as varied as the problems of his clientele. Ballplayers, Harvey notes, are as screwed up as the rest of us. And like the rest of us, their problems can sometimes interfere with their performance. "Self-consciousness will fuck you up," says Harvey. "Function over feeling." See the ball. Hit the ball. Throw the ball. Catch the ball. He has deconstructed each at-bat, for example, and can talk many minutes about the proper and improper uses of the eyes. He can describe the "tendency of eyes to move ahead of objects they are tracking," which makes "eyes jump to the hitting area. They don't track the ball in the middle of the zone," he says, which can lead to an overswing, as the batter is late picking up the ball in the zone. He has written and spoken extensively about the preparations a hitter must make to see the ball. Likewise, he talks with pitchers about executing their pitch no matter the count or the game situation. "I get pissed when he starts talking to the hitters," says Maddux. "What is he talking to them for?"

So here are all these multimillion-dollar platinum egos searching for the psychological underpinnings to their struggle. "For some of these guys, this is the first time they have had to admit they are not the world's greatest expert on themselves. This is their first recognition of their own humanity," Harvey explains. "They've been coddled their whole lives, worshiped in every setting, told they were exceptional, and all along, they were deficit." (Harvey says "deficit" a lot; it is a catchall to refer to any of our shortcomings.) "They were deficit and they didn't even know it." That's when players take the plane trip to Harvey Dorfman's couch.

"He told me it's normal to feel frustrated," says Raul Ibanez, a free-agent outfielder whose career took off after visiting Dorfman. "He told me, 'It's normal to feel the fear, to feel down. It's normal to feel this way.' Not a split-second pause later, though, he said, 'You're not normal; you're a professional athlete' . . . One of my issues was I was concerned about what the manager thought, what the front office thought, what the media was saying, the fans. If I went up and had a bad at-bat, I would think, Oh, they're going to send me to Triple A."

Yet as famous as Dorfman is among baseball people, he has remained largely unknown among the general public. That's no accident: if ballplayers did not trust him to be discreet, they wouldn't come to see him. Harvey, they know, has no ulterior motive. He is not looking to become known as the guy who revamped ballplayers, nor to cash in as some kind of self-help guru. He lives modestly with his wife of forty-nine years, Anita, in Brevard, North Carolina. Harvey says he's in it because he likes ballplayers, and when he sees a kid struggling—and from his seventy-four-year-old standpoint, they are all kids—he genuinely cares. "My priority is the person," he explains, "not the athlete."

Scott Boras first met Harvey when he was representing several members of the late-1980s Oakland A's. "I was fascinated by my initial conversations with Harvey," Boras recalls, "and I saw the results. Right then I knew I would attempt to hire Harvey. It took me a decade to get that to happen. He's tough to negotiate with."

Harvey's value to the Boras organization is both to keep existing clients performing at the top of their game, and to help lure prospective clients, part of what Boras calls his total conditioning package. "This clearly gives us an advantage over other agents," says Boras. "We are the only people representing baseball players who provide psychological services, and we believe that's important, because our job is to get the player performing at optimum levels."

*

The ballplayer winds up here, on this leather sofa, sitting across from Harvey, who is leaning forward from a wingback chair. This is clearly a baseball man's office. There is a glass-fronted cabinet filled with signed balls: Johnny Mize, Lou Boudreau, Van Lingle Mungo. A bookcase is piled with biographies of Cobb, Ruth, and Gehrig, plus *Ball Four* and scores of other baseball books. But there are also hundreds of novels: Gore Vidal, Arthur Koestler, William Styron.

The player looks around the room, at this diminutive man seated before him, and he wants sympathy, he wants understanding. Isn't that why he has come? To be reassured, to be made to feel great all the time, all over, on his insides as well as his outsides? He's not paid $10, $15, $20 million a season because he is shit. So, come on, little man, tell me I'm the frickin' bomb.

Instead, the little man says, "Are you seeing the ball good?"

"Um, yeah."

"Bullshit."

You see, this little man don't work like that. He can tell a guy has a problem before he even calls. Harvey watches baseball every day, and he can tell when a guy is going right and when a guy is hurting.

And the player thinks, What have I gotten myself into? Why am I here, locked up in this little lake house with this cranky old man who seems unwilling to believe anything I say?

"If you were seeing the ball good, you would never have called me."

Harvey is right, of course. The player takes a look around the room, then looks right at the attentive man across from him who is gazing back with big round eyes. Harvey often says, "One week I'm Hamlet, the next week I'm Bozo. You come to me with a certain disposition; I better know who to play . . . I am neither an asshole nor a saint, in totality. I am whatever is required at the moment."

So here he is, gazing back at this superstar, projecting sympathy and parental love. Unload on me, his wide eyes, open expression, and eager posture all seem to urge.

And so the player sighs, and he tells Harvey the truth.

How is it that Harvey can coax an otherwise vain and inarticulate athlete to reveal embarrassing truths? He wrote in a memoir that as "a sickly child, suffering from frequent and severe asthmatic attacks before the age of two, my world was, for the most part, my room—my bed." The young boy, born in the Bronx in 1935, attended school only sporadically; his mother allowed him to while away his days listening to the radio, to Gershwin and Irving Berlin, to radio serials, and, of course, to baseball.

It was then, secluded in bed, that baseball took over his imagination. He developed what he would call "a passive, vicarious involvement." He learned to keep score, to study box scores. The boy was surrounded by grave concern, pills, potions, tubes up his nose and down his throat, poultices to chest and neck, vaporizers, nebulizers in his bed tent, suppositories. The ailing child naturally came to admire hale and hearty ballplayers. "I'm six years old and I'm in bed," says Harvey today, "and I'm counting cars, listening to ball games and music on the radio. In terms of influence, experience isn't what happens to you—the boy in bed, alone—experience is what you do with what happens to you. I am gratified with what I did as a result of my experience."

Slow-footed and gasping, Harvey set out to join the boyhood fray one summer morning. On Gun Hill Road in the Bronx, he found a game of "All Across," where boys run from one curb across the street to the other, until all are tagged and the last one becomes "it." Harvey watched and asked to play. He was welcomed, but told, as any newcomer would be, that he would have to start as "it." Harvey was the quintessential "it," faked out of his Buster Browns.

He does not recall how much time elapsed in such humiliation, but in retrospect it has expanded to fill a disproportionately large amount of neural hard drive. But then, a miracle occurred: two boys taunting Harvey crossed in front of him and collided, one of them falling. Harvey immediately pounced, and pummeled the fallen player. The other players pulled him off, and Harvey burst into tears and ran home. But there had been a breakthrough. For the first time, he remembers, "he was the prey. I had become the hunter." Harvey had become a participant.

From his asthmatic condition, he developed a keen insight into how our fears can define us. "I understood how people limit themselves," he says. "I hitched my wagon early on to that ailing horse, meaning my affliction, and then I started to learn, Don't hitch your wagon to that horse; hitch your wagon to the horse that you want to be."

His own athletic career was a wheezing triumph of his will. He regularly took part in sandlot baseball and football, and majored in physical education at Brockport State Teachers College, where he played goalie for a Co-National Championship soccer team in 1955, all while being excused from running laps or even switching goals when his team was practicing shots.

He graduated with a degree in education and went on to earn a master's in educational psychology before commencing his career as a highly regarded teacher at Wheeler Avenue School in upstate New York, where he would meet his wife, third-grade teacher Anita Wiklund. He then taught at Burrs Lane Junior High in Dix Hills, Long Island, before moving to Manchester and Burr and Burton Academy. He has two children, daughter Melissa, forty-four, and son Dan, forty-two, and three grandchildren.

"This is the last one of these I'm ever going to do," Harvey told me as we sat on his back porch, overlooking the lake and the Canadian geese who were swimming back and forth, jerkily changing direction. He hasn't sat for an interview in almost ten years and is worried that I will portray him as some kind of "self-help guy." He stresses to me that he doesn't actually care how a player feels: "I only care how you behave." Anita comes out on the porch and tells us it's getting cold. Harvey stands up on unsteady legs. He is going in for hip replacement surgery in a few weeks, and the impending trauma has him feeling his age. He says there are a few myths he wants to dispel: one is that he "fixes" ballplayers. "I don't 'fix' guys; I hate that expression. It's like saying I'm a shrink. I'm not a shrink; I'm a stretch. I don't diminish—I expand."

Later, we are seated in his office, watching the playoffs on television. Harvey doesn't root for teams, he roots for players, for guys he's worked with and knows. There's Carlos Pena, the Tampa Bay first baseman and a client. There's Jason Varitek. There's Roy Halladay. All of them have either made the pilgrimage here or have met up with Harvey at some point in their career. Calling all afternoon on the phone are other ballplayers, seeking a little advice or just checking in. Chan Ho Park, Rick Ankiel, Raul Ibanez, and others leave messages on Harvey's machine, asking him to call them back.

We begin talking about why some players need to visit Harvey to become reacquainted with the most basic physical and functional aspects of their professions. "It's because muscles are morons," he says, and by that he means that muscles only do what we tell them to do, so it's imperative for even the most gifted of athletes to tell their muscles to behave correctly—keep the chin tucked in, and so on.

The instruction then radiates outward into the player's whole psyche, and that's when it can get interesting, when secrets and confidences must be revealed so that Harvey can help the player overcome his obstacles. There was the superstar who was afraid to confront his landscape architect about being overbilled. The catcher who couldn't throw the ball back to the pitcher and would make up pretenses to go out to the mound so he could hand the ball over. The slugger who believed the world was conspiring against him, in part because his alcoholic father had abused him. Another player, linked to steroids, who was considering a comeback and admitted that yes, he had been juicing, and now his fear was that without it he would never be any good. The relief pitchers who live in a state of permanent fear. "When Dennis Eckersley made the Hall of Fame," says Harvey, "I called him and said, 'Congratulations, you soiled yourself all the way to the Hall of Fame.'"

The truth, when it finally emerges, brings forth a torrent of tears, of painful confession, of relief, of unburdening. Finally, the player can tell another soul of his hurt. This little man in his sweats—listening, quiet, almost docile, but always respectful—he nods because he understands. He has stood in the locker room and helped a ballplayer pull on his shirt because he was so paralyzed by fear he couldn't dress. He has massaged the shoulders of a Dominican slugger who was homesick and missed his mother. He tells the player, You know what, it's okay to feel all this stuff, you're human, but you also have to perform, because you're a professional.

Harvey always takes stock of the player. "What I have to determine is whether this guy would benefit from an aggressive approach or a lighter hand. I ask a bunch of Columbo questions. 'Tell me what you are going through right now.' You don't ask questions a guy can answer with yes or no; it's always, 'Why?' The guy's like, 'Well, I came to ask you that.' You can tell if a guy is aggressive. If he's aggressive with me, then I can be aggressive with him. If he's lost, confused, intimidated, why would you want to be aggressive with a guy like that?"

And the player, now seated with Harvey out on the back porch, engages this old man, tells him his darkest secrets, and, together with Harvey, starts to see much more than just the ball.

ERIC NUSBAUM

The Death of a Pitcher

FROM PITCHERSANDPOETS.COM

I.

THEY RAN THE BASES for Jaime Irogoyen. His family, his friends,
and his teammates were all there at Estadio Carta Blanca in Juarez,
Mexico, at 11 A.M. on January 17. I like to imagine they were still
dressed up from the funeral; that they came straight from church.
I like to imagine that they filed out of the dugout in their suits and
lined up behind home plate like Little Leaguers.

In my version they all stand silently for a while, unsure of what to
do. There is no pitcher to get things started. No base coach to
windmill them around the diamond. They stand silently in the
quiet sanctuary of the empty stadium. They scratch their heads and
ponder life and death and the way a baseball field can make everything outside its lines or walls or fences disappear. Finally an old
man (maybe a grandparent or a coach) grumbles impatiently; he
knows death well. Let's do something, he says. *Vamanos.*

The first person to run is Jaime Irogoyen's sister. She jogs with
her eyes on the dry clay in front of her, rounding each base perfectly, so that her foot only barely touches the inside corners of the
bags. The old man who grumbled before nods at her technique.
The next mourner runs and the next one. Each waits for the person before to reach first base before taking off. Each runs with his
or her head down so as not to offend the imagined pitcher. After
all, Jaime Irogoyen was a pitcher.

II.

Estadio Carta Blanca was built in the early 1970s, an era of rapid and unregulated economic growth for Mexico. Oil production and manufacturing rose sharply, but rampant corruption and poor fiscal management marred all that. Times that should have been prosperous became trying; as jagged and hard to navigate as the Sierra Madre mountain range that begins just a couple hundred miles southwest of Ciudad Juarez.

The reason for Estadio Carta Blanca's construction was hopeful: the return of big league baseball to Juarez. The city hadn't had a franchise in the top league, La Liga Mexicana, since los Indios de Juarez of the 1930s. Now, after years of second-tier American minor league and Mexican semipro clubs, los Indios de Juarez were coming back. They threw their second first pitch as a franchise in 1973.

Like any expansion team, los Indios struggled their first few seasons. But in 1976, they tied for first in their division. In '82, led by former Dodger and Red pitcher Jose Pena, they won the championship. Celebrations were short-lived. At the end of the '84 season, after two years of hectic swirling rumors, the franchise was sold and moved to Laguna. After just a dozen seasons, seasons that saw a stadium built, a championship won, and a fan base develop, the Indios de Juarez were defeated for good.

But the name of the team, like the stadium, still lingers. Now the name, los Indios de Juarez, belongs to a local university. In the springtime, you can watch the kids play under the lights at Estadio Carta Blanca. You can close your eyes and imagine all the empty bleachers are full of screaming fans from a bygone era. It seems that in Mexico, the institutions of baseball can outlive governments. Regardless of the times, history is echoed through stadium speakers even as it is occurring.

III.

More than seven thousand people have died in Mexico's drug war since 2007. A plurality of those deaths, nearly two thousand of them, have occurred in Chihuahua, the border state in which Juarez is the largest city and Estadio Carta Blanca the largest baseball stadium. The persistent, increasingly macabre march of murder in Juarez is almost cinematic in its over-the top gruesomeness. But this is not a movie. Decapitated heads really are being found in ice chests across the country. Bodies really are piling up in the alleyway behind the Starbucks in Tijuana. Morgues really are overflowing. A *New York Times* headline called Mexico's drug war a "Wild Wild West Bloodbath."

To be sure, not all of the dead have been innocent. Many of the faceless (or headless) corpses belong to corrupt police officers, wily drug-runners, and gutless gunmen. But many more don't. Many are mothers struck by stray bullets, innocents misidentified by flailing cops and soldiers, well-meaning immigrants trekking to America, robbed, raped, and killed by their hired protectors. Some even are students and baseball players.

IV.

There was precious little media coverage of Jaime Irigoyen's death. In the United States, our press has not yet begun putting human faces on the bedlam below our southern border. In Mexico, there are so many dead, so many exceptionally tragic stories, that it is hard for journalists to single them out. Why is Jaime Irigoyen's death more notable than that of any other innocent civilian caught in the crosshairs of anarchy?

From what is available, in both English and Spanish, it becomes possible to piece together a story. Jaime Irigoyen was nineteen years old, a law student at Universidad Autonoma de Ciudad Juarez, and a pitcher for the school's baseball team, los Indios. Judging from available information, he was a good one too. As he got ready for bed on the night of January 12, 2009, that was his reality: baseball, school, girls probably.

But those interests were soon to become historical facts; the kind that are recollected in obituaries and recalled years later by nostalgic relatives. As the Irigoyen family watched television in their Juarez townhome, just miles from the Texas border, a group of masked commandos approached their house and knocked the front door down. They surrounded the family in the living room. "Him with the glasses," a soldier said, pointing at Jaime who sat quietly in just his shorts and socks and those glasses. They dragged him from the couch, gagging him and blindfolding him as his family stood by screaming. Then, with no explanation they took him away.

The soldiers forced his son into an unmarked SUV and sped off down the dark residential streets. Jaime's father was able to follow them at first. But after ten or fifteen desperate minutes, the captors lost him and disappeared into the Juarez night.

Jaime's mother reported that like many of the three thousand soldiers patrolling Juarez on President Felipe Calderon's orders, the men who took her son spoke in southern Mexican accents. But otherwise, the family had no clue as to who they were or why they had come. Her son was merely a student, a baseball player. He was just a good kid.

The next day, with some friends, the Irigoyens staged a protest outside a local military base. Jaime's parents demanded to know the whereabouts of their son. But the military denied any involvement, releasing the following statement:

> That whoever deprived him of liberty were dressed in military-style uniforms in no way says they were soldiers. We call on the general public not to be fooled by criminal gangs.

As if it made any difference to Jaime's family whether the men who took him were soldiers or not. As if criminal gangs were somebody else's responsibility completely, and the military had more important things to worry about. Regardless, it was not long before the Irigoyen family got its answer. Just thirty hours after he was taken, as his family stood outside the chain-link fence that kept helpless desperate people like them from spoiling orderly military procedure, Jaime Irigoyen's body was found dumped on a Juarez street. His eyes were still blindfolded and his mouth was still gagged.

The military never accepted responsibility for Jaime's death, but most in the media have chalked the murder up to a case of mistaken identity. Some speculate that a low-level informant, perhaps under the strain of torture, misinformed some police or military officer. But nobody will ever really know. Nobody but the men in the masks.

V.

The memorial at the stadium did not happen quite as I imagined. The real version is much more organized. Jaime Irigoyen's casket is brought to home plate on the shoulders of his teammates. The teammates, dressed in jeans and their blue caps and jerseys crowd alongside family and friends. There are strangers there, come to mourn the death of a pitcher, the death of potential, the state of a nation so unraveled it could let things come to this. Photographers from local and national newspapers take pictures, and reporters try to make themselves invisible but still get a sense of things.

The bleachers really are empty, and some of the mourners really are dressed up in suits. The service at the church is to take place right after the baseball stadium memorial. Once everyone has spoken, everyone who was going to cry has cried, and every available memory has been shared if not digested, Jaime's teammates lift the casket once again.

They hoist the heavy box upon their shoulders, in it their friend and the idea of their friend and the weight of symbolism nobody can help but feel. They make their way around the base paths; a gesture they realize is cumbersome and ironic. After all, Jaime Irigoyen was a pitcher. But nobody says anything like that.

VI.

December 2, 2008. Forty-six days before the kidnapping.

An editorial by Luis Carlos Martinez on out27.com, a Mexican baseball website, addresses the growing violence in his city of Juarez. He suggests that fans turn to baseball for comfort, for relief. In the column, he refers to a promising young pitcher named Jaime Irigoyen.

> Talk is unavoidable, but in the midst of these violent outbreaks that reign in our city, we must turn to something that offers a more flattering panorama. Baseball continues as an interesting alternative to divert our attention from these lamentable events.
>
> Bullets come and bullets go, but the sport is still king. Those of us who love baseball are convinced that the show must go on, that praying to our Creator, we can remain a part of this baseball family. And through

it all, the various tournaments in all categories and of all ages will continue to unfold throughout our beleaguered city.

Our most recent major tournament went off without a hitch. Behind great work on the pitcher's mound by youngster Jaime Irigoyen, los Indios de La Universidad de Juarez, won the first division at the third annual Hector Molina Interleague Baseball Tournament.

A nation can't let violence get in the way of living, especially when living is sometimes the only thing one can do to escape from the mental prison that violence creates. Bullets come, bullets go, but baseball stays. What other option do we have? Even when those bullets are spraying the infield dirt, splitting bats, and landing in the bleachers, baseball has to go on. Even as war plucks off baseball's innocents and blood seeps over its innocence, it must go on. Even as the clubhouse ranks are thinned, baseball must go on.

Luis Carlos Martinez could never have known that less than two months after his column was published, Jaime Irigoyen, the youngster who led his Indios to victory, would become a casualty. He could have never known that the game he turned to as a refuge from tragedy would soon bear witness to one. Or that Jaime Irigoyen would soon become a story much more prescient than any strikeout or tournament victory. He could have never known that so soon, the only option left on earth would be to run the bases and try to forget.

MIKE SIELSKI

Dream Derailed

FROM THE BUCKS COUNTY COURIER TIMES

DREXEL HILL — There is nothing on or near Harry O'Neill's grave marker that hints at the full scope of his story. He is buried at Arlington Cemetery here, underneath a giant pine tree that shades his stone and softens the heat of a July afternoon. The cemetery is set amid a neighborhood of row houses, not far from the Laundromats and beer distributors that line West Chester Pike, but from Harry O'Neill's grave, past a canopy of verdant trees, there is a clear view of a lovely little street of single-family homes.

"It's a beautiful spot," says one of the directors of Toppitzer Funeral Home, headquartered at the cemetery.

The words on O'Neill's marker provide the rudimentary details of his life: that he was born on May 8, 1917; that he was a first lieutenant in the Fourth Marine Division; that he served in World War II; that he died at age twenty-seven on March 6, 1945. The date of his death offers a small clue about him, for it suggests that he was killed in action. And he was, at Iwo Jima.

What the marker does not mention is this: seventy years ago, on July 23, 1939, Harry O'Neill played his only game as a major league baseball player. More specifically, he played his only *inning* as a major league baseball player, catching the bottom of the eighth for the Philadelphia Athletics in an otherwise unmemorable 16–3 loss to the Detroit Tigers. He never batted that day in Detroit, and he never played in an official major league game again.

If that aspect of O'Neill's story sounds familiar, it's because another player's similar tale has been immortalized in literature and film. In 1982, W. P. Kinsella published *Shoeless Joe* and introduced the world to Archibald "Moonlight" Graham, who played one inning of one game for the New York Giants in 1905 before retiring from baseball to become a doctor. Seven years later, Burt Lancaster played Graham in *Field of Dreams,* the now-famous screen adaptation of Kinsella's book. *Sports Illustrated* recently marked the twentieth anniversary of the release of *Field of Dreams* by calling it "the quintessential moving-image expression of why we love baseball." In fact, the popularity of the film led authors Brett Friedlander and R. W. Reising to write a biography of Graham, *Chasing Moonlight,* that was published earlier this year.

Harry O'Neill hasn't been resurrected as a character in an Academy Award–nominated movie, and he doesn't have his own link on barnesandnoble.com. For being one of two major league baseball players to die in combat during World War II, for his unique journey from Philadelphia to a deadly battle on a faraway island, he has a beautiful spot in a cemetery. That is all. In fact, the shards of Harry O'Neill's story survive still in only a few sources—in dust-covered boxes of microfilm that contain blurry replicas of broadsheets and tabloids, in a Pennsylvania college's archive, and in the fading memories of old men.

Born in South Philadelphia but raised in the Delaware County neighborhood of Darby, Harry O'Neill cut the admirable figure of the All-American athlete. He played three sports—football, basketball, baseball—at Darby High School and at Gettysburg College. By the time he was a senior at Gettysburg, he stood at least six foot two (depending on newspaper reports) and weighed two hundred pounds. In his senior-year photograph in the *Spectrum,* the college's yearbook, he wore a look of wariness on his oval face, his hair swept in a part from right to left and held there, presumably, by a dollop of pomade.

As he had been at Darby High, O'Neill was an excellent three-sport athlete at Gettysburg, but baseball was where he was at his best. During his junior season, 1938, he singled in a run in the ninth inning to beat Penn State, 5–4—an upset as surprising then as it would be today—and "behind the plate, he showed himself to be a heady receiver," according to the 1939 *Spectrum.* He batted .500 in his senior season with six extra-base hits, including a long home run against Lebanon Valley College. He graduated in 1939 and was immediately a major league prospect, and the A's signed him on June 5 for a monthly salary of $4,200.

Al Brancato, who played twenty-one games that season for the A's as a third baseman and shortstop, has only a vague recollection of O'Neill. "I thought he came up at the end of the year," says Brancato, who just turned ninety and still lives in Delaware County. "I'm surprised I don't remember."

At the time O'Neill joined them, the A's were 17–24. They would finish the 1939 season with a 55–97 record, the midpoint of a horrid nine-year stretch in which they never lost fewer than ninety-one games in any season. O'Neill's signing would seem to have been a nice opportunity for some good press and public relations for the A's: here was a local kid signing with his hometown franchise. Why not play him once or twice just for the sake of novelty? But even on a team going nowhere, O'Neill would have to wait forty-eight days before he caught a single pitch.

The game in which O'Neill played was the A's season distilled into nine awful innings. Earle Mack—the son of Connie Mack and the team's interim manager—used nineteen players in the game. By the end of the fourth inning, the Tigers had a 12–1 lead, and James C. Isaminger, who covered the game for the *Philadelphia Inquirer,* pointed out that the 9,772 fans at Briggs Stadium were "enjoying the cool breezes" and their team's easy victory.

Of the reporters from the four Philadelphia newspapers covering the game—the *Inquirer,* the *Daily News,* the *Bulletin,* and the *Record*—Isaminger was the only one who took notice in print that Earle Mack inserted Harry O'Neill into the game to replace Frankie Hayes.

"Harry O'Neill, of Gettysburg, Pa., went behind the plate in the eighth for his major league christening," Isaminger wrote in his game story. "He did not bat and had little to do behind the plate."

With O'Neill catching him, pitcher Chubby Dean walked two Detroit hitters in the bottom of the eighth but did not allow a run. After the game, the A's split into two traveling parties. One went back to Philadelphia. O'Neill was part of the second, which took a train to Cooperstown, New York, to help celebrate "Connie Mack Day" at the Baseball Hall of Fame by playing an exhibition game against the Penn Athletic Club, a semipro team.

The next day, as Pennsylvania Governor Arthur H. James and 3,500 other spectators at Abner Doubleday Park looked on, the A's beat the Penn Athletic Club, 12–6. O'Neill, however, went 0-for-4. Based on that performance, apparently, Earle Mack didn't consider O'Neill worth a second look.

The last man to see Harry O'Neill alive lives in Vineland, New Jersey, in a little red-brick rancher with an American flag flapping in the front yard and Marine memorabilia—caps, photos, metallic emblems—strategically placed around his living room. Private First-Class James Kontes doesn't like to talk much about his experience at Iwo Jima, but he has agreed to share what he remembers about the day O'Neill died.

Three weeks before his brief moment in the majors came and went, O'Neill already had begun preparing for his life after pro baseball. Upper Darby Junior High School had hired him as a history teacher and as its head football, baseball, and basketball coach. After one school year there, he gave the game one last try, playing minor league and semipro ball in Harrisburg. He then enlisted in the Marines in September 1942—less than a year after Japan's attack at Pearl Harbor.

Once he graduated from the Marines' Officer Candidate School at Quantico, Virginia, O'Neill was assigned to the Fourth Marine Division, training at Camp Pendleton, near San Diego. His wife, Ethel, visited him there in January 1944, staying until her husband and the rest of the Fourth Division boarded the USS *Calloway*, bound for the Pacific Theater.

As part of the division's Twenty-fifth Weapons Company, O'Neill followed the fighting from island to island—Kwajalein, Saipan, Tinian—returning to a San Francisco naval hospital for a month after sustaining a shell-fragment wound to his right arm.

"Everybody liked Harry," says Kontes, ninety, who adds that O'Neill didn't often mention his short time as a major league player. "After each operation, we'd come back to the base to get more training and get ready for the next one."

On February 19, 1945, the Fourth Marine Division landed on the black, volcanic sand of Iwo Jima. The Japanese, hunkered down along the beach, were waiting for them. "At the end of the fighting, the American dead totaled 6,821," according to Larry Smith, who authored an oral history of the battle. "It was the only campaign the Marines ever fought in which they took more casualties than the enemy."

The Fourth Division had launched an assault on the morning of March 6, and by the evening, the men had struggled to advance forward through small-arms and mortar fire from Japanese forces. Deep in a crater, as the sun began to set, Kontes found himself next to O'Neill. Neither of them knew a sniper's sight was trained on them.

"We were standing shoulder to shoulder," Kontes says. "Harry was on my left. We were looking out at the terrain in front of us. And this shot came out of nowhere.

"I think the guy must have been in a tree or something. That was their favorite place to shoot from. They got Harry. They took him out because he was taller. He didn't suffer. The corpsman and a couple of guys showed up with a stretcher and picked him up and carried him away."

On May 31, 1945, in her family's modest home at 618 Pine Street in Darby, Harry's mother, Susanna, took hold of a pencil and a small slip of white paper.

Henry Bream, Harry's football coach at Gettysburg College, had contacted Susanna and her husband to offer his condolences over their son's death. Bream's gesture clearly had touched Susanna. In response, she wrote him a thank-you note.

> Dear Mr. Bream,
> Mr. O'Neill and I thank you for your kind words of sympathy.
> We are trying to keep our courage up, as Harry would want us to do, but our hearts are very sad and as the days go on it seems to be getting worse. Harry was always so full of life, that it seems hard to think he is gone. But God knows best and perhaps someday, we will understand why all this sacrifice of so many fine young men.
> It gives us some comfort to know you thought so well of Harry and that he had so many nice friends.
> Sincerely
> Susanna O'Neill

Gettysburg College keeps a copy of Susanna's note to Bream on file in the special collections room of its library. Ethel O'Neill has since died, and she and Harry had no children. So aside from the note, there are only so many people and places left now where one can flush out the skeletal story of Harry O'Neill's life with some flesh and color.

"It should be a big deal," Al Brancato says. "You'd think I'd remember something like that."

Some still do. The *Philadelphia Inquirer* ran a column about O'Neill before Memorial Day. Baseball historian Gary Bedingfield is including a chapter about O'Neill in his upcoming book about professional ballplayers who fought and died in World War II. And the Philadelphia Athletics Historical Society in Hatboro has a black-and-white, 8½-by-11 photograph of O'Neill in its archives, though a scribble of pen across the top misidentifies him as "Henry O'Neill."

It is perhaps the only existing photo of Harry O'Neill in his Philadelphia A's uniform, and there is a bitter irony in the moment that the photo captures. His right foot is twisted and perched on its toes, like a ballet dancer's. His hips have rotated counterclockwise. His right arm has jerked across his chest as if he has thrown a punch. His eyes stare straight ahead, following something in the distance. In the photograph, Harry O'Neill has just done the one thing that he never had the chance to do in the majors.

He has just swung a bat.

RICHARD HOFFER

The Revolutionary

FROM SPORTS ILLUSTRATED

JUST BECAUSE HE WAS from the right side of town (and in little
Medford, Oregon, there was a right and a wrong side), Dick Fosbury was no more insulated from adolescent angst than the next
teenager. He was tall, gangly to the extreme—"a grew-too-fast kid,"
his coach would say—and not good enough at anything he did to
keep above the hallway fray.

Here's how it was at Medford High: Say Steve Davis (right side of
town) spotted Bill Enyart (wrong side), first day of school. He'd
grab Enyart by the neck and turn his collar inside out, exposing
the source of shame right there on the label for all to see. "JC Penney!" he'd howl. And keep in mind, Enyart was the Medford High
fullback, on his way to becoming Earthquake Enyart, an NFL career down the line. Social-class distinction offsets brawn any day.
But do you think Davis would recognize Fosbury's shared aristoc-
racy? (Fosbury's father was a truck sales manager, his mother a secretary.) If Davis caught Fosbury loitering by Fosbury's locker, he'd
punch him in the shoulder.

Medford's bucolic charms—peach and pear orchards spreading
beyond the modest cityscape (population 25,000)—were no con-
solation. Loving parents were great, but not as much use as you'd
think when it came to the ritual humiliation of simply growing up.
Did Dick Fosbury have it made? Of course. Was his every need ful-
filled? Sure. But he was a child of yearning, of insufficient achievement, of bad skin, his talents such that nobody could take him seriously. He was beginning to understand the curse of the bell curve:
he might very well be average. And when his head hit the pillow,

no matter how soft the bed, he was as miserable as the next thirteen-year-old.

Fosbury hoped to play basketball. In fact, being six foot four, he fully expected to. But Medford High was loaded and had six guys who could dunk. (Steve Davis, a bigger and better athlete than Fosbury, was one of them.) Fosbury sat on the bench. His senior year, 1965, when the team went to the state tournament, he remained at home so that more promising underclassmen could gain the experience. He played football, a third-string end (Davis was the primary receiver) until his junior year, when Enyart came up under him during a blocking drill and knocked out his two front teeth. Enyart was his great pal. In the cold of winter, when the coed PE classes would be given over to dancing in the gym, the two would stand together on the sideline, trying to remain invisible, which was complicated by their height. (Enyart stood six foot three.) Come ladies' choice, though, Big Lois would pick Fosbury, and that would be quite a scene, the two of them doing the Freddie, their long arms and legs flapping like hinged two-by-fours. So Enyart felt bad about those teeth.

Fosbury's real love was track. Although he quickly recognized that he wasn't going to amount to much in races, his lankiness was not as big a handicap in the high jump. This was something he could do, sort of. Beginning in the fifth grade he made the high jump his event, using his height and long legs to get a quarter-inch a year out of the antique Scissors jump, the one in which you run at the bar on a diagonal and more or less hurdle it, scissoring your legs over the bar and landing on your feet. The technique had been considered outdated since 1895, when straddling jumps were introduced. Still, Fosbury had gotten as high as 5′ 4″ in junior high, and he'd even won one or two meets a year.

In high school it was a different story. His varsity coach insisted on the Western Roll, in which a jumper also runs in from an angle but kicks his outer (rather than inner) leg over the bar and crosses the bar sideways, usually landing on his feet. Fosbury couldn't get the hang of it. The takeoff foot seemed wrong. The whole thing was awkward. His first competition as a sophomore was an invitational, a meet of perhaps twenty teams, as many as sixty high jumpers involved, and Fosbury failed to clear the opening height of five feet on all three chances. He was going backward! If he maintained this level of improvement, he'd be tripping over curbs. Steve Davis, meanwhile, was clearing six feet pretty easily.

Maybe there comes a time in every kid's life when he confronts his mediocrity and submits to the tyranny of normality. A life without expression: just another guy, not a single trait or talent to mark him in a crowd. Fosbury, all of fifteen now, wasn't there yet. He hadn't been crushed. On a twenty-five-mile bus trip to Grants Pass, Oregon, for a rotary meet with a dozen schools, he stared out the window and decided he was going to do whatever it took, make one last jump. If he finished the year at 5' 4", the same as he jumped in ninth grade, he was done, doomed to a third-string life.

Fosbury reverted to the Scissors for his first jump that day (his coach, sympathetic, had given him grudging permission) and was relieved to clear 5' 4". But that wouldn't be enough. The other jumpers were still warming up, waiting for the bar to be set at an age-appropriate height, while Fosbury continued to noodle around at his junior high elevations. If they, or anybody else, had been interested, though, they might have seen an odd transformation taking place, more like a possession, really. Fosbury was now arching backward ever so slightly as he scissored the bar, his rear end now coming up, his shoulders going down. He cleared 5' 6". He didn't even know what he was doing, his body reacting to desperation. His third round, his body reclined even more, and he made 5' 8".

The other jumpers began to gather; the coaches looked up from their charts. There was something odd about this, crazy even. On his fourth attempt Fosbury took a surprisingly leisurely approach to the bar and—My God! He was completely flat on his back now! —cleared 5' 10". The coaches began arguing. Was this legal? Was it safe? Should it be allowed? What, exactly, had they just seen? The high jump was an event that measured advancement by fractions of an inch, sometimes over a year. Fosbury, conducting his own quiet defiance, had just improved a half-foot in one day.

There have not been many breakthroughs in the annals of personal locomotion. Running forward, for example, is still considered the quickest unassisted way to get from point A to point B. Perhaps early man experimented with backpedaling as a means of escape, but the technique probably did not survive the first saber-toothed tiger. All the important means of fleeing and chasing were established early on, and with a certainty that only life-and-death consequences can provide.

This rather obvious reality has frozen sports—most of which are just highly stylized versions of getting from here to there—in time. If a cartwheel had been the most efficient way for our forebears to leap a chasm, then today's long jump competition would look much different. Some movements are simply beyond improvement.

Consider, then, the Fosbury Flop, an upside-down and backward leap over a high bar, an outright—an outrageous!—perversion of acceptable methods of jumping over obstacles. An absolute departure in form and technique. It was an insult to suggest, after all these eons, that there had been a better way to get over a barrier all along. And if there were, it ought to have come from a coach, a professor of kinesiology, a biomechanic, not an Oregon teenager of middling jumping ability.

And yet Dick Fosbury was the perfect, maybe the only, vehicle for innovation when it came to the high jump. All athletes recognize a performance imperative, a drive to exceed their limits, to explore upper boundaries. It's why they train and tweak. But Fosbury had the additional impetus of being a teenager. There is no swifter, more terrible saber-toothed tiger than the ritual humiliation of adolescence. He felt that animal's breath on his neck every day, and he felt it more keenly than his peers: he had picked the one sport that might return the favor of his determination but had gotten embarrassment instead.

In sport, the rarest kind of innovation is true, elemental change. The catalog of tinkering, or invention, that has produced substantive departures in form is slim indeed. Candy Cummings's "skewball" in the 1860s, the progenitor of the curveball? Notre Dame's forward pass in 1913? Paul Arizin's jump shot in the 1950s? The core movements of athletics, grounded in so much human history, do not easily, or very often, yield to change. Modern sports are somewhat amenable to improvement, but the rewards of experimentation diminish in proportion to the antiquity of the event. And few are older than the high jump.

Ancient though it was, the high jump at least seemed agreeable to experimentation. Jumpers found that they could throw themselves over the bar, more or less forward, by tucking their takeoff legs under their bodies. The Eastern Cutoff (which combined the Scissors motion with a headfirst approach), first seen in 1892, gave way to the Western Roll in 1912. By 1930 the last great change had occurred, although it was only a change by degrees. Now jumpers, still flinging themselves over headfirst, did not tuck their legs anywhere but stretched them horizontally. The facedown technique —like throwing your leg over a saddle—became known as the Straddle and produced another inch or two in height.

And that, except for some fooling around with run-up speeds and arm movements (the Russians were particularly good at putting all these little elements together, winning Olympic gold in 1960 and '64), was where the event remained until Fosbury's day. All jumpers used the Straddle. It was the only way to go.

When Fosbury jumped 5' 10" at that rotary meet at Grants Pass in 1963, he was in a back layout position, his shoulders going even farther back in reaction to his lifting hips. It was on-site engineering, his body and mind working together, making reflexive adjustments with only one goal, getting over the bar. In an act of spontaneity, or maybe rebellion, he created a style unto itself.

Fosbury's coach, Dean Benson, was not about to insist that he give up six inches on account of tradition. The improvement was too sensational. The next season, his junior year, Fosbury continued to refine the jump. His arms and legs were still all over the place, but what looked like an airborne seizure was actually Darwinian activity. Those tics and flailings that served to get him even a quarter-inch higher survived. The rest were gradually pared away. During that next full year of his upside-down layout, Fosbury began to lean with his shoulder, about forty-five degrees to the bar, and broke the school record of 6' 3". By his senior year he had introduced a curved approach, turning his back to the bar, completing the rotation, arching, lifting his hips, and kicking his feet clear in a final motion. He finished second in the state, now able to clear 6' 5½", well ahead of Steve Davis.

Fosbury was gaining attention, but more as a novelty than as the next new thing. In 1964 a photographer captured this craziness, and the shot went around the world, Des Moines to Johannesburg. "World's Laziest High Jumper" was the caption in one newspaper. A better caption, appearing under a staff photo in the *Medford Mail-Tribune,* was "Fosbury Flops over the Bar." A reporter returned to the phrase in a meet story, saying Fosbury looked like nothing more than a fish flopping into a boat. Fosbury was tickled by the connotation of failure. He was a contrarian at heart. The Fosbury Flop was born.

You might ask, If this was a far superior method, why hadn't somebody invented it before Fosbury? First, it wasn't necessarily a far superior method. For some past champions, it might not have been the least bit superior. But for a certain kind of jumper, one who just couldn't combine all the elements of conventional technique—a fast run-up, exaggerated arm action, or, more important, the straight-leg kick at takeoff that seemed to lift the jumper over the bar—Fosbury's new method might be more rewarding. Fosbury was a bent-leg jumper. In his upside-down leap it didn't matter where his legs were, as long as they kicked free at the end.

As to why nobody had come across this before, well, somebody had. In 1959 Bruce Quande, a kid at Flathead County (Montana) High, had started with the Scissors and had gradually rolled it over. Just like Fosbury. But Quande was not driven the way Fosbury was—the best part of being on the track team for him was stopping for ice cream on the trip back from meets—and he never made much of it. Nobody did.

There was good reason for that. Completing the Flop successfully was only half the battle; the return to earth still had to be negotiated. Few would even consider such an experiment in flight knowing they'd have to land on their necks. During Fosbury's sophomore year, the landing pit was only a pile of wood chips and sawdust. It was safe but not comfortable. By his junior year, though, his school had installed a foam pit, and the idea of a head plant, while still daunting, was a bit more palatable.

Still, even with a jump named after him, Fosbury was mostly unknown and mostly unwanted. Even after finishing second at the state meet in his senior year, college coaches were not calling. It wasn't discrimination, just performance. Not until the summer after graduation, when Fosbury won the national junior championship with a jump of 6' 7", did he get the first call. Berny Wagner, the new coach at Oregon State, took a chance on Fosbury and got him a small scholarship. That was all Fosbury was looking for anyway, an education, a chance at an engineering career. If the Flop could help get him a degree, it would have done its job.

Wagner knew Fosbury had jumped 6′ 7″; he just didn't know how. The coach wasn't hidebound, but he wasn't going to encourage something as crazy as the Flop. Let's get back to the Straddle, Wagner said. "You're the coach," Fosbury said. "You line out a program, and I'll follow it." But the Straddle didn't work for him in college any more than it had in high school, and he regressed. Wagner had taken a 6′ 7″ jumper and turned him into a 5′ 6″ stumbler.

So Fosbury began flopping in meets. It was strictly a face-saving maneuver. What did Wagner care, anyway? He had since acquired a couple of bona fide Straddle jumpers, and his investment in Fosbury was small enough not to trouble him further. But finally something happened. In the spring of Fosbury's sophomore season, Wagner took him to a three-way meet in Fresno. Using the Flop, Fosbury jumped 6′ 10″, not only an increase of three inches from the season before but also an Oregon State record. Wagner took him aside after the meet and said, "Okay, that's it. I'm not sure exactly what you're doing, but it's working for you. So stick with it, I guess."

Sports can be generous like that, overruling biases in favor of results. With wins and losses at stake, Wagner hedged his bets. By the end of the season he was teaching some of the other jumpers how to do the Flop.

Except for the fact that nobody could teach him any of the historical methods of jumping, Fosbury was extremely coachable. When Wagner told him he needed more conditioning, Fosbury ran and hopped the eighty-three rows in Parker Stadium. You couldn't appeal to tradition with Fosbury, but you could fire his competitive neurons. That was something else about him, that need to win. Fosbury was not intrigued by benchmarks. In fact, after his event was won, he never continued jumping just to set a record. "He jumps against people, not heights," Wagner said.

At the end of his sophomore season Fosbury placed fourth in the college nationals but was still not a world-class high jumper; he was maybe in the top twenty-five in the United States. But he was at least gaining renown for his style. Meet promoters who got a look at the Flop began inviting him to their events—the Oakland Indoor, the San Francisco All American Games. They didn't care how high he jumped, just how much hype he could generate. And the press loved it. A *Los Angeles Times* headline: "Beaver Physics Student to Show Unusual Jumping Form Today."

Since Fosbury hardly ever practiced the Flop ("There's no use wearing myself out," he said), the additional meets offered yet more opportunity for improvement. With higher grades of competition he was literally raising the bar on his event. In Oakland he cleared seven feet for the first time. *Track and Field News* put him on its cover in February 1968, as much to herald a format change for the magazine as a sea change in the high jump.

As a junior Fosbury became the country's most consistent seven-foot jumper. He won the 1968 NCAAs with a jump of 7′ 2¼″. Up to then the attention he had been getting was for the character of his jump, not its magnitude. Fosbury had found it amusing to supply feature writers with a variety of origin myths, telling some he'd graphed out the Flop on paper first, others that he'd stumbled backward on his takeoff. But now, with these kinds of heights, it was getting more serious. "So, Dick," a sportswriter asked him, "any plans on going to the Olympics?" Fosbury had never registered that ambition, and he'd never been to a single international meet. Could his first be an Olympics? Wild!

Avery Brundage, president of the International Olympic Committee, had come back from the Little Olympics, a fact-finding meet in Mexico City in 1966, and proclaimed the site of the '68 Summer Games safe. "I have seen the runners at high altitude," he announced, "and no one fell down dead." As reassuring as this was, members of the U.S. Olympic Committee decided on a program of altitude acclimation closer to the actual Games.

And so male track and field athletes were gathered at South Lake Tahoe, California, in early September 1968 and asked to breathe air at a Mexico City–like elevation of 7,370 feet. Some of the men who showed up thought it might as well have been for the scenery, maybe a little tuning up, but certainly not to make the team. They had done that in the last week of June, when they qualified at the Olympic trials in Los Angeles. According to the rules, at least as far as anyone understood them, the top ten or twelve from each event in Los Angeles went to the high-altitude camp for further winnowing, but the winner had automatically qualified for the Olympic team. So they thought.

After winning the NCAA championship in mid-June, Fosbury had gone 7' 1" to win the high jump at the trials. He had returned to Oregon, goofed off a bit, then packed his bags and set forth for Lake Tahoe in his Chevy II, no hurry. But upon checking in he learned that his spot on the U.S. team was up for grabs after all. The USOC had decided that the sea-level trials at Los Angeles might be a poor predictor of success in Mexico City. Even the winners would have to qualify anew. Fosbury felt a panic rising in him.

He was jumping erratically—"Hit-and-miss," he said—and the competition was bunching up around him. Fosbury needed all three tries to make 7' 2", at which he joined Olympic veteran Ed Caruthers, high schooler Reynaldo Brown, and John Hartfield. But because of his misses, Fosbury was in fourth place. Hartfield, without any misses, was in first. Since none of the four had ever jumped 7' 3", it was unlikely that the standings would change. Hartfield could not lose, and Fosbury could not qualify.

The bar was lifted an inch, which might have been a foot as far as they were concerned. But the weather was warm, and the juices were flowing. Caruthers, running ever so slowly, straddled the bar, just ticking it, but making it over safely. Brown likewise touched the bar on his attempt but also made it. Hartfield missed. Fosbury corkscrewed over the bar cleanly and came up out of the foam pit grinning madly.

But he hadn't made the team yet. Hartfield could still close him out on misses if he made the height. As Hartfield lined up, though, Fosbury's coach had a sudden inspiration. Since 7' 3" would have been an Oregon State record, Wagner asked to remeasure, so that it would qualify. Hartfield didn't notice this and started for the bar, stopping only when he saw the congestion of officials under the standards. It shook him up.

After the officials finally cleared out, Hartfield missed his remaining jumps. It was over. His sure trip to Olympic glory had just been canceled, and he ran into the woods, disappearing into a thick stand of Ponderosa pines. It was years before Fosbury saw him again.

Gary Stenlund was a good man to know at an Olympics. He'd arranged for friends to bring his VW bus down to Mexico City. It was a 1965 camper, a cream-colored pop-top beauty, perfect for the escapades he had in mind. When Stenlund and Fosbury toured the city, beer cans rattling in the back, it was usually in the company of two young women—former swimming gold medalists, as a matter of fact. Stenlund had laid that groundwork back in South Lake Tahoe. He was basically a one-stop party, Stenlund, anticipating all the requirements of fun.

Fosbury was not in Stenlund's league when it came to partying, wasn't even in the same sport. Stenlund's event was the javelin, but he liked to boast he was a decathlete when it came to the consumption of spirits. He was twenty-eight and had been hitting them hard for ten years, even while competing at an elite level. He could drink a case of beer, or a gallon of wine, or a fifth of whiskey, and throw the javelin 260 feet the next day. Often, anyway. When it mattered, he could cut back. The night before finals qualifying in Mexico City he held himself to only four beers, although as it turned out —he finished seventeenth—he might as well have drunk his full schedule.

But the days leading up to the Games were a good time to have wheels and women. There was plenty to explore, and the people were so hospitable, so friendly. Mexico City was dedicating itself to the amusement and amazement of its visitors, and you would have been a very poor guest to ignore such an offer.

An event that the guys and gals of Stenlund's camper definitely wanted to see was the arrival of the Olympic torch at the Pyramid of the Moon, thirty miles away in the pre-Columbian ruins of Teotihuacán. Mexican organizers had used some imagination in designing the ritual torch relay, choosing the paths of early explorers such as Cortés. On Saturday, Mexico's torchbearer, Enriqueta Basilio, a twenty-year-old hurdler, would carry the flame up the steps to the cauldron in the Olympic Stadium and start the Games. But the Friday-night ceremonies at Teotihuacán, Mexico's first great city, offered considerably more authenticity.

The Pyramid of the Moon is located on the Avenue of the Dead, but it was a very lively place when Stenlund and Fosbury and the girls got there. Tens of thousands of Mexicans had gathered at the pyramid for song and native performances. (There were 1,500 brightly costumed dancers on hand.) The four Americans ate chicken tacos and bean soup, drank the local beer, listened to the mariachis, and settled in for the arrival of the torch. This was not going to be just another stop for the sacred fire either; Sylvania had rigged the site with 1,900 flashbulbs, and the instant the runner lit the flame, the entire pyramid would light up. When the runner bent his torch to the cauldron, it was like a lightning strike. Stenlund, Fosbury, and the women were thoroughly seduced by the scene and decided to stay there the night, at the base of the ancient pyramid, under the stars.

Back in Mexico City, meanwhile, all roads within a mile of the Olympic Stadium were closed to everybody but officials, taxis, and buses for the opening ceremonies. But even sanctioned traffic exceeded the event's parking capacity. Cars and buses were simply abandoned as close to the destination as possible. Try as he might, Stenlund could not get his group to the ceremonies. He beeped his little horn and maneuvered as best he could, but it was no use. He and Fosbury and the girls laughed all the way.

Ed Caruthers was nineteen years old at the 1964 Olympics, and he was without a coach or friends in Tokyo. About all he could do was rattle around the athletes' village. He played some Ping-Pong, but mostly he hung out in the dining room. He had three weeks before his event, and it seemed forever. So what if he was going back and forth to the ice cream machine? What else did he have to do?

Caruthers gained ten pounds, and even if the weight was distributed invisibly along his six-foot-five frame, it was quite a disadvantage. Jumping over a bar set at 7′ 1″, which he had been doing that season, tops in the country, was never easy. Doing it with the equivalent of a Thanksgiving turkey tucked under his arm might be impossible. Despite a crash diet of breakfast cereal in the final days before his event, Caruthers could not return to form, and he jumped almost three inches beneath his personal best to finish eighth.

At least Caruthers could return for a second Olympics still very much in his prime. This time he would know better than to subsist on soft-serve ice cream. But the Olympics are subject to a terrible serendipity and do not always yield to determination. Caruthers would find that self-sacrifice, at the dairy bar or anywhere else, would count for little and that at the Mexico City Games, in a year that honored idiosyncrasy above all else, even the jump of his life wouldn't get him gold.

Because who could have anticipated Dick Fosbury? Caruthers had first seen him at the NCAA championships in 1967, employing a "goofball kind of thing" to get over the bar. He had not been impressed. But at the Los Angeles trials the next year, when Fosbury won with a leap of 7′ 1″, Caruthers was obliged to take notice. *Sport* magazine called Fosbury "our best bet" to win the Olympic high jump. But tradition always prevails, and Caruthers liked his own chances. After all, he'd won the trials in Tahoe, the ones that counted.

In Mexico City, Caruthers was mindful of diet and nutrition, and Fosbury conducted preparations that were almost daffy in comparison. He and Stenlund were always tearing around the city. They liked to rumble up to the Hotel del Ángel off Reforma Boulevard, where they'd go to the penthouse bar and hang out with the ABC crews. They'd sit at the feet of Howard Cosell and Jim McKay and absorb their stories. As far as training went, well, Fosbury had his own program.

The one thing he didn't like to do in practice was jump. He was a dedicated athlete, but he simply did not believe in jumping without proper incentive, or even atmosphere. It was only in competition, with the adrenaline flowing, that Fosbury could make a jump that mattered. And the crowd: he required attention to perform. In practice, with nobody watching him and nothing on the line, it was all he could do to make a few desultory repetitions.

Wagner had made the trip to Mexico City and insisted that Fosbury jump at least once. "Look," he said, "you've got a month here, you're getting rusty, you gotta do something." So Fosbury put off his adventures with Stenlund for a day and went to the practice field for a quick session. He just went through the motions until a rainstorm rolled through, forcing everyone to run for cover. Under a tarp he found himself shoulder to shoulder with Valentin Gavrilov, the Soviet Union's number-one jumper. They nodded, then engaged in a stumbling conversation. Gavrilov was the enemy, not only in sport but also in every way possible. Because of Gavrilov's government, Fosbury had had to duck under his school desk for air-raid drills. He'd had to worry about nuclear clouds poisoning his family. Yet there they were, chatting away, Gavrilov in his halting English, about events in Mexico, conditions at the athletes' village, everything. The storm cleared out after an hour, but Fosbury and Gavrilov, mortal enemies, remained under the tarp a while longer, chewing the fat.

Saturday night, the eve of the high jump finals, was not restful for Fosbury. He was still worked up from the qualifying rounds earlier that day, which chopped the field down to a dozen finalists. He visualized his jumps over and over. The nocturnal filmstrip played across his eyelids, keeping him awake.

Sunday was a perfect clear, crisp October day, temperature in the midseventies by 1 P.M., when the high jumpers filed onto the infield. The Olympic Stadium was full, eighty thousand fans on hand for the Games' track and field windup. Besides the high jump, there were two men's relays, the 1,500-meter race, a women's relay, and the marathon. It was going to be a wild day, though nobody could have guessed how wild.

Poor Ed Caruthers. He had a plan—usually important but, in an Olympics, likely irrelevant, perhaps laughable. Caruthers figured on a jump of 7' 3", maybe even 7' 4", an Olympic record, by his fifth pass, and he'd have his gold. What he didn't consider was the size of the field, which included many lesser jumpers, guys who had no shot but filled out the finals. To accommodate their numbers, the competition was begun at a height of 6' 6", four inches lower than Caruthers's planned entry point. To get even there was taking forever.

Fosbury, on the other hand, had no grand plan, hoping to start at 6' 8" and to increase his height two inches at a time to seven feet. It was slow going as the field remained intact nearly to that height. Then, at 6' 11½", it started to thin; five failed to clear. Everybody else made the next height, 7' ¼", but Caruthers needed all three tries while Fosbury made it on his first attempt. Caruthers, Fosbury, and Brown, the other U.S. jumper, passed at 7' 1", while Italian and West German jumpers could not scrape over and left the competition. It was now a Cold War showdown, three Americans and two Soviets, the way the Olympics were meant to be. The bar was set at just under 7' 2". The sun was getting lower, and the fans were starting to get interested.

Fosbury cleared the bar cleanly. When he jumped, though, the spectators laughed. Brown missed on all three tries, as did the Soviet Union's Valery Skvortsov. Gavrilov passed. Caruthers, having missed his first two tries, stared at the bar on his third attempt and flew over it by a full two inches.

Only the three medal winners remained to sort out the podium order. The sight of Fosbury, rocking back and forth on his heels the entire two minutes allowed for his approach and then exploding over the bar upside down, was now generating a lot of excitement. As he came to look more like a champion and less like a circus clown, the crowd's giggles were replaced by cheers. Few fan favorites ever developed in less time.

All three jumpers made 7' 2½" on the first try. Now, at 7' 3¼", the bronze medalist was determined. As the men's 4×100 relay teams wandered through the jump area, Fosbury took his stance, rocked back and forth, and dived over. The crowd went wild. Caruthers made it on his second try, but Gavrilov, Fosbury's new buddy, could not clear, and he was out.

It was nearly twilight, four hours into the competition. Shadows were touching the outside of the track, and the air was cooling. Caruthers's strategy was now "out the door," he said. Fosbury had yet to miss a jump, and Caruthers knew that having had to make ten attempts to Fosbury's six, he was fading. The crowd had swung entirely to Fosbury. "The press, usually reserved even at these emotion-charged Olympics," reported *Track and Field News,* "cheered at his every jump." The *Los Angeles Times*'s Jim Murray was agape at the journalistic gift that was being handed to him. "Fosbury," he wrote, "goes over the bar like a guy being pushed out of a 30-story window." A German writer exclaimed, "Only a triple somersault off a flying trapeze with no net below could be more thrilling."

The bar was set at 7' 4¼", not a world record but a U.S. and Olympic record, a touch more than either Fosbury or Caruthers had ever cleared. Fosbury's heels ticked the bar on his first attempt, for his first miss of the competition. Caruthers missed too. Fosbury missed again. Caruthers missed. The fans were on their feet.

For his third attempt Fosbury went through his usual deliberations—that interminable rocking back and forth, the wiggling of his fingers—eating up the allowable two minutes. He used this time not only to psych himself up but also to review the mechanics of the jump, which required untold adjustments as he converted horizontal force into vertical. He was always fighting his takeoff, which threatened to turn his pass into a long jump instead of a high jump. He rocked, and the fans counted with him, "One, two, three," and kept counting. "Forty," they chanted, "forty-one." Fosbury thought just a little more and then, satisfied with his preparations, began his looping jog to the bar.

As he did so, the first marathoners entered the stadium. Usually this is a moment of catharsis. The runners' appearance, which is always a surprise, touches off what is generally the biggest cheer of the Games. But not this time. The marathoners got just a smattering of applause. The crowd was devoted to the gangly guy floating upside down.

Fosbury veered off, threw his left shoulder to the bar, and lifted, peering sideways over that shoulder. He was registering everything now: the eerie quiet of the stadium, the slight whoosh of his shorts, the clap-clap-clap of the marathoners as they worked their way to the finish. The air really was thin up there. Fosbury watched the bar glide under him, completed his ideal parabola, and crashed backward onto the Port-a-Pit. From the foam landing he could look up and see that the jump was clean, but he hardly had to witness it for himself. Some eighty thousand people had already told him it was good: "Olé!"

Fosbury sprang out of the pit, flashing a victory sign and a wide grin. U.S. marathoner Kenny Moore, entering the stadium on his way to a fourteenth-place finish, looked around, trying to understand the crowd's sudden reaction. What was going on? Seeing his friend Fosbury loping around, his hands high, Moore understood. Continuing down the straightaway, he began dancing a jig.

Less happy was Ed Caruthers. His only chance at a gold medal had been for Fosbury to miss and for him, jumping next, to make the height. That couldn't happen now. Even if he made the height —he debated passing, moving the bar up a notch—it had been settled on misses. He took his turn all the same. He brushed the bar on his way down, knocked it off, and lay in the pit for minutes, realizing he'd have an altogether different life from the one he'd imagined for himself, that difference made by a half-inch.

Fosbury and Stenlund stuck around Mexico, but just as they had missed the opening ceremonies, so did they miss the closing. The two of them, along with the two women swimmers they'd camped out with in Teotihuacán weeks earlier, set off in Stenlund's VW camper for a resort in the mountains. Fosbury was tired of the attention, exhausted from being asked his opinion, his reaction, how he named his jump. He was glad to be somewhere with a pool and a few beers and some pals with whom to enjoy them.

Fosbury's new status as an Olympic champion, coupled with his determined idiosyncrasy, made him a national hero of sorts. When he went home to Medford, a ticker-tape parade was held for him, but because there were no buildings taller than two stories, kids had to run alongside his car to shower him with confetti.

He went on *The Tonight Show* and tried to teach Johnny Carson and fellow guest Bill Cosby how to do the Flop. (Performing in dress shoes, he memorably slipped on his own try.) He went on *The Dating Game*. But his heart wasn't in it. It wasn't even in the high jump anymore. He competed for Oregon State for one more season, but it was a forced march, satisfying an obligation to his school. As soon as he completed the season, finding enough fire to win the NCAAs again, he quit the sport and rededicated himself to his engineering studies. All he'd wanted in the first place was a degree.

Meanwhile, Stenlund cruised through the rest of the '60s and into the '70s in his VW camper, high as could be. He says he went seven years without cutting his hair, taking the camper on cross-country trips, Ken Kesey style.

One night, "stoned and tripping," Stenlund says, he rolled that van in an Ohio cornfield. There was nothing he could say to the cops, especially as he was nude, except for a black sheepskin seat cover. In later years, it must be reported, Stenlund sobered up, stayed sober, and returned to track and field, competing in USA Masters events. But that was it for the camper.

S. L. PRICE

The Ever Elusive, Always Inscrutable, and Still Incomparable Bobby Orr

FROM SPORTS ILLUSTRATED

Of COURSE THE PARENTS try to stay cool. But when the phone rings and that voice says, "This is Bobby Orr . . . ," some can't help themselves. "No!" they'll say, or giggle and talk too loud: just the idea of telling the cousins, the folks at work, *You won't believe who called last night,* is enough to get the nerves jangling.

Still, this is their boy's future at stake, so they usually recover and manage a few hard questions, and then the conversation will start sailing along and, *Why, he's just so easy to talk to, so down-to-earth, like everyone said,* and soon it's just two people gabbing, no starry-eyed stuff until the voice says something about coming by to talk a bit more. Then it sinks in: *Come by? Him?* And, still listening, now there's this quick scan of that family room in Thunder Bay or Hull or whatever Canadian town happens to have produced the next raw piece of hockey talent, a desperate glance at the stains on the coffee table, the drapes that long ago needed replacing . . . *Here?*

"It's unbelievable," says Barbara Tavares, mother of top Canadian junior John Tavares. "Your legs are like jelly."

Bobby Orr—for many the greatest hockey player ever, the defenseman who altered the essence of the game—has been making his living as an agent for thirteen years now, and he's become, as celluloid agent Jerry Maguire put it, good in the living room. He and partners Paul Krepelka and Rick Curran incorporated his Orr Hockey Group in 2002 and have built a clientele of thirty-three active NHL players (fourth most of any agency) that includes Ottawa center Jason Spezza, Carolina's Eric Staal and Cam Ward, and Philadelphia forward Jeff Carter, who last June signed a three-year, $15 million extension. Neither lawyer nor marketing expert, Orr leaves negotiations to his partners, serving as all-around adviser, player counselor, exemplar, and conversation stopper. "We were talking to different agents, but once I met him, my decision was pretty much made," Spezza says.

Who, after all, could better understand the pressure of becoming a national darling at fourteen, the psychic toll exacted by injuries, the threat of business "advisers" ever ready to sink their teeth into an athlete's balance sheet? Who better to remind overpaid kids of their responsibilities to their talent, teammates, and public?

Indeed, "Bobby Orr: Agent" might make perfect sense, except there's simply no precedent for a generational icon to enter this long-derided trade and even less reason to think the fiercely reticent Orr would be the first. Even now, it's no secret that he regards player representation as a generally dirty business; in 1996, when Orr began working as an agent, the irony was lost on neither friend nor foe.

"I found it hard to believe," Alan Eagleson says.

Yet here Orr is, despite — or perhaps, because of — the fact that Eagleson, the fallen power broker whose hockey empire grew out of his role as Orr's agent, left him all but broke as part of one of sports' most spectacular financial scandals. Here Orr is, knees and fortune rebuilt, sixty years old and rounding a corner in 2009. He has now been an agent for longer than his run as an NHL star and with his clientele growing and his firm embroiled in a big-time fee dispute with Islanders goalie Rick DiPietro, Orr is playing hardball. And on his terms: all agents alternate between vocal advocate and secret-keeping consigliere, but Orr has taken the public-private shuffle to new extremes, keeping his face before the Canadian public in TV ads that highlight his self-deprecating humor and that eternally boyish Bobby-ness, while keeping any thoughts on the league, his business, and his life under tight wraps.

Orr hasn't given a substantial interview in nearly two decades and doesn't need to. Thirty years after the Boston Bruins retired his number 4, the hockey world is still dazzled by the magic of his name: parents will always take his call, team execs and coaches who played against or idolized him will always agree to meet. And once inside, Orr works to defuse any hero worship. He'll giggle and tell jokes at his own expense, recall how it was for him to be young and homesick and crying, how it felt rising so fast. He'll steer the conversation to what he can do for your boy. Sometimes, though, the family will want a little more. And when, in the case of a prospect like Spezza, whose Canadian junior career nearly matched Orr's for bated-breath mania, a cocky little brother pipes up at the dinner table, "I bet you can't score on *me!*" well, sure, Orr will take that bet: ten shots, score fewer than five, and the kid wins.

So it was that, in the fall of 1998, eleven-year-old Matt Spezza found himself scrambling down to the basement in his Mississauga, Ontario, home to strap on goalie pads, gloves, and mask. Finally Orr pushed away from the table, hobbled downstairs in his golf shirt and slacks, and picked up one of Jason's sticks. He flipped the first two shots up, easy to block, but Matt was cocky and started taunting the man who scored 296 goals, the player known in practice to gather a puck off the ice as if with a spoon and with back to the goal swat it on a line into the top corner of the net. "Is that it?" Matt said. "Come on, let 'em go."

It happened fast: *Boom, boom, boom.* One low, right under the glove, then another and another; everybody laughing, but the room getting warm. "You could see it," Matt says. "He could put it wherever he wanted." Then, as quick as it came, the moment passed. Orr eased up, let the kid knock away the last pucks and win by one, done with remembering what Bobby Orr could do.

"He ran a tight room," former Bruins center Derek Sanderson likes saying about the man who helped save his life, but that doesn't do the matter near enough justice—not with Orr's first Boston coach, Harry Sinden, calling him the Godfather and his last, Don Cherry, relating how teammates shortened it over the decade that Orr played a kind of hockey no one had ever seen. "God here yet?" the other Bruins would say, or "Where was God last night?" But not to Orr's face. Not once.

God came to Boston in 1966, eighteen years old, and within two seasons the once-pathetic Bruins had been transformed into a spectacular, mean, winning bunch. Some of that was due to the '67 trade that brought in scoring machine Phil Esposito and forwards Ken Hodge and Fred Stanfield, but it was Orr, the working-class product of Parry Sound, Ontario, who set the tone. His on-ice artistry—coupled with a willingness to hurl that six-foot frame in front of any slap shot, into any opponent—endowed him with ultimate authority. He barely had to say a word.

Game days, Orr would arrive at 2:30 for a 7:30 start, play cards, bang around the emptiness, sort through the 144 sticks sent him every few weeks—weighing them, selecting two, maybe three, discarding the rest—getting himself ready. His teammates would file in at five or six o'clock. He'd wander about then with one stick weighted with lead or with pucks taped to the blade, shifting it from hand to hand. Locker room music rarely played. "I have never run into any player who brings the intensity that he brought," says Sinden, who spent forty-five years as a coach or front-office executive. "His silence, his looks, were enough to tell you if he didn't like what was happening. And he made the rest of us the same way. You could not be around him without feeling that and getting in line."

If you had a bad period? Or dogged it? Sanderson's locker was by a pillar, and he'd set his chair so the pillar would block Orr's view from across the room. "Is he looking?" Esposito would whisper. Always, Orr would be staring lasers. Sanderson only felt worse when Orr would wait until he was alone, come over, and mutter, "You got to pick it up. We need you."

Then Orr would hit the ice again, and it was wondrous to see— for the fans, yes, but even opponents found themselves entranced. When Bobby Clarke was a rookie center for the Philadelphia Flyers—the team that later raised the ante on Boston's bruising ways —he found himself all but cheering Orr's speed and control; he couldn't help himself. It wasn't just the end-to-end rushes, Orr's thick legs pushing him to a gear few could match, to scoring levels unheard of for a defenseman. It was his style. There was just one strip of black tape on Orr's stick and the puck seemed glued to it, that fine detail so compelling that Boston strippers took to sporting the equivalent of today's French bikini wax—a thin strip of pubic homage dubbed "a Bobby Orr."

During one penalty kill against the old Seals in Oakland, Orr swooped behind goal in possession, tussled with an opponent, and lost a glove. "He went around by the blue line, came back, picked up his glove—still had the puck," Esposito says. "[Goalie] Gerry Cheevers was on the bench, and I'm standing there and I hear Cheesy say to me, 'Espo, you want *The Racing Form?*' I said, 'Might as well; I'm not touching the puck!' Bobby killed about a minute and ten, twenty seconds of that penalty—and then . . . ," with even the Oakland players cheering now, ". . . he scored. Greatest thing I ever saw."

In 1969–70 Orr became the only player to sweep the league's top awards—MVP, defenseman, playoff MVP, and scoring title—and capped it off by scoring the Stanley Cup–winning goal over St. Louis in overtime. The following season, the Bruins scored 124 more even-strength or shorthanded goals than they gave up when Orr was on the ice, and that remains his most lasting monument; the man most mentioned as Orr's rival for the title of greatest ever, Wayne Gretzky, never cracked +100.

Yet Orr bristled at the attentions of superstardom, would tell coaches to find reasons to bawl him out like the rest. His last good season, 1974–75, he scored forty-six goals but probably gave away a half-dozen more by insisting that teammates had deflected the puck in. It's no accident that his signature play—and the one that won the first of his two Stanley Cups, against the Blues—was a give-and-go. Orr's best rushes were never look-at-me affairs but a storm he brewed on one end of the ice, gathering in his fellow Bruins for the inexorable sweep forward. When he began to move, says former Montreal goalie Ken Dryden, the sensation was unique: all the Canadiens began backpedaling in a small panic, like beachgoers sighting a coming monster wave.

"He brought others with him; he *wanted* them involved," says Dryden. "That's what made him so different: it felt like a five-player stampede moving toward you—and at his pace. He pushed his teammates, [because] you're playing with the best player in the league and he's giving you the puck and you just can't mess it up. You had to be better than you'd ever been."

Lord, do they remember. For hard men of a certain age, and for Canadians, especially, the mere mention of Orr can undam a rush of feeling. "Guys make fun of me because I'm always talking about him," says Cherry, whose second life as a hockey broadcaster gives him plenty of opportunity. "My son made [an Orr highlight] tape to Carly Simon — "Nobody Does It Better" — and I cry every time I see it. I don't know why."

It's no mystery. Orr did it all: blocked shots, dealt out punishing blows, endured the swooping hits of players desperate to stop him, somehow. When it came time to defend a teammate or himself, he fought. Gladly. "Too much," Esposito says. "He didn't have to, but he had a temper."

The fact is, despite his schoolboy haircut and shy grin, Orr was a killer on the ice. He laid out the Blackhawks' Stan Mikita with a perfect forearm cheap shot, hammered the hell out of Mikita's teammate Keith Magnuson at every opportunity, waited a year to get his revenge on Toronto's Pat Quinn — Orr jumped him in a brawl — after Quinn knocked him unconscious with a riot-sparking hit in the '69 playoffs.

"Pound for pound, he might've been the toughest guy in the game," Quinn says. "He wasn't a hold-and-throw like a lot of guys. He could go with both his hands, like a prizefighter."

A game-changing talent, a taste for blood: those were enough to make Orr a hockey hero for life. But vulnerability is what makes him resonate still. A recent TV ad shows Orr sitting silently while a lengthening scar on his famous left knee serves as a time line of victory, and loss; he played, really, only eight full seasons, and operations on both knees left him a near cripple at thirty. Ever since, commentators have made him the equivalent of Jim Brown, Sandy Koufax, even John F. Kennedy, shooting stars who left the world wondering what might have been. His last hurrah, the 1976 Canada Cup series, provided the perfect, bittersweet coda: Orr in so much pain that he couldn't practice, beating the Russians on one leg, outplaying the Czechs single-handedly, "the most courageous that I've ever seen a hockey player," says Clarke, the captain. Hockey nation didn't disagree.

"He *is* Canada," says Barb Tavares, whose son nevertheless ended up signing with another agent. But if Orr is how a certain segment of Canadians want to see themselves — self-effacing, self-sacrificing, quietly great — there's a glint of recognition too in what lies beneath the forced politeness, the goofy charm. In any conversation there's a tension that never leaves Orr, the feeling that his spring-loaded temper might snap and turn the warmest banter to ice. When first contacted by *Sports Illustrated*, Orr couldn't have been more welcoming, shuffling through his calendar for interview dates; in a second phone conversation he declared that he didn't want, as he has told many journalists, "a story about the agent business." He never returned another call.

Cherry has felt more than one freeze-out as Orr's coach in the 1970s and even after the two battled as celebrity coaches in the annual Top Prospects Game a few years ago. That time Orr didn't speak to him for six months. "Great heart, but he hates pretty good," Cherry says, and when asked how Orr was to coach, he pauses.

"I got to be careful here," he says finally. "You had to handle him right. You had to know when to talk to him; he was not an easy guy. He could spot a phony a mile away. There were so many people after him all the time that he became suspicious; he was never really friendly with a lot of people. When I first went there, I made the mistake: he was eating alone, and I made conversation. How was the fishing this year? And he picked up right away that I was just making conversation, and he didn't like that. He didn't like any bull——, and you know what? He's exactly like that today. He's pretty unforgiving. If you cross him, you will never get the chance to cross him again."

Eagleson crossed him the worst, of course, exposing a weakness as damaging as any knee injury. Once the cocky and high-flying master of the hockey universe, an irresistible force who rode Orr's celebrity into a multi-hatted—and conflict-ridden—position as executive director of the NHL Players' Association, hockey's most powerful agent and chairman of Hockey Canada's international committee, Eagleson would be accused of pilfering money from player pension funds and disability payments, and in 1998 he pleaded guilty to multiple counts of fraud, including those involving the theft of hundreds of thousands of dollars in Canada Cup proceeds. He served six months in a Toronto jail, was disbarred, got kicked out of the Canadian sports hall of fame.

Eagleson's bargaining tactics had made Orr the NHL's highest-paid player as a rookie, and Orr expected to be a millionaire when he retired in 1978: Eagleson had promised him, after all. But in '90 Orr told a Canadian newspaper in detail how, in blindly following

Eagleson's tangled financial advice, he had ended up with just $450,000 in assets—and tax bills that wiped him out. He had his homes in Boston, Cape Cod, and Florida and a name to sell, but a wife, Peggy, and two sons, Darren and Brent, to support. And the money was gone.

For press and public, Eagleson's crime against Orr was best summed up by the pair's final contract negotiation with the Bruins in 1976. Boston offered a multi-year deal that included an 18.5 percent ownership stake in the team, worth an estimated $49 million today. Though Eagleson made that offer public, Orr insisted that he didn't know about it until years later and, more to the point, believed Eagleson when he said there was a better deal to be gotten with the Chicago Blackhawks—owned, it just so happened, by Eagleson's close friend Bill Wirtz. Such obliviousness seems incredible, but then Orr had known Eagleson for fifteen years. "He had total control," Orr said in '90. "He said we were brothers. And I trusted him like a brother."

For his part, Eagleson won't talk about specifics and says, "I wouldn't do anything differently. That's how I was and that's how it is, and in the long haul of life the truth will eventually out."

What's not in dispute is the depth of Orr's trust. Esposito didn't like Eagleson, but Orr wouldn't hear a harsh word against him, and the tension between the teammates became palpable anytime his name came up. One day in the spring of '76, with negotiations at an impasse—Orr would eventually sign a five-year contract with the Blackhawks, but injuries limited him to just twenty-six games in two seasons—Cherry was alone at one end of the Boston Garden dressing room, fixing a stick for his son, when he noticed Bruins president Paul Mooney walk in and approach Orr as he sat pedaling on an exercise bike.

"Bobby, can I speak to you a minute?" Mooney said, puffing on a pipe.

"F—— off, Paul," Orr replied. "You're trying to drive a wedge between Al and I."

"Just let me talk to you for thirty seconds."

"F—— off. Don't talk to me."

Mooney shook his head and walked out.

"They were going to offer Bobby all that money, 18 percent," Cherry says. "Nope: 'F—— off.' That's how loyal he was to Eagleson. You couldn't convince him. Once he made up his mind? Forget it."

Rick Curran first heard the question six years ago, after he became Bobby Orr's business partner. Does Bobby participate? He's got the name, and you guys do all the work, right? Come on, Rick: is he *involved?*

"You don't understand. This guy gets up five-thirty, six o'clock every morning," Curran says. "By the time I talk to him—and we talk every day between seven and seven-thirty—I can tell by the sound of his voice whether our clients had a good or bad night the night before. He knows how everybody did; if someone's minutes are down, we know he's either injured or hasn't done what he should've been doing. And by the end of the conversation we have a list of seven or eight items for that day that we're going to address. Involved? He still lives and breathes it."

Endorsement contracts and public relations work had lifted Orr out of the financial ashes left by Eagleson, and in 1996 Orr bought into the Boston agency created by Bob Woolf. Now agenting gave him a chance to attack business as relentlessly as he did the game. "Dozens of calls every day—to players, to scouts, to skill coaches: How's our guy doing?" says Jay Fee, who worked at the agency before going out on his own in 2002.

Orr also drew a clear line: his agency would not handle—as Eagleson had—player finances. "Being victimized by a bad agent, I think Bobby wanted to run a business that would never do that to anybody," Fee says.

Still, Orr leaves much of the on-the-ground detail to his partners. The Flyers' Jeff Carter—handled primarily by the Philadelphia-based Curran—emerged as a breakout star for the firm this season, and he has scarcely any relationship with Orr. Meanwhile, Orr's Boston-based partner, Paul Krepelka, is the agent of record in DiPietro's case; he represented the Islanders goalie up to and including the moment DiPietro signed a record fifteen-year, $67.5 million contract in 2006. The relationship frayed soon after and DiPietro fired the firm, refusing to pay its percentage because he had never signed a standard player agent contract. Last summer, Orr filed a grievance with the NHL Players' Association, but DiPietro—who declined to speak to *SI*—says he owes nothing.

Krepelka agrees that DiPietro didn't sign a contract with the Orr Group, but says he negotiated the pact and should be paid. The grievance is expected to be heard this spring and "could segue into a lawsuit," Krepelka says.

Orr's role, though, was never about pen and paper. Then and now, he has traveled widely to take in college and pro games, bundled golf rounds with contacts in coaching and broadcasting, used his stature to gain an entrée denied rival agents. He often showed up unannounced at the Maple Leafs' offices when Pat Quinn, his old sparring partner, was coach and general manager from 1998 to 2006. Quinn usually didn't deal with player reps, but he always welcomed Orr. Eventually talk would turn to a client like defenseman Tomas Kaberle, and Quinn says, Orr would "get to where he wanted to go. And it was always about the kid, about his best interest." When, during Kaberle's 2001 holdout, hockey analyst Gord Miller of The Sports Network in Canada took an on-air shot at Kaberle's defense, Orr got in Miller's face, stats at the ready, snapping, "You'd better rethink that!"

Orr's loyalty to the faithful is just as fierce. If he has refused to donate signed pictures or gear to a desperate fan, or refused a charity golf tournament or hospital visit, no one has heard of it. In 2006 a story ran in the *Boston Globe* about a high school hockey player, Bill Langan, who played in a regional title game on the day of his mother's wake; the kid mentioned that his mother used to watch Orr play. Orr called, asked if he could help. Langan asked him to come to a team dinner. Orr made no promises. But he showed up without warning and stayed an hour.

As for the big, bad — and now old — Bruins, Orr is, Sinden says, "still the Godfather." When the flamboyant and reckless Sanderson showed up in Chicago in the winter of '78 stoned and unable even to hold a cup of coffee steady, Orr personally checked him into a hospital and was there when Sanderson woke up with three doctors staring at him. "Who's going to tell him?" one said.

"I'll tell him," Orr said and then leveled with Sanderson: "You're a full-blown alcoholic and a drug addict. It's over. You've got to go to rehab." Orr paid for that first stint. When Sanderson relapsed, he says, Orr paid to send him back. And then again. "He never left me," Sanderson says.

When Sanderson finally cleaned up, and began a new life as a financial adviser for athletes in the 1990s, Orr invested with him, gave Sanderson the chance to work with Orr's clients too.

Orr also paid for rehab stints for former Bruins trainer John "Frosty" Forristall, his roommate during his first years with the Bruins and an irreverent bon vivant whose alcohol problems led Esposito, then the general manager of the Tampa Bay Lightning, to let him go in 1994. Forristall returned to Boston jobless, and soon after he was told he had brain cancer. Bobby and Peggy took Forristall into their home for a year until he died in '95 at fifty-one.

"I'm glad somebody was there for him," says Frosty's older brother, Bill, from Florida. "He wouldn't come down here. I was a little too hard-nosed; I wouldn't put up with his drinking." Orr stood by Frosty to the end, hovering over him in the hospital, serving as a pallbearer at his funeral. But he wouldn't speak to Bill.

"Bobby wasn't too happy with me," Bill says. "John apparently said something that put me in a bad light. I've never been able to figure it out."

Maybe it was the fact that he'd just turned sixty, or that two knee-replacement surgeries had freed him of cane and pain. Maybe he figured he could finally take the onslaught of memories without breaking. But on November 27, Orr relented at last, stood on the ice at the General Motors Centre in Oshawa, Ontario, and allowed the junior team he left in 1966 to retire his number.

Still, he could barely sleep for two nights before. Oshawa, after all, had known him all the way back in 1962 when Orr was raw, wide-open, fourteen years old, and missing his parents, Doug and Arva, up in Parry Sound. Oshawa was where Wren Blair, a GM in the Bruins system, planted him and where the Eagle got his hooks in.

But Arva died in 2000 and Doug in '07, both in winter, and when Orr took the microphone that night, his voice quavered and his eyes filled. "I know my, uh, mom and dad are watching tonight," he said. "I know they're very, very happy . . . very proud. My mom and dad were the perfect minor hockey parents. Their whole philosophy was, Look, go out and play, have fun, and let's see what happens. And I wish there were more parents that thought like that when it came to their kids playing hockey . . ." And the standing crowd cheered the dig at hockey parents gone wild, cheered how things used to be.

Yet as much as he doesn't like being called an agent—"He'd rather it be, 'family representative,'" Sinden says—that's what Orr is. He famously never put either of his sons on skates, but he has his oldest, Darren, thirty-four, working for the Orr Group in Boston. Bobby Orr is now part of the machinery of parents, media, teams, and agents dedicated to finding the next Bobby Orr.

In January, Orr returned to Oshawa to coach against Cherry in the 2009 Top Prospects Game, the annual showcase for top junior talent. It was Orr's tenth appearance; he took part in the inaugural event in 1996 as a celebrity, but once he became a player rep, competing agents cried conflict of interest—he would, after all, be coaching a game designed to help determine draft order, salaries, and the size of an agent's commission. Orr offered to withdraw. Organizers wouldn't hear of it.

On the morning of this year's game Orr and his team of prospects posed for the traditional team photo. Afterward, the coaches and players scattered to the locker room, leaving their chairs and platforms and mess behind. Orr didn't say a word. He grabbed two chairs and skated them off the ice. Then he went back for a riser, bent over, and shoved it slowly to one end of the empty rink: wrong door. He wheeled and shoved it the length of the ice again, leaving it at the right one so the arena crew would have a bit less work.

The players returned after a few minutes and began circling the ice counterclockwise. Orr joined in, dipping into the flow and skating hard again, reversing time if only for a few laps. Cherry hadn't seen Orr on the ice pain-free in thirty-five years. "Before, it was push and glide, really sad to see," he said. "Now? You would never know."

Orr gathered up a puck and wristed it low into the empty goal, making the net shiver. He stopped, began feeding all the young men as they swooped past, clockwise now: Foligno, Holland, de Haan, Tavares, O'Reilly. He tapped gloves with one, cracked a joke with another. Now Eakin, McNabb, Roussel flashed past, and now Schenn, and Orr motioned with his stick, and Schenn passed back the puck, maybe three inches wide. "Hey!" Orr snapped, and banged his stick on the ice to say, right *here,* and Schenn got closer with the next one. Orr gave him a grin.

He came off the ice later, and the press gathered and someone asked if he remembered what it felt like to be that young. He spoke about playing as a kid, outdoors mostly, shooting through the fierce cold on the Seguin River, on Georgian Bay, scrapping on icy parking lots. "No coaches, no parents," he said. "Get the puck and just go.

"It was never a job for me. Even during my pro days, it was never, ever a job. That's what these kids have to understand: just enjoy it, keep that love and passion for the game. I think what sometimes we do—we, the pressures, the coaches and parents—we just suck that love and passion from our kids. And I think that's wrong."

He and Cherry had a bet on the game, $100. That night Orr's side won 6–1, and Cherry gave it up at the handshake. "Money goes to money, you see that?" he said.

And then Orr, icon and agent and coach all in one, raised the bill over his head and waved it in triumph. Thousands roared. Thousands laughed. Their Bobby was back, no limp, and eyes shining. It felt perfect, the way any church does when the ceremony goes off without a hitch and the light streams just so.

Life Throws Bernie Kosar for a Loss

FROM THE MIAMI HERALD

THE IRS AND THE CREDITORS and an angry ex-wife and an avalanche of attorneys are circling the chaos that used to be Bernie Kosar's glamorous life, but that's not the source of his anxiety at the moment. He is doing a labored lap inside his Weston mansion, the one on the lake near the equestrian playpen for horses, because he wants to be sure there are no teenage boys hiding, attempting to get too close to his three daughters. He shattered a Kid Rock–autographed guitar the other day while chasing one teenager out of his house because he doesn't mind all of the other boys within the area code thinking the Kosar girls have an unhinged dad.

"There are a million doors in this place," he says. "Too many ways to get in."

So up and down the spiral staircases he goes, a rumpled mess wearing a wrinkled golf shirt, disheveled graying hair, and the scars and weariness from a lifetime's worth of beatings. He has no shoes on, just white socks with the NFL logo stitched on because he's never really been able to let go of who he used to be. He is coughing up phlegm from a sickness he is certain arrived with all the recent stress of divorce and debt, and now he doesn't walk so much as wobble his way into one of the closets upstairs, where he happens upon some painful, wonderful memories he keeps sealed in a plastic cup.

His teeth are in there. So is the surgical screw that finally broke through the skin in his ankle because of how crooked he walked for years. He broke that ankle in the first quarter of a game against the Dolphins in 1992; he threw two touchdown passes in the fourth quarter anyway. Don Shula called him the following day to salute him on being so tough, but Kosar is paying for it with every step he takes today on uneven footing. The old quarterback shakes the rattling cup, then grins. There are about as many real teeth in the cup as there are in what remains of his smile.

"I never wore a mouthpiece," he says. "I had to live and die with my audibles. We played on pavement/AstroTurf back then. Getting hit by Lawrence Taylor was only the beginning of the problem."

So much pain in his life. He heads back downstairs gingerly.

"I need hip replacement," he says.

He pulls his jeans down a bit to reveal the scar from the surgery to repair his broken back.

"Disks fused together," he says.

Concussions?

"A lot," he says. "I don't know how many."

He holds out all ten gnarled fingers. "All of these have been broken at least once," he says. "Most of them twice."

Broke both wrists too.

The game was fast and muscled. He was neither. He was always the giraffe trying to survive among lions. Still is, really. He has merely traded one cutthroat arena in which people compete for big dollars for another, and today's is a hell of a lot less fun than the one that made him famous. More painful too, oddly enough.

Kosar holds up his left arm and points to the scar on his elbow.

"Have a cadaver's ligament in there," he says.

And that's the good arm. He bends over and lets both arms hang in front of him. His throwing arm is as crooked as a boomerang.

"I can't straighten it," he says. "I started breaking at thirty years old. Once you start breaking, you keep breaking."

The doorbell rings. It's his assistant with the papers he needs to autograph. She puts all the legalese from four folders in front of him on a coffee table that is low to the ground. A groaning Kosar, forty-five, gets down very slowly onto the rug until he is symbolically on his hands and knees at the center of what used to be his glamorous life. And then he signs the documents that begin the process of filing for bankruptcy.

"Let me tell you something, bro," he says. "It was all worth it."

Until the Bitter End

Brett Favre has made a spectacular public mess of his career, because of how very hard it is for even the strongest among us to leave behind the applause for good. It is difficult for any man to retire when so much of his identity and self-worth and validation is tied up in his job, what he does invariably becoming a lopsided amount of who he is. But it is especially hard on quarterbacks because of how much of America's most popular game they literally hold in their hands. That kind of control—over other strong men, over huddles, over winning, over entire swaying stadiums and their surrounding cities—is just about impossible to let go . . . as is the attendant attention, ego, importance, popularity, fun, and life. Running backs retire early sometimes because of the beatings, but quarterbacks never do. Joe Namath finished wearing a Rams helmet, Joe Montana ended with the Chiefs after forty, and Dan Marino got pushed out after losing 62–7—and now Favre wanders the earth so lost and searching that he's about to put on the uniform of his greatest enemy. Kings don't quit kingdoms voluntarily.

But there's no preparing you for the silence that comes after all you've heard is cheering. A quarterback will never feel more alive anywhere than he does at the conquering center of everything in sports. His is by consensus the most difficult job in athletics, and it requires an obsessive-compulsive attention to detail. The most diligent and consumed become Peyton Manning and Tom Brady; the talented and lazy become Ryan Leaf. And sometimes they sculpt their singular and all-consuming skill to the detriment of the balance needed for the rest of life's tacklers. Bills? Errands? Adulthood? Those things get handed off sometimes because, whether it is the offensive line or family and friends huddled around their income source, the quarterback must always be protected or everyone loses.

On and Off the Field

Kosar was one of the smart ones. He graduated from the University of Miami in two and a half years. He was smart enough to go a record 308 pass attempts without an interception. Smart enough to help build several businesses after football, with a 6 percent interest in a customer-service outsourcing company that sold for more than $500 million. Smart enough to have a wing of the business school at the University of Miami named after him. But now that the maids and wife are gone, you know how he feels walking into a grocery store by himself for the first time?

"Overwhelmed," he says.

He is like an embryo in the real world. The huddle gave him strength and purpose and enough fame and money that he never had to do much of anything for himself. Never had to grow, really, as anything but a quarterback. He says his kids (ages seventeen, sixteen, twelve, and nine) grew up in a world where "their idea of work was telling the maid to clean their room." And even the live-in maids had assistants. So now they're all trying to figure it out together, four kids led by a forty-five-year-old one.

Do you know how to wash clothes, Bernie?

"No," he says.

Iron a shirt?

"No," he says.

Start the dishwasher?

"No," he says.

He just learned the other day, after much trying and failing, how to make his own coffee. This is a man who owned his own jet and helped found companies, plural. But when his new girlfriend came over recently and found him trying to cook with his daughters, she couldn't believe what was on the kitchen island to cut the French bread. A saw.

"I was twenty-five and everyone was telling me that I was the smartest; now I'm forty-five and realize I'm an idiot," he says. "I'm forty-five and immature. I don't like being forty-five."

He still finds himself doodling plays on napkins in the kitchen. Running companies doesn't feel as rewarding as working with a high school or college tight end on routes. The only post-quarterback jobs that have given him any sort of joy are the ones near football: broadcasting Cleveland Browns games; running a company that created football websites and magazines; buying an Arena Football League team. But it isn't the same. Not nearly. As he tries to reorganize his life in a dark period that leaves his mind racing and sleepless, the people he quotes aren't philosophers and poets. They are coaches.

Like when he was at the University of Miami, for example. He was the weakest kid on the team. He was mortified when his statuesque competition, Vinny Testaverde, walked onto campus and bench-pressed 325 pounds a bunch of times. Kosar got 185 up just once, with arms shaking. So he went to Coach Howard Schnellenberger and, sweating and trying not to tremble, told him he was going to transfer. And now he quotes the old pipe-smoking coach and applies those lessons from nearly three decades ago to today: "Son, I'm not going to lie. It doesn't look good for you. But wherever you go in life, there's competition. The guys who run home to Mommy tend to be quitters their whole life."

Kosar won. Won huge. Won the job and the national championship in a flabbergasting upset of Nebraska to begin Miami's unprecedented football run through the next two decades.

That seems like so long ago. As creditors close in and his divorce has gotten messy in public, Kosar has had some suicidal thoughts, but he says, "I couldn't quit on my kids. I'm not a quitter. I'm not going to quit on them or me. I got here with hard work. I'll get out of this with hard work. No wallowing. No 'woe is me.' I'm great at making money. And, as we've found out, I'm great at spending it. What I'm not great at is managing it."

The Pangs of Loss

It is hard to believe he filed a bankruptcy petition on Friday, but a bad economy, bad advice, a bad divorce, and a bad habit of not being able to say no have ravaged him. He says financial advisers he loved and trusted mismanaged his funds, doing things like losing $15 million in one quick burst. There's a $4.2 million judgment against him from one bank. A failed real estate project in Tampa involving multifamily properties. A steakhouse collapsing with a lawsuit. Tax trouble.

His finances have never been something he controlled. He graduated on July 14, 1985, was at two-a-day NFL workouts six days later, and immediately got on the learning treadmill at full speed, always feeling like he was catching up because his team wasn't very good; and his receivers were worse than the ones he had at UM, and everyone on the other side of the ball was very fast, and he was very slow, and the only advantage he would have was being smarter. Dad would handle the bills; the son had to handle the Bills.

And he was always rewarded for being consumed that way. That's how the weakest and least physically gifted guy on the field once threw for 489 yards in an NFL playoff game. But that huddle eventually breaks, and the men who formed it break too. Depression. Drugs. Drinking. Divorce. You'll find it all as retired football players cope with the kinds of losses teammates can't help you with—a loss of identity, self-worth, youth, relevance.

A recent *Sports Illustrated* article estimated that within two years of leaving football, an astounding 78 percent of players are either bankrupt or in financial distress over joblessness and divorce. And over the years, a lot of those old teammates have asked Kosar to borrow a hundred grand here, a hundred-fifty grand there. He knew then that he wouldn't be getting it back. But, as the quarterback—always the quarterback—you help your teammates up.

How much has he lent teammates over the years without being repaid?

"Eight figures," he says.

Friends and family?

"Eight figures," he says.

Charities, while putting nearly one hundred kids through school on scholarships? "Well over eight figures."

When it became public earlier this month that the Panthers hockey team would be sold and that Kosar would be getting a minority-owner percentage of the $240 million price, his phone rang all weekend with people asking for help. Calls after midnight on Friday. Calls before 7 A.M. on Sunday.

"Everyone with a sob story came flooding back," he says. Then there's the divorce. It has been a public disaster, with him being accused of several addictions, of erratic behavior, and of giving away the couple's money. Bernie says he has no interest in fighting with his estranged wife publicly or privately because "I can't live vengefully in front of my kids. Why subject them to that? I don't want to fight anybody. I don't want hate or anger in their life. I may hurt me, but I wouldn't hurt anybody else." He speaks with a slur and admits there has been drinking and pain medication in his past, but says the only thing he's addicted to is football.

Drugs? Alcohol? "Would my kids be living with me if that were really the case?" he asks. "If I did 10 percent of things I'm accused of, I'd be dead."

He says the divorce has cost him between $4 million and $5 million already.

"That's just fees," he says. "And they keep coming. Attorneys charge $600 an hour just to screw things up more."

And here's the worst part: "I don't want to get divorced," he says. "I'm Catholic, and I'm loyal, and I still love her."

Challenges Ahead

He has poured himself into being Dad, but it isn't easy. Kids listen more from two to ten years old. But now there are the perpetual parental concerns of cars, driving, drinking, drugs, sex.

"I'm outnumbered now," he says.

And he has no clue how to help girls become women, although he gets moved to the brink of tears when his girls tell him they appreciate how hard he's trying. He wept like a child when his daughter painted him a picture of herself smiling and signed it with love. He has found therapy in learning how to clean the house with the kids and dealing with life's smaller headaches. Just the other day, while in a ten-hour bankruptcy meeting with ten attorneys that left him "humbled and in pain and feeling betrayed" as he took a detailed inventory of his life, he excused himself with a smile because one of his daughters—the oldest of his children lives with him full-time, the others part-time—was calling with some sort of popularity crisis.

"The worst feeling in the world is being Dad on Friday night at home at midnight and they haven't gotten home yet," he says.

His daughter rolled her car the other day, getting ejected as it sank into a lake.

"Memorial Day, I should have been doing the funeral for her," he says. "This other chaos is just stuff. Money. I'll make more. It feels bad. It sucks the life and energy out of you and is a relentless drain. But I'm going to come out of this fine. I always get up."

There are photos all over his mansion. Many of them are not up. They are on the floor, leaning against the walls. He'll learn how to hang them soon enough. He goes over and grabs the one by the fireplace. In it, he is in the pocket with the Browns, and everything is collapsing all around him. You can see Kosar's offensive linemen either beaten or backpedaling. His left tackle is on the ground, staring as his missed assignment blurs toward the quarterback's blind side. But the ball is already in the air, frozen in flight, headed perfectly to the only teammate who has a step in a sea of Steelers. It is a work of art, that photo. You can see clearly that the play is going to work. And you can see just as clearly that Kosar is going to get crushed.

Kosar runs his fingers along the frame. This is what his life once was and what it is now—a swirl of chaos and pain and danger surrounding a man who has to remain in control for the people around him as everything feels like it is falling apart.

"I just wanted to play football," the old quarterback says.

A laugh and a pause.

"Actually, I still do."

MIKE SAGER

The Man Who Never Was

FROM ESQUIRE

THE FALLBROOK MIDGET CHIEFS are fanned out across the field on a sunny autumn day in southern California, two dozen eighth-graders in red helmets and bulbous pads. Whistles trill and coaches bark, mothers camp in folding chairs in the welcoming shade of the school building, younger siblings romp. Fathers hover on the periphery, wincing with every missed tackle and dropped pass.

Into this tableau ambles a tall man with faded-orange hair cropped close around a crowning bald spot, giving him the aspect of a tonsured monk. His face is all angles, his fair skin is sunburned and heavily freckled, his lips are deeply lined, the back of his neck is weathered like an old farmer's. He is six foot five, 212 pounds, the same as when he reported for duty twenty-one years ago as a redshirt freshman quarterback at the University of Southern California, the Touchdown Club's 1987 national high school player of the year. The press dubbed him Robo Quarterback; he was the total package. His Orange County record for all-time passing yardage, 9,182, stood for more than two decades.

Now he is thirty-nine, wearing surfer shorts and rubber flip-flops. He moves toward the field in the manner of an athlete, loose-limbed and physically confident, seemingly unconcerned, revealing nothing of the long and tortured trail he's left behind.

A coach hustles out to meet the party. He is wearing an Oakland Raiders cap. "Todd Marinovich!" he declares. "Would you mind signing these?" He produces a stack of bubble-gum cards. As Todd signs, everybody gathers and cops a squat. Somebody tosses him a football, like a speaking stick.

"Hi, my name is Todd. I played *waaaay* before you guys were even born." Without his sunglasses, resting now atop his head, his blue eyes look pale and unsure. Raised much of his life on the picturesque Balboa Peninsula, he speaks in the loopy dialect of a surfer dude. He once told a reporter in jest that he enjoyed surfing naked at a spot near a nuclear power plant. Thereafter, among his other transgressions — nine arrests, two felonies, a year in jail — he would be known derisively for naked surfing. "One thing that I am today and that's completely honest," he tells the Midget Chiefs. "I wouldn't change anything for the world."

As he speaks, Todd fondles and flips and spins the ball. It seems small in his hands and very well behaved, like it belongs there. When he was born, his father placed a big plush football in his crib. Marv Marinovich was the co-captain of John McKay's undefeated USC team of 1962. He played on the line both ways. The team won the national championship; Marv was ejected from the Rose Bowl for fighting. After a short NFL career, Marv began studying Eastern Bloc training methods. The Raiders' colorful owner, Al Davis, made him one of the NFL's first strength-and-conditioning coaches. Before Todd could walk, Marv had him on a balance beam. He would stretch the boy's little hamstrings in his crib. Years later, an ESPN columnist would name Marv number two on a list of "worst sports fathers." (After Jim Pierce, father of tennis player Mary, famous for verbally abusing opponents during matches.)

At the moment, Marv is sitting at the back of the Midget Chiefs gathering, resting his bum knee, eating an organic apple. Nearly seventy, he has bull shoulders and a nimbus of curly gray hair. His own pale-blue eyes are focused intently on his son's performance, as they have been from day one.

"I was the first freshman in Orange County to ever start a varsity game at quarterback," Todd continues. "I broke a lot of records. Then I chose to go to USC. We beat UCLA. We won a Rose Bowl. It's quite an experience playing in front of a hundred thousand people. It's a real rush. Everyone is holding their breath, wondering, *What's he gonna do next?* After my third year of college, I turned pro. Here's a name you'll recognize: I was drafted ahead of Brett Favre in the 1991 draft. I played for three years for the Raiders. I made some amazing friends — we're still in touch."

Todd surveys the young faces before him. In about a minute, he has summarized the entire first half of his life. He looks down at the football. "Any questions?"

One kid asks Todd if he fumbled a lot. Another wants to know how far Todd can throw. The coach in the Raiders cap—they call him Raider Bill—asks Todd how he got along with his coaches, eliciting a huge guffaw from both Todd and Marv, which makes everybody else crack up too.

Then Todd points the football at a boy with freckles.

"You said you only played three years in the NFL," the boy says, more a statement than a question.

"Correctamundo," Todd replies, at ease now, playing to the crowd, not really thinking about what's coming next—which has always been his biggest strength and maybe also his biggest weakness.

"What ended your career?" the boy asks.

"What *ended* my career . . ." Todd repeats. His smile fades as he searches for the right words.

The Newport Beach Cheyennes were scrimmaging the best fourth-grade Pop Warner team in Orange County. It was September 1978. Todd was nine years old, playing his first year of organized tackle football.

Todd was the quarterback, a twig figure with flaming-orange hair. The opposing team was anchored by its middle linebacker, one of those elementary school Goliaths, physically mature for his age. With time waning and the score close, the game on the line, the Cheyennes' coach opted to give his second-string offense a chance. In this scheme, Todd moved to fullback. Over in his spot near the end zone, Marv's eyes bugged. *Why isn't this idiot going for the win?*

The Marinovich family had recently returned from living in Hawaii, where Marv, after coaching with the Raiders and the St. Louis Cardinals, had done a stint with the World Football League's Hawaiians. As Marv sorted out his work status, his family of four was living with the maternal grandparents in a little clapboard house on the Balboa Peninsula. Once a summer beach shack, it had been converted over the years into two stories, four bedrooms. The Pacific Ocean is two long blocks from the front deck; Newport Harbor is two short blocks from the back door, its docks crowded with yachts and pontoon party boats. In summer come the throngs: a nonstop party.

Todd's mom is the former Trudi Fertig. In high school, she held several swimming records in the butterfly. A prototype of the late-fifties California girl, Trudi was a Delta Gamma sorority sister at USC; she quit college after her sophomore year to marry the captain of the football team. Trudi's father, C. Henry Fertig, was the police chief of nearby Huntington Park. German-Irish, the son of a blacksmith, he was the one who'd passed down the carrot top. The Chief, as he was known to all, was the "most visible of all the Trojan alums," according to the *Orange County Register*. Before every USC game you'd find him, wearing his cardinal-colored shirt and bright gold pants, tailgating in his regular spot in front of the L.A. Coliseum, where the Trojans play their games. (After the Chief's death in 1997, at the age of eighty, the alumni laid a brass plaque on the hallowed spot.)

The Chief's son was Craig Fertig, a former USC quarterback, responsible for one of the greatest Trojan victories of all time, a comeback against undefeated Notre Dame in 1964. He was associated with the program for nearly fifty years as a coach, assistant athletic director, TV commentator, and fan until his death, the result of organ failure due to alcoholism.

Marv Marinovich grew up with his extended family on a three-thousand-acre ranch in Watsonville, in northern California. The spread was owned by his Croatian grandfather, J. G. Marinovich. According to family lore, J. G. was a general in the Russian army, a cruel man who'd overseen the battlefield amputation of his own left arm. After high school, Marv played football for Santa Monica City College. The team went undefeated and won the 1958 national junior-college championship. From there Marv transferred to USC. He was known for foaming at the mouth. After the championship, he was named Most Inspirational Player. He still has the trophy.

Drafted by the L.A. Rams of the NFL and by the Oakland Raiders of the AFL, Marv "ran, lifted, pushed the envelope to the nth degree" in order to prepare for the pros. One exercise, he says: eleven-hundred-pound squats, with the bar full of forty-five-pound plates, with hundred-pound dumbbells chained and hanging on the ends because he couldn't get any more plates to fit. "And then

I would rep out," he recalls. "I hadn't yet figured out that speed and flexibility were more important than weight and bulk. I overtrained so intensely that I never recovered."

After a disappointing three-year career with the Raiders and Rams, Marv turned to sports training. Over time, he would develop his own system for evaluating athletes and maximizing their potential. Much of the core- and swimming-pool-based conditioning programs in use today owe nods to Marv's ideas. His latest reclamation project: Pittsburgh Steelers safety Troy Polamalu. (See Polamalu and Marv on YouTube.)

With the birth of his own two children, Traci and Todd, came the perfect opportunity for Marv to put his ideas into practice. "Some guys think the most important thing in life is their jobs, the stock market, whatever," he says. "To me, it was my kids. The question I asked myself was, How well could a kid develop if you provided him with the perfect environment?"

For the nine months prior to Todd's birth on July 4, 1969, Trudi used no salt, sugar, alcohol, or tobacco. As a baby, Todd was fed only fresh vegetables, fruits, and raw milk; when he was teething, he was given frozen kidneys to gnaw. As a child, he was allowed no junk food; Trudi sent Todd off to birthday parties with carrot sticks and carob muffins. By age three, Marv had the boy throwing with both hands, kicking with both feet, doing sit-ups and pull-ups, and lifting light hand weights. On his fourth birthday, Todd ran four miles along the ocean's edge in thirty-two minutes, an eight-minute-mile pace. Marv was with him every step of the way.

Now, late in one of Todd's first games in Pop Warner, the coach sent a play into the huddle, a handoff to the halfback. As fullback, Todd's job was to be lead blocker.

The ball was snapped. Todd led the halfback through the hole.

He'd just cleared the line of scrimmage when Goliath-boy stepped into the gap and delivered a forearm shiver very much like the one that had gotten Marv ejected from the Rose Bowl. Todd crumpled to the ground. Blood flowed copiously from his nose.

The whistle blew. As Todd was being cleaned up, Marv convinced the coach that Todd needed to go back in the game. Immediately. At quarterback.

Todd stood over center, his nose still bleeding. Part of him felt like crying. The other part knew that it was the last few seconds of the scrimmage and the team was down by only a few points. For as long as he could remember, no matter what sport he played, he always had to win.

He took the snap and faded back, threw a perfect pass into the back corner of the end zone. "That has always been my favorite route," he says now, sitting outside a little coffee shop on Balboa Boulevard, drinking a large drip with six sugars and smoking a Marlboro Red. He tells the story from a place of remove, as if describing something intimate that happened to someone else. "I remember seeing the ball. It was spiraling and there was blood just flying off of it, splattering out into the air."

When the catch was made, there was silence for a beat. "And then I remember the parents cheering."

Six years later, on the opening night of the 1984 football season, Todd once again gathered himself as best he could, rising to one knee on the turf at Orange Coast College. There were seven thousand fans in the stadium. He'd just been blasted by two big studs from the celebrated front line of the Fountain Valley High School Barons.

Three days before he'd even set foot in a ninth-grade classroom, the six-three, 170-pound freshman was the starting quarterback for the varsity team at Mater Dei High School in Santa Ana, the largest Catholic high school west of Michigan. In a sports-mad county known for its quarterbacks—from John Huarte and Matt Leinart to Carson Palmer and Mark Sanchez—Todd's freshman start was a first.

Todd fought for breath. His head was ringing, his vision was blurred, he wanted to puke. Later he would recognize the symptoms of his first concussion. Marv's conditioning was designed to train the body and the mind to push beyond pain and fear. Throughout his career, Todd would be known for his extraordinary focus and will—qualities that would both enable and doom him. Two years from now, the left-hander would lead a fourth-quarter rally with a broken thumb on his throwing hand. Five years from now, he would throw four college touchdowns with a fractured left wrist. Sixteen years from now, he'd throw ten touchdowns in one game, tying an Arena Football League record, while suffering from acute heroin withdrawal.

Acting on instinct, fifteen-year-old Todd rose to his feet and peered out of the echoing cavern of his helmet. He searched the sideline, looking for the signal caller, his next play. A teammate grabbed him by the shoulder pads, spun him around to face the Mater Dei bench. "We're over *here,* dude," he told Todd.

Back in seventh grade, Todd had set his goal: to start on a varsity team as a ninth-grader. Marv made a progress chart and put it up in the garage; they worked every day. "It was brutal," Todd recalls. "Sometimes I didn't want anything to do with it. He'd give me the look, like, 'Well, fine, but you're gonna get your ass kicked when you start to play.'" Along the way, Marv consulted a series of experts: Tom House, the Texas Rangers' innovative pitching coach, found Todd's throwing motion to be 4.53 inches too low. A vision specialist in Westwood made Todd wear prism glasses, stand on a balance beam in a dark room, and bounce a ball while reciting multiplication tables.

By the summer before ninth grade, Todd was penciled in as Mater Dei's fifth-string quarterback. His typical week, as reported by the *Register:* Four days of weightlifting, three days of light work and running. Daily sessions with Mater Dei's assistant basketball coach. Twice weekly with a shooting coach. Two hours daily throwing the football. Twice weekly with a quarterback coach. Thrice-weekly sprint workouts with a track coach. There were also Mater Dei basketball club games and twice-daily football workouts.

"I don't think any of the kids were ever jealous of Todd, because they knew that when they left that field or court or gym, Todd was still going to be there for many, many hours," Trudi recalls. When Todd and Traci were growing up, Trudi worked as a waitress during the periods when Marv wasn't employed. Sometimes she secretly took Todd to McDonald's. The Chief fed him pizza and beer. Though Traci once wrote of hearing Todd cry in his room, nobody wanted to butt heads with Marv. Like an obsessed scientist, he had tunnel vision. "He didn't do reality too well," Trudi says.

Todd lost that first game against Fountain Valley, 17–13, but he showed promise. Shut down completely after that blow in the first quarter, he gained composure as the evening progressed, completing nine of seventeen passes for 123 yards and two interceptions, the second of which foiled a fourth-quarter drive that could have won the game. The *Register* would report: "If not for Marinovich . . . the Monarchs wouldn't have had an offense to speak of."

After the final gun, Todd stood with his parents. His new team-mates drifted over and surrounded him. "When I was growing up, the term my mom used was 'terrifyingly shy,'" Todd says. "That's why I always loved being on a team. It was the only way I could make friends. It was really amazing to have these guys, these upper-classmen, come over. And they're like, 'Hey, Todd, let's go! Come out with us after the game. It's party time!'"

Todd looked at Marv. The old man didn't hesitate. "He just gave me the nod, you know, like, 'Go ahead, you earned it.'

"We went directly to a kegger and started pounding down beers," Todd recalls.

It was January 1988, opening night of basketball season. With fifty-eight seconds left, the score was 61–all. Todd flashed into the key, took a pass from the wing. He made the lay-up and drew the foul. Whistle. Three thousand fans in the arena at the University of California–Irvine, went nuts. The six-five, 215-pound high school senior pumped his fist in celebration.

During his two years at Mater Dei, Todd had thrown for nearly 4,400 yards and 34 touchdowns. But the Monarchs' record was me-diocre; they had no blocking to protect Todd. So Marv had engi-neered his son's transfer to Capistrano Valley High, a public school in Mission Viejo. The team's head football coach, Dick Enright, was a USC alum and longtime friend of Marv's. As head coach at the University of Oregon, Enright had groomed quarterback Dan Fouts. Under Enright, Todd would go on to break the all-time Or-ange County passing record. He was named a *Parade* magazine All-American and the National High School Coaches Association's of-fensive player of the year.

Then the January 1988 issue of *California* magazine hit the stands with Todd's picture on the cover. The headline: "Robo QB: The Making of a Perfect Athlete." A media onslaught ensued. They called Todd the bionic quarterback, a test-tube athlete, the boy in the bubble. All over the world, people were talking about Todd's amazing story. In truth, he was leading a double life.

"I really looked forward to giving it all I had at the game on Fri-day night and then continuing through the weekend with the par-tying. It opened up a new social scene for me—liquid courage. I wasn't scared of people anymore," Todd says.

At Mater Dei, Todd had also begun smoking marijuana. By the

time his junior year rolled around, he says, "I was a full-on loady."
His parents had divorced just before his transfer, and he was shar-
ing a one-bedroom apartment with Marv near Capistrano. "Probably the best part of my childhood was me and Marv's relationship
my junior and senior years," Todd says. "After the divorce, he really
loosened up. It was a bachelor pad. We were both dating."

Every day before school, Todd would meet a group at a friend's
house and do bong hits. They called it Zero Period. Some of the
guys were basketball players, others were into surfing, skateboarding, and music — the holy trinity of the OC slacker lifestyle.

"Pot just really relaxed me. I could just function better in public," he says. "I never played high or practiced high. It wasn't as
hard on my body as drinking. I thought, Man, I have found the secret. I was in love."

Now it was January of his senior year, the opening game of basketball season. Todd was a swingman, the high scorer. The Capo
Cougars were one of the top-ranked teams in the county. The contest against archrival El Toro High School had come down to the
wire. Todd had just broken the tie with a lay-up. Then he hit the
foul shot: 64–61.

El Toro inbounded the ball; Capo stole it. Pass to Todd. Hard
foul in the paint. Todd went to the line again, two shots. Thirty-
seven seconds left to play.

The crowd was screaming, pounding the floor. Behind the basket, dozens of El Toro students were wearing orange wigs to mock
the carrot-topped Robo Quarterback. As Todd went through his
foul-shot ritual, something broke his focus. The opposing fans were
chanting: "Marijuana-*vich!* Marijuana-*vich!* Marijuana-*vich!*"

"I was supposed to be shooting free throws, but I was really glancing into the stands. I was trying to see if my father was noticing,"
Todd told the *Los Angeles Times* later.

He put it out of mind and nailed both shots. Game over.

No matter what the teams' record or national ranking, UCLA versus USC is always the biggest game of the year. The sixtieth meeting occurred in November 1990. From the opening kickoff, the
advantage seesawed. With less than a minute to go, the score was
42–38 in favor of UCLA. Todd and his Trojan squad began operating on their own 23. A field goal wouldn't do.

On third down, Todd completed a twenty-seven-yard pass to his favorite target, five-foot-nine Gary Wellman, a future Houston Oiler. On the next play he hit Wellman again for twenty-two yards.

With sixteen seconds left, the football was spotted on the UCLA 23-yard line. USC coach Larry Smith called for a time-out. Todd and his corps of receivers jogged to the sideline. A hush fell over the Rose Bowl crowd of 98,088.

Although he was recruited by every notable college, no other school really had a chance over USC. Todd's sister was a senior and his first cousin was planning on attending. His uncle Craig Fertig was an assistant athletic director. When Todd had visited USC that year, he'd been taken down on the field of the empty Coliseum — where he'd watched games with the Chief his entire life — and they put his name up on the scoreboard, complete with piped-in crowd noise. After that, Todd was taken by his All-American escort to a party on campus. "There was a three-and-a-half-foot purple bong. I was like, 'I'm home.' I even had my own weed on me," Todd recalls.

Todd redshirted his first year at USC. His second year he started every game, completing 62 percent of his passes for 2,600 yards and 16 touchdowns, leading the 1989 Trojans to a 9–2–1 record, a Pac-10 title, and a Rose Bowl victory over Michigan. Todd was named freshman player of the year. There was Heisman talk, speculation he'd leave early for the NFL.

At the opening of the next season, however, Coach Smith told reporters he wasn't yet decided on his starting quarterback. Smith was a flinty Ohio native who stressed discipline. Of all the coaches he'd ever had, Todd says, he hated Smith the most. Smith seemed determined to break the kid, going so far as to outlaw flip-flops on road trips. Smith told Marv privately he suspected Todd was using drugs. During the two months leading up to the UCLA game, Todd had been repeatedly drug-tested but never failed. He'd been suspended from the team for missing classes. He'd been benched as a starter for one set of downs. (When he returned to the game, the crowd booed; he threw a seventy-seven-yard touchdown pass.)

Now Todd and his receivers reached the sideline. "What do you want to do?" Coach Smith asked his quarterback.

Todd's face flushed to hot pink. "You're asking *me* what *I* want to do? Why start *now?*"

Todd turned to his receivers standing behind him. They believed in him. They'd seen his magic. His last-minute comeback against Washington State the previous season is still remembered as "the Drive": a textbook ninety-one-yard march downfield—with eleven crucial completions, including a touchdown pass and a two-point conversion—it prompted a call from former President Ronald Reagan.

Todd turned back to his coach. "This is what we're gonna do," he told Smith, yelling over the crowd. "*You're* gonna stay the fuck over here while *we* go win this game."

Todd and his boys jogged back to the huddle. Todd called the play. The ball was on the 23; sixteen seconds left. Wellman was in the slot. The pass was designed to go to him. But as Todd took the snap, he saw Wellman get jammed at the line.

"Whenever a receiver doesn't get a clean release," Todd recalls, "you got to go away from him, 'cause it just screws up the timing. So I looked back to the other side, and I saw Johnnie Morton on his corner route. He was supposed to run an eighteen-yard come-back, but we'd changed it at the line of scrimmage. Now he was making his move. When Johnnie went to the post, I saw the safety just drive on it, thinking I was throwing there. That's when I knew I had it."

Morton caught the ball deep in the left corner of the end zone, in front of the seats occupied by the Chief and his wife, Virginia. "It's been my favorite pass since Pop Warner," Todd said. "You really can't stop it."

On the evening of Saturday, January 19, 1991, Todd hit the bars on Balboa with his cousin Marc Fertig, a former USC baseball player, and two Trojan footballers. Coming home at 4:00 A.M., the boys were less than ten yards from the family beach house when two cop cars came screeching through the alley.

"I had a little nug on me," a marijuana bud, Todd says. "And a bindle of coke this guy had given me, this fan. It was half a gram. The cop went right for the drugs. Somebody must have tipped somebody off."

Todd was charged with two misdemeanors and allowed into a program for first-time offenders, but his USC career was finished. He declared himself eligible for the NFL draft and signed with

IMG, a big agency. For the first time since freshman summer, Todd went back into training with Marv.

Six weeks later, Todd walked onto the field at East Los Angeles College to show NFL scouts what he could do. His long locks had been sacrificed in favor of a bright-orange Johnny Unitas buzz cut, an image makeover suggested by his agent. There were representatives from eighteen teams. Trudi set up a table with lemonade and pastries. Todd was in the best shape of his life. With the help of a former NFL receiver, Todd says, "We put on an aerial show."

The only NFL owner in attendance was Al Davis of the Los Angeles Raiders. Arriving late, Davis climbed up into the stands and sat between his old friends Marv and Trudi. "I kind of knew right then that the Raiders were gonna pick me," Todd says. "I was totally psyched."

At the conclusion of Raider training camp that summer, as tradition dictated, the first draft pick threw a party. Todd had gone twenty-fourth in the first round and signed a three-year, $2.25 million deal, including a $1 million signing bonus. He rented a ranch and hired a company that did barbecue on a huge grill on a flatbed truck. He turned the barn into a stadium with hay-bale seating. He hired strippers, ten white and ten black. The grand finale: three porn stars with double-headed dildos. "They say in the history of the Raiders, it was the best rookie party ever," Todd says.

He made his first professional appearance on no smaller a stage than *Monday Night Football,* an exhibition against Dallas on August 12, 1991. Entering the game with fifteen minutes remaining, he moved the Raiders crisply downfield, completing three of four passes for sixteen yards and a touchdown.

As the season opened, to reduce the pressure on the rookie, coach Art Shell made Todd the third-string quarterback. Seeing little action on the field, he seemed determined to live up to his reputation as an epic partyer off it. Arriving at a hotel for an away game, he'd go with the rest of the players to a club. When they returned, he'd go out again. There were women, raves, Ecstasy, coke. Vets would save him a seat at the pregame meal just to hear his stories of the night before. "The cities started running into one another," Todd recalls.

Sometimes, for fun or hangover relief, Todd took pharmaceutical speed before the games. "I wasn't playing, so the warm-ups were my game. They'd have these great stereo systems in the stadiums; they'd be blasting the Stones or whatever. I'd take some Black Beauties and be throwing the ball seventy-five yards, running around playing receiver, fucking around — and then I was done for the day. I never played. Some guys did play on speed. Or they mixed with Vicodin. They could run through a fuckin' wall and not feel a thing."

The fifteenth week of the season, Todd made his first trip to New Orleans. After a long night of rum drinks in the Quarter, he ended up in bed with two stewardesses; he barely made it back for the pregame meal. The Superdome held seventy thousand screaming fans. "The noise was deafening. My *head*. I was in hell," Todd remembers now. "I was barely able to make it through warm-ups. I was sweating profusely, trying not to vomit."

Midway through the game, the Raiders' first-string quarterback, Jay Schroeder, was hit simultaneously from both sides, injuring an ankle. "Coach Shell looks at me, like, *Are you ready to go?*" Todd recalls. "I shook him off like a pitcher on the mound. I was like, *Are you fucking kidding me?*"

The following week, with Schroeder still sidelined for the final game of the regular season, Todd made his official debut against the Kansas City Chiefs. Marv was reported to have arrived at the stadium before the gates opened, waiting in line with the other fans to see his boy get his first start. Though the team lost 27–21, Todd completed 23 of 40 passes for 243 yards. Crowed *Los Angeles Times* sports columnist Mike Downey: "Sunday was Marinovich's football bar mitzvah. The boy became a man."

The next day was a Monday — five days before the Raiders were due to appear in the AFC wild-card game, also against the Chiefs. Ready to leave home for practice, Todd went to his refrigerator and discovered that he'd run out of clean urine.

As a consequence of his arrest, the NFL had been requiring Todd to take frequent urine tests. Todd felt he couldn't function without marijuana. "It just allowed me to be comfortable in this loud, chaotic world. Especially the world I was living in. I couldn't fathom being sober," he says. To reconcile these conflicting realities, he kept Gatorade bottles of clean urine, donated by non-pot-smoking friends, in the refrigerator at his Manhattan Beach townhouse, one block from the ocean, that he'd purchased for $900,000.

All season long, this had been his pretest routine: Pour the refrigerated pee into a small sunscreen bottle. Go to practice. Put the bottle in a cup of coffee and leave it in his locker to warm up while attending a team meeting. Come back, stash the bottle inside his compression shorts, beneath his package. Usually he'd ask the supervisor to turn on the water in the sink to aid his shy bladder. "I got it down to a science," he says.

But now he was out of clean pee, another critical responsibility blown off—like the time at USC when he couldn't be bothered to fill out his housing paperwork and ended up a homeless scholarship athlete. Like Marv, the real world wasn't really his thing.

Luckily, on this Monday morning, one of Todd's former USC teammates was still at his house, left over from the weekend's partying. He didn't do drugs. Unbeknownst to Todd, however, he'd been drinking nonstop since his own game on Saturday.

Soon after, the Raiders got a call from the NFL: Todd's urine sample had registered a blood-alcohol level of .32—four times the legal limit. "They're like, 'This guy is a fucking full-blown alcoholic,'" Todd says. "They made me check into Centinela Hospital in Inglewood for alcohol detox—and I hadn't even been drinking." The team left without him; he flew later. This time the Chiefs were ready for Todd. He threw four interceptions, fumbled once.

After the season the team held an intervention. Todd spent forty-five days at a rehab facility. The next season, Todd tried to stop smoking pot. Instead, for six weeks, he took LSD after every game—acid didn't show up on the tox screen. After one poor performance, coaches complained that he wasn't grasping the complex offense. Finally, he failed an NFL drug test. Strike two. Back to rehab.

The next August, 1993, near the end of his third training camp, Todd failed a third drug test for marijuana. Al Davis brought the kid into his office. After two seasons, eight games, eight touchdown passes, Todd's NFL playing days were over.

"I was like, Fuck it. I'd been playing my whole life. I'd accomplished my goals. I never said I wanted to play forever. I just wanted to play at the highest level. Even in college, it felt like the shit you had to put up with in order to play wasn't worth it. Those few amazing hours on Sunday were being outweighed by all the bullshit."

Todd packed up his Land Cruiser and drove to Mexico to camp and surf. "I thought I had a ton of money," he says.

It was shortly after Swallows Day in San Juan Capistrano, March 24, 1997. Todd lived in a small house near the beach; a few friends were hanging out. At one point, somebody got the idea to go to the grammar school next door and play dunk hoops on the low baskets.

As the game got going, the motley crew of loadies transformed themselves into ballers. As always, Todd couldn't miss. He was by now twenty-seven. After traveling the world for two years, he'd attempted to return to football, only to blow out his knee on his first day of training camp with the Winnipeg Blue Bombers of the Canadian Football League. During his recovery, an old buddy from Zero Period at Capo had introduced him to the guitar and then later to heroin. Their band, Scurvy, achieved modest success, playing at clubs on the Sunset Strip. Then the bassist was busted, ruining hopes for a record deal. For the past three years, Todd had been a full-blown addict.

Going up for a rebound, one guy hurt his back. John Valdez was twenty-nine and weighed about 275 pounds: he went down like a slab of beef. With much difficulty, the guys hauled him back to Todd's bed. Valdez had no money; the emergency room was not an option. In agony, he appealed to his host: "You got anything to help the pain?"

Todd left the room and retrieved his stash of Mexican black-tar heroin. "I fixed myself first," he says. "I remember it being strong stuff, so I just gave him a fraction of the amount." A few minutes later, returning from a cigarette break on the front porch, he checked on Valdez. "He's frothing from the mouth. He's fuckin' blue."

Todd ran outside and retrieved the garden hose—it was easier than lugging Valdez to the shower, as he'd seen in movies. When that didn't help, Todd started slapping him in the face.

"I'm fucking hitting this guy with everything I've got," he recalls. "And I swear, I could see his spirit struggling to leave his body. I don't tell this story much; people think I was hallucinating. But on heroin you don't hallucinate. You do *not* fucking hallucinate on fucking heroin. The only way I could describe it is like when you see heat waves on the beach—when the heat waves eddy up and warp your vision. It was like that, and it was colorful. I actually saw it, the life force or whatever, as it would leave the top of his head, and he'd become this fleshbag, and then I would smack the shit out of him and I would see it actually coming back into him."

The friends had scattered; there was one guy left with them in the house. Todd yelled, "Call fuckin' 911!"

As the other guy cleaned up the drugs and the syringe, the dispatcher coached Todd through CPR. Finally the paramedics arrived, along with sheriff's deputies.

The day before, Todd had helped a buddy harvest his marijuana crop. As a thank-you, he'd gotten a trash bag full of cuttings, not bud but still smokable. He'd stashed the bag in his garage rafters with his surfboards and promptly forgot about it. As the paramedics wheeled out Valdez on a gurney, one of the deputies came into the room holding the trash bag of pot. "Where are the plants?" he demanded.

"I'm not a grower," Todd tried to explain. "See, this buddy of mine—"

Just then, another deputy entered the room. He was carrying two half-dead pot plants that Todd had set up in his laundry room with a drugstore-variety grow light.

Todd was charged with felony marijuana cultivation. He served two months in jail and a third at a minimum-security facility in OC known as the Farm.

In April 1999, just shy of his thirtieth birthday, Todd was finally cleared to play again by the NFL. He promptly herniated a disk playing pickup hoops. That summer, he worked out for several teams. The Chargers and the Bears showed real interest, but he failed the physical; no deals could be made. He ended up signing as a backup quarterback with the B.C. Lions of Vancouver, in the Canadian Football League.

Except for a little pot, Todd was drug-free for the first time in years. His roomie was Canadian. About two weeks into his stay, he asked Todd if he wanted to go with him "to check his babies."

It turned out he was growing potent B.C. bud. On the way home,

Todd stopped at a head shop to buy a bong. There were little vials scattered everywhere on the ground. His junkie warning system sounded a shrill alarm.

Todd had arrived in his own personal land of Oz, a place where junkies bought and used heroin openly and cops only got involved if somebody OD'ed. The heroin was called China White. It was infinitely more potent than the black tar Todd had used before—and relatively cheap. He got into a routine: "The day before every game, we would do a walk-through in the dome—that was my day for needle exchange. All my years of being a dope fiend, the hardest part was always getting needles. I was getting good coke and really pure heroin and combining them. That's all I wanted to do. I woke up, fixed, went to practice. Thank God I was just backing up. I was just the clipboard guy, playing the opposing quarterback in practice."

Once, during halftime at a home game, Todd retrieved a premade rig out of his locker and went to the bathroom to shoot up. Sitting on the toilet, half listening to the chalk talk, he slammed the heroin. As the team was leaving the locker room for the second half, he struggled with the screen in his glass crack pipe—he wasn't getting a good hit. Then the pipe broke, and he lacerated his left thumb. By the time he got out onto the field, his thumb wrapped in a towel, the game had already started. He took up the clipboard, his only duty. "I didn't even know what play they were calling," Todd says. "Nobody looked at the shit I wrote down anyway."

At the end of the season, the team had a party. Todd was "gowed out of my mind," meaning that he was "somewhere between a nod and full-on slumber." His weight had dropped to 176 pounds. "I was a celibate heroin monk. I would go downtown, cop, come back to my pad, and not leave till the drugs were gone," he says. "There was no furniture in my place, just a bed and a TV. I wasn't eating. I spent a lot of time in this Astro minivan I had. I'd just climb into the back and fix. My life revolved around dope and my dog."

Now, at the party, Todd became aware that the general manager of the Lions was motioning for him to come over. The GM was a good guy who'd recruited him to come to B.C. He shook Todd's hand. "I know we signed you for one year with an option for another year—" he said pregnantly, looking grave.

And then he issued a toothy, *gotcha* grin: "We'd like to pick up that option!"

"You have to be fuckin' crazy," Todd said. "I can't stay here."

Todd returned to football for the last time in the spring of 2000—a mercurial stint with the Los Angeles Avengers in the Arena Football League. His first year, he tied the record for most touchdowns in a single game despite undergoing severe heroin withdrawal; after shitting his pants during warm-ups, he came out and threw ten touchdowns to win a game against the Houston Thunderbears. That same year, at age thirty-one, he was named to the all-rookie team. The next season, he became L.A.'s franchise player. The day he picked up his signing bonus, he was busted buying heroin. With him in the truck was $30,000 cash in an envelope. Toward the end of the season, he was ejected from successive games for throwing a clipboard and a hand towel at officials. Finally, he was suspended from the team.

"At that point, heroin became my full-time job," Todd says.

By 2004, he was broke and living again on the Balboa Peninsula, haunting the beaches and alleyways of his youth. In the summers, he often lived on the beach, washing at the bathhouse. Sometimes he couch-surfed with friends. Different from many junkies, he seemed to have a knack for being a good guest. Even at his worst, he maintained the sweet and vulnerable quality that makes people want to embrace him. He didn't go to his family's place often. He hated the way Trudi looked at him. At some point, his uncle Craig would accuse him of stealing and Trudi would change the locks.

Because he'd lost his car and license, Todd had trouble scoring heroin. He couldn't afford it anyway. There was a ton of speed around Newport Beach, though. "People were practically giving it away," he recalls.

When he was high, he loved to skateboard. "It was a way to burn off all that energy that I had from the meth. It was like surfing on fucking concrete. I would skate for eight hours a day. I'd be just carving up and down the street for miles and miles. It was probably the most fun I've ever had on drugs. That and sex. Meth makes you just fucking perv. It turns normal people with some morals into just fucking sick perverts. That's all I wanted to do, you know, is look at porn or create my own."

A ghostly, six-five redhead living on the same tiny peninsula where he grew up so prominently, Todd was an easy mark. In August 2004, he was arrested by Newport Beach police for skateboarding in a prohibited zone. Police found meth and syringes on him. In May 2005, he was rousted from a public bathhouse by police; he fled on his beach cruiser and was apprehended fifteen blocks away. Police found drug paraphernalia in his toiletry kit but no drugs. One of the cops was an old Capo Valley teammate. Todd was charged with violating probation. In June 2005, thanks to twenty-three of his former USC teammates who put up the $4,600 required for him to enter an inpatient treatment program, Todd avoided going back to jail. For the next year, he was in and out of rehab facilities.

At a little past one in the morning on August 26, 2007, a pair of Newport police officers riding in an unmarked minivan spotted Todd, by now thirty-eight years old, skateboarding on the boardwalk. He was carrying a guitar case and wearing a backpack; he had just been to his hook spot. As Todd knew well, skating is not permitted on the boardwalk.

"One cop started running at me. The other one's crossing the boulevard, trying to head me off. I popped off my skateboard, dropped my guitar case, and fucking ran down this alley. One of them yelled: 'Todd! Freeze!' I heard a *pop pop pop*. I thought they were fucking *shooting!*" It turned out to be a taser. The projectile imbedded itself in the lower part of his backpack. "My leg started spasming, but it wasn't too bad. I just kept running." He ended up on a second-floor balcony. "I saw the fucking light come on, and a guy came out, looked at me, and shut the door real fast. I was like, *Oh fuck!*"

By then there were helicopters with spotlights. He could hear the dogs. "That's when I gave up. I've seen too many people come into fucking jail tore up from dogs. So I just laid down on the fucking ground and they found me."

It was his ninth arrest. He was charged with felony possession of a controlled substance and misdemeanor counts of unauthorized possession of a hypodermic needle and resisting a police officer. He did his second stint at the Farm, where he picked vegetables and repaired irrigation equipment.

*

Evening in the suburbs, September 2008. The dishes have been put away, the washer in the garage is cycling through another load. A fifteen-year-old boy sits at the dining room table, doing his honors geometry homework.

Todd saunters into the room. He stands over the kid for a moment, places his large freckled mitt on his shoulder. The knuckles are raw from his part-time job scraping barnacles off the bottoms of boats. It is a tough, physical job. He likes that it tires him out; he always seems to be a little jittery and on edge, generally ill at ease in the world. He wears a wetsuit and goggles, uses a long air hose, makes his rounds from motor yacht to sailboat in a dinghy. He'll be down there all alone for a half-hour at a time, his bubbles slowly circling the hull, lost in repetitious physical effort, cocooned by the silent, salty water. He compares it to the soothing feeling of heroin.

As of tonight, he's been sober thirteen months. Following his last arrest, he was diverted to a special drug court run by a county judge. Hanging over Todd's head is a suspended sentence of two years in jail. His schedule is nearly as crowded as it was during the summer before ninth grade. Pee testing three times a week. Weekly drug-court sessions, one-on-one therapy, group therapy, sessions with his probation officer, thrice-weekly AA meetings. If he completes the program, in another eighteen months, he could have his felonies dismissed or reduced, opening up his opportunity for coaching at a public school. With all the responsibilities, he is expected to cobble together a new life. It is a difficult task.

Besides the barnacle scraping, for which he makes about $40 a boat, Todd leads a weekly group meeting at a rehab facility; people seem to respond to both his celebrity status and his easygoing manner. He's also been painting murals in people's houses. There is a local gallery that wants to show his work; a website is planned for direct buying. His other source of income is private coaching. Over the past year, he's become known as somewhat of a "quarterback whisperer." This past summer he worked with Jordan Palmer, brother of Carson; both Palmers are on the roster at Cincinnati. USC coach Pete Carroll recently told him he'd try to get Todd some work next summer at a football camp. There will be an interview for a job as offensive coordinator at a local junior college. Right now, Todd has four students, kids of varying ages. All of them have promise; Jordan Greenwood is one of his most talented.

"Dude. You got a minute?"

Jordan looks up attentively. He is five foot eleven and a half, 150 pounds. He's a freshman at Orange Lutheran, one of the schools that competes in the Trinity League against Todd's old team Mater Dei. Jordan started playing tackle football at age eight. He has always been a super athlete. One time in a soccer game, he had three goals in the first ten minutes.

About a year ago, Jordan was referred to Marv. Todd was brought in on day two. Though he hadn't been sober long, Todd watched Jordan throw and thought to himself, *I could really help this kid.* The first order of business: completely remake Jordan's throw—which nearly gave Jordan's father a heart attack. For the next six months, every night, Jordan had to stand in front of the mirror and repeat the new motion a thousand times. Each rep had to be perfect. It was up to Jordan; nobody could do it for him.

The first three exhibition games of the new season, the freshman team coach rotated four quarterbacks. Fleet of foot, Jordan was perfect for the veer offense; he scored fifteen touchdowns, including a seventy-yard run against an inner-city team. Then came the fourth exhibition. The entire extended Greenwood family was on hand to watch. Jordan did not play.

Now, after a nice dinner of strip steaks and salmon and double-stuffed potatoes, with all the other adults out of the room, Todd folds himself into the chair next to Jordan. His orange hair is not so bright anymore, like a colorful curtain faded over the years by the sun.

"What's the worst part of your experience over there at Orange?" Todd asks.

Jordan drums his pencil on the open pages of his math book. "I don't know," he says.

"Not playing?"

Jordan makes eye contact. "Yeah, mostly."

"What else?"

Shrug. "I dunno." This is the biggest thing in his life. You can tell he's trying not to cry.

"Listen, dude," Todd says, as warm a *dude* as was ever uttered. "Things can look pretty overwhelming right now because you're so young, but believe me, you can have a great career—possibly at Orange Lutheran. I wouldn't cash my chips and be bitter just yet.

Some days, stuff just looks all wrong—take it from me. You're gonna be fine. You just have to believe in yourself."

Jordan nods his head, brightening.

Todd gives him a little shove. Next game, Jordan will run for three touchdowns and throw for another. Before the season is over, he'll be promoted to JV and win the team's most valuable offensive player award.

Todd and Marv Marinovich are at a self-storage facility in San Juan Capistrano. Most of Marv's equipment is inside, odd-looking machines and exercise stuff. Somehow, in the haste of the initial rental, the key was lost. After attempting to drill out the lock—it looks so easy in the movies—they await a locksmith.

Todd is squatting on the hot asphalt like a gang member in a prison yard. Marv is standing against the building in a sliver of shade. Ending his seventh decade, he looks twenty years younger. He lives alone, eats only organic food. Despite his ferocious reputation, he seems a sweet man who loves Todd very much. After two divorces, he has only Todd and Traci, who lives several hours away, and Mikhail, his son with his second wife, a former dancer. Mikhail is a six-foot-four sophomore defensive end at Syracuse, about as far as you can get from OC. Last year Mikhail made news when he was arrested for getting drunk and breaking into the college's gym equipment room with a friend. Todd advised: "Don't be stupid. You're a Marinovich. You have a target on your back."

Marv's stuff is in storage because he was asked to leave the private high school out of which he'd been working for nearly two years. There was a beef with his young partner. After a display of temper, Marv was asked to vacate by school authorities. The partner stayed. Todd and a friend went with a U-Haul to claim Marv's equipment.

Now, because it's the end of the month, they have to pay or move. A friend of Todd's has volunteered a garage. Todd has taken care of everything. Since he's been straight, he's spent a lot of time helping Marv. He's helping him get his driver's license back—a long tale of red tape. He helped him buy a computer. He's helping with visits to the doctor; there are indications of heart arrhythmia. "All those years I was so out of it. It feels good to be the one helping," Todd says. "He's always been there for me."

When Todd was born, he was listed as Marvin Scott Marinovich on his birth certificate. Trudi changed it a few years later to Todd Marvin. Later—an inside joke after a long day of training—Marv started calling his son Buzzy, after Buzzie Bavasi, the legendary Dodgers general manager. For some reason, Todd began calling Marv Buzzy too. Nowadays, when Marv calls Todd's cell phone— Todd's ringtone is the opening bars of the *Monday Night Football* theme song—Todd will pick up and say, "Hey, Buzzy, what's up?"

Now, waiting for the locksmith, needing talk to fill the time, Todd begins telling Marv about the art history course he's taking at Orange Coast College. The other night in class, Todd explains, they were learning about dadaism, the anti-art movement born in Switzerland during World War I. One of the icons of the movement was this dude named Marcel Duchamp. He did a cool painting called *Nude Descending a Staircase.* "When he was coming up, his older brothers and his friends were the ones recognized as the famous painters. They thought Marcel sucked," Todd explains. "But in the end, everybody recognized that Marcel was the true master."

"After he was dead, I'm sure," Marv says.

"When I heard that," Todd continues, ignoring his father's comment, "the first thing I thought of was you, Buzzy. Someday people will realize what a genius *you* are."

Marv looks at him. He's not sure if Todd is goofing or serious. He raises his thick eyebrows archly. "Have you been drinking something?" he asks.

And then the two of them, Buzzy and Buzzy, share a big laugh.

Driving north on I-5, past the rugged mountains of Camp Pendleton, Todd and I are returning from off-loading Marv's stuff. The large U-Haul truck judders wildly on the uneven asphalt. Even at fifty miles per hour in the slow lane, the ride is torturous. It has been a full day; the mood in the cab could rightfully be called slaphappy. Todd has noticed that if he sings a note and holds it, the pounding of the road will make his voice quaver rhythmically. It is a silly, joyful thing that turns the discomfort of the ride upside down. I remember my son doing the same on this stretch of road when he was about five.

You could say Todd missed his childhood. Sports took away his first twenty years. Then drugs took the second twenty, the decades of experience and personal growth that shape most men as they near forty, which Todd will turn this upcoming July 4. When Todd was young, Trudi used to tell him that the Independence Day fireworks were all for him. Today she estimates that since he's been straight, these past thirteen months, Todd has matured from an emotional age of about sixteen to maybe twenty-five, the same age as his fiancée.

Alix is an OC girl with pretty blue eyes. She is pregnant. They are expecting a boy. They plan to name him Baron Buzzy Marinovich. They have cleaned out the Chief's trophy room on the first floor of the beach house and made a little nest for themselves, complete with a new mini-kitchen where the bar used to be.

Todd says he's finished with drugs—the frantic hustle, the lies, the insidious need, the way the world perceives you as a loser. Each time he went to jail, he walked the gauntlet of deputies, many of them former high school football players. "You had everything and you threw it away," they said. It was hard to hear. He knows they were saying the truth.

Three months from now, in early February, feeling pressure from all directions—the deaths within two weeks of his uncle Craig and grandma Virginia, the upcoming gallery show, Marv's health problems, a new life with his fiancée, questions about his future —he will drive on a Sunday afternoon to his old hook spot in Santa Ana and buy some black tar. As soon as he smokes the first hit, he will throw the dope out the window and call his probation officer, then drive directly to the county offices to give himself up. Sixteen months of sobriety lost in an instant. His penalty will be one week at the Farm; it could have been two years. As he drives across town to surrender, he will see in his mind a picture of Alix, the swell of her belly. He wants to be a father to his son.

"I'm gonna get through this program," he says now, his voice quavering comically as we bounce up the road in the U-Haul. "The day is coming when I'm not gonna have to piss in a fucking cup."

From the driver's seat, sensing his good mood, I ask: "How much effect do you think that Marv and sports and all contributed to you turning to drugs?" I'd been saving this line of questioning since our first interview, six months earlier. "If you look at your life, it's interesting. It appears that to get out of playing, you sort of partied away your eligibility. It's like you're too old to play now, so you don't have to do drugs anymore. Has the burden been lifted?"

Todd looks out the windshield down the road. The truck bounces. Thirty full seconds pass.

"I don't know how to answer that," Todd says at last. "I really have very few answers."

"That's kind of what it seems like. A little."

Twenty seconds.

"No thoughts?"

"I think, more than anything, it's genetic. I got that gene from the Fertigs—my uncle, the Chief. They were huge drinkers. And then the environment plays a part in it, for sure."

He lights another Marlboro Red, sucks down the first sweet hit. He rides in silence the rest of the way home.

PAT JORDAN

Chasing Jose

FROM DEADSPIN.COM

I HAVE BEEN PURSUING JOSE, like the Holy Grail, for three months now, trying to nail him down for a magazine profile he'd agreed to do in January, partly because, as his lawyer/agent had told me, "Jose's on the balls on his ass," and partly because Jose was trying to interest a publisher in his second steroids-tell-all book, which existed only as a two-page proposal of typos that had yet to interest any publisher. This second book would be titled *Vindicated,* and it would "encompass approximately 300 pages and will require six months to complete."

My pursuit of Jose began in January when I called him in California. His girlfriend, Heidi, answered the phone. I told her that I was writing a magazine story about Jose writing a book. "And a movie," she said. "Jose is writing a book and a movie about himself." I said, "You mean a screenplay?" She paused a beat, then said, "No, a movie." I said, "Of course."

I tried to picture Jose writing his book and his movie. Hunched over, his broad shoulders casting a shadow across his desk like a raptor's wings, his brow furrowed in concentration, his massively muscled body tensed in anticipation of that torrent of words about to flow out of him like urine for one of the many steroid tests he'd been forced to take during his baseball career. I wondered, just how *does* Jose write? Like Shakespeare, with a quill pen on parchment? Like Dickens, wearing a green eye shade while seated at a clerk's desk? Like Hemingway, standing at a lectern in Finca Vigia, with a stubby pencil and unlined paper? Like Thomas Wolfe, in his Victorian house in Asheville, pounding away on a tall, black, manual Underwood? Or maybe the words flow out of Jose in such a torrent, ten thousand an hour, that he can relieve himself adequately of his thoughts only by tap-tap-tapping on a lightning-fast computer, like Stephen King?

Anyway, as Heidi said, Jose is writing a book, and a movie, about his life, which he will star in, as himself. Jose is also going to star in a kung fu martial arts movie. That's what Rob told me. "Jose is fielding offers," said Rob. Rob is Jose's lawyer and agent. He's a Cherokee Indian from North Carolina. In the four years that Rob has been Jose's agent, Jose has racked up about a half-a-million dollars in legal fees. Rob hasn't been paid anything yet, although he said that Jose did give him his five World Series rings, worth about $50,000, as a down payment.

Heidi, Rob told me, is Jose's girlfriend/publicist. She's a "cute, little junior college graduate, who lives with Jose," said Rob. "She likes to let Jose think she's working hard for him when really all she is doing is fucking things up for him." Rob said Heidi lives with Jose without paying anything, which may be literally true, but not figuratively. The price women pay for living with Jose is actually quite high. All those boring days and nights during which Jose rarely speaks, except to say, "Where's the Iguana?" because of Jose's fervent belief that when "women talk only bad things can happen." All those needles and vials of performance-enhancing drugs around the house which his woman of the moment must learn to differentiate, winstrol from deca-durabolin from HGH, and then draw the proper amount of fluid into each syringe and inject that needle and its fluid into Jose's buttocks. All those variations of his moods from steroid-fueled anger to steroid-withdrawal depression. All those startling changes in his genitalia, his penis swelling with steroid use at the same time his testicles are shrinking from steroid use. All those strange women's messages on Jose's cell phone. All those trips to the gynecologist to cure the STDs Jose brought back with him from one of his road trips. And, finally, most depressing of all, all those perfunctory sex acts with Jose, doggy style in front of a mirror so Jose can watch himself perform, his chest muscles and biceps twitching as he works. Which is why Jose's first two wives, Miss Miami, and Miss Fitness America, divorced him.

After a little prodding, Rob did admit to me that as of the moment no *actual* offers for that kung fu movie have come Jose's way, which, considering his fielding prowess (he once camped under a fly ball which hit him in the head and bounced into the bleachers for a home run), might be a good thing. Still, Jose spends his days at his house in Sherman Oaks, California, off the Ventura Freeway near the San Fernando Valley, home of the porn industry, waiting for producers to call to inform him that the time is ripe, America is now hungry for a kung fu movie starring a steroid-inflated, Cuban ex-baseball player in his forties. In anticipation of that call, Jose showed off his martial arts moves to the man who choreographed *Crouching Tiger, Hidden Dragon*. The man watched Jose's 250-pound body spin and kick and leap into the air for a few minutes and then he told Jose that his moves "were stiff, not very fluid, and you don't kick very well." Jose told Rob, "That guy doesn't know what the fuck he's talking about."

Jose always knows best. He's the master of everything he undertakes and he can point as proof to his baseball success, 462 home runs in seventeen years, based on a simple philosophy, "see ball, hit ball." Jose has carried over this philosophy into everything in his life. "See girl, fuck girl." "See Ferrari, buy Ferrari." "See money, take money." Admittedly, Jose's philosophy of life has brought him some success with girls and fancy cars, but it has not, of late, brought him much success with money. Rob said, "Right now, Jose has zero money." In fact, Rob has a lien on one of Jose's two houses, and "whenever Jose pisses me off, I threaten to foreclose."

Rob has yet to foreclose because he has the stoic patience of his ancestors who made that terrible trek from North Carolina to Oklahoma, which was called "the Trail of Tears." But that doesn't mean that Jose hasn't "pissed off" Rob a lot over the last four years that he has been Jose's lawyer. When Rob was defending Jose and his twin brother Ozzie a few years ago in a civil suit brought against the two brothers by a man they had beat up in a Miami bar, he told Jose to keep a low profile and not buy anything because Rob planned on pointing out to the court that Jose was broke. A week before the trial began, Jose leased a $300,000 Rolls-Royce and bought a $2.6 million house, in addition to the $1.7 million house he already owned in Encino. "I had to admit in court that all those things Jose owned," said Rob. The jury returned a verdict that required Jose to pay the man he and Ozzie beat up 90 percent of $1.5 million. Ozzie, who is also broke, had to pay the other 10 percent. "Jose still hasn't paid a cent," said Rob.

Rob told me that after the trial Jose put his expensive house in

South Florida up for sale, turned down offers of over $1 million, then swapped his house for some Mexican stocks that were supposed to be worth millions in a few years. By the time Jose sold those stocks, they were worth a small fraction of that amount.

Over the years, Rob told me, he had negotiated numerous prospective deals for thousands of dollars for Jose to promote a fast-food franchise (he'd hold up a huge sandwich and exclaim, "This thing's gotta be on something!"), appear in a reality TV show, and have a movie made based on Jose's life. But no matter how much money Jose was offered in those deals, it seems it was never enough. He demanded more, and all the offers vanished, to Rob's chagrin.

"I just can't get him to do what's best for him," said Rob. One of the things Rob thought would be best for Jose was to let me write a profile of him for a national magazine, which would help him sell his book, and the movie about his life, neither of which had been sold yet. (Even the ever-optimistic Rob didn't hold out much hope for the kung fu movie.) When I agreed to write the profile and found a magazine that would publish it, Rob told me to call Heidi to work out the details of my trip to Sherman Oaks. "I cleared it with Jose," said Rob. So I called Heidi.

"What interview?" Heidi said. I told her. She said, "Jose's too busy now, he's writing a book, and a movie, about his life." I called Rob. He called Heidi. Then he called me to tell me that he'd "straightened Heidi out." So I called Heidi. She said, "Will it be a cover story?" No. "Then Jose's not interested. He's too busy writing a book, and a movie, about his life." I called Rob. I told him Heidi was not quite "straightened out." He called her. Then I called her. She said, "Will you pay Jose?" No. She said, "Then Jose's not interested. He's too busy writing his—" I said, "I know," and hung up.

During the marathon of my negotiations with Heidi, the Mitchell Report was published. Jose's name figured in the report based on the allegations he had made about steroid use he'd instigated with some of his teammates in his first book, *Juiced.* In fact, Jose tried to crash the press conference when Mitchell announced the findings of his report. He was intercepted by security and escorted from the hearings because he didn't have press credentials. But now that Jose was experiencing the last five minutes of his fame before he retired to the anonymity of his future job as an official greeter at a San Fernando Valley Gentleman's Club, a book publisher surfaced like the Loch Ness Monster, and offered to publish Jose's as-yet-unwritten second book, *Vindicated,* if it included new revelations about baseball's steroid users. There were coy hints from Jose that he would mention such names as Roger Clemens and Alex Rodriguez. The publisher agreed to shell out $250,000 for such a tome if it could be written in ten days so it could be published in April, on baseball's opening day. Rob called and asked me if I wanted to write that seventy-thousand-word tome in ten days. I said, "You said it would take six months in the proposal." Rob said, "Ten days." I said, "Rob, I can't write two thousand words in ten days. I'm not a *fucking* typist!" Besides, I added, I was still committed to the magazine profile. Rob said, "Call Heidi." I called Heidi. (By now my wife had begun to be suspicious about my whispered telephone conversations with this mysterious Heidi. "Who is this broad?" she said. I shrugged.) Heidi answered the phone. She said, "Jose can't do the interview now because his book publisher doesn't want him to reveal anything that will be in his book." Click. Buzz.

Apparently, there wasn't as much new dirt in Jose's second book as he had promised. Not a day after the press reported that he had signed a contract to write a second book, Jose's ghostwriter, a former *Sports Illustrated* writer, informed the press that he was withdrawing from the project because, after he had reviewed Jose's material, he'd decided that Jose couldn't produce the goods on A-Rod's supposed drug use. Jose's publisher then dropped his book and Rob scurried around to do damage control. He claimed that Jose had canceled the deal with his publisher because he had got a better offer from another publisher that no one in Jose's camp would identify. Then, a third ghostwriter (if you can count me as the first) was impressed into Jose's service on the strength of his impeccable writing credentials—a stint at the *National Inquirer,* and the authorship of O. J. Simpson's sterling effort, *If I Did It,* in which Simpson described how he would have killed his wife, Nicole, and Ron Goldman, if he had actually killed them, which he hadn't. *Vindicated* was begun, and just as quickly finished, seventy thousand words in ten days (I am in awe!), and will be published April 1 by that phantom book publisher, which, it would later be revealed, was to be Simon & Schuster.

Jose was paid $100,000 for *Juiced,* which sold about 200,000 copies. He has received about $850,000 in royalties so far, but he claims he is owed $1.4 million. The book was a bestseller despite the fact that many people questioned the veracity of Jose's claim about rampant steroid use in baseball for a number of reasons, not the least of which was Jose's unsavory reputation as a wife-beater (Miss Fitness America), a baseball slacker (his teammates accused him of not hustling), a gun-toting, sports car–speeding, steroid-crazed solipsist who cared nothing about anyone else on earth, except himself. He had a reputation for not showing up at benefits for children and card shows as he'd promised. In fact, Rob said that one of the reasons why he had so much difficulty selling Jose's second book was because "he never showed up for interviews" for his first book. "I had to go get him out of bed for interviews." Jose even managed to turn his penchant for refusing to get out of bed into a moneymaking scheme when he was sentenced to house arrest after a steroid-use conviction. He simply offered his fans a chance to spend the day with him, hanging out at his house in South Florida, for $2,500, while Jose slept.

It is no wonder then, that Jose's steroid revelations were met with a jaundiced eye, despite the fact that those revelations were essentially proven true. Still, the *L.A. Times* was not impressed, calling *Juiced* "the worst book in three centuries," which may, or may not, have been an exaggeration, but which prompted me to buy a copy of *Juiced* and, with much trepidation, dip my toes into its fetid waters.

In *Juiced*, Jose dismisses his baseball achievements and the $45 million he made, and writes, instead, about those subjects that warmed his heart: fast cars and loose women. He lists all the fancy cars he owned and raced dangerously on public roads, and all the many women he bedded (baseball players are constitutionally unable to be faithful to wives and girlfriends, he claimed), which, curiously, did not seem to give him much pleasure. These women he referred to, decorously, as "road beef" and "slump-busters" if they were outrageously homely, and "imports" if they were classy enough, like Miss Fitness America, to import to the city where he was employed. Jose even talked about his relationship with Madonna, with whom he once had a flirtation that did not go much beyond the teenaged make-out stage because he found her so unattractive. (Jose is ever the gentleman.)

Jose's most explosive revelation in the book concerned his team-mate with the Oakland A's, Mark McGwire. They were called "the Bash Brothers" because of all the home runs they hit for the A's in the eighties. Jose claimed that he convinced Mark to take steroids after his rookie year, and that often in the clubhouse he and Mc-Gwire would retire to a stall in the bathroom where they would each drop his drawers and bend over while the other injected him with steroids. Jose and Mark seemed to spend more time in club-house bathrooms, bent over, exposing their buttocks, than Congressman Larry Craig did in the Minneapolis Airport restroom.

After I finished *Juiced,* and thoroughly washed my hands, I learned from Rob that Jose's second wife, Miss Fitness America, had written her own book about her life with Jose, after they were divorced. It was called *Juicy,* and, curiously, it was published by the same publisher that had published *Juiced,* Regan Books. "Jose negotiated the deal for his ex-wife's book with Judith Regan," said Rob, "so he could pay for the child support he owed her for their daughter." After Jose got his ex-wife her book contract, he told her, "Go ahead, knock yourself out." And she did.

Although *Juicy* is every bit as depressing as *Juiced,* it does have one literary quality *Juiced* never aspired to. *Juicy* is a *very* funny book, although I'm not so sure that Miss Fitness America, a breast-implanted young woman named Jessica, as in Rabbit, intended it to be.

In *Juicy,* Jessica describes herself as a failed Hooter's waitress whose claim to fame, before she became Jose's "road beef," was that she *almost* gave Lars Ulrich of the band Metallica a blow job, to which news her sister replied, "So cool!" Jessica wrote that she always wanted to be a dancer (she did not specify, with pole or without) but knew that dream was beyond her because she was too lazy. So she rechanneled her ambition toward being a veterinarian, but abandoned that dream before she even embarked on it because she had Attention Deficit Disorder. (Unlike Jose, at least Jessica was self-aware.) Then she met Jose. It was a "meet cute" at Hooter's, and a match made in the heavens of such matches.

At first, Jessica loved being Jose's "road beef" and then his "import," because he spent a lot of time buying her clothes she couldn't afford on her Hooter's salary. Then they set up house-keeping at Jose's Coral Gables mansion with its rock waterfall pool and its cougars and giant Iguanas roaming the grounds and, sadly, Jessica discovering that living her life with Jose was "a total fucking bore." Her daily calendar of their activities reads something like this: sleep, wake, fuck, eat, lay by the pool, find Iguana, eat, fuck, shop, watch TV, fuck, sleep (for Jose anyway), and masturbate, all, of course, without Jose ever speaking. This last activity on Jessica's daily to-do list she was forced to resort to because Jose's sexual performance left a lot to be desired, at least by Jessica. The way it worked was, Jose had sex with Jessica in front of a mirror until he had an orgasm, then spilled off her and went to sleep. While her big lug snoozed, Jessica slipped out of bed and repaired to the bathroom where she made love to herself. Jessica claimed she didn't have an orgasm with Jose during their first two years of sex. She wrote, "If he noticed, he didn't care." So, she began faking orgasms, "but I can't honestly say he noticed that either."

When I finished reading *Juicy*, I had only one thought: how do such people, so perfectly right for each other, meet? Craigslist? Divine intervention? A database reeking of fire and brimstone? It astounded me that Jessica and Jose ever even got divorced. Probably they did, because, as Jessica wrote, when Jose was no longer rich and famous after he left baseball she found him *less* interesting, damning herself in the process by admitting that at one time she had actually found such a man *interesting*.

Today, Jose is not only less interesting, but also broke. Which is why his second tome, *Vindicated,* is so important to him. It is his last chance in life to forestall, for a few more years anyway, that looming downward spiral of his life when he will be forced to confront his future as an official greeter at that San Fernando Valley strip club. Rob, ever Jose's Sancho Panza, and ever conflicted, said, "I want to put Jose on a path to enjoy the fruits of his athletic labors. He's genuinely a nice guy. I desperately want to help him. Still, he *is* my most frustrating client." Most frustrating *and* most frustrated, for now, after years of steroid abuse, Jose has been confronted with one more unpleasant fact of his life (all those bills that eventually come due). Jose's own testosterone level is now so low that, in order to maintain erections, he must now take testosterone, irony of all ironies, *legally,* under a doctor's supervision. I wonder if he'll write about *that* in *Vindicated.*

Rob said that like all men Jose has changed over the years, learning, I presumed, that an unexamined life is not worth living. Rob said, "Yeah, Jose has evolved. But it hasn't been a positive evolution. He's still as opportunistic and self-absorbed as ever. Only now, he's even more desperate." So desperate, in fact, that before Jose sold his second book to Simon & Schuster, he, or one of his emissaries, allegedly tried to extort money from Detroit Tigers outfielder Magglio Ordonez by promising not to accuse Ordonez of steroid abuse in *Vindicated* if Ordonez invested $5 million in one of Jose's movies. (Jose didn't specify which movie, his autobiography or his kung fu extravaganza.)

"Jose is one step from homeless," Rob told me in early March. It seems that Simon & Schuster is holding up Jose's book advance until he performs his required book tour, S&S having learned a lesson from the publisher of Jose's previous book, which set up interviews and book signings that Jose blew off.

In mid-March, Rob called to tell me that my interview with Jose was back on.

I said, "Why?" The interview couldn't be published now until early June, two months after *Vindicated* would be published. Rob said, yes, but that June story would give the book a secondary bounce after the initial flurry of publicity died down. Rob was worried that after the names of the steroid abusers were culled from *Vindicated,* the book would die a quick death in maybe two weeks. That's where I came in.

"Call Jose," Rob said. "He's expecting your call." So, I called Jose. Mercifully, he answered the phone, and not the inscrutable Heidi. In a surprisingly mute voice, Jose agreed to an interview at his house in Sherman Oaks on the following Saturday. Before I left for California I insisted Rob give me Jose's address in case Jose failed to meet me at my hotel, as he'd agreed to. Rob also gave me his original two-page proposal for *Vindicated.* In it, I was shocked to learn, there was no mention of the new names of drug abusers Jose would mention in *Vindicated,* except as an afterthought in the last line of the proposal. It seems that the Mitchell Report and its attendant publicity had jogged Jose's memory of the many PED abusers he'd left out of *Juiced.*

When I got to my hotel in Sherman Oaks on Saturday afternoon, I called Jose. Heidi answered the phone. "What interview?" she said. "Jose is too busy writing . . ." I called Rob. He called Jose, then he called me back. "He's busy tonight, but he'll pick you up in front of your hotel at noon Sunday and take you to his house."

I woke at 7 A.M. on Sunday and drove out to Jose's house on my own, just to prepare myself for the eventuality that Jose would not show up at my hotel. And if he didn't, what would I do? Break down his front door? Jesus, Jose was making me as crazed as he was.

Anyway, Jose was renting a nondescript house in a neighborhood of faux, vaguely Mediterranean houses that looked out over a dry water viaduct, littered with detritus, and beyond that the Ventura Freeway. There was a FOR SALE sign on the front lawn, and a black BMW in the driveway. Through the house's many windows I could see nothing on the walls. No prints or photographs or mirrors. It was the kind of rented house that people use as a way station, before they move on to a bigger house, or to living in their car underneath the Ventura Freeway. I went back to the hotel and waited for Jose to pick me up at noon.

At 10 A.M., L.A. time, Rob called to tell me the interview was off. Jose had changed his mind yet again. I was apoplectic. Rob tried to calm me down with these reassuring words, "Pat," he said, "why are you so upset? You and I both know Jose's a piece of shit."

Contributors' Notes

JOHN BRANT is a longtime writer-at-large for *Runner's World*. He is a frequent contributor to numerous national magazines and is the author of *Duel in the Sun: Alberto Salazar, Dick Beardsley, and America's Greatest Marathon*. Brant lives in Portland, Oregon, with his wife and two children. This is his fourth appearance in *The Best American Sports Writing*.

STEVE FRIEDMAN is the author of *The Gentleman's Guide to Life, Loose Balls* (with Jayson Williams), and *The Agony of Victory*, and he is writer-at-large for *Backpacker, Bicycling,* and *Runner's World*. A St. Louis native and graduate of Stanford University, he lives in New York City. This is his eighth appearance in *The Best American Sports Writing*. Much of his work can be seen at Stevefriedman.net.

MALCOLM GLADWELL has been a staff writer with *The New Yorker* since 1996. From 1987 to 1996, he was a reporter with the *Washington Post,* and then served as the newspaper's New York City bureau chief. He graduated from the University of Toronto, Trinity College, with a degree in history. He was born in England, grew up in rural Ontario, and now lives in New York City. He is a past winner of a National Magazine Award and the author of three books: *The Tipping Point: How Little Things Make a Big Difference, Blink: The Power of Thinking Without Thinking,* and *Outliers: The Story of Success.*

CYNTHIA GORNEY is a contributing writer for the *New York Times Magazine* and *National Geographic* and is on the faculty at UC–Berkeley's Graduate School of Journalism. She is the author of *Articles of Faith: A Frontline History of the Abortion Wars,* and her work has appeared in *The New Yorker, Sports Illustrated, Runner's World, Harper's, O, Bazaar, Mother Jones, Glamour,* and many other publications. She lives in Oakland.

KARL TARO GREENFELD is the author of four books: *Boy Alone*, about his autistic brother Noah, *Speed Tribes, Standard Deviations*, and *China Syndrome*. A longtime writer and editor for *The Nation, Time*, and *Sports Illustrated*, he served as the editor of *Time Asia* from 2002 to 2004 and was among the founding editors of *Sports Illustrated China*. He has also written multiple times for the *New York Times, GQ, Vogue, Condé Nast Traveler, Wired, Details, Men's Journal*, the *Washington Post, Outside, Condé Nast Portfolio*, and *Salon*. His articles and essays have been selected for *The Best American Sports Writing, The Best American Travel Writing, The Best American Nonrequired Reading*, and *The Best Creative Nonfiction*. His fiction has appeared in *The Best American Short Stories, The Paris Review, American Short Fiction, The Missouri Review, Commentary*, and *The Sun*. Karl was born in Kobe, Japan, has lived in Paris, New York, Hong Kong, and Tokyo, and currently lives in Pacific Palisades with his wife, Silka, and two daughters, Esmee and Lola.

RICHARD HOFFER was a senior writer at *Sports Illustrated* for twenty years. He is the author of three books: *A Savage Business: The Comeback and Comedown of Mike Tyson, Jackpot Nation: Rambling and Gambling Across Our Landscape of Luck*, and *Something in the Air: American Passion and Defiance in the 1968 Mexico Olympics*.

BOB HOHLER is a sports enterprise reporter for the *Boston Globe*. A Boston native, he joined the *Globe* in 1987 after reporting for two New Hampshire papers, the *Concord Monitor* and *Monadnock Ledger*. He covered news throughout New England before covering government and politics, including President Clinton's impeachment case, while serving in the *Globe*'s Washington bureau from 1993 to 2000. He served as the *Globe*'s beat writer for the Boston Red Sox from 2000 to the 2004 championship season. He has received numerous writing honors, including the 2010 Dick Schaap Excellence in Sports Journalism Award from Northeastern University's Center for Sport in Society, the 2009 Award for Excellence in the Coverage of Youth Sports from the John Curley Center for Sports Journalism at Penn State, and the 2007 Salute to Excellence Award from the National Association of Black Journalists. He was also cited by the Associated Press Sports Editors in 2005 for the nation's best investigative reporting. He is the author of *I Touch the Future . . . The Story of Christa McAuliffe*.

SKIP HOLLANDSWORTH was raised in Wichita Falls, Texas, and graduated with a BA in English from Texas Christian University. He has worked as a reporter and columnist for newspapers in Dallas, and he also has worked as a television producer and documentary filmmaker. Since joining *Texas Monthly* in 1989, Hollandsworth has been a finalist four times for a National Magazine Award and received the award in 2010 for the piece included here.

PAT JORDAN is a contract writer for the *New York Times Magazine*. He says of his story "Chasing Jose" that "it was the most frustrating story I've ever been involved in, for the obvious reasons I delineated in the story, and others. After I decided to write a story about chasing Jose Canseco, I realized how funny it was becoming each day.

"My friend and the editor of my last book, *The Best Sports Writing of Pat Jordan*, Alex Belth, told me he'd send it off to *Deadspin*. I had no idea what *Deadspin* was, or anything about publishing online. Anyway, Will Leitch, then the editor, published 'Chasing Jose,' and it made a stir online, I guess. Writing for *Deadspin* was a wonderful experience, despite the fact that they don't pay for stories. A vanity press for me, I guess, but still worth it. Now that 'Jose' is in print, I couldn't be happier. I am, after all, a print and paper kind of writer."

JENNIFER KAHN has been a contributing editor at *Wired* magazine since 2003 and a feature writer for *The New Yorker, National Geographic, Outside, Discover, Mother Jones,* and the *New York Times,* among others. Since 2008, she has taught long-form writing in the Magazine Program at the UC–Berkeley Graduate School of Journalism.

THOMAS LAKE lives in Atlanta and writes regularly for *Atlanta* magazine and *Sports Illustrated*. This is his second appearance in *The Best American Sports Writing*. He met his wife, Sara, at Gordon College in Massachusetts, where she was a star on the softball team, and he is sure she would have done the same thing Mallory Holtman did, if she ever had the chance.

JEANNE MARIE LASKAS is the author of five books, including *Growing Girls, The Exact Same Moon,* and *Fifty Acres and a Poodle*. Her next book project, *Hidden America: The Unseen World of People Who Make Everything Work,* will be published by Putnam in 2011. The book examines the lives of people who do the hands-on jobs that make America work. From 1994 to 2008, Laskas was a regular syndicated columnist for the *Washington Post Magazine*. She has been a contributing editor at *Esquire,* and most of her magazine feature stories now appear in *GQ,* where she is a correspondent. Her stories have appeared in numerous anthologies, including *The Best American Magazine Writing 2008* and *The Best American Sports Writing 2000, 2002, 2007,* and *2008.* A professor in the creative writing program at the University of Pittsburgh, she lives with her husband and two daughters on a horse farm in Scenery Hill, Pennsylvania.

DAN LE BATARD is a columnist for the *Miami Herald*.

MICHAEL LEWIS is the author of *The New New Thing, Liar's Poker, Money-ball, Coach,* and *The Blind Side.* In 2006 he served as guest editor for *The Best American Sports Writing.*

MIKE MAGNUSON is the author of two novels, *The Right Man for the Job* and *The Fire Gospels,* and two books of nonfiction, *Lummox: The Evolution of a Man* and *Heft on Wheels: A Field Guide to Doing a 180.* His stories and arti-cles have appeared in *Bicycling,* where he has been a contributing writer since 2003, *Backpacker, Gentlemen's Quarterly, Esquire,* and a number of other publications. He lives in Los Angeles.

ERIC NUSBAUM is a freelance writer and editor of PitchersAndPoets.com and RoguesBaseballIndex.com. He attended the University of Washing-ton and has recently lived in Seattle, New York, and Los Angeles.

DAVID OWEN is a staff writer for *The New Yorker* and a contributing editor of *Golf Digest.* His most recent book is *Green Metropolis.*

BILL PLASCHKE is a columnist for the *Los Angeles Times,* a regular panelist on the ESPN daily talk show *Around the Horn,* and author of a collection of his columns entitled *Plaschke: Good Sports, Spoil Sports, Foul Balls, and Odd Balls.* He was born in Louisville, Kentucky, and worked in Fort Lau-derdale and Seattle before joining the *Los Angeles Times* in 1987.

S. L. PRICE has been a senior writer at *Sports Illustrated* since 1994. His third book, *Heart of the Game: Life, Death, and Mercy in Minor League Amer-ica,* was published in paperback in May. This is his fifth appearance in *The Best American Sports Writing.*

A writer and columnist for the *Boston Globe* since 1968, BOB RYAN was named National Sportswriter of the Year by the National Association of Sportscasters and Sportswriters in 2000, 2007, 2008, and 2009. He is also a past winner of the Curt Gowdy Award from the Naismith Basketball Hall of Fame, a member of the USBWA Hall of Fame, and a charter member of the New England Basketball Hall of Fame. The author of eleven books, Ryan is a regular on ESPN's *Sports Reporters,* a frequent contributor to ESPN's *Around the Horn,* and a frequent guest host on ESPN's *Pardon the Interruption.*

MIKE SAGER is a bestselling author and award-winning reporter. A former *Washington Post* staffer under Bob Woodward, he worked closely with gonzo journalist Hunter S. Thompson during his years as a contributing editor for *Rolling Stone.* Sager is the author of three collections of non-fiction and one novel. He has served for more than a decade as a writer-at-large for *Esquire.* Many of his articles have been optioned for film. He lives with his wife and son in La Jolla, California. For more information, please see www.MikeSager.com.

ROBERT SANCHEZ is a staff writer at *5280* in Denver, writing mostly long-form features and narrative stories. A former newspaper writer for the *Denver Post,* the *Rocky Mountain News,* the *Philadelphia Inquirer,* and the Associated Press, Sanchez has won or been nominated for multiple state and national awards, including the Livingston Awards for Young Journalists and the City and Regional Magazine Association's Writer of the Year. He graduated from the University of Missouri School of Journalism and is married to his high school sweetheart, Kristen. The two have a daughter, Alexandra, and a son, Michael.

MIKE SIELSKI is a sportswriter for the *Wall Street Journal.* From 2003 to 2010, he worked as the sports columnist for Calkins Media, a chain of daily newspapers in suburban Philadelphia. His columns appeared regularly in the *Bucks County Courier Times,* the *Intelligencer,* and the *Burlington County (New Jersey) Times* and on www.phillyburbs.com. A 1997 graduate of La Salle University and a 1998 graduate of the Columbia University Graduate School of Journalism, Sielski is also the author of *Fading Echoes: A True Story of Rivalry and Brotherhood from the Football Field to the Fields of Honor.* Released in late 2009, *Fading Echoes* received starred reviews from both *Publishers Weekly* and *Library Journal,* and *Booklist* called it "an emotionally charged book that offers a profound understanding of American life in the first years of the twenty-first century."

MICHAEL SOKOLOVE is a contributing writer for the *New York Times Magazine,* as well as the author of two books: *The Ticket Out: Darryl Strawberry and the Boys of Crenshaw* and *Hustle: The Myth, Life, and Lies of Pete Rose.* He has appeared on numerous national television and radio news shows, including ABC's *Good Morning America* and *Prime Time Thursday,* ESPN's *Outside the Lines,* and CNN's *Paula Zahn Now.* He has been a guest on the National Public Radio shows *Fresh Air, The Tavis Smiley Show,* and *Only a Game.*

WRIGHT THOMPSON is a senior writer for ESPN.com and *ESPN: The Magazine.* He lives with his wife, Sonia, in Oxford, Mississippi.

ALEXANDER WOLFF is a senior writer for *Sports Illustrated* and the author of six books, including *Big Game, Small World: A Basketball Adventure,* which was named a *New York Times* Notable Book in 2002. A former Ferris Professor of Journalism at Princeton, he lives with his family in Addison County, Vermont.

To find stories by some of these authors that have appeared in previous editions of *The Best American Sports Writing,* see the index at glennstout.net.

Notable Sports Writing of 2009